Possible Worlds

'This is a well-organized, thoroughly argued and intelligent book – the most comprehensive study of the metaphysics of possible worlds that I have ever seen.'

Theodore Sider, *Syracuse University*

'*Possible Worlds* provides a lucid, thorough and fair-minded treatment of the debate – both over the last thirty years and up to the minute – between different sorts of realist about modality.'

Fraser MacBride, *University of St Andrews*

Our world – the actual world – being but one of a vast infinity of possible worlds is an idea that is increasingly familiar in fiction and natural science. Over the past forty years philosophers have recovered this image from its venerable philosophical history in order to address deep and serious issues that are central to the subject. Talk of possible worlds promises explanations of possibility, necessity, essences, properties, counterfactuals, supervenience and much more. But what do philosophers mean when they talk about these possible worlds? Are they speaking of a realm of abstract entities or of a multitude of other universes that differ in various ways from the one that we inhabit?

Possible Worlds presents the first up-to-date and comprehensive examination and assessment of all the issues pertaining to realism about possible worlds. John Divers examines prevalent philosophical positions and subjects them to a detailed exposition and evaluation, including extensive discussions of genuine and actualist realists. This is a comprehensive, critical account of forty years of literature on realism about possible worlds, enhanced by many original developments and insights, and will prove a valuable introduction to the topic.

John Divers is Senior Lecturer in Philosophy at the University of Leeds.

The Problems of Philosophy

Editors: Tim Crane and Jonathan Wolff, *University College London*

This series addresses the central problems of philosophy. Each book gives a fresh account of a particular philosophical theme by offering two perspectives on the subject: the historical context and the author's own distinctive and original contribution. The books are written to be accessible to students of philosophy and related disciplines, while taking the debate to a new level.

Recently published:

TIME
Philip Turetzky

VAGUENESS
Timothy Williamson

FREE SPEECH
Alan Haworth

THE MORAL SELF
Pauline Chazan

SOCIAL REALITY
Finn Collin

OTHER MINDS
Anita Avramides

CIVIC REPUBLICANISM
Iseult Honohan

PERCEPTION
Howard Robinson

THE NATURE OF GOD
Gerard Hughes

SUBSTANCE
Justin Hoffman and Gary Rosenkrantz

DEMOCRACY
Ross Harrison

THE MIND AND ITS WORLD
Gregory McCulloch

POSSIBLE WORLDS
John Divers

Possible Worlds

John Divers

London and New York

First published 2002
by Routledge
11 New Fetter Lane, London EC4P 4EE

Simultaneously published in the USA and Canada
by Routledge
29 West 35th Street, New York, NY 10001

Routledge is an imprint of the Taylor & Francis Group

© 2002 John Divers

Typeset in Times by RefineCatch Limited, Bungay, Suffolk
Printed and bound in Great Britain by
TJ International Ltd, Padstow, Cornwall

All rights reserved. No part of this book may be reprinted or
reproduced or utilised in any form or by any electronic,
mechanical, or other means, now known or hereafter invented,
including photocopying and recording, or in any information
storage or retrieval system, without permission in writing
from the publishers.

British Library Cataloguing in Publication Data
A catalogue record for this book is available from the British Library

Library of Congress Cataloging in Publication Data
A catalogue record for this book has been requested

ISBN 0–415–15555–X (hbk)
ISBN 0–415–15556–8 (pbk)

*To my mother, Betty,
and to the memory of my father, Robert*

Contents

Preface   xi
Acknowledgements   xv

Part I: Introduction   1

1   Where possible-world talk is used   3
(1.1)   Modalities   3
(1.2)   Intensions   9
(1.3)   Relations over intensions   10

2   What possible-world talk means   15
(2.1)   Possible-world discourse (PW)   15
(2.2)   Interpretations of PW   16
(2.3)   Applications of PW   18
(2.4)   Abstentionism, realism and antirealism   19
(2.5)   Realisms   21
(2.6)   Antirealisms   22

3   Why possible-world talk is used   26
(3.1)   Conceptual applications of PW   26
(3.2)   Ontological applications of PW   32
(3.3)   Semantic applications of PW   34
(3.4)   A Sketch of a Kripkean PW-semantics for QML   36
(3.5)   Other applications of PW   39

Part II: Genuine realism   41

4   Genuine realism: exposition and applications   43
(4.1)   Interpretation   43
(4.2)   Ontology and primitive concepts   45

(4.3)	Conceptual applications 47	
(4.4)	Ontological applications 51	
(4.5)	Semantic applications 57	
(4.6)	Justification 57	

5 Genuine realism: quantification over non-actuals — 59
- (5.1) Non-existent entities 59
- (5.2) Analytic actualism 62
- (5.3) Genuine worlds are not proper individuals 65
- (5.4) From possibilia to impossibilia 67
- (5.5) The incalculable costs of impossibilia 76
- (5.6) The impossibility of singular reference to non-actual individuals 77

6 Genuine realism: worlds — 86
- (6.1) Non-individuals 87
- (6.2) Disconnected times 90
- (6.3) Temporally disconnected dual existences 91
- (6.4) Island universes 93
- (6.5) Non-actual spatiotemporal relations 99
- (6.6) Recombination 100
- (6.7) Unworldly genuine realism 103

7 Genuine realism: unanalysed modality — 106
- (7.1) Accurate analysis 106
- (7.2) Conceptually modal analysis 108
- (7.3) Doxastically modal analysis 110
- (7.4) Ontologically modal analysis 112
- (7.5) The infinitude of alien properties 114
- (7.6) From infinitude to incompleteness 117

8 Genuine realism: counterparts — 122
- (8.1) Irrelevance 124
- (8.2) Concern 133
- (8.3) Intuitions of truth and validity 139
- (8.4) The consequences of deregulation 144

9 Genuine realism: epistemology — 149
- (9.1) The utilitarian case for GR knowledge 151
- (9.2) Utility as warrant in ontology 155
- (9.3) Obstacles to a prioricity 158
- (9.4) Scepticism about epistemological objections to GR 164

Part III: Actualist realism 167

10 Actualist realism: exposition 169
(10.1) Plantingan realism (PR) 173
(10.2) Combinatorial realism (CR) 174
(10.3) Nature realism (NR) 177
(10.4) Book realism (BR) 178

11 Actualist realism: conceptual applications 181
(11.1) BR and primitive modal concepts 182
(11.2) CR and primitive modal concepts 189
(11.3) NR and primitive modal concepts 191

12 Actualist realism: ontological applications 196
(12.1) Ontological identification 196
(12.2) Truthmaking 201

13 Actualist realism: semantic applications 210
(13.1) The D-problem 211
(13.2) D as the actual individuals 213
(13.3) D as the actual singular terms 216
(13.4) D as the individual essences 219
(13.5) The V-problem and its existentialist solution 223

14 Actualist realism: safe and sane ontology? 227
(14.1) The actual world 228
(14.2) Abstractness 229
(14.3) Unrealized existence 231
(14.4) Criteria of identity 232
(14.5) Properties 237
(14.6) States of affairs 239

15 Actualist realism: paradox 243
(15.1) PW-paradoxes 243
(15.2) Kaplan paradoxes 245
(15.3) PW-paradox and the species of AR 246
(15.4) Restriction solutions 249
(15.5) Proper class solutions 251
(15.6) Non-maximality solutions 252

16 Actualist realism: transworld identity and transworld identification — 257
- (16.1) Distinguishing transworld identity theses 258
- (16.2) The discernibility argument against transworld identity 261
- (16.3) The Adam–Noah example 263
- (16.4) GR, haecceitism and non-trivial essentialism 265
- (16.5) AR, haecceitism and non-trivial essentialism 268
- (16.6) The transworld identification problem 270
- (16.7) Semantic stipulation and modal epistemology 272

17 Actualist realism: representation — 275
- (17.1) Misrepresentation by linguistic AR 275
- (17.2) Linguistic AR revitalized 278
- (17.3) Misrepresentation by GR 284
- (17.4) Magical representation by AR 286
- (17.5) *Tu quoque* 289

Part IV: Conclusion — 293

18 Summary and evaluation — 295

Notes 298
Extended bibliography 361

Index 373

Preface

I set out to write a book about possible worlds which would have a first half devoted to introductory material and a summary of the ins and outs of realism about possible worlds, and a second half devoted to the systematic exposition and evaluation of the antirealist options. I believed, and still believe, that progress in the philosophy of modality is blocked by the absence of a comprehensive discussion of the antirealist options. I was keen to set about that work but I became convinced that the literature on possible worlds as it stood did not offer an appropriate basis on which to proceed. So the work on antirealism was postponed, and the present book emerged in an attempt to clear the ground for that work.

I thought that work was needed to clarify some fundamental, but often disregarded, distinctions and issues that ought to shape philosophical discussion of possible worlds. Part I offers what I hope will be a useful tour of the modal and intensional territory over which talk of possible worlds holds sway. But more importantly, I try to spell out the options for interpreting talk about possible worlds, and relate those options to the different kinds of explanations that the use of possible-world talk is supposed to afford and to the question of commitment to the existence of possible worlds. Here I attempt to prime against a range of vices that are detectable in the literature. There is the undifferentiated offer of a possible-world account of this or a treatment of that in the possible-worlds framework. Are we being offered, to pin down but three possibilities, an attempt at conceptual analysis, a specification of truthmakers or a bit of applied model-theoretic semantics (and don't ask why)? There is the bland assurance that, for the purposes at hand, appeal to possible worlds is merely 'heuristic'. Does this mean that the 'account' on offer would succeed even if there are no possible worlds and no matter what account we give of the meaning of possible-world talk in order to explain away apparent commitment to possible worlds? In order to guard against these and other vices, we must always be careful in discussions of possible worlds to keep two questions clearly in view. When a 'possible-world' account (of modality, counterfactuals, propositions, etc.) is on offer, exactly what kind of explanation is it supposed to afford, and exactly how is the possible-world talk supposed to be interpreted? That is the moral of Part I, and as such I hope that the introductory material will serve both the philosophy undergraduate who comes to the topic anew and those more familiar with the subject matter who would value a general perspective on the taxonomy and evaluation of the realist and antirealist positions.

I also felt that work was needed by way of summary and assessment of the debate between the two great traditions of genuine realism and actualist realism about possible worlds – hence Parts II and III. Having researched in the field for over fifteen years I approached the realist literature with the presumptuous expectation of 'filling in the gaps' in my reading and dealing summarily with the realist positions on the basis of the opinions that I had, by and large, already formed. However, I found that the literature was far more extensive than I had realized. (In reaction to this discovery I have opted to include an extended bibliography rather than a shorter list of works cited.) The quantity and quality of the literature that I found convinced me that there was call for a systematic, book-length and up-to-date treatment of the debate between the two realist camps – especially since a wealth of important work has been published in reaction to the appearance in 1986 of the definitive work in the field, Lewis's *On the Plurality of Worlds*. Also, in attempting to provide that treatment, my opinions changed. I had previously thought there to be several strong objections against Lewis's genuine realism and that some of these were (all but) decisive. I have come to think that most of these objections are weak or can be rebutted, that those that are any good aren't as good as I had thought or that they survive in only qualified form. In sum, I have come to think that the objections against genuine realism, even taken collectively, are not convincing. Since I had formed fairly negative views of the credibility of actualist realism and these were enhanced in the process of writing, the upshot is that I here take genuine realism to be more credible than actualist realism and I think that genuine realism may be credible *tout court*.

I give the (conditional) verdict to genuine realism over actualist realism having attempted to treat the actualist realist options in a completely systematic way. After reading Lewis's exposition and defence of genuine realism in *On the Plurality of Worlds* one becomes keenly aware that the exposition of the rival actualist realist positions is invariably less comprehensive. One might find that the actualist realist cause is prosecuted by providing an informal possible-worlds semantics for a modal language without any clear statement about what the conceptual and ontological implications of the semantic theory are supposed to be. One might find that a frequently cited source of the view that possible worlds are – say – sets of sentences, or (even more generally) abstract objects, turns out to be a few undeveloped remarks that are made in the context of a presentation of a very specific application of possible-world talk and in order to distance the author from genuine realism. One might find that an application of possible-world talk is proposed with the assumption that *any* species of actualist realist interpretation will sustain its success. In order to ground comparison with genuine realism, I have tried to distinguish specific versions of actualist realism and to force each version to face up to all of the fundamental conceptual and ontological questions which one might ask of a fully and properly developed interpretation of possible-world talk – questions to which the genuine realist provides answers. Perhaps in trying to force the actualist realists to go systematic and comprehensive I have commended an answer to a question which has (inadvertently) weakened a position and which a more skilful or more sympathetic exponent of actualist realism would not give. Perhaps in trying to force the actualist realists to go systematic and comprehensive in the ways indicated, I have begged questions in favour of the philosophical methodology that underpins genuine realism. Perhaps I have asked questions of certain versions of actualist realism which they were never intended to answer. However, I trust that the questions which I have put to the actualist realist are fair and straight enough to allow me to be put right by others if I have gone wrong in any of these ways, and I hope that we will all learn more about actualist realism if so.

I emphasize that the verdict of the final chapter is conditional: *if* we are to be realists about possible worlds then we should be genuine realists. Whether we are to be realists at all is a question which I believe we can only answer with reasonable justification once the antirealist alternatives have been considered. So I advertise again the need for that work on antirealism to be done. But I hope that there is now a better foundation for that work than there was before.

I conclude my writing in the shadow cast by the very recent death of David Lewis. The ensuing tributes suggest rightly that we have

Preface

seen the passing of a great philosopher. I will add only that the topic of possible worlds will be dominated by the name and the work of David Lewis for as long as it is discussed and that it is a profound intellectual pleasure to engage with that work.

John Divers
4 January 2002

Acknowledgements

I have had many opportunities to present and discuss ideas about modality and related matters in the period during which this book was written. For discussion in various groups and seminars within my own department at Leeds, I thank Otavio Bueno, Peter Mott and Scott Shalkowski. For various other discussions and comments, I thank the philosophers who attended when I gave talks at the following venues: The Aristotelian Society; Birkbeck College, London; Bled (Philosophical Analysis Conference); University of Bradford; University of Bristol; University of Cambridge (Moral Sciences Club); University College, London; University of Durham; University of Glasgow; University of Prague (Czech National Science Academy Colloquium on Possible Worlds); Queen's University, Belfast; Trinity College, Dublin; University of St Andrews; St David's University College, Lampeter and the University of York. I am especially grateful to the Philosophy departments of the University of Birmingham and the University of Helsinki at which I had the opportunity to give a series of seminars on realism and anti-realism about possible worlds. In the latter case, I would like to acknowledge the wonderful hospitality shown to me by Janne Hiipakka, Markku Keinanen, Anssi Korhonen and Gabriel Sandu and the subsequent philosophical correspondence I have enjoyed with Markku and Anssi. I have been fortunate enough to benefit from extensive comments on the draft manuscript and so for their most helpful efforts I thank Jim Edwards, Bryan Frances, Bo Meinertsen, Alexander Miller, Mark Nelson, Peter Simons, Alan Weir, Anthony Wrigley and two anonymous readers for Routledge. I thank the editorial staff at Taylor & Francis, especially Zoe Drayson and Muna Khogali, and the series editors, Tim Crane and Jo Wolff, for tolerating my failure to meet various submission deadlines. I thank Tim in particular for the good advice that led to the emergence

Acknowledgements

of the book in its present form. Finally, my special thanks go to Joseph Melia for his contribution to discussions at Leeds and elsewhere, for detailed comments on the entire draft manuscript, for permission to use the material from our joint article and – perhaps most importantly of all – for giving his time and expertise so generously and consistently over the last two years in hundreds of conversations and comments that have improved the book in so many ways.

Material from J. Divers, 'A Genuine Realist Theory of Advanced Modalizing', *Mind*, 1999, 108: 217–39 and J. Divers and J. Melia, 'The Analytic Limit of Genuine Modal Realism', *Mind*, 2002, 111: 15–36 are reproduced by kind permission of Oxford University Press.

Part I

Introduction

CHAPTER 1

Where possible-world talk is used

To show why philosophers find it congenial to talk in terms of possible worlds, I will begin by presenting in this chapter a picture of where such talk is used – this is a picture of what possible-world talk is supposed to elucidate or explain. The remaining chapters of the introductory section will be concerned with the fundamental philosophical issues that underlie possible-world talk. In Chapter 2, I will consider the different ways in which possible-world talk might be interpreted. There the central distinction is between *realist* interpretations that reflect acceptance of the existence of many possible worlds and *antirealist* interpretations that reflect resistance to that commitment. In Chapter 3, I distinguish the different kinds of elucidation or explanation – conceptual, ontological and semantic – that possible-world talk might be supposed to provide.

In seeking to cover the territory over which possible-world talk ranges in a fairly systematic and comprehensive way, I propose to divide it into three regions: the modalities (1.1), the intensions (1.2) and relations over intensions (1.3).[1]

(1.1) MODALITIES

The primary target of possible world discourse is modality. Philosophers typically recognize four central and interrelated *cases* of modality: possibility (can, might, may, could); impossibility (cannot, could not, must not); necessity (must, has to be, could not be otherwise); and contingency (maybe and maybe not, might have been and might not have been, could have been otherwise). The cases are standardly regarded as definitionally interrelated in the following ways. Possibility rules out impossibility and requires (exclusively) contingency or necessity. Impossibility rules out possibility, rules out necessity and rules out contingency. Necessity requires possibility, rules out impossibility and rules out contingency. Contingency requires possibility, rules out impossibility and rules out necessity.

Philosophers also recognize different *kinds* of modality. Charitable interpretation and appropriate context suggests that I might speak truly in making any of the following impossibility claims: 'It is impossible that the number of chairs in the room is both even and not even'; 'No one can both be married and be a bachelor'; 'Michael could not have had any parents other than those he actually has'; 'Nothing can travel faster than light'; 'It can't be the case that I don't exist'; 'A player cannot be in an offside position while in his or her half of the field of play'; 'I won't be able to keep our appointment this evening'; 'You can't pay people different rates for doing the same job just because one is male and the other female'. This intuitive variety of kinds of impossibility reflects that there are different kinds of consideration that exclude something from the realm of possibility. If the salient excluding considerations are logical (no proposition is such that both it and its negation are true) we might speak of logical impossibility. If the considerations are rooted in the meanings of words (nothing is both married and a bachelor) we might speak of analytic impossibility. Aside from the logical and analytic modality, contemporary philosophical interests also highlight metaphysical modality (fixed by the natures and identity conditions of things), nomological modality (fixed by the laws of nature), epistemic modality (fixed by what is known), doxastic modality (fixed by what is believed) and deontic modality (fixed by what satisfies a certain norm or rule). Yet, the picture seems naturally extendable so that we can recognize a kind of modality arising from any reasonably circumscribable set of considerations, no matter how trivial or parochial. Thus the truth of my saying that I won't be able to keep our appointment this evening, may be grounded in the consideration that my keeping of the appointment fails to conform to or comply with my current set of actual social priorities and preferences. The salient kinds of modality are intuitively, but not uncontroversially, interrelated. It seems right to say that the laws of nature are in no position to permit what logic rules out. Thus, logical impossibility entails nomological impossibility. Yet even if the actual laws of nature rule out that a body should travel faster than light, logic appears to exert no such constraint. Thus, logical possibility does not entail nomological possibility.

Possible-world talk is invoked to elucidate these distinctions of both case and kind among the modalities.

We begin with the idea of the totality of the possible worlds across which all of the genuine possibilities (and no impossibilities) are represented. One of these possible worlds – the actual world – is special, closer to our hearts and distinguished somehow from the others that are 'merely' possible. Given this conception of a plurality of possible worlds, a modality of a given case and kind is characterized in terms of what is the case at a specified range of the possible worlds. In general, the M-possible worlds (logically possible worlds, analytically possible worlds, nomologically possible worlds, etc.) are those among the genuinely possible worlds that conform to or comply with the set of M-constraints (the laws of logic, the strictures of meaning, the laws of nature, etc.). Then, what is M-possible is true at some M-possible world; what is M-impossible is not true at any M-possible world; what is M-necessary is true at all M-possible worlds, and what is M-contingent is true at some but not all M-possible worlds. That basic characterization offers elucidation of the interdefinability of the cases of modality and their interrelations by way of principles governing the underlying quantifiers over possible worlds. For example, that necessity requires possibility is underpinned by the requirement that what is true of all (possible worlds) is true of some; that impossibility rules out necessity is underpinned by the requirement that what is true of none is not true of all. The basic characterization also promises elucidation of the interrelations between the kinds of modality. That nomological possibility entails logical possibility, for example, is reflected in a certain relation between the two sets of possible worlds. All of the nomologically possible worlds are logically possible worlds – the set of nomologically possible worlds is a subset of the logically possible worlds, the region of the logically possible worlds includes all the region of the nomologically possible worlds. That nomological necessity fails to entail logical necessity is reflected by there being a logically possible world that is not a nomologically possible world. It is not the case that all of the logically possible worlds are nomologically possible worlds (the set of logically possible worlds is not a subset of the nomologically possible worlds). It is a matter of controversy whether we can identify the collection of all the genuinely possible worlds with the collection that is circumscribed by any given M-specification. Thus it is controversial whether the collection of all (and only) the genuinely possible worlds can be identified with the logically possible worlds, or with the analytically possible worlds, or with the metaphysically possible worlds, etc.[2] However, once we help ourselves to the idea of a collection of all and only the genuinely possible worlds which contains the actual world then, whether that collection is subject to more informative characterization or not, the modality that is captured by that collection of possible worlds is supposed to be both *alethic* and *absolute*. I now turn to these characterizations of the modalities and their possible-world elucidations.

As we have seen, various constraints that we take to hold over the actual world seem apt to be expressed in modal terms. But these constraints give rise to 'musts' that differ intuitively in various ways. Here is one such difference.

With the logical 'must' the relevant constraint holding over the actual world is a matter of non-modal truth (or falsehood) at the actual world. What logically must be true is actually true so that, for example, it is actually true that nothing is both green and not green. But with the moral 'must', for example, matters stand otherwise. Moral constraints that hold over the actual world do so in a way that is not directly reflected in non-modal truth (or falsehood) at the actual world. What morally must (or ought to) be true is (often) not actually true so that, for example, it is not true at the actual world that no one commits rape even though it ought not to be the case that anyone does so. In possible-world terms, we put the matter as follows. Corresponding to each world and to a set of constraints M, we have the set of M-possible worlds that conform to those constraints by having all of the relevant non-modal statements hold true at them. The alethic modalities are those kinds of modality for which the actual world is always one of the M-possible worlds that it generates: the constraints generated from the actual world are always satisfied by the actual world. All other kinds of modality are non-alethic. It follows from this brief characterization and from the earlier definitions of the various cases of modality that the following inferences are characteristically valid for the alethic modalities and invalid for the non-alethic modalities:

(1) $\dfrac{\text{Necessarily P}}{\text{Actually P}}$ (2) $\dfrac{\text{Actually P}}{\text{Possibly P}}$

In possible-world terms, we infer in (1) what is true at the actual world from what is true at all M-possible worlds and we infer in (2) what is true at some M-possible world from what is true at the actual world:

(PW1) $\dfrac{\text{At all w, A}}{\text{At w*, A}}$ (PW2) $\dfrac{\text{At w*, A}}{\text{At some w, A}}$

The inferences will be valid, and so the relevant modality alethic, just in case the actual world, w*, is one of the M-possible worlds.

Among the kinds of modality that are usually reckoned to be alethic are the logical, the analytic, the metaphysical and the nomological. Prominent among the modalities that are usually reckoned to be non-alethic are the broadly deontic modalities – modalities that primarily guide action, prescribing what must, must not or may be done in order to satisfy certain precepts, norms or rules. Among the deontic subclass of non-alethic modalities are not only the moral modalities but legal modalities and other modalities of permission and obligation generated by various bodies of policy, codes of practice and sets of imperatives; drivers must not exceed 70 m.p.h., passengers may smoke on the upper deck and season tickets must be purchased in advance. Corresponding to these we have our classes of M-possible worlds from which the actual world may be absent in virtue of actual speeding drivers etc. The other major subclass of non-alethic modalities are those that correspond to the non-factive propositional attitudes – i.e. attitudes, φ, that do not sustain the validity of the inference:

(3) $\dfrac{X \; \varphi\text{'s that P}}{P}$

Prominent among these is the attitude of belief and the associated doxastic modalities. The 'might' of a doxastic modality, to pick on one case by way of example, is what the belief system (of an individual, at a time) does not rule out. A doxastically possible world is one that conforms to my actual belief system by making it true. Similarly, a connatively possible world is one that conforms to my actual desires by making them come true. But since, no doubt, some of the things that I believe about the actual world are not true at the actual world, and since some of the things that I desire for the actual world will not come true at the actual world, the actual world will not number among my doxastically possible worlds or among my connatively possible worlds. However, for those special types of attitude that are factive, the related modalities are alethic. The factive status of knowing, reflected in the validity of the inference from my knowing that p to p, is reflected by the inclusion of the actual world in the class of all my epistemically possible worlds. For what I know to be true of the actual world is, invariably, true at the actual world. In the remainder of the book, I will be concerned almost exclusively with the alethic modalities.[3,4]

Introduction

Within the range of the alethic modalities, I turn now to the possible-world elucidation of the distinction between absolute and relative modalities. Simply, a modality of kind M is absolute iff (i.e. if and only if) all and only the genuine possible worlds are M-possible worlds. Consequently, a modality of kind M is not absolute (it is restricted or merely relative) if there are some genuine possible worlds that are not M-possible worlds. What is necessary in only a relative or restricted sense is what holds throughout some proper subset of the genuinely possible worlds. Thus the genuine modality that is captured by the collection of all of the possible worlds is an absolute modality. The difficult questions, as indicated earlier, concern which kinds of modality should be accorded absolute status. In that matter opinion ranges from the austere position of identifying the unrestricted totality of possible worlds as those that are constrained only by the holding of the logical truths of some given logical system, through to the far more permissive position on which all logical, analytic, metaphysical and even some nomological modalities are absolute. For present purposes it does not matter which philosopher is right about where the line between absolute and relative modality should be drawn. What is important is that, due to the proliferation of modalities, all philosophers who take the modalities seriously will regard the distinction between absolute and relative modalities as non-trivial. The need to articulate the distinction is then served well by the distinction between unrestricted and restricted quantification over the genuine possible worlds. Finally on this point, the discussion of the distinction between absolute and relative modalities presents the best opportunity to mention one further aspect of possible-world talk that is congenial for certain purposes – talk of worlds being possible relative to others, or of worlds being accessible from others. To illustrate the point, let us think of the absolutely possible worlds as all and only those that respect first-order logic. What logic demands, then, does not change from possible world to possible world. There is no question of a claim being a logical truth at one possible world but a non-logical truth or even a falsehood at another. Because logical modality is absolute (we assume) in these ways, we may say that every possible world is logically accessible to and from every other possible world. Let us now take nomological modality as our example of a restricted or relative modality so that the absolutely possible worlds differ from one another with respect to the laws of nature that hold true at them. We may say then that a possible world w is nomologically accessible from a possible world v just in case all of the laws of nature at v are laws of nature at w as well.[5] The relation of nomological accessibility is not an equivalence relation on the absolutely possible worlds. For example if all of the v-laws and some extra laws hold at w, then v is accessible from w but not vice versa, the accessibility relation is not symmetrical. It seems now that such definitions of accessibility relations, and such observations about the logical features of the relations promise some insight into questions about iterated modality that may otherwise seem doomed to intractability. Does it follow quite generally that something is possible from it being possibly possible? For a given univocal modality, M, the question may now be formulated as follows. If p is true at a world, w, which is accessible from a world, v, which is accessible from the actual world, is p thereby true at some world that is accessible from the actual world? If the accessibility relation is a transitive relation, as in logical accessibility, the answer is positive. If the accessibility relation is not transitive, the answer is negative. So thinking in terms of accessibility relations over possible worlds helps us to deal with questions of which principles of iteration are valid for various kinds of modality.[6] In the remainder of the book I will be concerned almost exclusively with modality that is absolute as well as alethic, and all unqualified talk of modality is to be understood as such.[7]

(1.2) INTENSIONS

The wider modal territories include those of the *intensions*. The rough and ready idea is that entities of a kind are usually counted as intensional iff (a) they are associated with extensions in the actual world and (b) the associated extensions are not sufficient to distinguish what are intuitively distinct entities of that kind.[8] Thus, it has been held, *propositions* are intensions (or intensional entities) since the extension of a proposition in the actual world is its truth-value at the actual world and distinct propositions have the same truth-value at the actual world. The English sentences, 'The Earth has several moons' and '5 is the smallest odd prime number' have the same truth-value, but (intuitively) do not express the same proposition. Equally it has been held that *properties* are intensional entities since the extension of a property at the actual world is the set of all and only the actually existing individuals that have the property, and one such set is the extension of distinct properties. The property of being human and the property of being a featherless biped have (we may presume) the same extension, yet they are distinct properties. It has also been held that *states of affairs*, *events* and other kinds of entity that we intuitively accept are intensional.

Talk of possible worlds promises philosophical illumination here through the proposal that intensional entities can be distinguished by appeal to divergence of extension across the totality of possible worlds. The basic and natural criteria of identity that are suggested by this strategy include the following: the same proposition is expressed by two sentences iff those sentences are true at exactly the same possible worlds; the property X = the property Y iff, at each possible world, all and only the individuals that have X also have Y. In that light, the thought goes, sentences such as those in our example – 'The Earth has several moons' and '5 is the smallest prime number' – do turn out to express different propositions since there are possible worlds at which one is true and the other false. Equally, divergence in extension at some possible world – where there are featherless bipeds that are not human – ensures that being human is not the same property as being a featherless biped. The categories of proposition and property figure most prominently in discussions of intensional entities. Where possible-world talk is used to elucidate further categories of intensional entity it is typically by forging relations between them and the primary categories in some way. One such relation is identity and, for example, states of affairs have been identified with propositions and events identified with properties of spatiotemporal regions in which they occur. Moreover, properties may be taken as the single primary sort of intension with propositions construed as special cases of these, i.e. as properties of possible worlds.

(1.3) RELATIONS OVER INTENSIONS

The further modal territories that are covered by possible-world talk also include various phenomena that may be presented by way of relations over intensions.

One prominent range of relations over propositions are those expressed by *non-material conditionals*. A material conditional holds in the actual world so long as it is not the case at the actual world that the antecedent is true and the consequent false. When we try to capture the conditional relation of *entailment* between propositions or the conditional relation of *counterfactual dependence*, the material conditional seems inadequate. We do not want to say that an entailment relation holds between any arbitrary pair of propositions – say, that no American is a philosopher entails that Quine is a philosopher – just because either the antecedent is false or the consequent true. Nor do we want to say indiscriminately that just any counterfactual conditional is true – say, that if Quine had been a footballer then Kripke would have been a footballer – just because the antecedent condition (Quine being a footballer) does not actually obtain. To put the point otherwise, entailment claims and counterfactual conditionals are not material conditional claims, but if so, how are they to be understood? Talking in terms of possible worlds promises a way forward by allowing us to characterize the various non-material conditional relations between propositions in terms of the truth-values of antecedent and consequent, not just at the actual world, but at a certain range of possible worlds. Conditionals that are intended as capturing relations of entailment are to be treated as strict conditionals. We then say that the strict conditional relation holds between the antecedent proposition A and the consequent proposition C iff there is (absolutely) no possible world at which the antecedent holds and the consequent fails to hold. Counterfactual conditionals may be treated as a case that is intermediate between material conditionals and strict conditionals. We say that an intermediate conditional relation holds between the antecedent proposition A and the consequent proposition C iff there is no possible world among a selected subset of the possible worlds at which A is true and C is false. What is special about counterfactual conditionals is that, even for different tokens of the same sentence type, the set of worlds that is relevant to their truth is something that varies with context of utterance. In virtue of their difference from strict conditionals and the contextual aspect of their truth-conditions, counterfactual conditionals may otherwise be classified as *variably strict conditionals*. Counterfactual conditionals may be regarded as having truth-conditions, or only as having acceptability or assertibility conditions; selection may be constrained to the selection of a unique world or not; selection of possible worlds from the standpoint of the given world may be presented, with relative neutrality, in terms of proximity or in a more committed fashion – for example, in terms of a family of similarity relations that are supposed to range over possible worlds. But these are variations on the standard treatment in terms of possible worlds as presented.[9]

Also within the category of relations over intensions, we find that possible-world talk is invoked to elucidate various relations of property covariance or perhaps more accurately, relations of covariance between families of properties. These are the kinds of relations to which philosophers appeal in attempting to characterize the

Introduction

connection between, say, the mental and the physical, or the moral and the natural. The relations in this group are sometimes envisaged as ranging over collections of propositions (truths), facts or entities of other sorts. But let us focus initially on the property application. Relative to a kind of possibility M (metaphysical, nomological, etc.) and a corresponding set of M-possible worlds we can elucidate the salient conceptions of such covariance as follows. One prominent conception of property reduction centres on co-extensiveness of properties across all possible worlds. The A-properties are reducible to the B-properties iff, for any possible world w, and any individual x that exists at w, if x has the maximal A-property A* then, at w, x has some maximal B-property B* and in any possible world v, any individual that exists at v has A* iff it has B*.[10]

To say that the A-properties *supervene* on the B-properties is to say that there could be no A-differences without B-differences. But that characterization of covariance is ambiguous, and it can be disambiguated by appeal to possible-world talk. The notion of strong supervenience is captured by the following inter-world formulation: for any possible world w, for any individual x that exists at w, for any possible world v and for any individual y that exists at v, if at w, x has some maximal A-property, A*, then there is some maximal B-property B* such that, at w, x has B* and if, at v, y has B* then at v, y has A*. The notion of strong supervenience is weaker than that of the notion of reduction that was specified above since strong supervenience does not require that just any possible individual that has A* also has B*. The notion of weak supervenience is captured by the following intra-world formulation: for any possible world w, for any individuals x and y that exist at w, if at w, x has some maximal A-property, A*, then there is some maximal B-property B* such that, at w, x has B* and if, at w, y has B* then at w, y has A*. The notion of weak supervenience is weaker than that of strong supervenience in that the former exerts only a ban on mixed worlds – i.e. there is no world within which some x is B* and A* and some y is B* but not A* – while the latter exerts a ban on such mixtures both within and across worlds. Thus, consider the case in which the intended basic family of properties is the family of physical properties and the intended associated family of properties is the family of mental properties. Weak supervenience dictates that, within each world, no things that are the same in all physical respects differ in any mental respect – it rules out worldmates that are physically indiscernible being mentally discernible, it rules out worldmates with the same maximal physical property having different maximal mental

12

properties. Strong supervenience dictates that, even when we compare things across different worlds, no things that are the same in all physical respects differ in any mental respect – it rules out things (worldmates or not) that are physically indiscernible and mentally discernible, it rules out things (worldmates or not) that have the same maximal physical property but different maximal mental properties.

The idea that A-properties are independent of B-properties is just the idea that A-properties are not even weakly supervenient on B-properties – that is, there is a possible world w, and individuals x and y that exist at w such that, at w, x has maximal A-property A* and either lacks any B-property or has a maximal B-property B* such that at w, y has B* but does not have A*. Aside from strong and weak supervenience a third notion of supervenience, global supervenience or world supervenience focuses on possible worlds themselves rather than the individuals that exist at the worlds. The notion of global supervenience is captured by the following (rather vague) formulation: for any possible worlds w, v, if w and v are the same in all B-respects then w and v are the same in all A-respects.[11]

There are two notable aspects of these formulations. First, as presented in these standard formulations, none of the supervenience relations are asymmetric – it is not ruled out in any case that the X's supervene on the Y's and that the Y's also supervene on the X's. But if an asymmetric concept of supervenience is required it can be constructed from the basic concept in the obvious way – i.e. by conjoining the basic supervenience thesis with the negation of its 'converse'. Second, the various prominent relations of property covariance have analogues that are not restricted to range over properties in particular or even intensional entities more generally. Thus possible-world talk is invoked in adjacent territory since – for example – certain notions of ontological interdependence, dependence and independence can be articulated in line with the possible-world format for reduction, supervenience and independence respectively. For example, the claim that a set ontologically depends on its members may be articulated as the supervenience claim that there is no possible world at which each member of the set exists and the set itself does not exist; the claim that the soul is ontologically independent from the body with which it is actually associated may be articulated as the independence claim that there is a possible world at which the soul exists and the body does not; if independence is mutual then there is a possible world at which the body exists and the soul does not.

Other property-centred concepts that are articulated in possible-world terms are the venerable metaphysical concepts of essential property and essence. For any metaphysically possible world w and for any possible individual x, F is an essential property of x iff, at w, x exists iff x has F. Intuitively, then there could be a property – say, humanity – which is essential to more than one individual. But there is a further notion of an individual essence which is intended to be essentially unique to the possible individual that has it, thus: for any possible individual x, (complex) property E is an individual essence of x iff, for any possible world w, at w there exists some y such that y has E iff y is identical to x. Derivative concepts can be constructed for kinds rather than individuals. For any (metaphysically) possible world w, any possible individual x, any possible kind K, any property F: F is essential to K iff at w, for all x, if x is of kind K then x has F. For any (metaphysically) possible world w, any possible individual x, any possible kind K, any property E : E is an essence of K iff at w, for all x, x is of kind K iff x has E.

Causation is another target for elucidation in possible-world terms, and it too may be counted as a case of a relation over intensions since it is often conceived as a relation between events (of certain types). In one popular sort of approach, the specification of either the necessary or sufficient conditions of A causing C invokes the counterfactual that if A had not occurred then C would not have occurred. Thus, causal relations are elucidated ultimately in terms of patterns of events – not just in the actual world or in every possible world, but in a sphere of suitably close possible worlds. More generally, and without commitment to the foregoing direction of explanation, it is widely accepted that causation is a member of a close-knit family of categories that includes not only counterfactuals, but also laws of nature and dispositions. Accordingly, if talk of possible worlds is invoked in order to provide elucidation in any one of these cases, we should expect that it will enter directly or indirectly into the elucidation of the others.

By considering the modalities, the intensional entities and relations over the intensional entities, it has been easy to show that possible-world talk covers a substantial and important range of philosophical territory. Moreover, given the aim of elucidating the modalities in terms of possible worlds, it is clear that possible-world talk will be found to have a role wherever the modalities are afoot. As such, a proper conception of the range of application of possible-world talk is one that ought to remain open-ended.[12]

CHAPTER 2

What possible-world talk means

In this chapter I begin by drawing a three-fold distinction: possible-world talk or possible-world *discourse* is one thing; an *interpretation* of possible-world discourse is another thing; and an *application* of the interpreted discourse is yet another thing (2.1)–(2.3). I then chart the varieties of realism and antirealism about possible worlds in relation to the interpretation of certain contested sentences of the discourse (2.4)–(2.6).[1]

(2.1) POSSIBLE-WORLD DISCOURSE (PW)

Possible-world discourse – hereafter, PW – is just a fragment of English. Very roughly, and no more is required, it is that fragment which contains all the sentences involving the phrase 'possible world', all of the other elucidating sentences of the previous chapter and whatever relevant expansions of these elucidations might be adduced. So PW includes, for example, the following sentences: 'There are possible worlds other than the actual world'; 'There are other possible worlds in which there are several counterparts of one actual thing'; 'There are more possible individuals than there are actual individuals'; 'There are some remote possible worlds in which bodies exceed the velocity of light'; 'There are pairs of possible worlds that are both accessible from the actual world but inaccessible from each other'; and 'Propositions are sets of possible worlds'. It does not matter that the boundaries of PW are not sharply drawn here, nor that PW may have to be conceived rather extensively to include all of the intended sentences. The important point concerns the philosophical status of the discourse that has been, no matter how roughly, circumscribed. That point is that since the use of PW is susceptible to interpretation in a number of different ways, the mere use of the discourse leaves open a number of philosophically contentious questions – questions about the semantic structure and logical form of sentences, questions about their conceptual content and questions about ontological commitment. The use of PW is available to any philosopher. But when the chips are down, we want to know exactly what the talk is supposed to mean and exactly what kind of application the discourse, so interpreted, is supposed to afford. Unless both of these questions are answered, one who invokes PW achieves nothing of any philosophical substance. Consequently, the initial elucidations presented in the first chapter achieve nothing of any philosophical substance by themselves. They merely serve to suggest that a given subject matter might be explained in some, as yet unspecified, way by drawing on some, as yet unspecified, features of the explaining discourse, PW. The claim that the mere use of PW leaves open – or is neutral among – various philosophically informed interpretations is not supposed to be controversial: it is supposed to be a claim that might plausibly be made about any discourse that attracts philosophical attention. In the cases of, say, colour discourse, moral discourse or mathematical discourse, we would not expect any substantial philosophical commitment, including commitment to any form of realism or antirealism, to be established immediately by the mere fact that a philosopher is prepared to call things 'blue', or 'wrong' or to use numerals for the purposes of calculating.[2] Substantial philosophical commitments, and ontological commitments in particular, ensue from commitment to an interpretation of the relevant discourse. However, in the case of PW, it is not always clear when we are supposed to be dealing with a specific interpretation of the discourse as opposed to the discourse itself. For the literature is replete with phrases that connive to conflate discourse with interpretation, and to conflate either of these with some kind of application to which the interpreted discourse may be put – phrases such as 'the possible worlds approach', 'the possible worlds framework' and 'the possible worlds treatment'. I hope that the danger inherent in such conflation will emerge more clearly once the notions of an interpretation and an application of PW have been pinned down.

(2.2) INTERPRETATIONS OF PW

Distinct from the discourse itself are the interpretations of PW, each of which is a philosophically sensitive and informed account of the meaning of the sentences of PW. Philosophers may mean different things by their uses of PW sentences, even on the occasions where they attain verbal agreement. So there is no question of there emerging a unique, descriptively accurate interpretation of PW that captures what we all univocally and really mean. Rather, in associating herself with one of the many available interpretations of PW, a committed philosopher is making a normative commitment – a judgement about which interpretation of PW is best. The interpretation of PW that we associate with a philosopher is the interpretation that she applies to her own usage of PW for serious explanatory purposes and which she commends to others. If a philosopher thinks that her serious explanatory purposes are not served by PW, however interpreted, then she is bound, when the chips are down, to abstain from its use. Otherwise, she is bound to give an account of what her serious usage amounts to. To that end, a full interpretation of PW discourse must issue a verdict on all of the following aspects of the discourse, especially concerning certain crucial, contested sentences: the truth-aptitude of sentences; the pattern of truth-values of sentences; the semantic structure of sentences; and the meanings of key theoretical terms they contain.

The question of truth-aptitude is whether the declarative sentences of PW are apt to be evaluated for truth and falsehood. The marks of truth-aptitude are often taken to include considerations of illocutionary force or of psychological antecedence – e.g. that the sentences articulate assertions, that they have a descriptive function or that they present mental states which are properly classed as beliefs.

If the declarative sentences of PW are rated as truth-evaluable, the next question is whether, among these, any in a special class of contested sentences of PW is true. It is necessary to focus on a special range of sentences for present purposes since any philosopher who finds a class of sentences truth-evaluable is bound, for trivial reasons, to hold that some are true.[3] A *contested* sentence of PW is one that meets two conditions: (a) it looks as though its use would conventionally be taken as (or as entailing) an assertion of the existence of a possible world that satisfies a certain non-modal condition and (b) it is accepted (and may be presumed known) by all parties that the actual world does not satisfy the non-modal condition in question. Thus, among the contested sentences of PW, I will assume, are:

(1) There is a possible world at which there are no humans.
(2) Some possible worlds have Newtonian space and time.
(3) There are possible worlds other than the actual world.
(4) There is a possible world at which there are talking donkeys.[4]

Given that a contested sentence, S, is truth-apt, our third question concerns its semantic structure. Specifically, the question is whether the sentence really has a semantic structure that permits valid inference to the existence of a possible world of the kind that satisfies the condition in question (that there is a possible world at which there are no humans, that there is a possible world that has Newtonian spacetime, etc.).

The remaining questions concern the meaning of any special, theoretical terms that figure in PW sentences and – more pragmatically – whether, on occasion, apparent quantification over worlds is to be construed as restricted in light of any prevailing contextual factor. Among the former, the salient question is what the 'possible world' expression is to be taken to mean. A fully satisfactory answer to this question would deliver verdicts on the question whether 'possible world' functions as a sortal predicate. If so, what are the criteria of identity and difference for things of that sort and, as we would ask of any predicate, what marks the difference between things that are of that sort and things that are not?

The stance that a philosopher takes on the matter of the interpretation of PW is crucial for two related reasons that will be developed presently. First, because commitment to an interpretation of PW will locate a philosopher as either a realist or an antirealist about possible worlds. That is, such a commitment will reflect either a belief in the existence of a plurality of possible worlds or the lack of such a belief. Second, because commitment to an interpretation of PW will determine whether or not a philosopher is entitled to claim that her use of PW affords certain kinds of philosophical application. Before substantiating these claims, it remains to complete the presentation of our three-fold distinction by commenting briefly on the notion of an application of PW.

(2.3) APPLICATIONS OF PW

An application of PW is a specific theoretical or explanatory purpose for which PW, under a given interpretation, is deployed. To anticipate further development, the central and broad kinds of PW application that must replace the earlier, uncommitted, talk of 'elucidations' are the conceptual, the ontological and the semantic. Within these respective kinds of explanation, we can identify more specific projects such as that of providing an analysis of the modal concepts, that of identifying certain kinds of (intensional) entity with entities of a more basic kind, that of specifying the truthmakers of modal sentences and that of providing a Kripkean semantics for some specific modal logic or language. This initial comment is intended only to convey an idea of what an application of PW is and how that contrasts with the discourse itself or an interpretation of it. I will expand on these matters of application, and their relation to realist and antirealist interpretations of PW, in Chapter 3. In the remainder of the present chapter, I will substantiate my earlier claim concerning the relationship between the interpretation of PW and the ontological issue of realism about possible worlds.

(2.4) ABSTENTIONISM, REALISM AND ANTIREALISM

The patterns of response to our questions of interpretation sort philosophers into the primary categories of abstentionists, realists and antirealists.

The most radical option available – one for which we should allow, even though it has not proved popular – is abstentionism. Therein, a philosopher resolves, when push comes to shove, to shut up rather than put up, and abstain altogether from PW talk. The abstentionist, in contrast with the philosopher who persists in the use of PW, has no obligation to provide an interpretation of PW since she proposes no application of the discourse for which she can be held to account. There are, undoubtedly, more things to be said about the varieties of abstentionism and their motivation. One might be drawn to abstentionism on the grounds that the philosophy of the modal and the intensional is a legitimate enterprise that is not best served by the use of PW. On the other hand, abstentionism about PW might be motivated by the more radical conviction that the modal and the intensional make a thoroughly bad lot that cannot coherently be represented, either in PW or otherwise. Since the abstentionist is a relatively minor character in what will unfold, I will not attempt to anticipate here the subtle variations that this position may afford.

Realism, as the term will be used throughout without further qualification, is the ontological thesis that there exists a plurality of possible worlds (of some kind or other). An interpretation of PW that yields positive answers to our first three questions, in respect of some contested sentences, is an interpretation that commits its proponent to realism in my sense. One who offers positive answers to the questions of truth-aptitude and semantic structure holds that some contested sentence of PW, S, is truth-apt and that the sentence entails an assertion of the existence of some possible world other than the actual world. This puts our interpreter in the position of having a conditional commitment to the existence of some non-actual possible world. Commitment to realism follows, then, when a positive verdict is returned on the truth of any contested sentence. Since a pattern of positive responses to all three primary questions of interpretation commits one to realism, any philosopher who wishes to avoid commitment to realism must withhold a positive verdict on at least one of the key questions of truth-aptitude, truth-value and semantic structure.

The philosophical character who persists in the use of PW, contra the abstentionist, under an interpretation that is intended to avoid commitment to realism is an *antirealist*.

Much more might be said about this way of carving out the options and by way of emphasizing exactly what realism and antirealism amount to. But before proceeding to further exposition of the main interpretational options, I will make four comments.

First, being an antirealist interpreter in the present sense is a matter of intent. The antirealist interpreter does not believe in a plurality of possible worlds and consequently she intends to avoid commitment to the ontological thesis of realism. But she may fail in this intention and really be committed to the ontological thesis of realism. Second, it may seem peculiar to identify realism as a thesis about the existence of *many* things of a kind rather than a thesis about the existence of some things (at least one thing) of a kind. However, it is not unprecedented that ontological disputes focus on a claim of the existence of many rather than a claim of the existence of at least one. Consider the cases of minds and times, where the question of the existence of 'others' might be held open once it is accepted that there exists one such thing – a 'one' to which (it might be supposed) we have special epistemic access. That feature of these cases is also relevant to the case of the existence of worlds. Third, and consequently, since realism is the thesis that a plurality of possible worlds exist then – even relative to a fixed conception of what 'possible world' is to be taken to mean – an antirealist may hold any of the following views: (a) no possible worlds exist; (b) exactly one possible world exists; (c) at least one possible world exists and we should be agnostic about the existence of others; (d) we should be agnostic about whether there are any possible worlds. I will have cause to distinguish these positions occasionally as we proceed. Fourth, strictly speaking, what our antirealist refuses to assent to is really a conjunctive claim of the type: the possible worlds are (all and only) the F's & there exists more than one F. For we ought to allow that the antirealist about possible worlds might, for quite independent reasons, believe that there are many entities of a type F that *others* wish to identify as the possible worlds, without herself being prepared to identify those entities as the possible worlds. That is, the antirealist may accept that a concept has many instances – say, maximal sum of spatiotemporally related individuals, or maximal consistent set of propositions – without accepting that any possible world falls under that concept. In that case our antirealist focuses her rejection on the first conjunct – that possible worlds are the F's – rather than the second – that there exists more than one F.

By characterizing the positions of realist and antirealist in relation to the interpretation of contested sentences of PW, we can chart the species of realism and antirealism in (what I hope is) an illuminating and fairly comprehensive way.

(2.5) REALISMS

Realism is reflected in an interpretational stance according to which: (a) PW sentences are truth-apt; (b) some contested sentences are true; and (c) such sentences have a semantic structure that permits valid inference to the existence of some non-actual possible world. The question of the nature of the possible worlds thus accepted is correlated with the further question concerning the meaning of the theoretical terms, and in particular that of the 'world' predicate. The two most familiar and distinct answers to this fourth question separate our realists into the camps of genuine realists and actualist realists.[5] Here I offer a brief, initial statement of each position.

The *genuine realist* (GR) takes unrestricted first-order existential quantification to range over a domain of individuals among which only some actually exist.[6] The GR concept of a world is that of a concrete object – an individual which is, in some sense, maximal. One such world is actual, and the many others are non-actual.[7] GR will be discussed at length in Chapters 4–9.

The actualist realist (AR) takes unrestricted quantification to range over all and only the things that actually exist. AR is significantly heterogeneous and affords (at least) four paradigm conceptions of the sense of the 'world' predicate. According to these respective paradigms 'world' refers to: (a) a certain kind of state of affairs (Plantingan realism, PR); (b) a certain kind of recombination of the actual individuals and the actually instantiated properties (combinatorial realism, CR); (c) a certain kind of complex property (nature realism, NR); or (d) a certain kind of collection of interpreted sentences (book realism, BR). AR holds that all of her worlds actually exist but only one is actualized. Typically, some AR worlds are possible and some impossible. Typically, AR worlds are abstract. Broadly, GR conceives of the possible worlds as a vast plurality of non-actual, concrete things while AR conceives of the possible worlds as a vast plurality of actual, abstract things.[8] AR will be discussed at length in Chapters 10–17. This covers the varieties of realism that will figure significantly below.

The debate between these two species of realist has been the dominant issue in the metaphysics of modality over the last three decades. The task undertaken in Parts II and III of this book is to provide a systematic account and evaluation of that debate.

(2.6) ANTIREALISMS

In contrast with the realist positions, the antirealist positions on possible worlds are severely underdeveloped. This is not to deny that the antirealist cause has been prosecuted on various fronts and even in some detail. However, there is, as far as I know, no systematic treatment of the options for antirealism about possible worlds. Indeed, as far as I know, no attempt has been made even to assess the capacity of any one species of antirealistic interpretation of PW to deliver the range of beneficial applications that are associated with the use of the discourse. Such a substantial treatment of antirealism about possible worlds lies outside the scope of this book. However, before proceeding to concentrate on the debate between genuine realists and actualist realists, I will conclude this chapter by indicating the strategies of interpretation that are available to the antirealist.

Antirealism requires an interpretational stance that stops short of affirming the following conjunction: that the declarative sentences of PW are truth-apt, that some contested sentences are true and that some have a semantic structure which permits valid inference of the existence of non-actual possible worlds.

The first and most radical antirealist strategy of interpretation denies that the declarative sentences of PW are truth-apt.[9] Such a strategy might aptly be described as non-cognitivist antirealism, expressivist antirealism or non-factualist antirealism (NFA). The definitive and negative dimension of non-factualism is the claim that the declarative sentences of a target discourse are not truth-apt and this is typically complemented by a positive account of the role or function of such sentences as something other than that of articulating assertions, describing anything or stating beliefs. This strategy of interpretation is familiar from many other philosophically interesting regions of discourse for which a realistic (usually, face-value) interpretation threatens troublesome ontological commitments. Prominent among such cases are those of discourse about morals, the mental, scientific unobservables and meaning.[10] Non-factualism about modality is a venerable doctrine that predates modal philosophers' preoccupation with possible worlds. Blackburn (1984: 213–16, 1986) has drawn reflectively on the pre-worldly modal non-factualist tradition in order to indicate, albeit very briefly, how and why a non-factualist strategy of interpretation might be focused on the discourse of PW.

The second antirealist strategy of interpretation is that of factualist antirealism (FA). FA grants that the sentences of PW, and especially the contested sentences, mean what they appear to mean in respect of illocutionary status (contra non-factualism) and semantic structure (contra structure-based antirealism below). The characteristic stance of FA is, rather, to decline to assent to the truth of any contested sentence. The FA strategy encompasses both error-theoretic and agnostic strands. The characteristic commitment of the stronger, error-theoretic strand of FA is that all of the contested sentences of the discourse are, and can justifiably be asserted to be, false. Prominent among the cases in which error theory has been prosecuted with a view to avoiding problematic ontological commitments are those concerning morals, colours, the past and the future, the mental and the mathematical.[11] The characteristic commitment of the weaker, agnostic strand of FA is that none of the contested sentences are known or can justifiably be asserted to be true.[12] In the case of modality, the FA tradition is barely detectable, and for PW in particular, such an interpretation has yet to be developed.

The final broad strategy of interpretation that is available to the antirealist invites the title of structure-based antirealism (SA). In this case, avoidance of commitment to a plurality of possible worlds rests on refusal to accept that the contested sentences have a semantic structure which permits valid inference of the existence of non-actual worlds. It is to be expected that the denial that contested sentences have such a semantic structure will be complemented by a positive account of semantic structure. In the two known species of SA about PW, the common form of positive account has it that quantification over possible worlds in contested sentences occurs semantically within the scope of some non-factive construction.[13] In the simplest type of case, then,

(4) There is a possible world at which there are talking donkeys

has a semantic structure of the type

(SA4) O[∃x(Wx & ... x ...)]

in which 'O' is a certain non-factive sentential operator.[14] The fictionalist and modalist species of SA are distinguished from one another by the selection of different non-factualist constructions to play the role.

In the case of fictionalist antirealism the non-factive operator is a story prefix or fictive prefix of the type, 'According to T _' where 'T' refers to a theory that postulates a plurality of worlds. In its most prominent specification, Rosen (1990), the supposed fiction occupying the 'T' place is taken to be a version of genuine realism about possible worlds. Thus, (4) emerges as having semantic structure

(F4) According to GR, [∃x(Wx & ... x ...)].

Obviously enough, 'fictionalism' is so-called precisely because it is a strategy of interpretation that has been invoked in service of antirealism about the entities that paradigmatically fictive discourses appear to be about (hobbits etc.). Moreover, such fictionalism is reminiscent of the kind of antirealist strategy in mathematics that proposes to interpret apparently unconditional mathematical claims as disguised or elliptical expressions of claims about what is, or would be, true given the truth of a certain set of axioms.[15,16]

In the case of the second species of SA, i.e. modalist antirealism, the ontologically deflating, non-factive operator is taken to be a primitive possibility operator, 'It is possible that _' ('◇'). Thus, (4) emerges as having semantic structure:

(M4) ◇[∃x(Wx & ... x ...)].

This kind of modalism might usefully be further specified as worldly modalism since it is a non-abstentionist position that invites us to embrace PW, and hence worldly expressions, under a primitively modal interpretation. By contrast, unworldly modalism is a position that commends abstention from using PW in favour of using traditional, primitively modal but worldless forms of expression. Modalism has had many recent proponents but the contemporary statement and defence of the position is primarily associated with Prior.[17] Relatedly, and more generally, as with all of the other antirealist strategies of interpretation that we have considered, the reading of ontologically problematic sentences as occurring within the scope of a (presumed) non-factive possibility operator is familiar from the mathematical case.[18]

Thus, as advertised, we have versions of antirealism about possible worlds that are correlated with a non-positive answer to either the question of truth-aptitude, the question of truth or the question of semantic structure concerning the contested sentences of PW. However, although an interpreter's antirealist convictions are expressed through an answer to one of these questions, the view that she takes on the fourth question of interpretation – concerning the meaning of 'possible world' and related theoretical terms – cannot be presumed irrelevant to the defensibility of her interpretation. Since the antirealist proposes an interpretation of PW which she applies to her own serious usage of the discourse and commends to others she thus presumes about the discourse under her favoured interpretation what the abstentionist is wont to deny about it under any interpretation – namely that PW is coherent and equipped to sustain some application. Consequently, we should anticipate that there will be something at stake when the antirealist interpreter chooses, say, to enter into agreement with GR rather than AR (or vice versa) about the concept that 'possible world' is to be taken to express. For we should anticipate that both the coherence of an antirealist interpretation of PW and at least some of the kinds of application that it may be supposed to afford are matters that are sensitive to a decision about the concept that 'possible world' expresses even once it is assumed, as by the antirealist, that the concept has at most one instance. However, present ambition concerning the illumination of antirealism about PW is limited to the basic taxonomy of the interpretational strategies and indication of where these have been developed, if at all, in the case of PW.

Hereafter, as indicated previously, I will be concerned exclusively with the debate between the two kinds of realist about PW.

CHAPTER 3

Why possible-world talk is used

Chapter 1 presented a picture of the modal and intensional territory that talk of possible worlds has been supposed to elucidate. But why exactly is PW used? What kinds of elucidation or explanation does such talk bring? What kinds of philosophical project does PW serve? What kinds of application does PW afford? Here I present an inventory of such applications in order to ask subsequently which can be sustained by the realist interpretations of PW. The three categories into which applications will be divided are the conceptual (3.1), the ontological (3.2) and the semantic (3.3)–(3.4).

(3.1) CONCEPTUAL APPLICATIONS OF PW

PW may be applied in order to elucidate modal and intensional *concepts*. In general, the objects of conceptual elucidation are – naturally enough – concepts. However, the immediate focus of any attempt at conceptual elucidation is typically and standardly some range of sentences containing items of vocabulary that are taken to express those concepts. Thus, attempts to elucidate – say – moral, mental or mathematical concepts typically take the form of attempts to define, to give the senses of, or to elucidate the meanings of families of moral, mental or mathematical terms or sentences. In that spirit, the general form of a PW conceptual elucidation of given modal or intensional concepts will take the form of a PW articulation of the meaning of some such terms.[1] Such a PW articulation of the meaning of a modal or intensional expression may be intended as explicit or implicit, as modal or non-modal, or as intensional or extensional. I will say something about each of these distinctions in turn.

An explicit account or analysis of a concept (the explicit definition of a term) is articulated by way of a biconditional. The left-side of the biconditional contains some item of vocabulary taken as the canonical means of expressing the concept that is the intended analysandum. The right-side of the biconditional expresses the analysans which is taken to be appropriately 'free' of the concept that is the analysandum. Thus, in cases where the relevant concept is expressed by a predicate we might encounter attempts at explicit analysis such as:

(1) $\forall x[x \text{ is good iff } A_1(x)]$
(2) $\forall x[x \text{ is a natural number iff } A_2(x)]$

in which – at least – no use of 'good' figures in the sentence that takes the place of '$A_1(x)$' and no use of 'natural number' figures in the sentence that takes the place of '$A_2(x)$'. To present a case in which the relevant concept is expressed by a sentential operator, rather than by a predicate, we might encounter an attempt at explicit analysis such as:

(3) $(\text{If P then Q}) \text{ iff } A_3(P,Q)$

in which – at least – no use of the 'if ... then ...' construction figures in the sentence that takes the place of '$A_3(P,Q)$'. The typical intention behind such explicit analysis or definition is that the right-side of the biconditional in question should provide the means for replacing any occurrence of the canonical expression of the concept under analysis ('good', 'natural number', etc.).[2] It should not be ruled out that analyses may be successful and useful even if they do not permit the means of invariably replacing analysed terms as explicit analysis. To put the point otherwise, a proposal may succeed as an implicit analysis even if it does not succeed as an explicit analysis. But, having noted this point, I will focus henceforth on the case of explicit analysis.[3]

In the case that concerns us, PW might be supposed capable of articulating explicit analyses of the concepts of property, possibility, counterfactual dependence, etc. by supplying sentences (in which the key left-side expressions do not figure) to take their places on the right-sides of the following biconditionals:

(4) $\forall x[x \text{ is a property iff } A_4(x)]$
(5) $(\text{It is possible that P}) \text{ iff } A_5(P)$
(6) $(\text{If it had been that P then it would have been that Q}) \text{ iff } A_6(P,Q)$.

This is not, of course, to say that just any such sentences will do the job. There are further conditions that would naturally be thought necessary for any such explicit analysis to be successful – most notably, that the analysing biconditional should be analytic (hence necessary) and, perhaps, that some sort of priority should attach to the intended analysans. However, these considerations aside, there is one further point that merits emphasis if the role of PW in conceptual analysis is to be made clear.

In the special case of (broadly) functional analysis a concept is presented as the concept that satisfies a certain higher-order description or, to put the point more naturally, as the concept of a property that plays a certain complex role. Thus philosophers present functional analyses of concepts such as, say, pain in biconditionals of the form:

(7) $\forall X[X = \text{Pain iff } R_1(X)]$

in which '$R_1(X)$' articulates a complex role – specified, in this case, by reference to sensory input, other mental states and behavioural output. Similarly, one might present a functional analysis of the concept of a property, or of being-a-property, thus:

(8) $\forall X[X = \text{Being-a-Property iff } R_2(X)]$.

The functional specification might invoke the sub-roles of properties as semantic values or as the grounds of similarity or whatever – the details do not matter here. What does matter is that the conceptual project of functional analysis is commonly allied to, but is to be distinguished from, the ontological project of identifying the thing that actually plays the role in question as an entity of some familiar kind – typically, a kind that is already recognized in the analyst's ontology. It is, perhaps, not out of the question that a philosopher might seek to apply PW in discharging the conceptual task of spelling out the roles in question. However, in a 'functional theory' of the intensions – the properties, the propositions, etc. – PW is much less likely to figure directly in the conceptual project of specifying roles than it is to figure directly in the related, ontological project of identifying role-players (see (3.2) below). In any event, conceptual analysis, via specification of functional roles or otherwise, is one prospective application of PW; ontological identification is another.

I turn now to the distinction between modal and non-modal conceptual elucidations. Obviously any PW elucidation of a modal concept is modal in the trivial sense that it is elucidation of a concept that has been identified as modal. The issue is whether interpreted PW sentences are to be counted as modal analysans when they are used for the purpose of providing a conceptual elucidation of given modal or intensional analysanda. At first approximation, an analysans might be counted modal either because of its use of an explicitly modal term (perhaps, 'possible') or because of its use of some term whose meaning could only adequately be explained by use of a modal term.[4] Successful explicit and non-modal analysis requires that the modal concept that is the analysandum should not itself figure as an element of the analysans. But an explicit analysis of one modal concept might be counted illuminating and successful if the analysans involved the use of another modal concept. So PW, under an interpretation, might be applied for the purpose of intra-modal conceptual analysis or elucidation. When the aim is intra-modal conceptual analysis, it then becomes a challenging and interesting question how many distinct modal concepts interpreted PW must contain if it is to furnish successful analyses of the entire family of modal and intensional concepts. In the limiting case of intra-modal analysis, PW under a given interpretation may embody only one primitive modal concept and thereby afford adequate analyses of the entire family of modal and intensional concepts. Such a body of analyses might be said to be circular with respect to the family of concepts as a whole but non-circular with respect to all but one of the member concepts. It is a distinct and clearly stronger claim that appropriately interpreted PW may be applied to yield a thoroughly extra-modal analysis of the family of modal and intensional concepts. That would be to claim – at least – that an explicit analysis can be given of any of the modal or intensional concepts in which the (interpreted) PW analysans contains neither any explicitly modal term nor any term whose meaning can only be adequately conveyed by using some explicit modal term. The topic of thoroughly non-modal, i.e. extra-modal, analyses is discussed at length in Chapter 7 and Chapter 11.

Finally, just as PW may be applied with a view to providing either modal or non-modal analyses, so it may be applied with a view to providing either intensional or extensional analyses of modal and intensional concepts. Indeed, when the benefits of PW are listed, the feature of extensionality is very often invoked and even given pride of place (see e.g. Blackburn 1984, Lycan 1991a and Yagisawa 1988). However, the issue is complex, for the distinction between intensional and extensional is conceived in various ways in the literature. I

Introduction

propose to deal with the issue of 'extensional analysis' by (a) identifying three prospective applications of PW, each of which speaks to one version of the distinction between extensional and intensional, and then (b) assigning each of these various 'extensionalizing' applications of PW to a category other than the conceptual – i.e. the ontological or the semantic.

Sometimes an ontological distinction is intended – there are intensional entities and extensional entities. It is not entirely obvious exactly how the intended ontological distinction might be spelled out. But I venture that the underlying ontological issue is that of safe and sane ontology and, in particular, where that issue is conceived at least partly as a matter of whether a putative kind of entity has been supplied with appropriate criteria of identity. One major challenge presented by the formidable critique of modality due to Quine (1947, 1951, 1953a, 1953b and 1961) is that of purging modal language (and logic) of semantically generated commitment to 'dark' intensional entities such as essences that are held dubious (unsafe or insane) on such grounds. Among the respectable extensional entities, it is supposed, are individuals and sets. Subsequently, analyses that purport quantification over only such things might be deemed 'extensional' in virtue of that fact. That is one way in which extensional analysis might be thought advantageous and associated with PW. But I would prefer to deal directly with the underlying ontological issues – i.e. issues of safety and sanity of ontology, and of how questions of criteria of identity bear on these.[5]

Sometimes a logical distinction seems to be intended – there are extensional logics and intensional logics. Spelling out that distinction might involve fiercely complex, controversial and technical issues. But there is some hope that these issues can be bypassed. I presume that ordinary first-order predicate logic will count as extensional if any logic does. Moreover, if PW affords a Kripkean semantics (see (3.4) below) for a given modal logic or language then I presume that this will be enough to justify the use of the methods of first-order predicate logic – and so, by hypothesis, extensional methods – in evaluating relevant modal inferences. Perhaps the provision of such a semantic theory might be presented as a victory for extensional analysis but, again, I would prefer to deal directly with the issue of whether, or to what extent, an interpretation of PW can deliver such a semantic theory.

Sometimes a linguistic or semantic distinction is intended – there are intensional and extensional expressions.[6] This version of the distinction concerns the preservation of truth-value under substitution of actually extensionally equivalent expressions. In the case of sentential operators, extensionality is (partially) expressible thus:

(E) A sentential operator 'O' is extensional only if [(O(p) iff O(q)) iff (p iff q)].

So judged, all of the standard modal sentential operators are non-extensional (intensional). To take one case as an example, any possibility operator will fail of extensionality given that *only some* falsehoods are (in that sense) possible – thus the falsehood of (9) and the truth of (10):

(9) (It is possible that there are talking donkeys) iff (It is possible that $1 = 0$)
(10) (There are talking donkeys) iff $(1 = 0)$.

It is therefore natural to say that such a possibility operator and other explicitly modal operators are non-extensional expressions. To cut sharply across a very formidable corner, I venture that the underlying issue here has been the very semantic coherence of modal languages. The failures of substitutivity that constitute the intensionality of the modal operators appear to show that the semantic value of a modal sentence is not, in general, a function of the semantic values (e.g. truth-values) of its constituent expressions (and their mode of composition). This would suggest that we can have no systematic account of the truth-conditions of modal sentences and, in turn, that the modal expressions, and the sentences in which they occur, are deficient in sense. Another major challenge presented by Quine (1947, 1951, 1953a, 1953b and 1961) is that of vindicating the coherence of modal languages by providing an adequate compositional semantics for such languages in face of the apparent and characteristic intensionality of the modal expressions.[7] Accordingly, we might subsequently use the term 'extensional analysis' to dignify a representation of the truth-conditions of modal sentences that avoids the problems of substitutivity and affords a compositional semantics. Such an account might be construed as presenting the original failures of substitutivity as a phenomenon of the surface syntax of the modal sentences of natural languages – a phenomenon that has no analogue at the important level of regimentation where semantic structure is made perspicuous. I will take it, then, that an interpretation of PW meets the challenge posed by the intensionality of modal expressions when it affords an appropriate, compositional,

Introduction

semantic theory for modal languages. And so this is another aspect of 'extensional analysis' that I propose to deal with under the heading of semantic applications of PW.[8]

I will take it that the notion of 'extensional analysis' is drained of interest once we have dealt with the ontological and semantic applications of PW that have been identified. Consequently, I will deal with these applications directly and comment explicitly on the matter of extensionality only occasionally and briefly in doing so.

(3.2) ONTOLOGICAL APPLICATIONS OF PW

PW may be applied to serve at least two distinguishable kinds of *ontological* aim.

The first case is the aim of *ontological identification* in which PW articulates the identification of some familiar kind of entity as a certain kind of construct out of possible worlds. Typically, although not invariably, it is a kind of intensional entity (proposition, property etc.) that is so identified. There are three kinds of claim that one has to be in a position to make in order to articulate a thorough and proper (non-trivial) ontological identification. First, there is an equivalence thesis of the form:

(11) $\forall x[Ix \text{ iff } Qx]$

in which 'I' expresses the kind that is the target of ontological identification and 'Q' expresses a kind of construction out of possible worlds and their elements – e.g. anything is a property iff it is a set of possible individuals. Such an equivalence thesis is not in itself a piece of conceptual analysis.[9] But the conception of an equivalence thesis as grounding an ontological identification is inevitably informed by some conception of the analysis of the concept. For example we should expect the analysis of the concept of a proposition (e.g. a specification of the proposition-role) to exert some constraints on the kind of thing that a proposition can be. Such constraints are conditional. They are of the form: if there are things that play the proposition-role then they must be thus and so. Neither such claims nor equivalence theses, such as (11), entail the existence of I's. To that extent, one can use PW to give an ontological account of the kind I – what it *would be* to be such a thing – without commitment to realism about I's. Second, given an appropriate equivalence thesis, it is necessary and sufficient for realism about I's that a further non-emptiness condition should hold, e.g.:

(12) ∃x[Qx]

where (12), of course, is an interpreted sentence of PW. Third, and finally, in this regard, among the constraints on the adequacy of a proposed ontological identification (if there are things that play the proposition-role then they must be . . .) constraints of numerical adequacy deserve a special mention. The adequacy of any proposal to identify the natural numbers with (say) sets of a certain kind, requires that there are – and that the proponent of identification is in a position to say that there are – enough of those sets to be the natural numbers. Moreover, we might expect that what is enough in this respect might be a matter about which an analysis of the concept of natural number would inform us. Of course we do not require that the analysis of every concept should determine on its own how many distinct things fall under that concept. But the analysis of a concept, along with other considerations may constrain that, if there are such things as I's, then, whatever the I's are, there have to be at least n distinct such things. So one who proposes to use PW to articulate an ontological identification of the propositions (say) had better be in a position to assert that there are enough possible-world constructs to be the various and distinct propositions.[10]

The other kind of ontological application that PW might be thought to afford is that of specifying truthmakers for modal truths. But there are substantial obstacles in the way of a clean and straightforward account of this issue. Realist interpreters of PW have not claimed explicitly or often that the specification of truthmakers for modal truths is a benefit that (suitably interpreted) PW delivers.[11] Nonetheless, I believe many are drawn to this claim or, at least, have entertained it. In that light, a discussion of PW as a means of specifying truthmakers for modal truths will be largely exploratory but not, I trust, uncalled for. The particular case of modal truth aside, there is an enormous range of questions that bear on the matter of how an adequate specification of truthmakers should proceed. Is truthmaking always purely existential – is it always a matter of the existence of a something, the existence of which is necessary and sufficient (in some sense) for the sentence in question to be true? When truthmaking is existential, for which kinds or categories of entity does existence make for truth? Is there one–one correspondence between truths and truthmakers, or can the correspondence be many–one or one–many – relatedly, what is the relationship between sentential complexity and the complexity of truthmakers?[12] In demanding truthmakers for truths are we to consider reaching beyond contingent truth or treating non-contingent truth differently? These difficulties – the want of explicit advocates of a truthmaker-specifying role for PW, and general questions about the detail of the truthmaker-specifying programme – are jointly formidable. But I believe that one can cut a path through them in order to make some substantial points about the capacity of the different interpreters of PW to speak to the issue of truthmakers. The most effective way of cutting such a path is, I believe, by focusing on one major question. Is the proponent of a given interpretation of PW in a position to endorse the existence of a kind of entity, the existence of which is plausibly necessary and sufficient for some claim of non-actualized possibility to be true?

Before leaving the topic of ontological applications, I note that ontological applications of PW tend to be completely overlooked in the antirealist literature. The antirealist literature is dominated by concern with the semantic and conceptual applications of PW. There is an obvious diagnosis of why that should be so. By resisting realism, the antirealist interpreter simply deprives herself of the ontological resources that are required to underpin the ontological applications of PW. If (other) possible worlds are not in one's ontology then one cannot plausibly maintain the existence of intensional entities and their identity with constructions out of possible worlds, and one cannot hold that certain modal claims are true and are made true simply by the existence of such things.[13] So antirealist interpreters have ignored or neglected ontological applications of PW because their interpretations afford no such applications. Perhaps so. But let us not be too hasty in judging that this puts antirealists at a disadvantage to realists, for the extent to which the realists can maintain these putative ontological applications of PW remains to be seen.

(3.3) SEMANTIC APPLICATIONS OF PW

PW has *semantic* applications. There are, of course, semantic aspects of the conceptual and ontological applications that have already been outlined. But what I have in mind here are applications of PW in presenting relatively rigorous, systematic or 'formal' semantic theories of modal and intensional languages (or logics). In charting this territory we broach a range of issues that have more to do with general considerations of semantic methodology than with semantical theorizing of the modal (and intensional) *per se*. In order to concentrate on the latter, I will deal briskly with the former.

Systematic semantics is about identifying certain explanatory aims, matching explanatory aims to a certain style of theory and then constructing an adequate theory in that style. In the case of the systematic semantics of modality, the range of relatively well known explanatory aims includes the provision of some or all of the following: the logically or semantically perspicuous expression or regimentation of natural language sentences; a theory of meaning for a natural language – perhaps a theory that demonstrates the learnability of the language and the coherence of some of its controversial modal idioms; a characterization, and perhaps even an explanation, of the valid modal inferences in a language; the demonstration of metalogical results (completeness, soundness, etc.) for various modal logics; a justification for using first-order logical methods to evaluate modal arguments.[14] The semantic theories for modal languages that are most familiar to philosophers come in two styles. One is a broadly Kripkean, model-theoretic semantic theory for quantified modal logic and the other a Tarskian theory of absolute truth for variously strong modal languages.[15] The general idea behind a systematic semantic application of PW, then, is that interpreted PW should provide a metalanguage in which a theory in one or other of these styles, and adequate to one or other of the explanatory aims, can be constructed for a suitable modal object language. The legitimacy of many of the explanatory aims listed is in dispute as is the capacity of one or other style of semantic theory to meet them. However, rather than attempt to engage with such general methodological issues or justify any particular combinations of explanatory aim and style of theory I will settle on one issue of semantic application to pursue throughout the remainder of the book. The issue is whether a given interpretation of PW affords the presentation of an adequate semantic theory in the (broad) style of the Kripke (1963) model theory for quantified modal logic (QML).[16] Discussion of this style of semantic theory dominates the philosophical literature, but the decision to focus on it does not rest only on the consideration of familiarity. More importantly this style of semantic theory is typical, since the most important and immediate philosophical challenges that it poses are those posed by 'possible-world' semantic theories in general.

As in the case of the ontological applications, it is not either kind of realist but the antirealist who is naturally and immediately called to account over her entitlement to use semantic theories in either of the styles described.[17] The primary philosophical question that is raised by a PW presentation of a semantic theory, in either style, is

Introduction

how one can assert the theory in question without commitment to realism about possible worlds. For all such theories *appear* to involve quantification over sets and sequences whose members are possible worlds. The next philosophical question that is raised by a PW presentation of a semantic theory, in either style, is how one can assert the theory in question without commitment to realism about possible individuals. For all such theories also *appear* to involve quantification over sets and sequences whose members are possible individuals. Both of these major philosophical questions arise whether the semantic theory is Kripkean in style or Tarskian in style. So, in the present context, I let the former do philosophical duty for both.

In the next section, I will sketch a semantic theory for QMLs in the style of Kripke (1963) in order to establish both the notation and the philosophical aspects of the theory that will figure in subsequent chapters.[18]

(3.4) A SKETCH OF A KRIPKEAN PW-SEMANTICS FOR QML

I will first sketch the Kripke semantics as a pure semantics.[19] We begin by distinguishing the syntax of a certain kind of object language under study from its semantics. Syntactically, our first-order modal language, L, is that of an ordinary non-modal predicate logic (predicates, names, quantifiers, variables, sentential connectives of negation, conjunction, etc.) extended by two sentential operators – a box, '$\Box$', and a diamond, '$\Diamond$', that make (open) closed sentences when you prefix them to (open) closed sentences. So among the closed sentences of the object language we find – e.g.:

$\Diamond$Fa, $\Box$Fb, $\Diamond\Box$Fa, $\exists$x$\Box$Fx, $\Diamond\forall$yGy, $\Box\Diamond\exists$x[Fx $\vee$ ~ $\Box\forall$y[Gy & Hxy]].

In the semantic theory, a model for L is a sequence <W, w*, R, D, Q, V> whose elements are characterized minimally as variously inter-related, but otherwise arbitrary, set-theoretic entities. W is a non-empty set, w* is a member of W, R is a relation on the members of W, D is a non-empty set and Q is a function from W to subsets of D. V is a function that takes <n-place predicate, W-member> pairs to n-tuples of members of D, takes each variable and name to a member of D and takes each <closed sentence, W-member> pair to exactly one member of {0, 1}. This last point about V is important and bears some expansion. The idea is that V assigns to each <closed atomic sentence, W-member> pair one of the elements in {0, 1} and then assigns to each <closed non-atomic sentence, W-member> pair one of the elements {0, 1} according to certain recursive principles – e.g. for any closed sentences A, B and any W-members, w, v:

(V,~) $V<\sim A,w> = 1$ iff $V<A,w> = 0$; otherwise $V<\sim A,w> = 0$
(V,&) $V<A \& B, w> = 1$ iff $V<A,w> = 1$ and $V<B,w> = 1$;
       otherwise $V<A \& B, w> = 0$.

In the case of the quantifiers, we have to proceed indirectly. We proceed through assignments of values in {0,1} to triples of open sentences, assignments (I) of elements of D to variables, and W-members – thus:

(V, ∀) $V<\forall x[A(x, y_1 \ldots y_n)], I_k, w> = 1$ iff
        for all I_i, $V<[A(x, y_1 \ldots y_n)], I_i, w> = 1$;
        otherwise $V<\forall x[A(x, y_1 \ldots y_n)], I_k, w> = 0$.[20]

Then, returning to the easier kind of case involving closed sentences, we have, in particular:

(V,◇) $V<\Diamond A, w> = 1$ iff there is a v such that Rvw and
       $V<A,v> = 1$; otherwise $V<\Diamond A,w> = 0$
(V,□) $V<\Box A, w> = 1$ iff for all v such that Rvw, $V<A,v> = 1$;
       otherwise $V<\Box A,w> = 0$.

We then have the following definition:

(VAL) For all L-sentences, A, A is valid iff
       for all models, M, and for all W-members, w:
       $V<A,w> = 1$.

Given various judicious, but non-*ad hoc* restrictions on models, it is subsequently demonstrable that various independently familiar sets of inference rules for the object language – i.e. various modal logics – are sound (all of the theorems that they produce are valid sentences of L) and complete (that all the valid sentences of L are theorems).[21]

I emphasize that the above statement of the pure semantic theory does not involve talk of possible worlds or any of the other distinctive vocabulary of PW. So there is no question of anyone who

Introduction

endorses this piece of algebra – as it is sometimes described – being thereby committed to the existence of many possible worlds. Anyone can endorse the pure theory so long as they believe in sets and the set-theoretic entities that the theory postulates.[22] The pure theory begins by presuming nothing about the meaning of the box and the diamond and ends by telling us no more than that they function semantically in the way that certain quantifiers do, and that certain sentences that feature those expressions are valid. The shift from a pure semantic theory to an applied semantic theory occurs when the theorist construes the box and diamond – and the other items of L vocabulary – as representing certain, antecedently meaningful, expressions of natural language. The thought is that we can gain certain semantic insight (explanation, illumination, vindication, etc.) in the case of natural languages by establishing semantic results about their formal analogues such as L. The application of the pure semantics to a fragment of modal English is based on the presumption that box represents 'It is necessary that' and diamond represents 'It is possible that'. Once that is presumed, however, the pure semantics has to be further articulated so as to specify, by way of a class of special intended models, the domain of the quantifiers to which these operators are semantically akin.[23] It is this further articulation that involves the use of PW, that gives us a semantic theory that is taken to apply to the modal expressions of English and which deserves to be called a 'possible-worlds' semantic theory.

The canonical articulation of the applied semantic theory proceeds as follows. W is the set of all possible worlds, w^* is the actual world, R is a relation of accessibility on the set of all possible worlds, D is the set of all possible individuals and Q is a function that assigns to each possible world a domain of individuals that exist at that world. V is a valuation function that assigns each predicate an extension at each possible world and assigns each closed sentence one of the truth-values T, F at each world (relative to each assignment of possible individuals to each name and variable). In particular, we have for any closed sentences A, B and any possible worlds w, v:

$(V, \Diamond)$ $V<\Diamond A, w> = T$ iff
there is a v such that v is accessible from w and $V<A,v> = T$;
otherwise $V<\Diamond A,w> = F$

$(V, \Box)$ $V<\Box A, w> = T$ iff
for all v such that v is accessible from w, $V<A,v> = T$;
otherwise $V<\Box A,w> = F$.

So articulated – i.e. when articulated in terms of PW – the theory is supposed to be apt to answer semantic questions about our familiar modal talk and reasoning. Such an applied semantics in this style – hereafter, simply a PW-semantics – is, therefore, a benefit that use of PW may afford if appropriately interpreted.

(3.5) OTHER APPLICATIONS OF PW

For our purposes, the kinds of application that PW may be supposed to afford can be limited to the ontological, conceptual and the semantic as outlined. But before advancing the main agenda, I would like to draw a line under the issue of applications of PW by commenting on the use of PW for various other purposes that will not figure significantly in what follows.

First, whilst PW has been widely held to serve various conceptual, ontological and semantic projects it is notable that PW has not widely been held to further the cause of modal epistemology.[24]

Second, the above inventory of ontological, conceptual and semantic applications of PW does purport to cover the central kinds of application but it does not purport to be exhaustive. For example, a further kind of metaphysical, rather than narrowly ontological, project that the discourse has been invoked to serve is that of articulating a priori cosmological explanations (cf. Schlesinger 1984, van Inwagen 1996).

Third, and following on from the previous point, talk of 'many worlds' and indeed of 'many possible worlds' figures prominently these days at the more empirical end of cosmology and in certain branches of theoretical physics. Thus, Skyrms (1976) cites the many worlds interpretation of quantum mechanics (DeWitt and Graham (eds) 1973) as a non-philosophical source of the idea that there is a plurality of (concrete) possible worlds. The worlds envisaged in such empirical theories are able to serve their empirical explanatory purposes since they are invariably conceived as having individual parts that overlap or otherwise stand in 'transworld' causal or 'transworld' spatiotemporal relations to one another. Moreover, it is presumably the case that the existence of many such worlds is a matter of absolute contingency since it is a matter of absolute contingency whether quantum theory is true. Although I will not argue the point, I take it that these considerations give strong grounds for holding that talk of possible worlds so construed is unsuited to serve the philosophical projects that have been outlined above. Whether PW can be interpreted in ways that have not been taken into account here and so as

Introduction

to afford empirical applications is a matter that has no bearing on the agenda that is pursued in this book.

Fourth, and finally, it is claimed in various ways that use of PW brings a certain quality of imaginative assistance to our thinking about modal and intensional matters – that the imagery of PW is vivid, that it is of heuristic value, that it aids the imagination, etc. This claim is hardly contestable. Consider as a typical claim involving iterated modality, articulated without the benefit of the distinctive resources of PW, the following:

(13)   It is necessarily contingent that there are kangaroos.

Consider now the standard PW 'translation' of (13):

(14)   At every world w there is a world u that is accessible from w at which there are kangaroos and there is a world v that is accessible from w at which there are no kangaroos.

The modal aspect of (13) fails to engage the pictorial imagination whilst the worldly aspect of (14) is apt to do so to some effect. More generally, the PW picture – the picture of many worlds, the one visually distinguished actual world, the many arrows of accessibility drawn among the worlds – is, indeed, psychologically compelling. This psychological benefit of PW might count, on the margin, in the dispute between those who advocate the use of PW and those who advocate abstention, but it counts for nothing in the competition among interpreters of PW. In particular, the picture itself is the common property of all realist interpreters of PW – if not of all interpreters of PW – and it is of no significance in settling any philosophical issue that arises among them. What will differ from interpreter to interpreter, of course, is the story about what in reality – if anything – corresponds to the elements of the picture and that is when the philosophical issues arise.

The most general and introductory phase of the book ends here. It is now time to consider the realist interpretations of PW in some detail and to attempt some evaluation of their relative merits. This evaluation will be based on an exploration of their capacity and effectiveness in sustaining the kinds of application that have been identified and on their philosophical virtues and vices more generally. GR is discussed in Part II and AR is discussed in Part III.

Part II

Genuine realism

CHAPTER 4

Genuine realism: exposition and applications

The most famous – perhaps, infamous – species of realism about possible worlds is the genuine realism (GR) of David Lewis. In the present chapter, I offer what I take to be the mature version of GR presented in Lewis (1986a) but drawing also on Lewis (1968, 1970, 1973, 1983a and b) (and – in one respect – Divers (1999a)).[1] In the remainder of Part II, I deal with the critical evaluation of GR discussing issues concerning quantification over non-actuals (Chapter 5), worlds (Chapter 6), primitive modality (Chapter 7), counterpart theory (Chapter 8) and epistemology (Chapter 9).

(4.1) INTERPRETATION

The GR interpretation of PW proceeds in different ways depending on whether we are dealing with a case of de dicto modality or a case of de re modality.[2] In a straightforward case of absolute, alethic de dicto possibility, we move from the English (1) to the neutral PW claim (1*) and then to the GR interpretation (G1*):

(1)   There might have been talking donkeys.
(1*) There is a possible world at which there are talking donkeys.
(G1*) $\exists x \exists y [Wx \ \& \ Pyx \ \& \ Dy \ \& \ Ty]$.[3]

In (G1*), a world ('Wx') being possible is construed as a matter of its unrestricted existence ('$\exists \ldots$ [Wx $\ldots$]') and the existence of talking donkeys at the world is construed as the world having such things ('Dy & Ty') among its parts ('Pyx'). In a straightforward case of absolute, alethic de re possibility, we move from the English, to the (neutral) PW claim and finally, to the GR interpretation, thus:

(2)   Carnap might have been a footballer.
(2*) There is a possible world at which Carnap is a footballer.
(G2*) ∃x∃y[Wx & Pyx & Cyc & Fy].

As before, the existence of a possible world is construed as the existence *simpliciter* of a world and what is the case at the world is a matter of what is in the world – i.e. how its parts are. However, what is required specifically of a world in order that it represents that Carnap is a footballer is: (i) that the world represents the existence of Carnap by its having a part that is a *counterpart* of Carnap ('Cyc')[4] and (ii) that part represents Carnap being a footballer by its being a footballer ('Fy'). Restricted alethic modalities are treated in terms of quantification over contextually variable, restricted spheres of worlds – just those in which actual laws of nature hold, or which are indiscernible from our own up until a counterpart of one of our times, etc. Insofar as my claim:

(3)   Nothing can travel at velocity v

is construed as a claim of de dicto nomological impossibility, it will be interpreted as the claim that there is no world that is nomologically accessible from this world α ('Rxα') and at which anything travels at velocity v ('Vyv'):

(G3*) ~∃x[Wx & Rxα & ∃y[Pyx & Vyv]].

In GR, expressions of actuality are interpreted as meaning 'this-worldly'. Such an interpretation presents 'actual' and its cognates as items whose function is to refer to, or to restrict quantification within, some given world. The expressions in question are treated as indexical since which world is the given world is determined by the context in which a sentence is uttered as well as its (context-independent) content. When such expressions occur with their primary sense, their function is straightforwardly token-reflexive – that is, in any world w (in any sentential context of any sentence token) the expression introduces the world in which the token is uttered. To call a world 'actual' in this primary sense, is like referring to this place as 'here', or to this time as 'now' or to oneself as 'I'. So the modal claim:

(4) There is something that actually exists which might not have existed

has, on the natural de re reading, as its worldly analogue:

(4*) Something exists at this world and at some possible world it does not exist

which – as uttered in α, with 'this world' interpreted in its primary token-reflexive sense – becomes

(G4*) $\exists x[Px\alpha \ \& \ \exists y[Wy \ \& \ \forall z[Pzy \rightarrow \sim Czx]]]$.[5]

In cases (1*) and (4*) GR presents us with an interpretation of a contested PW sentence as truth-apt, which we may take to be true and as involving wide-scope existential quantification in such a way that the truth of the sentence requires the existence of some non-actual possible world. Hence the realism of GR interpretation.[6]

(4.2) ONTOLOGY AND PRIMITIVE CONCEPTS

Salient among the ontological theses of GR are the following. There exists an infinite plurality of possible worlds. From the standpoint of each possible world, including our own, that world itself is actual and the other possible worlds that exist are non-actual. The possible worlds are causally and spatiotemporally closed, individuals. No world stands in any causal or spatiotemporal relation to any world other than itself or to any part of a world other than its own parts. Individuals are worldbound in that no individual is such that all of it exists in more than one world. However, we can pin matters down more firmly, for the ontology of GR lends itself to systematic presentation as a set of postulates which characterize the ontological primitives of the theory in kind, number and variety. These postulates also provide as constructs out of the primitive entities whichever entities feature in subsequent applications of GR.[7]

The ontological primitives of GR, then, are sets and individuals:

(O1) There are sets.
(O2) There are individuals.
(O3) Everything is either a set or an individual.[8]

Genuine realism

Individuals are formed from individuals according to a principle of unrestricted mereological summation:

(O4) For any individuals, there exists an individual which is the mereological sum of exactly those individuals.[9]

The variety of sets is characterized thus:

(O5) There is an empty set.
(O6) For every individual x there is a set y such that x is the unique member of y.
(O7) There exist ... (all of the sets in the standard set-theoretic hierarchy, these being constructed iteratively out of the empty set and the singleton sets of individuals).

Among the individuals are the worlds:

(O8) Some individuals are worlds.
(O9) An individual x is a world iff any parts of x are spatiotemporally related to each other, and anything spatiotemporally related to any part of x is itself a part of x.
(O10) Every individual that is a part of a world is a part of exactly one world.
(O11) α is the world of which we are parts.
(O12) For any individuals $x_1, x_2, \ldots x_n$ there is a world containing any number of duplicates of each, if there is a spacetime big enough to hold them all, and such that for any spatiotemporal relation, the duplicates in question stand in that relation.[10]

The conceptual position of GR can be put even more succinctly since the intention is that only the following proper theoretical concepts should be taken as primitive: *individual, set, part of, similar to* and *spatiotemporally related to*.[11] On this ontological and conceptual basis GR purports to offer a range of conceptual, ontological and semantic applications of PW.

(4.3) CONCEPTUAL APPLICATIONS

By way of conceptual applications, the GR interpretation of PW purports to offer explicit and non-modal analyses of the family of modal concepts. As with the ontological component of GR, we can envisage a series of postulates that do the work.

Some of these postulates of conceptual analysis deal with concepts of intensional entities and characterize those concepts in terms of certain theoretical roles, 'R', 'S', etc. – thus:

(C1) $\forall x(x$ is a property iff $Rx)$
(C2) $\forall x(x$ is a proposition iff $Sx)$.

Since many different roles are associated with the broad notions of property and of proposition, different species of these generic intensional concepts may have to be distinguished – e.g. natural properties, narrow propositions, etc.[12] Moreover, further generic kinds of intensional concept (state of affairs, possibility, etc.) will require other postulates. However, for my purposes, the generic postulates for property and proposition will suffice.

Central to the modal concepts is the case of absolute possibility, for which the basic postulate is:

(P) It is possible that A iff there is some world w, such that at w, A.[13]

(P) addresses the ordinary and default case in which the content of the non-modal statement, A, is intended or supposed to be restricted to individuals that co-exist in a single spacetime. However, not all modal claims are of that kind. In particular, from the standpoint of GR, all of the following kinds of modal claims may be read as cases in which the ordinary intention or supposition does not hold: modal claims that are explicitly about sets (say, that each has its members essentially); modal claims that are implicitly about sets (that every proposition is thinkable, that there could be natural properties) and claims about the plurality of worlds itself (it is not a contingent fact that there is a plurality of worlds). Modalizing in such extraordinary cases, I will argue, calls for special treatment.[14] The postulate dealing with the extraordinary content A is:

(A) It is possible that A iff A

Genuine realism

and the justification for invoking this distinct postulate proceeds as follows.

GR treats our non-modal claims about ordinary individuals such as donkeys, swans, planets, etc., as implicitly world-restricted claims. Thus

(5) There are donkeys

is to be interpreted – by default, in ordinary contexts of use – as the (true) claim that the actual world has donkeys as parts:

(G5*) $\exists x[Px\alpha \ \& \ Dx]$.

However, there are non-modal existential claims about properties, numbers, propositions which GR takes to be true – e.g.,

(6) There is a plurality of worlds.
(7) Natural properties exist.

GR cannot construe the quantifiers in these cases as (invariably) world-restricted, for if read that way, they express – what are from the GR standpoint – falsehoods, thus:

(G6*) $\exists x \exists y (Px\alpha \ \& \ Py\alpha \ \& \ Wx \ \& \ Wy \ \& \ \sim(y = x))$
(G7*) $\exists x(Px\alpha \ \& \ Nx)$.

(G6*) will be held false on the grounds that no world has distinct worlds as parts. (G7*) will be held false on the grounds that no set – recall that natural properties are sets – is part of any individual.[15]

If (6) and (7) are to express truths, as GR requires, the quantifiers they contain should be interpreted as unrestricted, and not just as ranging over the actual – thus:

(G6**) $\exists x \ \exists y[Wx \ \& \ Wy \ \& \ \sim(y = x)]$
(G7**) $\exists x[Nx]$.

In the ordinary case, modal claims are interpreted by GR as existential and universal quantifications into places held in corresponding non-modal claims by world-restricting terms. So we have the translations:

GR: exposition and applications

(8) There are donkeys iff $\exists x[Px\alpha \, \& \, Dx]$
(9) It is possible that there are donkeys iff $\exists y[Wy \, \& \, \exists x(Pyx \, \& \, Dx)]$
(10) It is necessary that there are donkeys iff $\forall y[Wy \to \exists x(Pxy \, \& \, Dx)]$.

But in the extraordinary case, sentences taken to express true modal claims cannot be regarded as expressing generalizations of previously world-restricted contents. In an extraordinary case, e.g.,

(11) It is possible that there is a plurality of worlds
(12) It is possible that there are natural properties

we have to allow for modal truth even though the non-modal sentences that the modal items modify, viz.:

(6) There is a plurality of worlds
(7) Natural properties exist

are not taken to express world-restricted contents in the first place. (Thus, see (G6**) and (G7**) above.) There is no world-restricting element afoot in the content of (6) or (7) to sustain subsequent existential or universal generalization. In the alternative, GR can say that in such modal cases, the modal modifiers are redundant, hence the schema (A) for extraordinary possibility. In the case of the extraordinary possibility claims that we have considered, that schema yields:

(13) It is possible that there is a plurality of worlds iff $\exists x \exists y[Wx \, \& \, Wy \, \& \, \sim(y = x)]$
(14) It is possible that natural properties exist iff $\exists x[Nx]$.

By invoking the classical definitions of necessity and contingency in terms of possibility, the realist can derive from (A) further schemas to deal with other extraordinary cases of modalizing – e.g.:

(AN) It is necessary that A iff A
(AC) It is contingent that A iff A and not-A.[16]

Intuitively, what holds of logical space unrestrictedly is not a contingent matter, and in non-contingent matters what is possible is also necessary. Such intuitions are captured by these extraordinary GR schemas.

GR appeals to the extraordinary interpretation of modal claims whenever she intends or interprets the associated non-modal content as content that is not world-restricted content. Otherwise, and by default, non-modal content is taken to be world-restricted and the ordinary interpretation merited. I proceed now with further conceptual postulates of GR.

In the case of the counterfactual conditional, the basic postulate is

(C3) If it had been the case that A then it would have been the case that C iff for any selected world w, at w, if A then C.

In the case of property supervenience, the basic postulate is

(C5) The A-properties supervene upon the B-properties iff it is not the case that there are x, y, such that (x is A-discernible from y) and it is not the case that (x is B-discernible from y).

Further postulates will deal directly with other modal concepts including non-alethic modalities, strict conditionals, essences, causation, laws of nature, etc. As is evident from the examples above, the postulates that deal directly with familiar modal and related concepts have analysans which express concepts that GR does not admit as primitive – e.g. at w, x is a selected world, etc. Accordingly, the explanatory component of GR will have to include various 'bridging postulates' to deal with intermediate, theoretical, non-primitive concepts that figure directly in those analyses. To illustrate the point the concept of counterparthood is prominent in GR analyses but is intended to be susceptible to analysis in terms of the primitive concepts beginning with the following:

(C6) For all x, for all y, x is a counterpart of y iff there are worlds w, v such that x is part of w, y is part of v and there is similarity in some respect R and some degree n such that x bears R in degree n to y.[17]

The intention is that all GR analyses should terminate in analysans that feature only the primitive proper concepts of individual, set, part-of, spatiotemporal relatedness and similarity.

(4.4) ONTOLOGICAL APPLICATIONS

The second major element of the explanatory component of GR consists in postulates of ontological identification. Typically, following the identification of an intensional concept with a certain theoretical role, a postulate of ontological identification identifies the kind of construct out of GR ontology that is supposed to play the role in question. Thus, GR includes postulates of kind identification such as:

(I1) The properties (the players of property-role R) are all and only the subsets of the set of all individuals.
(I2) The propositions (the players of proposition-role S) are all and only the subsets of the set of all worlds.

The relevant claims of non-emptiness that establish realism about the target kind are entailed by the ontological postulates of the theory – thus:

(I1.1) There are subsets of the set of all individuals.
(I2.1) There are subsets of the set of all worlds.

So, via the conceptual postulate and the ontological postulates for properties, the (generic) properties are identified as the subsets of the individuals.[18] A similar story can then be told through additional postulates in order to identify certain species of proposition, states of affairs, possibilities, etc. with certain subsets of worlds.[19] Since only individuals and sets are accepted as ontological primitives, the ambition of GR is to identify each kind of thing that exists with some construct – see ontological postulates (O4)–(O7) – out of individuals and sets.[20] In GR such constructs are many and various. The cardinality of the set of possible worlds and, a fortiori that of the set of possible individuals is at least that of the power set of the continuum.[21] GR does not rule out that the set of worlds is bigger than that insofar as she takes herself to lack compelling grounds for ruling out that each type of world might be replicated to a non-arbitrary infinite degree.[22] But the admission of indiscernible worlds does no work by way of generating any new types of construct.

Concerning the further type of ontological application that has been highlighted, it is initially tempting to think that GR might offer an account of truthmaking for modal claims. If we allow ourselves to speak momentarily and loosely in terms of facts, the following

Genuine realism

train of thought is seductive. First, it seems attractive to claim that acceptance of GR puts one in a position to say that certain modal facts are really just existential facts. Second, it seems a short step to the further thought that it is these existential facts that are the truthmakers for modal claims. Third, it seems right to hold that talk of existential facts can be replaced here with talk about the existence of individuals. Thus, it would seem, for GR, the truthmakers for:

(15) There could have been unicorns

– say – are the unicorns: the (unrestricted) existence of a unicorn is necessary for the truth of (15) and the (unrestricted) existence of any such individual is sufficient. The main objection to the thesis that GR offers an account of truthmaking for modal claims is a modal objection. I will address that objection to the case of de dicto possibility claims since, I believe, this is the case where the proponent of the thesis has greatest cause for optimism. But before stating the main objection, I would like to make a number of related observations in order to show that even if the main, modal, objection fails, one who would claim that GR provides truthmakers for modal claims still has a mountain to climb.

The most general, but perhaps the least damaging, observation is that GR accepts various modal truths, for she does not recognize the existence of any 'corresponding' individual. Most obviously, de dicto impossibility claims – e.g. it is impossible that there is something that is both uniformly red and uniformly green – are of this character, since GR postulates no corresponding impossible (red and green) individuals or impossible worlds.[23] However, GR treats such de dicto impossibility claims as negative existential claims (and, we might note, de dicto necessity claims may also fall under this heading since GR treats such necessity claims as universal generalizations and these are (classically) equivalent to negative existential claims). So one might regard this as but one case in which GR will have to provide an account of truthmaking for logically complex claims in terms of truthmaking for basic cases and that, after all, is a generic problem for the truthmaker project that stands independently of the modal case. Let us assume then, for the moment, that a satisfactory account of truthmaking is available in all cases of logical complexity, including those of impossibility and necessity claims, given a satisfactory account of truthmaking in the basic cases. The next thought is that if GR is to offer truthmakers for a class of basic modal claims they will *only* be individuals. For GR will not accept the existence of entities of any of those other categories that have been supposed right for the truthmaking job – e.g. primitive facts, or facts *qua* constructs out of properties (*qua* universals or *qua* sets) and individuals.²⁴ But how wide is the class of truths for which individuals will be adequate to serve as truthmakers? Let us begin by taking a step back. One type of statement that naturally comes to mind is that of, as it were, singular existential statements about possible individuals. In the case of actual individuals, what makes true

(16) Carnap might have existed

is just what makes true

(17) Carnap exists

viz. Carnap. The thought, then, is that GR is in a position to extend this account to the non-actual possible individuals. So if Brownie is one of the other-worldly talking donkeys, then what makes true

(18) Brownie might have existed

is Brownie. However, that thought faces a formidable obstacle in the consideration that there really are no singular terms that are apt to refer to non-actual individuals and so (18) has no proper truth-condition (see (5.6)). In seeking the basic modal claims that are made true by individuals, thoughts naturally turn away from cases in which the availability of singular terms for non-actuals is not an issue and turn towards the case of de dicto possibility claims. In that case, if GR individuals are conceived as serving as truthmakers for de dicto possibility claims in general, it must be because they are being conceived as thick individuals –(not thin or bare particulars without qualities) but individuals with certain qualitative features built in or encoded. Even in a case of simple predication, such as (15), it is the conception of an individual-in-its-unicornhood which sustains the intuition that the existence of an individual is a truthmaker for the claim that there could be talking donkeys. It is more obvious that individuals must be conceived thickly if we are to extend to cases of even slightly more complex predication, the picture of individuals as truthmakers for de dicto possibility claims – thus consider:

(19) There could have been blue unicorns.
(20) There could have been blue talking unicorns.

Genuine realism

But if the individuals are thick enough to make true such claims, are they thick enough to serve as truthmakers for de re modal possibility claims as well? Consider the following claim concerning an actually speechless donkey:

(21) Shergar could have talked.

GR provides for the existence of talking donkeys and the existence of any such thing is, in one sense, sufficient for the truth of (21), for such a thing is a counterpart of Shergar – a relevant counterpart, let us assume – and it talks. But should we think of the other-worldly donkey as a truthmaker for (21)? Having gone along with the story so far, there is no obvious reason why the other-worldly donkey should not be so thick an individual as to have built into it the non-relational features that make it a counterpart of Shergar. Moreover, since extraordinary interpretation is called for, it is not possible that our donkey exists and is not a counterpart of Shergar, for the individuals (unrestrictedly) co-exist and are counterparts. Yet perhaps to do justice to the (counterpart) relational aspect of the GR truth-conditions of de re modal claims we should allow that both of these 'internally related' individuals get in on the truthmaking act for (21). So perhaps the truthmaker for (21) should be construed as the very thick (transworld) individual that consists in the sum of Shergar and our donkey. So even if the main objection fails, many issues concerning GR and truthmaking remain to be addressed.

All previously intimated difficulties aside, the main objection to the capacity of GR to afford truthmakers is an objection from non-contingency. If we ask after the modal status of the truth that it is possible that unicorns exist, and so (on analysis) of the truth that (unrestrictedly) there are unicorns, then by GR lights the extraordinary interpretation is called into play and the truth emerges as non-contingent (necessary). As GR postulate (AC) reflects, in the realm of unrestricted content there is no contingent truth. But where there is no contingent truth, there is no room for the kind of non-trivial modal or counterfactual variation that we would expect to characterize the relationship between truth and truthmaker. The (other-worldly) unicorns, we suppose, are truthmakers for the claim – (15) – that there could have been unicorns. But consider now the matter of necessary and sufficient conditions. The existence of unicorns is indeed, an absolutely necessary condition for the truth of (15): it absolutely could not be the case that (15) be true and there should be no unicorns. But that is settled trivially by the absolute

GR: exposition and applications

impossibility of the second conjunct: it is impossible that (unrestrictedly) there should be no unicorns. But in virtue of the absolute necessity of such existence (unrestricted existence) and by this reasoning, the existence of the unicorns is a necessary condition of *any* claim being true. Equally, the existence of unicorns will be absolutely sufficient for the truth of (15): it absolutely could not be the case that unicorns exist and (15) fail to be true. But that is settled trivially by the absolute impossibility of the second conjunct: it is absolutely impossible that (15) fail to be true. But in virtue of the absolute necessity of such truth (truth about absolute possibility) and by this reasoning, the existence of unicorns is a sufficient condition for the truth of any truth that holds of absolute necessity. Combining the two points, the existence of the unicorns is necessary and sufficient for the truth of (15), but also for (22) and (23):

(22)   There could have been blue swans.
(23)   There could have been Newtonian spacetime.

Thus, when truthmaking is cashed out in terms of the existence of certain things (here individuals, but no matter) as (modally) necessary and sufficient for truth, what we get in the case of absolute possibility claims is the absurdity that the unicorns are truthmakers for (15) – and for (22) and for (23). Of course the modal articulation of the truthmaking relation need not take precisely the form of a claim about absolutely necessary and sufficient conditions for truth: it might take the form of a counterfactual claim or a supervenience claim. But the general problem of non-contingency pervades all such formulations. In the case of counterfactual formulations, any counterfactual – and a fortiori, any counterfactual in which the consequent is about the truth of modal claims – will hold when the antecedent supposition is that (*per impossibile*) absolutely non-contingent matters of unrestricted existence were otherwise. In the case of supervenience claims, truths of absolute possibility – being absolutely non-contingent truths – will supervene on anything. Since there could be no difference in truths about absolute possibility, then, a fortiori, it is not the case that there could be differences in truths about absolute possibility *and* . . . no differences in some arbitrary respect.

A characterization of the modal relationship between truthmaker and truth will be satisfactory only if it issues in a suitably discriminating matching of truthmakers to truths. Thus far, I cannot see how this might be achieved given the GR conception of both the modal status of the truths about absolute possibility and the modal status of the (unrestricted) existence of the putative truthmakers. The problem might be presented as that of earning the right to assert the kind of pattern of modal claims that would result in correct matching – e.g. the conjunction of (24) and (25):

$$\neg \Diamond \exists x Ux \; \Box\!\!\to \neg \exists x Ux$$

(24) If it had not been true that there could have been unicorns then there would have been no unicorns.

(25) It is not the case that [if it had been false that there could have been unicorns then there would have been no blue swans].

$$\neg (\neg (\Diamond \exists x Ux) \; \Box\!\!\to (\neg \exists x Bx \,\&\, Sx))$$

The only reasonable grounds for such assertion would be that we are dealing here with modalities that are not to be analysed in either the ordinary or the extraordinary way. But until some third way is motivated, specified and shown to issue in truth-conditions that will serve the intended pattern of modal assertion, the suspicion must be that GR would be saving – and only saving from the most immediate kind of objection – the project of providing truthmakers for modal claims at the cost of admitting mysterious and unanalysed modalities. In that light, it is obvious that the rational course for GR would be to eschew the project of providing truthmakers rather than sacrifice her claim on a comprehensive conceptual and semantic account of the modalities. This outcome is in perfect harmony with the explicit claim of Lewis (1992: 218) that the demand to specify truthmakers for possibility claims is wrong in the first place. But there is more to be said here, for the recently established triviality of all claims about the supervenience of (absolutely non-contingent) modal truth has further implications.

When the letter of the demand to specify truthmakers is felt too exacting – e.g. when a truthmaker is demanded for each truth – it is tempting to think that the spirit of the demand is preserved if one is in a position to assert, at least, that truth supervenes on being.[25] Indeed, Lewis (1992: 218–19) commends such a retreat and finds that various philosophical positions – including phenomenalism, Rylean behaviourism, Priorian presentism and the acceptance of nomologicality as an ontological primitive – flawed on the grounds that they violate the principle that truth supervenes on being. However, it is notable that Lewis does not appeal to the supervenience thesis in defending GR or in attacking rival theories of modality. What emerged above was not that GR is in violation of the requirement that truth supervenes on being, but rather that, by GR lights, the supervenience thesis holds trivially. So no *ad hominem* objection to GR lurks here. But to claim that GR provides truthmakers for modal claims would be to claim a further ontological application for GR on the flimsiest, most dubious, of grounds.

(4.5) SEMANTIC APPLICATIONS

GR does indeed offer a PW-semantics for QML and associated languages, even if she is ultimately sceptical of the adequacy of QML as a medium of regimentation of natural language sentences.[26] We shall find that all of our realist interpreters are motivated to modify or tailor the semantics of Kripke (1963) in one way or another. In the case of GR, it is the counterpart-theoretic treatment of de re modal claims that motivates the modifications.[27] Staying as close as we can to the general form of the models that were introduced in (3.4), a GR model for quantified modal logic is a 7-tuple

(GRM) <W, w*, R, D, Q, C, V>

in which the additional element C is a counterpart relation.[28] A GR applied semantics describes the models thus: W is the set of all worlds; w* (also known as α) is the actual world; R is the accessibility relation on the set of worlds; D is the set of all possible individuals; Q is the domain function taking subsets of D onto worlds; V is a valuation function; and the additional element C is a triadic counterpart relation (x is a counterpart of y in w). Further aspects of the metaphysics of GR and the distinctive aspects of counterpart-theoretic representation will be reflected on constraints on the admissibility of models. For example the world-boundedness of ordinary individuals – expressed in ontological postulate (O10) above – requires that the domain function from D to the worlds assigns disjoint subsets of D to each world and the valuation function will be characterized in terms appropriate to the counterpart-theoretic account of the truth-conditions of de re modal claims.

(4.6) JUSTIFICATION

Lewis offers two kinds of justification for GR. The earlier justification is the argument from paraphrase of Lewis (1973, Chapter 4). There it is argued: (a) that we ought to believe in possible worlds since our belief so stated is just a paraphrase of a belief we already

Genuine realism

have in ways the world might have been and (b) that construing the nature of possible worlds non-reductively proves a better strategy of interpretation than that offered by reductionist – i.e. AR – alternatives. The later justification is the argument from utility of Lewis (1986a: 3–5). There it is argued: (a) that if an ontological hypothesis has eminent utility (i.e. sufficient net utility and greater net utility than its rivals) then that gives us good reason to believe that it is true and (b) the ontological hypothesis of GR has such eminent utility with respect to total theory (and metaphysics in particular).[29] These two justifications can be linked.

The earlier justification, as Skyrms (1976) has emphasized, is caricatured if we read it, ignoring the (b) element above, as endorsing the principle of face-value interpretation of all existential locutions (e.g. 'there are ways things could not have been') at all costs. Rather, the explicit position, fleshing out the (b) element of the earlier justification, is that such a face-value interpretation ought to be regarded as affording the best semantic theory of the discourse if it does not lead to trouble and the alternatives do.[30] Lewis (1986a) shifts from treating competing theories as if they simply do or do not lead to trouble, to treating each theory as leading to some degree of trouble of some kind which constitutes a cost that is to be deducted, for the purpose of assessing credibility, from the value of the benefits that it affords. In that light, the difference between the (1973) and (1986a) justifications is only a matter of emphasis.

This concludes the exposition of GR and the account of the applications of PW that such an interpretation affords.

CHAPTER 5

Genuine realism: quantification over non-actuals

In this chapter, I discuss various objections to the coherence, or acceptability more generally, of GR (purported) quantification over non-actual individuals. Objections of this kind have often been accompanied by the suggestion that GR shares unwelcome features that are associated with Meinong's conception of quantification and existence. Orthodoxy, or perhaps caricature, has it that Meinong's thoroughly referentialist theory of meaning led him to countenance quantification ranging over entities that exist and entities – including non-actual possibilia and impossibilia – that do not exist (but subsist). So far as the evaluation of GR is concerned, the central question is not whether a properly Meinongian realism about possibilia is tenable, but whether, as many have alleged, the GR conception of quantification and existence is flawed in the ways that orthodoxy supposes the notorious 'Meinongian' conception of quantification and existence to be flawed.[1] The ensuing objections that I discuss are as follows: (5.1) GR is committed to logical inconsistency in asserting that there are things that do not exist; (5.2) GR is committed to analytic falsehood in denying that everything is actual; (5.3) GR worlds are not proper individuals since they lack accidental properties; and (5.4)–(5.5) GR is unstable insofar as it admits possibilia and excludes impossibilia. Finally, I present and discuss in (5.6) a neo-Fregean objection to the propriety of GR quantification over possibilia which is based on the claim that such quantification is not appropriately underwritten by the possibility of singular reference to such things.

(5.1) NON-EXISTENT ENTITIES

Some have taken the view that insofar as Meinongian quantification is not 'literal gibberish' (Lycan 1979: 290) it involves commitment to the logical falsehood:

(M) $\exists x[\sim\exists y[y = x]]$.

That GR suffers this Meinongian defect is variously considered or suggested by Richards (1975), Plantinga (1976, 1987), Haack (1977) and Lycan (1979). It is true that Lewis's earlier writings occasionally exhibit a paradoxical turn of phrase which, in the absence of qualification, promotes such a suspicion.[2] However, the mature GR account of quantification over non-actual possibilia (Lewis 1973: 86–7, 1986a: 98–9) allays the suspicion of commitment to logical falsehood and, as far as I am aware, that suspicion has not been directed explicitly on GR in the subsequent literature.[3] I will summarize the mature GR account of quantification and illustrate how it can be deployed in order to fend off the objection of commitment to the existence of the non-existent.

The mature GR account of quantification has the following salient features: (i) we begin by asserting that there is an otherwise uncharacterized domain of all individuals over which unrestricted individual quantifiers range; (ii) that domain of unrestricted individual quantification is then identified conceptually as the domain of all and only the possible individuals; (iii) the domain of actual individuals is identified – conceptually and via the indexical account of actuality – as the domain of individuals that includes us and all of our individual spatiotemporal relata; (iv) the domain of non-actual individuals is identified (conceptually) as the complement, in the unrestricted domain of individuals, of the domain of actual individuals; (v) norms of interpretation require that many token uses of quantificational idioms in general be understood as intimating restricted quantification over a contextually appropriate proper subset of all of the individuals; (vi) in cases of ordinary token uses of quantificational idioms – when concerns with modal metaphysics are not to the fore – the contextually appropriate domain over which quantification is intimated is to be understood, by default, as a restricted domain of actual individuals; and (vii) there are individuals that are not actual individuals.

Consider, then, the following argument of Plantinga (1976: 256) which seeks to convict GR – de facto Lewis (1972) – of harbouring a Meinongian commitment to the existence of non-existents.

Grant that possibly there is an object distinct from each object in the domain of the actual world. Then on the canonical conception of possible worlds, encoded in a Kripkean applied semantics where possible worlds have varying domains, there is a possible world w in which there exists an object x that is distinct from each of the things

GR: quantification over non-actuals

that exist in the actual world α. Since the domain of w contains an object that is not a member of the domain of α, the universal domain D that is the union of all world domains contains an object x that is not in the domain of α. So there exists an object x that does not exist in the actual world.[4]

So far so good. However, the subsequent and final move of the argument consists in the move from, 'this object, then, does not exist in the actual world' – which GR accepts – to 'and hence does not exist' – which GR rejects. GR is entitled to accept the former claim but reject the latter on the grounds that the alleged entailment of non-existence by non-existence in the actual world is question-begging. That entailment is sustained only if quantification over actual objects exhausts unrestricted quantification over objects, and that is precisely what GR denies. In the absence of further supporting argument for the entailment (see next section) the argument against GR fails.

Furthermore, although GR has no need of such misleading forms of expression as 'there are some things that do not exist', and is well advised to avoid their use, the mature account of quantification supplies a basis for a non-paradoxical and charitable interpretation of such sentences. The principles of interpretation governing token uses of quantificational idioms allow that different quantificational idioms within the same token sentence may be taken to express variously restricted (or unrestricted) quantifiers. A token of 'there are things that do not exist' might charitably be interpreted as expressing a truth if the first quantificational locution ('there are') is taken to express unrestricted quantification and the second ('do not exist') is taken to express (negated) restricted quantification. Then the unparadoxical proposition expressed is that there unrestrictedly are certain things that are not identical to any of a certain restricted number of things, i.e.:

(M*) $\exists x[\sim\exists y[Fy \ \& \ y = x]]$.

But that proposition is not faithfully represented by any formula which suggests univocal unrestricted quantification and, in particular, it is not represented faithfully by:

(M) $\exists x[\sim\exists y[y = x]]$.

Finally, Plantinga (1987: 314–16, 331) persists in attributing to 'the possibilist' and to advocates of the canonical conception of possible world semantics (see above) the thesis that there are things that don't exist. On these occasions, however, Plantinga does not attribute directly to GR or to Lewis the thesis that he considers objectionable, nor does he direct any argument against the mature GR account of quantification over non-actual individuals. One notable development in Plantinga (1987) is the contrast between an actualist conception of quantification with a Meinongian conception, with the former defined by the thesis that '... whatever there is *exists*' (Plantinga 1987: 92, his emphasis). But with 'actualism' so (idiosyncratically) understood – and so long as the idioms of quantification are read as univocally restricted or univocally unrestricted – GR is entitled to count herself among the actualists rather than among the Meinongians to whom Plantinga objects. But that is not actualism as we know it.

(5.2) ANALYTIC ACTUALISM

A critic might be convinced that the GR account of quantification is acceptable in all of the following respects. Existential quantification over an unrestricted, maximal domain of individuals is perfectly coherent and conceptually primitive. It is also perfectly coherent to identify a related domain of quantification as the subset of the maximal domain of individuals whose members are all and only the individuals that stand in some spatiotemporal relation to us. Moreover, the actualist critic of GR need not even deny that this 'related' domain of quantification is distinct, in extension, from the unrestricted domain of individuals. Let us reserve the neutral term 'multiverse' for a plurality of spatiotemporally disjoined island universes that models the ontological component of GR (see Chapter 4). The actualist opponent of GR may acknowledge that the existence of a multiverse is both epistemically and metaphysically possible – for all we know, such a multiverse exists, and even if there is no such multiverse, there might have been. So the actualist critic of GR may concede that quantification over a multiverse domain of individuals is coherent, intelligible and brings no commitment to logical falsehood. However, the critic may refuse to allow that the existence of such a multiverse has the modal significance that GR takes it to have. That is, what the critic may specifically refuse to allow is that other island universes of the multiverse are, or would be, alternative, non-actual possible worlds. If island universes existed, they would be parts of actuality rather than other possible worlds, and talk about possible worlds is not adequately interpreted as talk about such things.[5] This critical stance reflects the intuitive, pre-theoretical conviction that everything – the multiverse, its island universe parts and whatever else there is – is actual. But what is the basis of the intuition that everything is actual? One answer to that question is that the thesis of ontological actualism, that everything is actual, is analytic. Thus, the new objection emerges, even if the GR account of quantification and existence does not entail a commitment to the narrowly logical falsehood that there are things that don't exist, it does entail commitment to the broadly logical falsehood that there are things that are not actual.

This objection to GR is potentially lethal. If analytic actualism is true – i.e. if it is analytic that everything is actual – then key theses of GR are false in virtue of meaning alone and are, a fortiori, false. Naturally, then, Lewis (1986a: 99–101) rejects analytic actualism. The case that he makes locates the claim that everything is actual as one of three key theses that would command the assent of 'some spokesman for common sense' – viz.:

(1) Everything is actual.
(2) Actuality consists of everything that is spatiotemporally related to us, and nothing more (give or take some 'abstract entities'). It is not vastly bigger, or less unified, than we are accustomed to think.
(3) Possibilities are not parts of actuality, they are alternatives to it.

According to Lewis: (a) these theses are on an equal footing (with respect to analyticity); (b) they jointly fix the meaning of 'actual'; and (c) they jointly go beyond just fixing the meaning of 'actual'. Given (a), either all of the theses are analytic or none is. But since the conjunction of the theses is not analytic, it is not the case that all of the theses are analytic. So, none of the theses is analytic and a fortiori (1) is not analytic, i.e. analytic actualism is false.

Construed straightforwardly as an argument against analytic actualism, this case is unlikely to stall the critic. The selection of the key theses is at once dubiously inclusive and dubiously exclusive. Should we really expect the spokesman for common sense, one whose opinions reflect the communally settled meaning of 'actual' to take a view, far less a positive view, on (2) and (3)? On the other hand, in considering how the meaning of 'actual' and its cognates are fixed, one would expect to pay attention to the inferential role of cognate expressions as manifest in central and intuitively valid patterns of inference, e.g.:

(AE) $\dfrac{\text{It is actually the case that P}}{\text{P}}$

(AI) $\dfrac{\text{P}}{\text{It is actually the case that P}}$

Moreover premise (a) is objectionable since its acceptance gratuitously imposes an unwelcome commitment to the analyticity of (2) and (3) given a commitment to the analyticity of (1). However, even if Lewis fails to demonstrate the falsehood of analytic actualism, less is required in order to hold off the objection.

The point of the objection from the analyticity of actualism is that there is supposed to be something deeply defective with the GR conception of quantification and existence. In other words, if analytic actualism is true one would expect that we can make nothing intelligible of the thought that there are things that are not actual. That, after all, is the claim that one would naturally want to make about the negation of any claim that one held to be analytic – that there are male vixens or that there are things that don't exist. But GR does attempt to make something intelligible of the denial that everything is actual. In the context of GR, a substantive case is made that the denial of actualism is ontologically, semantically, epistemologically and otherwise philosophically coherent. It is, at this stage of the dialectic, an open question whether this substantive defence of the coherence of GR is successful, and if it is not, it may be fair on reflection to conclude – ultimately, and in due course – that it is the denial of actualism that is the ultimate source of the incoherence. But it seems unfair to attempt to deprive GR of the right to attempt such a substantive defence of the coherence of her position simply by insisting on the analyticity of what she denies. Here, it is worth considering how difficult it is to defend a philosophical thesis directly – as opposed to indirectly, by running with it – against the charge of analytic falsehood. GR might make this point to the actualist realist by lodging against actualist realism the 'objection' that it is in violation of the analyticity of thesis (3). Outside of the modal arena, the point might be brought home to the mathematical Platonist – say – by confronting her with the contention that it is analytic that everything is concrete. In either case, the likely and reasonable reaction would be to deny the claim of analyticity and get on with the substantive philosophical defence of the coherence (and utility) of the ontological hypothesis.⁶ I see no reason to deprive GR of that recourse at this stage.

Taking an alternative route, the objection from the analyticity of actualism may emphasize the reasons that are available for insisting that the thesis of actualism is analytic. However, this does not appear to be the kind of case where the analyticity of the thesis in question is likely to be supposed to be non-obvious as the analyticity of certain theorems of arithmetic, for example, is sometimes supposed to be. Insofar as the analyticity of actualism is plausibly derivable from any more basic analytic theses, it is derivable rather quickly by the substitution of 'is actual' for its alleged synonym 'exists' in (what we may presently suppose to be) the analytic:

(4)   Everything exists.

In this light, what the matter boils down to is whether GR is entitled to resist the claim that 'is actual' and 'exists' are synonymous. It is uncontroversial that most English speakers in most contexts, if not in all contexts, use the expressions interchangeably.⁷ Nor is it controversial that most, if not all, English speakers take the thesis of actualism (1) to be true. On the other hand, it is clear that GR finds agreement with the spokesperson for common sense on many of the judgements on which agreement is necessary to ensure that there is at least substantial overlap between the meaning of 'actual' as it is used in the wider English-speaking community and as GR proposes to use it: Mount Everest is actual, Santa Claus isn't actual, there aren't actually any golden mountains, there are actually other planets, etc. With these observations made it is not obvious how to judge the claim of synonymy short of embarking on a full-scale investigation into the metaphysics and epistemology of meaning. Since I do not propose to proceed down that road, I will take the view that the case has not been proved against or for the analyticity of the thesis of actualism. Consequently GR ought not to be prevented at the outset, as it were, from attempting to meet the challenge of demonstrating, in philosophically substantive ways, the broad intelligibility of the conception of existence and quantification that he endorses.⁸

(5.3) GENUINE WORLDS ARE NOT PROPER INDIVIDUALS

A third objection has it that the worlds over which GR purports to quantify share with Meinongian subsistents a failure to satisfy a certain necessary condition of proper individuality (McGinn 1981:

152–3).⁹ The mooted condition requires of any proper individual that '... its properties partition (non-trivially) into the essential and the accidental'. The subsequent claim is that '... what transpires in a world is essential to its identity; the identity of a world is fixed by its content' (McGinn 1981: 152). When confronted with this objection, GR will naturally be tempted to query the precise content, status and independent plausibility of the general condition on proper individuality that is invoked. However, it is not dialectically necessary to do so since GR is equipped to meet the objection head-on by establishing that worlds do have both essential and accidental properties.

The basis of this case is that claims about the essential properties of worlds should be treated just the same as claims about the essential properties of other ordinary individuals.¹⁰ That is to say both: (a) that whether a world has a given property essentially or accidentally is a matter of whether all, rather than only some, of its counterparts have that property; and (b) that the counterpart relation(s) relevant to the truth of a token essentialist claim about a world is a context-sensitive matter.¹¹ Of course one might, for various reasons, object to the counterpart-theoretic account of the truth-conditions of modal claims in general or of essentialist claims in particular (see (7.1) below). But the present objection is aimed at the modal status of the properties of worlds in particular and not the GR account of the truth-conditions of essentialist claims in general. So in the (present) absence of any objection to that general account, GR is presently entitled to apply that general account to address the particular objection. Then, the question is whether there are counterpart relations, i.e. similarity relations, such that worlds do not share all of their properties with all of their counterparts. There is no shortage of candidates, but let us consider only two.

If similarity of nomological character is the only contextually relevant consideration – a case which Bigelow (1990) emphasizes – the counterparts of any world will be all and only those worlds with the same laws of nature. Consequently, it will emerge as an essential feature of (say) the actual world that it is non-Euclidean and an accidental feature that it contains intelligent organisms. Other worlds will be essentially Euclidean and accidentally devoid of intelligent organisms. If we consider an extremely stringent counterpart relation that requires absolute intrinsic similarity of individuals, it will be an essential property of the actual world that it has human parts. But it will be accidental that the actual world is a world since, by recombination, other worlds have proper, non-worldly parts that are duplicates of the actual world. To change the emphasis, the claim that genuine worlds have all of their properties essentially is justified, from a counterpart-theoretic perspective, only if every essentialist claim about worlds invokes a counterpart relation that requires absolute indiscernibility. Given the availability of the other counterpart relations, and pressures exerted by interpretational considerations to allow variation of counterpart relations across contexts of utterance, the burden of proof shifts to the objector who must now show why the imposition of such a strict counterpart relation is always warranted in the case of worlds when it is not always warranted elsewhere. [12]

(5.4) FROM POSSIBILIA TO IMPOSSIBILIA

Lewis's (1986a: 7) rejection of impossibilia is, more precisely, the rejection of the (unrestricted) existence of genuine worldbound individuals that instantiate impossibilities. Each element of this more precise claim merits explanation.

First, the rejected impossibilia are conceived as ordinary, genuine individuals that exist wholly within one world. The principle of unrestricted summation, expressed in postulate (O4) of (4.2), generates transworld individuals out of individuals that exist in different worlds – e.g., take the head of any talking donkey from any other world and there is an individual that consists in the sum of that head and your body. By the ordinary possibility principle (P) it is possible that an individual exists (if and) only if it exists at some world. Since, it is natural to affirm, transworld individuals do not exist at any world, then by the lights of (P), it is not possible that such individuals exist – they are not possible individuals. Thus GR may find reason, as Lewis (1986a: 211) does, for characterizing some of the individuals he believes in as impossible individuals. My own view is that it is misleading and unnecessary for GR to call transworld individuals 'impossible'. The pressure to do so comes from the application of the ordinary possibility principle (P) to the claim that it is possible that such individuals exist. But as we have already seen, in Chapter 4, there is good reason for GR to apply a different, extraordinary possibility principle in cases where modal claims concern transworldly states of affairs. Applying the extraordinary possibility principle (A), it is possible that there are transworld individuals just in case there are transworld individuals. So by availing herself of principle (A), GR may reckon transworld individuals among the possible individuals, maintain the general principle of identifying possibility with unrestricted existence and avoid conveying the impression of believing in serious impossibilia (i.e. genuine individuals with incompatible properties).[13]

Second, the rejected impossibilia are conceived as absolute impossibilia rather than as (variously) relative impossibilia. GR may freely admit that certain kinds of individual exist only in a restricted class of alethically possible worlds that are not relevantly accessible from the actual world – e.g. nomological impossibilia such as individuals whose velocity exceeds that of light. Insofar as merely relative impossibilia, or relatively impossible worlds, are among the absolute possibilia, their admission is innocuous.

Third, the rejected impossibilia are conceived as genuine individuals that instantiate impossibilities – e.g. by being both blue and not blue, or by succeeding in squaring the circle. The rejection of such individuals ensures that impossibilities cannot be represented – as de dicto possibilities are for GR – directly, by instantiation.

The charge then is that GR rejection of impossibilia, so clarified, is not tenable alongside acceptance of possibilia. The arguments that I will presently consider have a conditional conclusion that is addressed, *ad hominem*, to GR: if acceptance of genuine possibilia is justified then acceptance of genuine impossibilia is justified. One might establish that conclusion and remain neutral about whether one ought subsequently to deny the consequent or affirm the antecedent. However, in line with majority opinion, I will take it that what is at stake here is a reductio of GR. Since the existence of genuine impossibilia is unjustified (unjustifiable), GR must avoid commitment to the conditional thesis on pain of refutation.

The first attempt to convict GR of commitment to the conditional thesis (see Naylor 1986 and Yagisawa 1988) is a 'parity of reasoning' case that proceeds from the Lewis (1973) 'paraphrase argument' for the existence of possibilia that was discussed at (4.6) above. If the paraphrase argument justifies belief in possible worlds, *qua* ways things could have been then, the case proceeds, the same form of argument justifies belief in possible worlds, *qua* ways things could not have been. The attempt fails since its advocates proceed from the caricature of the methodological stance of Lewis (1973) that was highlighted in (4.6). The explicit position of Lewis (1973) is that such a face-value interpretation ought to be regarded as affording the best semantic theory of the discourse if it does not lead to trouble and the alternatives do.[14] Given the latter condition, if an *ad hominem* argument is to succeed in imposing on GR a uniform ontological attitude to possibilia and impossibilia, it must look beyond the surface grammar of our modal locutions and consider the net theoretical utility – especially the costs – associated with accepting impossibilia.

The next argument from possibilia to impossibilia is based on the second strand of the justification of GR, viz. that the balance of theoretical benefits to costs, calculated so as to justify GR, further justifies its impossibilist expansion. In order to evaluate this argument we ought to envisage two competing GR theories. Possibilist GR (PGR) is GR as we know it thus far embracing possibilia and rejecting impossibilia. Impossibilist GR (IGR) is GR as we know it augmented by a commitment to impossibilia in addition to possibilia. Before considering how the shift from PGR to IGR is supposed to increase the theoretical benefits, I will begin by emphasizing how much serious work IGR must do in order to maintain the benefits that PGR purports to afford.

First, in order to characterize her ontology in a way that sustains the conceptual ambitions of PGR, IGR must find a way of adding non-modal postulates to PGR that generate a sufficient variety of worlds to match all of the impossibilities. If the claim to provide a thoroughly non-modal analysis of the family of modal concepts is to be sustained then, when the money is down, IGR can no more characterize her ontology by speaking of impossible worlds than PGR can in her own case by speaking of possible worlds. Second, IGR must also have a non-modal way of distinguishing the possible worlds from the impossible worlds. Once any impossible world is admitted, the ordinary possibility principle:

(P) It is possible that A iff there is a world, w, such that at w, A

is false (right to left). So what IGR requires is a surrogate principle that succeeds in restricting right-side quantification to the possible worlds without appealing explicitly or implicitly to modal concepts in order to effect that restriction. I do not say that this two-fold challenge cannot be met, but until it is PGR already has substantial reason not to risk the central conceptual benefit – and arguably the most important benefit of all – that she claims by admitting (for whatever reason) impossibilia.

Moreover, even if IGR manages to meet the challenge that has been set, the admission of impossible worlds brings no obvious improvement to the PGR theory of impossibility. To see this, allow that IGR succeeds in identifying non-modally the possible worlds (p-worlds) as a subset of all the worlds over which she quantifies and subsequently identifies non-modally the impossible worlds (i-worlds) as the complementary set of worlds. Consider now the PGR formulation of truth-conditions for impossibility claims:

(PI) It is impossible that A iff it is not the case that (there is a world, w, such that at w, A).[15]

It is, perhaps, superficially tempting to think that the admission of impossibilia allows RGR to improve on this situation by offering the alternative formulation:

(RI) It is impossible that A iff there is an i-world, w, such that at w, A.

The temptation may consist in thinking that (RI) is ontologically more perspicuous than (PI) in clearly presenting strong truthmakers for impossibility claims – entities whose very existence makes such claims true. The temptation may even consist in the more nebulous thought that (RI) enjoys some advantage over (PI) for bringing about a more unified treatment of the cases by having specified truth-conditions 'of the same form' as those that are specified for possibility claims. Any such thought, however, is doomed since it is based on the failure to note the extensional inaccuracy of (RI). In order to account for any truth of the form:

(5) It is impossible that (P and not-P)

for arbitrary possibility P, IGR requires the existence of an i-world at which P and not-P. However, it seems an obvious feature of the representational operator, 'at w' that it should distribute across conjunction so that any world at which (P & ~P) is a world at which P. In any event, so long as there is some impossible world w, such that at w (P and not-P) and at w, P, (RI) is false (right to left). So, given the existence of impossible worlds at which some possibilities hold, IGR needs further to circumscribe, in a non-modal way, the impossibilities as holding at some impossible worlds but not at any possible world – thus:

(RI*) It is impossible that A iff ((there is an i-world, w, such that at w, A) & (It is not the case that there is a p-world v, such that at v, A)).

GR: quantification over non-actuals

Clearly the price of so attaining extensional accuracy is to preserve whatever disadvantages of form, or lack of ontological perspicuity, that were supposed to attach to the possibilist principle (PI). Indeed, comparison of (PI) and (RI*) presents the postulation of impossibilia – so far as applications to impossibility is concerned – as an idle cog that does no work that is not already done by possibilia.

It has been argued by Yagisawa (1988), however, that there are two further areas of application – the intensions and extraordinary possibilities – that ought to convince PGR to extend her ontology and admit impossibilia.[16] I will deal with these in turn. Recall (from Chapter 1) that PW discourse promises adequate discrimination among, intuitively, distinct intensional entities. Recall also that GR purports to achieve this discrimination in a fully extensional way by identifying the different kinds of intensions – propositions, properties, etc. – as different kinds of subsets of all of the possible individuals (see Chapter 4). Yagisawa (1988) argues that the methodological principles that justify acceptance of PGR in light of such success – that it is worth expanding ontology in order to gain a simple, unifying, appropriately discriminating and extensional treatment of the intensions – also justify the acceptance of IGR. The argument proceeds from the claim that PGR fails to discriminate sufficiently among intensions. Intuitively, it may be felt that the impossible properties (propositions) that are all identified within PGR as the empty set of individuals (worlds) – e.g. being an irrational integer, being a married bachelor (two is odd, Willard is a married bachelor) – are really distinct. To put the point otherwise, the entities in question are not just intensional but hyperintensional – for such entities, even intensional equivalence is insufficient for identity.[17] In the case of propositions, the intuition can be bolstered by considering relevant pairs of attitude ascriptions. We would, for example, expect different patterns of behaviour and inference to ensue from one who falsely believes that there is a counterexample to Fermat's last theorem than from one who believes that $1 = 0$. Not least, we might expect the former to be broadly intelligible. Yet, the PGR treatment of propositions would deem the two belief states equivalent – they are the same kind of attitude to the same proposition.[18] The next thought is that such conflation can be avoided by maintaining the general form of the PGR treatment of intensions while extending the range of unrestricted quantification to include impossibilia. Thus, the admission of an impossible world, u, at which Fermat's 'conjecture' has a counterexample but it is not the case that $1 = 0$, allows us to distinguish extensionally between the two impossible propositions. For the first impossible proposition has u as a member and the second does not. Thereby, IGR allows us to maintain the unifying, simplifying and extensionalizing features of a PGR theory of intensions while increasing the discriminatory power of such a theory. So if PGR passes the cost/benefit threshold of credibility then – a fortiori – IGR does so also.

One defensive strategy that PGR ought to explore, but which will not be explored in any detail here, is attempting to undermine the first premise by questioning whether PGR really does lack the capacity to discriminate appropriately among intensional entities or contents. One element of the strategy will be to press the question of what degree of discrimination is appropriate, the other will be to exploit the discriminating capacities of PGR ontology. On one hand, PGR will take it that a conception of the appropriate variety of – say – the propositions requires us to distinguish the different roles that are associated with the notion and to consider, for each such role, how many and varied the players of the role in question would have to be. So where a propositional role – say that of intra-individual cognitive content – requires relatively fine discrimination, the allegation that PGR fails to distinguish suitably many propositions might be thought to have more force. In that light, however, it will be crucial to distinguish the theoretical cost of failing to generate enough distinct role-players for some such intensional roles from the, presumably greater, cost of failing to do so for all such roles. On the other hand, where PGR is prima facie vulnerable to the charge of conflating distinct intensional entities or attitudinal contents, it remains to explore the variety of representational discrimination that the PGR ontology affords. Thus, Lewis addresses problems of insufficient discrimination in his ontological account of properties (1986a: 55–7) and of propositions (1986a: 57–9) by invoking distinguishing aspects of the quasi-syntactic structure of linguistic items that express them.[19] To the extent that PGR succeeds in matching IGR in effectively discriminating among intensions in a fully extensional manner, the methodological case for IGR comes to rely increasingly on the claim to have provided a simpler and more unified treatment of the intensions.[20] Moreover, if IGR gains any advantage over PGR with respect to the discrimination of intensions, this is restricted to the sphere of ontological benefits. Analysing the concepts of property, proposition, etc., is, for PGR, a matter of identifying associated roles in advance of consideration of which entities are apt to play the roles in question. So although PGR and IGR offer competing accounts of ontological identification of intensional entities, they do not – for all we have seen and might expect – offer competing accounts of the intensional concepts. Equally, the variety of constructs that are available to GR for the purpose of identifying distinct intensions is a matter that appears to be somewhat removed from the concern to provide a PW-semantics for QML.

In sum, consideration of the intensions shows us the following. In light of some of the roles associated with some intensional concepts, it may be the case that IGR is superior to PGR in its capacity to provide an effective, or at least simpler and more unifying, ontological account of the intensions. However, the admission of impossibilia carries the risk – to put the point mildly – of undermining the ambitions of GR to provide thoroughly non-modal analyses of the modal and intensional concepts. It does so by requiring extra ontological postulates to generate all of the impossibilities, by requiring a way of distinguishing the possible worlds from the impossible worlds and by having no non-modal means of doing so on offer. So, I argue, PGR has as yet no compelling reason to think that conversion to IGR will result in an increase of theoretical benefits. However, there is a further application of impossibilia that PGR is bound to consider.

Yagisawa argues: (a) that there are various modal claims that cannot adequately be expressed within the resources of PGR and (b) that methodological principles to which PGR adheres compel her to postulate the existence of alternative logical spaces and impossible worlds over which we may quantify in order to remedy this expressive deficiency. I will argue that Yagisawa's claim (a) is false and then explore (b) with a view to demonstrating the costs of admitting impossibilia.

The claims that are supposed to demonstrate the expressive deficiency of conservative GR are these:

(6) w could have been inaccessible from w′ (where w is accessible from w′).
(7) There could have been more worlds than there actually are in our logical space.
(8) I could have been there instead of here (where 'there' refers in context to another possible world and 'here' refers in context to the actual world α).
(9) Logical facts (e.g. the law of excluded middle) could have failed to obtain.

It is immediately to be conceded that Yagisawa is correct to hold that these claims cannot adequately be treated in the manner that is appropriate for – what I have called – ordinary modal claims. But we have provided PGR with an alternative means of handling the interpretation of extraordinary modal claims – that is claims that involve modalizing about things other than individuals that all exist within a single space and time. By that criterion, as we shall see in turn, each of (6)–(9) is an extraordinary modal claim for which a satisfactory extraordinary interpretation can be provided.[21]

(6) is a case of modalizing about the obtaining of a relation between two individuals that are not spatiotemporally related. Recalling the accessibility predicate 'Rxy', the redundancy interpretation of extraordinary possibility claims applies straightforwardly here, to yield:

(P6)   ~Rww'.

(7) is a case of modalizing about a totality – the totality of worlds – that includes individuals that are not spatiotemporally related. The occurrence of 'actually' in (2) brings complications.[22] But skipping over these, and letting the occurrence of 'actually' become redundant, (7) may be construed as equivalent to:

(7*)   There could have been some world that is not identical to any of the worlds that exist (in our logical space).

Applying the redundancy interpretation to this extraordinary possibility claim we obtain:

(P7*) $\exists x[Wx \ \& \ \forall y[Wy \rightarrow y \neq x]]$.

Let us make explicit the intended referents of the locative terms 'here' and 'there' as they figure in (8) to give us:

(8*)   I could have been in world w instead of being in α.[23]

Transplanting his point from (8) to (8*), Yagisawa (1988: 187) insists quite correctly that (8*) has a legitimate reading that does not invite the ordinary truth-condition requiring that I have counterparts in some counterpart of w and lack counterparts in some counterpart of α. In our terms, and as Yagisawa intends, (8*) has a legitimate reading as a (transworld) modal claim about how logical space could have been different. Taking (8*) on the intended reading as initially equivalent to:

(8**) I am part of α and there is some world w which is distinct from α such that it is possible that I am part of w

and then applying the redundancy interpretation of extraordinary possibility claims to the final clause, we get:

(P8**) Piα & ∃x[Wx & x ≠ α & Pix].

Finally, since '... logical facts are not about any particular possibilia, not even possible worlds' (Yagisawa 1988: 187) (9) may be read as a claim about the totality of worlds – the claim that, as it were, the totality of worlds could have been such that the law of excluded middle failed to hold. It is not obviously sufficient, but it is necessary by PGR lights that for the totality of worlds to represent that A is a logical law, it is necessary that A. However, to simplify the case in a way that does not bear on the point at issue I will assume that the condition in question is sufficient as well as necessary.[24] Then the claim that PGR is challenged to express is equivalent to the claim that it might not have been absolutely necessary that P ∨ ~P. The redundancy interpretation of extraordinary modal claims reduces a claim of this form – it is possible that it is not necessary that A – to negation. So what emerges is the unrestricted claim:

(P9) ~(P ∨ ~P).

All of the claims as interpreted express falsehoods by PGR lights. (P6) is false since, by hypothesis, w' is accessible from w. (P7) is the classical logical falsehood that there is some world that is not identical to any world. (P8) is false, given the worldboundedness of ordinary individuals such as me (GR ontological postulate (O10) in (4.2)). (P9) is also a classical logical falsehood. So all of the possibility claims are false by PGR lights. But PGR has met the legitimate and appropriate challenge to express the content of claims and should dismiss as illegitimate and inappropriate any further insistence that they should be represented as expressing truths.

Here we reach an important point in the dialectic. PGR might now be tempted to rest her case, arguing that she need not embrace impossibilia since it has not been shown beyond reasonable doubt that IGR offers increased benefits. There may be some ontological advantage to be gained through a more discriminating identification of the occupants of certain intensional roles, but on the other hand the availability of an explicit non-modal analysis of the modal concepts is put in jeopardy. If the shift from PGR to IGR were cost-neutral, PGR may well be entitled to hold her ground. However, I will now argue, the shift from PGR to IGR cannot be presumed cost-neutral.

(5.5) THE INCALCULABLE COSTS OF IMPOSSIBILIA

The IGR hypothesis of impossible worlds is seriously deficient in detail. I have already indicated that we have no idea of how the ontology of impossibilia is to be characterized. To give a further example, Yagisawa (1988) proposes that the worlds be partitioned into logical spaces, our logical space consisting in the PGR plurality of possible worlds and the other logical spaces consisting in classes of impossible worlds. Logical spaces are supposed to consist in classes of worlds that are mutually logically accessible or which share a logic. Yet we are offered no account of what it is for a world to have one logic rather than another – an account that would have to inform us, how (if at all) the logical laws at a world w differ from the laws of nature at w or, indeed, from any other universal truths that obtain at w. But no matter how that fundamental issue is addressed, the most serious difficulty associated with IGR seems bound to persist.

Lewis (1986a: 7 n.3) rejects impossibilia because he is not prepared to accept the existence of any subject matter about which one would tell the truth by contradicting oneself. Yagisawa (1988: 202–3) defends the acceptance of such a subject matter by doing no more than: (a) pointing out that IGR does not claim that one can tell the truth about anything *possible* by contradicting oneself and (b) asking why one cannot tell the truth about an impossible thing by contradicting oneself. Regarding the former, it is true that IGR appears to be committed to a weaker claim than those actualist dialethists – e.g. Priest (1987) – who hold that contradictions are not only true in some possible worlds but, indeed, in the actual world. But what IGR shares with the actualist dialethist is a commitment to the existence of things about which we speak truly in contradiction, and so to an inconsistent hypothesis. The pressing question then is what the consequences of inconsistent hypotheses are supposed to be. One might think that it would be bad enough if the provision of an answer to this question involved, as is likely in the actualist dialethist case, a retreat to paraconsistentist account of logical consequence. The cost of such a retreat would be, at least, the abandonment of classical logic and the adoption of a paraconsistentist semantics. But it is far from obvious that the proponent of IGR should expect to be let off so lightly. The actualist dialethist postulates the existence of actual things about which we speak truly in contradiction and so in reasoning about all that there is, she takes it to be appropriate – *qua* actualist – to appeal to the dialethic logic of the actual world. But which logic will IGR invoke for the purpose of reasoning from his hypothesis? Why should we expect that the logic of any one logical space should be applicable? There is no more reason to expect the logic of the actual world, and 'our' logical space, to be appropriate than there is to think that we can apply the actual laws of nature to (unrestrictedly) all that there is. Moreover, if our logical space is classical or even intuitionistic, then the application of the logic of our logical space to the IGR hypothesis will produce the absurdity that anything is a consequence of the hypothesis (*ex contradictione quodlibet*). Is the logic that is to be applied to IGR, then, to consist in genuinely universal principles that hold over all 'logical spaces'? If there are such principles, why not stick with the conservative view that these characterize the maximal domain of absolute (logical) possibility and discount the variations between 'spaces' as variations of restricted, non-logical possibility? If there are no such universal logical principles, what then?[25]

In face of these mysteries PGR is entitled to hold that only gestures have been made towards presenting the content of IGR, and that no assessable competing hypothesis has emerged. Since we have no account, in general or in particular, of what the consequences of the hypothesis are we are in no position even to estimate the net theoretical utility, the balance of benefits to costs, associated with IGR. Consequently, the case that the net theoretical utility of PGR is matched or outstripped by that of IGR does not come close to having been made. Finally, then, GR is not convicted of the charge that her own epistemological and methodological principles commit her to impossibilia (and impending reductio).

(5.6) THE IMPOSSIBILITY OF SINGULAR REFERENCE TO NON-ACTUAL INDIVIDUALS

McGinn (1981: 151) points us towards another source of suspicion concerning the cogency of GR quantification over non-actual individuals. His two-fold observation is that there is in fact no clear

Genuine realism

referential apparatus for possible worlds and that it is hard to see how there could be. McGinn takes this observation to suggest only that we do not pre-theoretically recognize genuine worlds as proper individuals. However, there is potentially much more at stake here since the second part of McGinn's observation interacts with a venerable account of quantification to produce a new and more substantial objection to GR.

Let us reserve the term 'objects' for (all and only) the legitimate values of first-order variables of quantification. There is no doubt that individuals in general and the non-actual individuals postulated by GR in particular are supposed to be objects. However, the propriety of quantification over non-actual individuals is thereby put at risk from a substantive Fregean thesis which is, bluntly stated, that first-order quantification is legitimate only where singular reference to the elements of the domain is possible.[26] According to the ensuing objection, GR quantification over non-actual individuals is illegitimate since singular reference to such things is impossible – non-actual individuals are not legitimate objects.

I will pursue this objection without attempting any serious defence of the Fregean doctrine on quantification on which it presently depends.[27] I acknowledge that there is at large a no less prominent tradition, associated with Russell and Quine, which appears to subvert the Fregean approach by seeking to accord quantification 'priority' over singular reference. So, even if the Fregean objection can be developed successfully, nothing here will convince those who would reject the general principle governing first-order quantification on which the objection is based. I trust, however, that the Fregean doctrine on quantification is of sufficient interest and has enough advocates to sustain interest in the objection. Perhaps the doctrine will even be undermined by the present attempt to apply it. But in order at least to earn attention for this line of objection, I will deal immediately with certain predictable attempts to dismiss the whole line of objection in advance.

First, recall that the point is not to offer an argument for the non-existence of non-actual individuals but to offer an argument against the intelligibility of purported quantification over such things. The aim is consistent with a fairly robust attitude to ontological questions – whether non-actual individuals exist is one thing, whether we can refer to them is another, etc. The point is to exert a constraint on which existential claims we can properly assert noting, of course, that what cannot properly be asserted cannot truly be asserted.

GR: quantification over non-actuals

Second, perhaps the thought occurs that the force of the objection can be undermined by pointing out that if successful it would – embarrassingly – carry over to the case of a hypothesis of actual spatiotemporally isolated individuals. However, as the ensuing dialectic will bear out, the crucial question is whether singular reference is possible and it is (for reasons that will become clear in Chapter 6) inappropriate to apply the GR theory of possibility in the context of such a hypothesis.

Third, the ontological parity of actual and non-actual individuals might be invoked with a view to defusing the objection. If we can intelligibly quantify over the former (whether that is grounded in the possibility of singular reference or not), and the latter are things of the same kind, then we are entitled to quantify over the latter. However, this would be to misconstrue both the dialectical position and the nature of the objection. The dialectical position, we assume, is that we have a realist, GR, who believes in the existence of all, but not only, the entities her actualist opponent believes in. In such a case, objections must be focused on the contested class of entities and not on the whole class that the realist endorses. One might as well dismiss objections to existential claims about scientific unobservables or polytheism (versus monotheism) by pointing out that the realist takes the contested entities to belong to a more inclusive kind that has unproblematic members. In any event, insofar as it is correct to say that non-actual individuals are, ontologically, on a par with actual individuals, the parity resides in their intrinsic individuality. However, the present objection is not focused on any such intrinsic feature of non-actual individuals but rather on the relations in which the contested individuals could stand to us.[28]

I turn now to the development and evaluation of the claim that GR quantification over non-actual individuals is illegitimate since singular reference to such things is impossible.

The basic objection begins with a classification of singular terms into the three broad categories of proper names, (indexical, ostensive or) demonstrative expressions and descriptions. I assume that the possibility of successful reference to individuals by means of proper names is dependent on the possibility of singular reference by the other means. That is to say, there is no possibility of bare proper naming of an individual that could not be, in the same circumstances, an object of demonstrative or descriptive reference.[29] So if it is possible to achieve singular reference to non-actual individuals it must be possible to do so demonstratively or descriptively. In the

79

case of demonstratives, the obvious obstacle to successful reference is the spatiotemporal and causal isolation of actual referrer and non-actual referent, since such success appears to depend precisely on referrer standing in certain spatiotemporal or causal relations to referent.[30] In the case of descriptions, let us begin by considering descriptions which are (we believe) consistent, but which have no actual referent – e.g. 'the mountain that is made of gold', 'the oldest talking donkey', etc. GR advises us that such descriptions apply to individuals that (unrestrictedly) exist. However, the subsequent problem is that each such description applies to many things across many worlds so that the (semantic) definiteness of the description and the implied singularity of reference proves untenable. So we still cannot isolate any non-actual object by achieving unambiguous singular reference to it. One momentarily appealing response has it that we can steer a successful course by restricting the application of some relevant descriptive singular terms, to the context of a given non-actual world (or part thereof). But how is such a context to be specified? One might invoke descriptions such as 'the oldest talking donkey in W', where 'W' is an expression that refers to a certain non-actual world. But thereby vicious circularity ensues since to assume the availability of such a singular term would be to assume precisely what is at issue. Thus, the basic objection concludes, we have closed off all of the routes to the possibility of singular reference to non-actual individuals.

In attempting to meet the objection head-on GR will naturally consider two courses. The first is to acknowledge that there are no actual means of reference to non-actual individuals and subsequently dispute that such reference is impossible. The second is to insist that we do actually have the means of achieving singular reference to non-actual individuals.

The modal response emphasizes that the success of the present objection clearly does not depend merely on the absence of singular reference to possibilia, but on the impossibility of such reference. It is then open to GR to block the objection by arguing that despite the (timeless) absence of actual acts of singular reference to non-actual individuals, such reference is not – by her own lights – impossible. For GR, the possibility of successful acts of singular reference to non-actual individuals consists in the (unrestricted) existence of acts that realize that possibility. Furthermore GR may venture that there (unrestrictedly) are acts of this kind even if there are no actual acts of this kind. Thus, given that there are countless other-worldly talking donkeys, for example, that are the objects of successful proper naming, definite description and demonstrative reference on the part of their worldmates, GR is in a position to acknowledge the possibility of singular reference to non-actual individuals. This reply may encourage the objector to clarify and reformulate the basis of her objection as follows.

What matters for the legitimacy of our attempts – we, the actual people – to quantify over non-actual individuals is that those attempts be underwritten by the possibility of our achieving singular reference to those individuals. Even in light of that clarification, it seems that GR remains well placed to construe the other-worldly acts of reference that she has adduced as representing the appropriate possibility. The (doubly de re) possibility of us referring to non-actual individuals, it would seem, ought to be understood by GR as a matter of our counterparts referring to the counterparts of such things. In that case, the possibility of us referring to a particular non-actual talking donkey is already represented by the recently adduced worlds in which those who talk about the talking donkeys are apt to stand as our counterparts and any such donkey is apt to stand as a counterpart of itself. Moreover, this strategy appears to be available for quite general application to ensure that GR can even go a long way towards meeting a particularly strong version of the (under-specified) requirement that he should account for the possibility of singular reference to non-actual individuals – viz.:

(S1) For each individual x such that x is (wholly) in a world other than α it is possible that there is some individual y such that y is (wholly) in α and y refers to x.[31]

By generalization of the present strategy, what would make for the satisfaction of (S1) is: (a) that for each non-actual individual x there is a world w in which there exists some x* which is a counterpart of x and there exists some y* which is a counterpart, of some actual speaker and (b) x refers to y. Given the variety of worlds and the variety and flexibility of counterpart relations, GR may be allowed to presume in the absence of counterexamples that the conditions are in general fulfilled. Notably, the strategy may even be supposed to cover the possibility of actual reference to wholly alien non-actual individuals – individuals that instantiate only properties that are not instantiated in the actual world.

Despite its initial appeal the foregoing modal response fails since it involves a misconstrual of the kind of possibility that is in question.[32] The crucial point is that from the GR standpoint the thesis of the possibility of actual reference to non-actual individuals is a transworld claim.[33] As such, the thesis is an extraordinary modal claim and so, it was argued in Chapter 4, the extraordinary possibility principle (A) rather than the ordinary possibility principle (P) ought to be applied. The application of (P) wrongly renders the possibilities in question as being of the kind that can be represented within some world. The extraordinary possibility principle (A) construes the impossibility of transworld singular reference as a matter of there being (unrestrictedly) no cases of such reference. In particular, the appropriate truth-condition for (S1) is:

(S1A) For each individual x such that x is (wholly) in a world other than α there is some individual y such that y is (wholly) in α and y refers to x.

According to the basic objection, that condition is not fulfilled. Indeed, it would be surprising were (S1A) fulfilled since it requires no less than that actual reference be made to every non-actual individual. More of that shortly. However, as matters stand, the basic objection, if successful, would not only show the falsehood of:

(S1) For each individual x such that x is (wholly) in a world other than α it is possible that there is some individual y such that y is (wholly) in α and y refers to x

but also of the significantly weaker principle:

(S2) For some individual x such that x is (wholly) in a world other than α it is possible that there is some individual y such that y is (wholly) in α and y refers to x.

For the extraordinary possibility claim (S2) merits the truth-condition:

(S2A) For some individual x such that x is (wholly) in a world other than α there is some individual y such that y is (wholly) in α and y refers to x

and the basic objection has it that even that condition is not fulfilled. However, a second response on behalf of GR promises at least to improve on such comprehensive failure of singular reference to non-actual individuals.

GR: quantification over non-actuals

This second response proceeds from the contention that if there are no indiscernible worlds, then we can successfully refer to non-actual individuals.

Lewis rejects, on the grounds of their arbitrariness, the hypotheses (a) that only some worlds are replicated and (b) that all worlds are replicated to an arbitrary degree but he is agnostic about the hypothesis (c) that all worlds are replicated to a non-arbitrary degree. Given such indiscernible worlds, even the availability to us of an absolutely comprehensive description of any non-actual world – a description of the form, 'The world w such that Φw' – would not effect reference to a unique world since the condition Φ would be satisfied by many indiscernible worlds. So it is necessary to rule out indiscernible worlds if descriptive singular reference to non-actual worlds is to be possible.[34] Further argument shows that it is also sufficient.

Let v be some proper part of the actual world to which we refer by means of the name 'v' and then consider the (quasi-descriptive) condition 'x is a world and x is a duplicate of v'. The principle of recombination tells us that this condition picks out at least one individual, for the possibility of v existing without anything else is represented by the existence of at least one duplicate of v that has no worldmates – that is, by the existence of a v-duplicate that is a world. However, if there are no distinct indiscernible worlds, the quasi-descriptive condition picks out at most one individual – the ban on indiscernible worlds ensures that nothing else is both a world and a duplicate of v. Moreover, it is plausible that this process can be extended, in a recombinatorial manner to provide increasingly complex singular terms that refer uniquely to worlds – terms of the type, 'the world that consists in duplicates of this and that part of the actual world standing in such-and-such relations'. Once we have unique descriptions of worlds these can be deployed in order to achieve unique reference to sub-worldly individuals – e.g. 'the oldest talking donkey in V' (where 'V' is introduced as an abbreviation of some description that refers uniquely to some world). Thus we have singular terms that achieve reference to non-actual individuals – worlds and non-worlds alike – if there are no indiscernible worlds.

The next stage of the response consists in supplying a justification for GR ruling out the existence of indiscernible worlds.[35] The justification proceeds very straightforwardly from the general principles of net theoretical utility. Consider as rival theories minimal GR (MGR), in which the ontological component stipulates against indiscernible worlds, and a non-minimal, replicating GR (RGR), in which the ontological component stipulates the existence of non-arbitrarily many replicates of each type of world. Lewis's agnosticism is based on the absence of any reason to choose between MGR and RGR. But now we have such a reason. The quantification over non-actual individuals that is essayed in RGR is suspect – or so the objection has it – since it is not underwritten by the possibility of singular reference to any such individuals. The quantification over non-actual individuals that is essayed by MGR is not suspect in this way. Therefore, we have grounds to prefer MGR, *ceteris paribus*, over any version that postulates indiscernible worlds, or even a version that is neutral on the question. The point is generalizable. If agnosticism is merited in the first place, and no commitment to the existence of indiscernible worlds can be demonstrated, then any trouble associated with indiscernible worlds provides a reason for opting, *ceteris paribus*, for MGR, since that rules them out.[36]

The foregoing response, if successful, shows that we actually have singular terms that achieve reference to some non-actual individuals so that the Fregean requirement (S2), via truth-condition (S2A), is fulfilled.[37] However, the stronger requirement requiring that it be possible to refer to all individuals in the intended and contested domain remains unfulfilled and indeed, one might think, inevitably so.

Aside from whether (S1) is ultimately a reasonable requirement, the result of subjecting (S1) to the extraordinary possibility treatment – i.e. (S1A) – is extraordinarily demanding. The resultant requirement is that for every non-actual individual that exists, there exists in the actual world a singular term that refers uniquely to that individual. The chances of fulfilling such an onerous requirement might be improved if we allow reference to be a very weak 'representation' relation – the kind of relation that holds between unintelligent things, as in Lagadonian languages (see 10.4 below) where each individual refers to itself.[38] Yet even then the resources of actual reference are bound to be insufficient – at least, that is so if we accept the Lewis (1986a: Chapter 3) account of the limitations of the linguistic ersatzist's attempts to construct 'worldmaking' languages out of actual existents, according to which Lagadonian resources, managed in the way described, and even in the absence of indiscernible worlds, appear bound to fall short in two cases.[39] One case is where we have worlds that are symmetrical in all respects (and we can refer to some of these as combinations of parts that are duplicates of parts of the actual world), it seems that there is nothing we can do in order to achieve singular reference to any individual part of that world rather than the indiscernible individual that is its image. If such a world is minded, perhaps its inhabitants can do so in virtue of their occupying an appropriate spatiotemporal position but that, it has been argued, is irrelevant to the transworld possibility of our doing so. Another case is that of the alien individuals that instantiate properties that are not 'constructible' out of actually instantiated properties. These are not duplicates of any part of the actual world nor parts of any world that is a duplicate of any part of the actual world, so we cannot refer to them by the means that have been proposed nor by any other obvious means. Since no remedy of these referential deficiencies is in prospect, let us assume that GR will admit that she cannot defend the possibility of our referring to each individual in the intended domain of non-actual individuals.[40] The issue now is to consider the consequences of that position.

Even the harshest conclusion that might be drawn is not disastrous for GR. It is that GR quantification is intelligible only insofar as it extends to the non-actual individuals and worlds that are describable in terms of recombinations of parts of the actual world. In particular, it might be concluded that GR quantification lapses into illegitimacy where it purports to range over the realm of alien possibility.[41] This is significant for at least two reasons. First, as we shall see in Chapter 7, it is not the only case in which GR ambitions appear to run aground on the rocks of alien possibility. Second, the limited version of GR that emerges is significantly closer than the more ambitious version to certain species of AR with respect to the range of possibilities with which it can plausibly claim to deal. Perhaps there are other objections to be mounted and other lessons to be learned from what has been established about the limit of our singular reference to non-actual individuals. But I will not pursue the issue here.[42]

In (5.6) I have attempted to open up a new, neo-Fregean, line of investigation into the legitimacy of GR quantification over non-actual individuals but I do not claim to have secured a conviction. In that light, and recalling that I have argued that none of the other objections in this category are successful, I turn now to subject other aspects of GR to critical evaluation.

CHAPTER 6

Genuine realism: worlds

Every interpreter of PW is obliged to give an account of the meaning of the key theoretical term 'world' and of the kind of thing a world is. The GR story begins with Lewis (1968: 27) where the 'world' predicate is an official primitive of counterpart theory and worlds are subject to only partial and implicit characterization via the role of the predicate in the postulates of the theory. In Lewis (1973: 84–91) essentially the same picture persists although certain aspects of the partial explication are rendered more explicit and the account is more metaphysical than semantic in emphasis: other possible worlds are the same kind of thing as the world we inhabit and, consequently, none is a construct out of linguistic or mathematical elements. In Lewis (1986a: 69–78) world issues are addressed more directly and fully than before and according to the primary account (as I shall say) that emerges there: (a) worlds are sums of worldmates and (b) all and only individuals that stand in some spatiotemporal relations to one another are worldmates.[1] Indeed, this account gives rise to the following explicit definition of the 'world' predicate:

(GRW1) $\forall x[x$ is a world iff x is an individual & $\forall y[\forall z[((y$ is a part of x & z is a part of x) $\rightarrow$ (There is some spatiotemporal relation in which y stands to z)) & ((y is part of x & there is some spatiotemporal relation R in which y stands to z) $\rightarrow$ (z is part of x))]]].[2]

The concept of a world is then established as a fully-fledged sortal concept when it is associated with the mereological criterion of identity for individuals in general – worlds are identical just in case they have exactly the same parts, thus:

GR: worlds

(GRW2) $\forall x[\forall y[(x$ is a world & y is a world$) \rightarrow ((x = y)$ iff $\forall z[(z$ is a part of $x)$ iff $(z$ is a part of $y))]]]$.

The general form of objection to the primary account of worlds is that it interacts with the explanatory component of GR to produce a distortion of the modal facts. It is alleged, in the Kantian objection (6.2), that the nature of the distortion is to misrepresent the impossible as possible. Far more commonly, it is alleged that the nature of the distortion is to misrepresent the possible as impossible – as in cases concerning non-individuals (6.1), dual existences (6.3), island universes (6.4) and alien spatiotemporal relations (6.5). Beyond these questions about the nature of worlds, this is also the natural place to consider an objection to GR alleging that paradox is afoot within the principle of recombination and the commitments that it harbours concerning the number of worlds (6.6). In light of these difficulties I will consider in (6.7) the merits of a version of an unworldly GR that aims to do without identifying worlds as a special natural kind of individual. In what follows, I will follow common practice and focus on the temporal element of the primary account – times, temporal relations, the temporal dimension of the spatiotemporal manifold – rather than the spatial.[3]

(6.1) NON-INDIVIDUALS

Since the primary account conceptually determines that worlds are individuals it threatens to distort the modal facts by deeming impossible the existence of non-individuals.

Assuming that sets are not to be identified with individuals, the category of non-individuals divides exclusively and exhaustively into the sub-categories of sets and non-individual-non-sets. GR sees no need to believe in the latter since she identifies among the individuals and set-theoretic constructs thereof role-players for all of the roles that have tempted philosophers to postulate that there are non-individual-non-sets – the roles of number, proposition, property, state of affairs, etc. Of course, to the extent that such GR identifications are unsuccessful she is under pressure to admit *sui generis* entities – neither sets nor individuals – to play the roles. But even if she is successful, GR will still have the case of sets to deal with. Here I propose to concentrate on the case of sets which will, I hope, prove instructive as to how other cases of non-individuals might be handled.

The modal problem with sets unfolds thus. If, as GR acknowledges, sets exist – and perhaps even if they don't – then it is possible that sets exist.[4] However, the primary account of worlds threatens to combine with the ordinary possibility principle (P) to deem the existence of sets impossible. The primary account conceptually necessitates that worlds are individuals. (P) requires for it to be possible that sets exist that there is some world in which there are sets, and on the standard GR account of what it is to exist in a world that requires in turn that some world has sets as parts. But orthodoxy has it – and Lewis concurs – that no set is part of any individual. Therefore the existence of sets – and so by GR lights, that of propositions, properties, states of affairs, etc. – is impossible.[5]

The foregoing argument may be construed as a reductio of the primary account of worlds. But GR may rescue the possibility that sets exist by rejecting other premises. One such alternative course – that will not be pursued here – would be to reject the orthodox principle that forbids sets from being parts of individuals. The other two obvious courses are: (a) to revise the account of what it is for something to be in a world; and (b) to withhold application of the ordinary possibility principle (P) in this case.

Lewis (1983b: 39–40) emphasizes approach (a) and reconstrues being-in-a-world as a generic relation of which there are various species. As ever, an entity can be in a world by being a part of it. However, an entity can now be in a world by being partly in it – by having a part that is part of that world – and so extraordinary, transworld individuals are (partly) in many worlds.[6] Also, an entity can be in a world by existing from the standpoint of a world, which is to say by being included in the least restricted domain over which we would normally evaluate quantifications at that world, modal metaphysics being deemed abnormal. It is this third species of the relation that is geared to the rescue of the possible existence of sets. Given that, say, your singleton set is included in the least restricted domain over which we would normally evaluate actual world quantifications, that set exists from the standpoint of the actual world, so exists in a world and thereby its existence is possible. Pure sets such as the empty set and its iterations may thus be reckoned to exist in all worlds so that the existence of such sets – and such things (e.g. numbers) that are identified as constructs out of them – is not only possible but necessary.[7] Approach (b) identifies modal claims about sets as extraordinary modal claims and treats them accordingly. On that basis, it would be true to say of any set that exists (unrestrictedly) that it is possible and indeed necessary that it exists. Equally, it is possible and necessary that sets exist.

Approach (a) affords two advantages. First, given that actual existence is a matter of being in *this* world, it lets you say that numbers, etc. actually exist (cf. Lewis 1986a: 95–6). Second, it offers room to endorse the intuitive contingency of the existence of certain impure sets. For impure sets whose members exist contingently are good candidates for existing from the standpoint of some but not all worlds – indeed, existing from the standpoint of exactly all of those worlds according to which all of their members exist. The main disadvantage of this approach resides with the notion of existing from the standpoint of a world. That notion stands under suspicion of being at least ad hoc, worryingly vague and perhaps even so improperly explicated as to merit classification as a primitive.[8] Approach (b) has the complementary profile. The recognition and special interpretation of extraordinary modal claims is free of suspicion of ad hoccery, vagueness or of adding primitive concepts. In this last respect, recall that the strategy works by assigning no semantic content to appropriate occurrences of modal expressions. However, this approach looks likely to stand at odds with the intuitive contingency of the existence of impure sets. If treated as an ordinary modal claim it is not true that it is possible that my singleton set exists since no set is part of any world. If treated as an extraordinary modal claim it is true that it is necessary that my singleton set exists since it (unrestrictedly) exists. Equally, this second approach offers no immediate prospect of endorsing the actual existence of sets, since it provides no sense to that claim other than that the sets should be parts of this world.

Although both approaches face difficulties, in neither case are these serious or irremediable. The remedy that I commend to GR is to proceed by addressing the drawbacks of approach (a). GR can recognize effective variety within the being-in-a-world genus without resorting to the suspect notion of existing from the standpoint of a world. Thus, consider the following explication:

(D) $\forall w[\forall x[x$ is in w iff
    (i)   (x is an individual & $\exists y[y$ is part of x & y is part of w] $\vee$
    (ii)   (x is a set & $\forall y[(y$ is an individual & ((y is a member of x) $\vee$ (y is a member of a member of x) $\vee \ldots \rightarrow$ y is a part of w)]]].[9]

(D) is not vague and relies in its explanans only on the already accepted primitive concepts of GR. Certainly (D) is disjunctive. But (D) is not ad hoc since it makes dual provision for being in a world that corresponds exactly to the two fundamental ontological categories of GR ontology. (D) allows us to assert that the existence of impure sets is appropriately contingent and that impure sets actually exist so long as all of their individual *ur-elements* are parts of this world. Depending on how GR proposes to treat the empty set (see n.6 above) (D) may already accommodate pure sets. If it does not, then modal claims about pure sets can be treated as extraordinary modal claims and the one remaining bullet to be bitten is that GR must assert that, although pure sets exist – and it is both possible and necessary that pure sets exist – no pure set actually exists. But that is not an obviously embarrassing commitment and, indeed, it is a thesis with venerable precedent.[10]

The remaining problems for the primary account of worlds flow from its spatiotemporal element.

(6.2) DISCONNECTED TIMES

According to GR, there are many worlds and so, given the primary account of worlds, there are many disconnected times. Kant (1781) held it impossible that there should be disconnected times and others, such as Bennett (1966) and Rosenberg (1989) have sympathized. If the Kantian doctrine is correct then it appears that GR misconstrues the impossible – the existence of disconnected times – as possible.

It is as well to deal swiftly with the thought that GR does not really endorse the possibility that disconnected times exist. Certainly, if we treat as an ordinary modal claim the claim that it is possible that there are disconnected times, and subsequently apply the ordinary possibility principle (P), then the interpreted claim that emerges is that *some world* has disconnected times as parts. GR will, of course, deny the possibility so understood. However, the claim that it is possible that there are disconnected times is not an ordinary modal claim but a paradigm case of an extraordinary modal claim. Applying the extraordinary possibility principle (A) of (4.3), the interpreted claim that emerges is that there are disconnected times. So as we would expect, GR commitment to the existence of disconnected times entails commitment to the possibility of the existence of disconnected times. Subsequently, GR ought to respond to the Kantian position as Miller (1990) suggests. First, GR ought to concede to the Kantian that the *actual* existence of disconnected times is impossible. That ordinary, intra-world, modal claim is true for there is no world that has disconnected times as parts and so nor, a fortiori, is there any world containing a part that is a counterpart of our world and which has disconnected times as parts. Second, the kind of inconceivability claim that is supposed to support the impossibility of disconnected times can be accepted without accepting that it supports that, disputed, impossibility claim. GR might accept that – swiftly – we are unable to imagine ourselves as subjects of such experience as would justify belief in two disconnected times.[11] GR may even count such a failure of conception as evidence of impossibility.[12] Still, GR may hold that the impossibility in question is that of a temporally unified subject standing to two disconnected times in any way that would permit identification of both as parts of her own, reflexively and indexically identified, world. That is to say, the inconceivability claim need be taken to support no more than the thesis on which the Kantian and GR agree, viz. the impossibility of the actual co-existence of disconnected times.

(6.3) TEMPORALLY DISCONNECTED DUAL EXISTENCES

Other critics will argue that it is precisely because GR is bound to agree with the Kantian about the impossibility of the actual co-existence of disconnected times, that she is thereby bound to misrepresent the possible as impossible.

The first kind of scenario adduced in support of the possibility of actually disconnected times is a scenario of dual existence. The advocate of this case (King 1995) subsequently argues that GR ought to abandon the primary account of worlds in order to accommodate that possibility. The scenario that we are presented as a package of conceivable phenomena is one in which a subject experiences two radically different 'alternate' lives. The package in question involves the emergence of non-collusive, individually and mutually coherent, reports of the occurrence of events which we know, by exhaustive cognition, not to occur in our time. It is then proposed that the best explanation of this package is a hypothesis of the existence of disconnected times which are inhabited by the subject. Confronted by such a case, GR will naturally seek an alternative explanation of the package in which the dual existences are temporally connected so that no recalcitrant 'possibility' ensues.[13] However, and more interestingly, King suggests that GR ought to embrace the possibility of actually disconnected times and switch from a temporal to a causal account of worlds. In judging the viability of this option we have to weigh three considerations that count against it.

First (cf. Rosenberg 1989: 421) it has been held that facts of causal connectedness or disconnectedness, such as the causal isolation of worlds, are not good candidates to be primitive facts. Indeed, it has been held, and often for that reason, that causal relatedness supervenes on spatiotemporal relatedness. Second, a causal account of the unification of worlds, just like a (spatio)temporal account of the unification of worlds must face the allegation that it misconstrues the possible as impossible. Among the recalcitrant cases that will be presented are not only those in which there are actually some individuals that stand in no causal relation to one another, but that of the *chaotic* worlds in which no individual stands in any causal relation to any other.[14,15] Third, as noted by Bigelow and Pargetter (1990:190) and Rosenberg (1989: 420), the concept of *world* is prior to that of *causal relation* in the GR hierarchy of analysis given to us by Lewis. Causation is there analysed in terms of counterfactuals, which are analysed in terms of truth-values of material conditionals across spheres of proximate *worlds* – moreover, proximity is analysed in terms of similarity including similarity of laws, and laws are analysed in terms of *worlds*.[16]

Concerning the first consideration, King (1995: 545) observes quite reasonably that both elements – the non-primitiveness of causal relations and their supervenience on spatiotemporal relations – stand in need of supporting argument. So let us, for the sake of argument, discount that consideration entirely. Concerning the second consideration, it seems to me that the possibility of chaotic worlds is a far stronger prospect than the possibility of King's dual existences. But, let us, for the sake of argument concede a draw on that point. It is the third consideration that is crucial.

It would be a massive undertaking, with absolutely no guarantee of success, to show that the benefits available from a version of GR in which causal relations are taken as conceptually primitive is of comparable value to the benefits available from standard GR in which (spatio)temporal relations have that status. But in the absence of the demonstrable utility of causation-based GR we have no reason whatsoever to believe it. It would be madness for GR to risk all by altering so fundamental a part of her entire approach to philosophical explanation in an attempt to accommodate the findings of one slender thought experiment.[17] I take this threat to the utility and credibility of GR to be a decisive reason for resisting the causal account of world unity.[18]

(6.4) ISLAND UNIVERSES

The second kind of scenario adduced in support of the possibility of actually disconnected times is one in which there actually co-exist a multitude of island universes – that is individuals, just like Lewis's worlds, that are temporally, spatially and causally isolated from one another but which are co-actual. Lewis (1986a: 71) concedes substantial intuitive plausibility to the claim that there could be island universes and admits that he would rather not deny it. However, accepting that he must deny this possibility in order to maintain the primary account of worlds Lewis seeks to undermine the problematic modal intuition by presenting similar, surrogate possibilities that may account for the intuition but which are consistent with the primary account – worlds containing spatiotemporal regions that *only appear* to be disconnected or worlds containing spatiotemporal regions that are *all but* isolated.[19] Bigelow and Pargetter (1990: 189–93) are unconvinced by Lewis's resistance and attempt to bolster the island universes problem in three distinguishable ways which I will discuss in turn.

First, Bigelow and Pargetter – hereafter, BP – suggest that it is an epistemic possibility that the actual world contains island universes since the hypothesis that our world has disconnected temporal regions is compatible with accepted physical theory. Let the physical theory in question – the general theory of relativity – be true. Yet, GR ought not to abandon the primary account of worlds on these grounds.

Recall that GR accepts that it is an epistemic possibility that there are disconnected times and that our universe is but one of many such things – indeed, that is how she takes things to be. So far no conflict. It is then simply tendentious to claim further, in the present context, that general relativity is compatible with *our world* having disconnected temporal parts or the *actual* co-existence of disconnected temporal regions. 'Actual' and 'world' are not proper theoretical terms of general relativity. What significant role could be found for 'actual' or 'our world' except for the indexical role of picking out the local closed temporal region? Such a role would have the dual effect of making general relativity look like a non-empirical theory (one that claims potential jurisdiction beyond the actual) and which would undermine the point of the island universes example. It is not to be ruled out that 'world' might be introduced as a theoretical term with some other role into a recognizable formulation of general relativity. However, the meaning of 'world' would then be fixed by a set of empirical constraints that would simply render equivocal the use of the term in general relativity and the use of the same term in philosophical explanations of the modalities and the intensions. No doubt general relativity, like any other empirical theory, has models that are susceptible to metaphysically tendentious description – e.g. models that 'may be taken to represent' our world having many disconnected temporal regions. But the availability of such models and their susceptibility to such description is not very compelling for the epistemic possibility of controversial doctrines that philosophers take to be metaphysically impossible.[20]

Second, the primary account strikes BP (1990: 92) as arbitrary by admitting as worldmates individuals that share only a single common moment of time but ruling out as worldmates individuals for which there is a non-zero, non-realized, objective chance of their sharing some moment.

The charge of arbitrariness against the primary account of worlds is puzzling, for there are at least three aspects in which the account might naturally be characterized as non-arbitrary rather than arbitrary. First, the account offers *necessary and sufficient* conditions for individuals to be worldmates. Second, the condition is that individuals stand in *any* spatiotemporal relation. Third, the condition is categorical in content – of the form P – rather than probabilistic – of the form that there is a non-zero objective chance that P.[21] Other puzzles about the example arise from the consideration that ascriptions of objective chance seem to be, in various respects, essentially temporal. Here is one thought. It seems appropriate to say that at time t_1 the objective chance that P will not occur is m and that at time t_2 the objective chance that P will not occur is n ($\neq$ m). That being so, should ascriptions of objective chance not always, then, be relativized to a time? If so, what would be the effect on the example of making the relativization explicit? If not, how are we to make sense of the claim that there (timelessly) is a non-zero objective chance that two things be temporally related when they (timelessly) are not so related? These are genuine, although admittedly inchoate, questions. But rather than pursue them here or consider further the BP claims about objective chance, I will focus on the modal consequences of those claims.

That there is a non-zero, non-realized objective chance that two individuals be temporally related entails, I presume, that it is contingent whether the two individuals are temporally related. Understood as ordinary contingency, the GR interpretation of this claim is that there is a world at which the two individuals are not temporally related and a world at which the two individuals are temporally related. The objection against the primary account of worlds may then be that it determines the falsehood of the former conjunct, and so of the conjunction and so – wrongly – of the contingency claim. I am unsure whether there is any significant pre-theoretical modal intuition to the effect that (timeless) temporal relatedness is a contingent matter (see below). But in any event GR can accommodate such an intuition by assigning to the contingency claim a truth-condition which is not ad hoc and is fulfilled. Consider two individuals a and b which are, by hypothesis of non-realization of relevant objective chance, temporally disconnected. The claim that it is contingent whether a and b are temporally related may be represented as the conjunction:

(C) It is possible that a and b are temporally related &
It is possible that a and b are not temporally related.

If we construe the non-modal content of the first conjunct – that a and b are temporally related – as an intra-world content (in light of the primary account of worlds), then the first conjunct of (C) merits the ordinary possibility interpretation thus:

(C1) There is a world in which there is an a-counterpart x and there is a b-counterpart y and x is temporally related to y.

There is no obvious obstacle to (C1) being satisfied in the case where neither a nor b is a world. In the special case where, as BP intend, a and b are (according to the primary account) worlds, several approaches to the supply of appropriate counterparts are available. For the sake of brevity I will mention only the generic relation under which any world is the counterpart of any other. Thereby any world will satisfy (C1) since it can be both x and y and since temporal relatedness is reflexive. If a more restrictive counterpart relation is required, then only some (relevant) worlds will do, but the same explanation of the satisfaction of (C1) applies to any such world and so there is no problem. So we have an interpretation in which the first conjunct of (C) is true. Next, if we construe the non-modal content of the second conjunct – that a and b are not temporally related – as a transworld content (in light of the primary account of worlds), then the second conjunct of (C) merits the extraordinary possibility interpretation thus:

(C2)   a and b are not temporally related.

But (C2) is true by hypothesis, so the second conjunct of (C) is also true. So (C) is true under an appropriate non-*ad hoc* interpretation and GR can at least meet the modal dimension of the BP objection from non-realized objective chance of temporal relatedness.

It might be felt that the foregoing response amounts to cheating. I think that this charge can be resisted.[22] But suffice to say that if, for whatever reason, GR is constrained to interpret 'contingent whether' univocally, i.e. in terms of a univocal interpretation of the implicit possibility operators, it is indeed the case that GR is compelled to deny that it is contingent whether individuals are (timelessly) spatiotemporally related. Moreover, even if the foregoing response is legitimate, it does not deal with the next complaint that can be distinguished within the BP critique. There, I will argue, the best response for GR will be simply to accept an allegedly counter-intuitive modal consequence and seek to limit the damage. I note here that the same strategy of damage limitation is also available for application to the present case, if GR acceptance of the non-contingency of spatiotemporal relatedness is compelled.

The third distinguishable complaint that BP (1990: 192–3) make against the primary account is that it commits its proponent to the truth of certain counterfactuals which are 'clearly false'. In BP's crucial example, we are to imagine that the actual world is a last gasp world (as I'll say) that is unified by final momentary overlap between regions R and S, and that it is only in that last moment that 'we' from R meet Jane from S. Relative to that scenario, the crucial counterfactual that BP consider to be clearly false, and which they take GR to be committed to holding true is (CF):

(CF)   If Jane hadn't stood in any temporal relation to us, then Jane would not have existed.[23]

In essence, the BP argument in favour of a GR commitment to the truth of (CF) is as follows. On the standard GR account of truth-conditions for counterfactuals, falsification of (CF) requires that there is a world in which the antecedent condition be fulfilled – i.e. that there is a world in which there is a counterpart of Jane and there are counterparts of us and the counterpart of Jane stands in no spatiotemporal relation to the counterparts of us. But by the primary account there is no such *world* and so GR is committed to the truth of the counterfactual.

96

GR: worlds

This objection is tougher than its predecessor in that appeal to the extraordinary interpretation of modal claims, in addition to the ordinary interpretation, does not allow GR to succeed in 'weaseling away' commitment to the allegedly counter-intuitive modal claim. This is not to deny that GR has grounds for seeking an extraordinary interpretation. The antecedent of (CF) is:

(1) Jane stands in no temporal relation to us.

So, the case may go, given the primary account of worlds, (1) may be read as a transworld, unrestricted, content. And as such, there is a case for withholding from (CF) the ordinary interpretation that is applied to counterfactuals when antecedent and consequent are read as intra-world contents. However, the commitment to the truth of (CF) threatens to reassert itself even when that point is taken. For even in the absence of a detailed account of the truth-conditions of extraordinary counterfactual claims, it is predictable that any such account that GR is likely to find acceptable and continuous with the ordinary case, will have the feature of determining as true any counterfactual with an impossible antecedent. But since (1), *qua* unrestricted content, is false, (1), *qua* unrestricted content, is impossible. The point can be made more generally. It is necessary in order to falsify (CF) that GR should provide for the truth of an appropriate possibility thesis – viz.:

(2) It is possible that (we exist & Jane exists & there is no T such that T(us, Jane)).

What the foregoing considerations show is that GR cannot provide for the truth of (2) on either reading of the single possibility operator that is involved. The truth of the conjunction is not represented by any world (speaking to the ordinary case) nor by logical space as a whole (speaking to the extraordinary case).[24] So if GR is to defend the primary account of worlds – let us accept – she is compelled to accept the truth of the counterfactual, (CF), which the objector alleges to be clearly false. GR might then argue that for whatever cost she thereby incurs, there is an equivalent cost incurred by her rivals with respect to certain other, parallel, counterfactuals. Here is one way in which such a case might be made.

The counterfactual (CF) is determined to be true (and the antecedent possibility claim (2) is determined to be false) on GR interpretation because it exhibits the following pattern of features.

Genuine realism

Falsehood requires the existence of something which represents a possibility of the form $\sim\exists F(Fab)$ where $\exists F(Fab)$ is a necessary condition of anything representing any possibility for a and b. So truth is determined by an intractable conflict between, as it were, the form of the falsity-condition of the claim and its content. But the thought, then, is that most interpreters of PW will have trouble over some such counterfactuals – counterfactuals which might reasonably be thought false from a pre-theoretical standpoint but which have antecedents which the theory determines to be impossible. For given commitment to the classical semantic principle that all conditionals with impossible antecedents are true, the theorist will be committed to the truth of any such conditional.[25] Thus, for example, to speak to two species of actualist realist – the nature realist and the Plantingan realist respectively – we have:

(3) If there had been no states of affairs involving a and b there would have been no states of affairs.
(4) If there had been no properties whose instantiation entailed the existence of horses and mountains there would have been none whose instantiation entailed the existence of mountains.[26]

These counterfactuals would appear to have impossible antecedents, by the lights of the respective interpreters, and would thus (we assume) be determined to be true, given that the relevant entities – the properties and the states of affairs – are conceived, respectively, as necessary existents. The *tu quoque* move deserves further scrutiny in these cases and I do not claim, on behalf of GR, that all rival interpreters of PW are so vulnerable. But insofar as reticence in these respects is merited, that is largely because rival interpreters of PW offer no clear account of how such extraordinary counterfactuals and other modal claims are to be interpreted, and not because there are good grounds for thinking that they escape the charge. So it is simply unclear that GR has a special problem about counterfactuals with theoretically sensitive content.

In sum, BP develop the island universes objection against the primary account of worlds in some very interesting directions. But in doing so they broach considerations – such as atemporal objective chance and extraordinary counterfactual claims – that are not understood well enough at present to offer very promising grounds for rejecting an otherwise well defended account of the nature of worlds.

(6.5) NON-ACTUAL SPATIOTEMPORAL RELATIONS

Lewis's major worry about the primary account of worlds is that it is excessively constrained by the nature of the spatiotemporal relations that are instantiated in the actual world (1986a: 74–5). It is generally assumed that a Newtonian world is (absolutely) possible – a world that differs in an ontologically fundamental way from our own relativistic world in that two distinct types of distance relation, rather than one, obtain between its regions.[27] If the difference between such worlds and our own is a matter of our very own spatiotemporal relations being instantiated there, albeit behaving differently, there is no problem. To say that the worldmates of those worlds stand in 'spatiotemporal relations' to each and only each other is to say something true, since whatever 'spatiotemporal relation' means we know that it refers to the relations (our spatiotemporal relations) that unify that world. However, it is not clear how to answer the question whether the Newtonian possibility is a matter of our spatiotemporal relations behaving differently as opposed to distinct relations being instantiated. More generally, therefore, we ought not to presume that our spatiotemporal relations are so versatile that any way a world could be is invariably a matter of some pattern of those very relations being instantiated. Yet when we use the term 'spatiotemporal' in the primary account, we can only be confident of covering the worlds in which our spatiotemporal relations are instantiated. So it is at least doubtful that the necessary condition articulated in the primary account of worlds is adequate. For we cannot rule out that it is a contingent matter whether our spatiotemporal relations are instantiated or that worlds are unified solely by relations that are alien to our own.[28,29,30]

Lewis suggests that this objection calls for a retreat from the primary account to a secondary account in which it is necessary and sufficient for individuals to be worldmates that they instantiate some analogically spatiotemporal relation – the task is then to spell out how such relations are analogically spatiotemporal.[31] To that end Lewis (1986a: 75–6) suggests that such relations are: (i) natural (not gerrymandered or even mildly disjunctive); (ii) pervasive (relatedness within the system is transitive); (iii) discriminating (it is possible that all individuals are discernible from one another with respect to their place in the system); and (iv) external (they do not supervene on the intrinsic natures of the relata taken separately, but only on the intrinsic character of the composite of the relata). Since he claims no more than that (i)–(iv) capture '... at least some of the points of analogy ...', Lewis does not come close to attempting an explicit definition of analogical spatiotemporality. We know that Lewis (1986a: 76–8) is sceptical that external and natural relatedness alone is sufficient for individuals to be worldmates. But it is unclear whether he construes the addition of features (ii) and (iii), either individually or jointly, to amount to a plausible candidate for sufficiency. In any case, since there is a lack of cases to test the sufficiency of the conjunction of (i) and (iv) there is also a lack of cases to test the sufficiency of any extension of that conjunction. Yagisawa (1992: 85–6) attempts to cast doubt on whether pervasiveness and discrimination are necessary conditions for individuals to be worldmates. In the case of pervasiveness, the objection is that we do not even know whether the spatiotemporal relations in our worlds are pervasive. But the basis of this claim is just the alleged epistemic possibility that the actual world contains island universes as discussed in (6.4) above. In the case of discrimination the objection appears to be based on a misunderstanding. Yagisawa takes Lewis to allow that relations may be analogically spatiotemporal relations even if they are not discriminating since Lewis allows that such relations need not discriminate at every world in which they are instantiated. But Lewis construes what it is for a system of relations to be discriminating modally, defining the notion in terms of the *possibility* of such a system achieving discrimination. Such relations are discriminating in all worlds because they achieve discrimination in some.[32]

It is unclear how to proceed from these basic observations. Dialectically, the natural way forward for GR is to begin by defending the strongest construal of Lewis's suggestion. That is to construe relatedness as fixed by (i)–(iv) as an explicit definition of the worldmate relation and see whether any retreat is required. In the absence of counterexamples or of any other demonstration of the modal inadequacy of such a definition, let it stand.[33] In the event of a difficulty, see if the points of analogy can be martialled in a way that is not vulnerable to the objection. As far as I know, the opponents of GR have presented no new objections – that is no objections that were not already occasioned by the primary account – to an account of worlds in terms of analogically spatiotemporal relations that give due cause for retreat from the bolder position.

(6.6) RECOMBINATION

It is not only the GR account of the nature of worlds but also her account of the variety of worlds that is alleged to be problematic.

A principle of recombination appears indispensable to GR since such a principle is required to generate enough worlds to underwrite the non-trivial extensional accuracy of the crucial possibility principle:

(P) It is possible that A iff there is a world according to which, A.[34]

As a first attempt at stating the kind of recombinatorial principle that is supposed to generate the range of worlds in question, let us consider (R):

(R) For any (worldbound) individuals x and y and for any numbers n and m, there is world w in which there are n duplicates of x and m duplicates of y.[35]

Thus, if there (unrestrictedly) is a talking donkey and there (unrestrictedly) is a white swan then, by (R), there is a world in which there are duplicates of both, there is a world in which there are duplicates of neither (no talking donkeys and no white swans), there is a world in which there is a duplicate of one but not of the other (there are talking donkeys but no white swans), there is a world in which there is one talking donkey and two thousand white swans, etc. But such an unrestricted version of the principle brings trouble.

The original paradox of recombination presented in Forrest and Armstrong (1984) threatens the existence of a set of all genuine worlds and, a fortiori, the existence of a set of all genuine individuals. Lewis (1986a: 101–4) responds to a slightly amended version of the paradox by proposing a restricted version of the principle of recombination instead of the unrestricted principle of recombination on which the paradox depends. But I will pick up the story with Nolan (1996) who argues as follows. Since the kind of argument proposed by Forrest and Armstrong and considered by Lewis is subtly invalid, it fails to show that there is no set of all possible worlds. However, a simple, alternative cardinality argument does succeed in showing that there is no set of all possible individuals and the proper response to this conclusion – contra Lewis – is to accept an unrestricted principle of recombination and make theoretical adjustments elsewhere. The Nolan argument relies only on the principle of recombination being specified in some way which entails:

(R*) For any individual, x, and for any given number, n, there is a world in which there are at least n distinct duplicates of that individual.

Assume, then, that the cardinality (the number of members) of the set of (unrestrictedly) all individuals is c. By recombination, via (R*), there is for any arbitrary individual a, a world containing 2^c duplicates of a. Thus, the set of all individuals has at least 2^c members. But since $2^c > c$ (for $c > 1$) the cardinality of the set of individuals is not equal to c, contrary to the initial hypothesis. Thus the choice facing GR is that between rejecting the hypothesis that there is a set of all individuals and restricting the principle of recombination in some way so that it does not have (R*) as a consequence.

The restricted form of recombination principle that Nolan suggests has it that the extent of duplication of individuals is constrained by the maximum size of spacetime that (unrestrictedly) exists – thus:

(R**) There is some number N such that no spacetime is larger than N, and for all individuals x, y, and for all numbers n, m such that $(n + m) \leq N$, there is a world in which there are at least n duplicates of x and at least y duplicates of m.

So if C numbers all the individuals (including all of the spacetime points) then there is a number $C^* > C$ such that C^* lies beyond the scope of (R**). For if the set of all spacetime points is no larger than C then no single spacetime is larger than C, and (R**) does not entail the existence of a world in which there are more than C duplicates of any individual. However, the cost of imposing this restriction on recombination is commitment to a maximal size for any possible spacetime. To assert that there is some N such that there are (unrestrictedly) no spacetimes of size $> N$, is just to assert the GR interpretation of the claim that it is impossible for any spacetime be of size $> N$. The alternative strategy for GR is to persist with unrestricted recombination and operate with a revised ontological hypothesis in which it is denied that there is a set of all individuals, but all of the individuals are available as a maximal sum of individuals and as a proper class – a proper class usually being construed as a set-like entity that has members but is not itself a member of anything.[36] Nolan encourages GR to pursue the option of persevering with unrestricted recombination, but I would be inclined to advocate the alternative.

First, on the cost side it is to be admitted that commitment to a modal thesis that is not independently motivated (by considerations of logical status, analyticity, etc.) is unwelcome. But the commitment in question is not very strong, insisting only (de dicto) that spacetime has a maximal possible size. Second, by opting for the modal restriction on spacetime size we need not disrupt the simplicity of the ontological component of GR, by messing with the non-mereological part to give us classes rather than sets. Third, we need not threaten the fundamental ontological integrity and economy of categories that is characteristic of GR (see Chapter 9) by admitting – as Nolan suggests may be necessary – universals as a primitive category.[37] Fourth, there remains the very large question of whether the combination of mereology and proper class theory really does provide an adequate and comprehensive substitute for classical set theory both in terms of the account of quantification that it affords and in terms of the range of GR applications of PW that it will sustain.

Caution counsels GR to accept the mild embarrassment of a gratuitous, but apparently self-contained, modal commitment rather than risk coherence and utility by seeking a substitute for the set of all individuals. In that cautious spirit the ontological component of GR, as presented above, incorporates a version of the principle of recombination (O12) (in 4.2) that is restricted in the way that Lewis (1986a: 92) suggests and which Nolan's argument requires.[38]

(6.7) UNWORLDLY GENUINE REALISM

Yagisawa (1992) suggests that GR should release herself from the obligation to solve the problem of world identity by abandoning the concept of a world. The argument is that GR has no need to deploy the concept of a world since the roles that worlds are supposed by Lewis to play can be played adequately by entities whose identity conditions are unproblematic and to which GR is already committed. More specifically: (i) the two key roles that worlds are supposed to play within a GR semantics for modality are those of truth-relativizer (P is true at X) and possibilia localizer (y exists in X); and (ii) the possible individuals generated by unrestricted summation – including the transworld individuals as well as the ordinary, intra-world individuals – are apt to play these roles. In order to evaluate this claim let us contrast GR as we know it – worldly GR (WGR) – with the unworldly variant UGR.

On the plus side, UGR promises to provide truth-conditions that underwrite the truth of the crucial possibility claims that the primary account has been held deficient for presenting as false. The possibility of island universes would be underwritten by the existence of aggregates of individuals that are island universes – say, the aggregate of this WGR world and any other. The possibility of Newtonian relatedness is underwritten by the existence of aggregates of individuals – forget whether we ought to call them 'worldmates' – that are Newtonian interrelated. Yet, turning away for the moment from questions of application there are differences between worlds and aggregates in general that raise suspicions as to whether UGR would really be stable. One notable difference between indiscriminate aggregates of individuals and worlds is that the former overlap while the latter do not. So, to put the point mildly, careful consideration of the representational and other implications of overlap is in order.[39] Equally, once worlds drop out of the picture, must GR frame an unworldly surrogate for the worldly principle of recombination in order to ensure that there are 'truth-relativizers' enough so that each possibility is true at one?[40] These are but some of the matters, aside from questions of application, that a full defence of unworldly GR must address. However, questions of application appear decisive in showing that WGR has been given insufficient reason to convert to UGR.

The essential flaw in Yagisawa's case for UGR is most easily seen once we grant, for the sake of argument, the conclusion that the semantic applications of GR do not require recognition of worlds. Having made this concession, the point remains that no argument has been offered for the dispensability of the concept of a world in light of the conceptual or ontological ambitions of GR. Such a case might plausibly be made with respect to the ontological applications of GR, once the role-players for all of the various propositional roles are identified as sets of individuals. However, the role of the world concept in the WGR hierarchy of conceptual analyses stands as a major obstacle to demonstrating comprehensive dispensability. Recall from the recent discussion in (6.3) of the prospects of a causal account of the worldmate relation that the concept of causation is analysed in terms of counterfactuals, which are analysed in terms of truth-values of material conditionals across spheres of proximate worlds. In that 'truth-relativizer' capacity perhaps worlds are, as Yagisawa suggests, dispensable. However, worlds re-enter the picture since proximity of relevant 'truth-relativizers' is analysed in terms of similarity and, crucially, similarity of laws in particular, with laws analysed, in turn, in terms of worlds.[41] In the absence of a demonstration that the concept of a world is dispensable to GR in providing analyses of those concepts in which that concept of a world is presently implicated as analysans there is a major gap between Yagisawa's semantic and ontological premises and his unworldly conclusion.[42]

The objections to the primary account of worlds typically assign a weight to pre-theoretical modal opinion that is inappropriate when the modal claims in question involve the use of theoretical terms. Retreat to the secondary account of worlds, and so to analogically spatiotemporal relations, may be merited in face of uncertainty about how far the meaning of our term 'spatiotemporal relation' is constrained by the contingent facts about its actual extension (or uncertainty about the modal flexibility of actual spatiotemporal relations). If the secondary account does prove inadequate then GR has yet another problem about certain *alien* possibilities. However, as far as I am aware, no argument for the inadequacy of the secondary account has been offered. In any event, the case for GR retreating to an unworldly version of her doctrine is very far from having been made.

CHAPTER 7

Genuine realism: unanalysed modality

The major theoretical ambition of GR is that of providing explicit and non-modal analyses of the family of modal and intensional concepts. Central to that ambition is the provision of an explicit and non-modal analysis of the concept of possibility as expressed by the biconditional:

> (P) It is possible that A iff there is a world at which it is the case that A.[1]

I will address the questions of what it is for the GR analysis of possibility to be accurate (7.1) and appropriately non-modal (7.2)–(7.4) subsequently, defending the GR analysis against various charges to the effect that it fails to meet at least one of these criteria of adequacy. None of these unsuccessful charges is concerned with any special range of possibilities, but I will argue here that this matter of range is crucial. Insofar as GR analysis of possibility is trained on cases of 'local' possibility, I have no objection to offer. But I will present an argument (7.5) which aims to show that in so far as GR analysis aims to cover alien possibilities it is doomed to be either incomplete or modal.[2]

(7.1) ACCURATE ANALYSIS

Accuracy (in extension) requires from the GR analysis of the concept of possibility that the ontology of the theory should combine with prior modal opinion to underwrite the truth of (P). That is to say, more specifically: (i) that the ontological component of GR must generate a set of worlds that determines the truth-values of the existential claims about worlds that figure as the right-sides of instances of (P); and (ii) these truth-values must match the truth-values of the

GR: unanalysed modality

left-side possibility claims, the latter being assigned – by and large – on the basis of our prior modal beliefs.[3] So, the GR analysis of possibility is accurate only when the ontological component of GR determines the existence of a set of worlds that is *complete*, by containing worlds of sufficiently many different types to represent all of the possibilities, and *consistent*, by containing no world of any type that represents any impossibility.[4] If the ontological postulates of GR fail to determine a consistent set of worlds then GR permits the existence of a world at which P even though (by pre-theoretic lights) it is impossible that P. If the ontological postulates of GR fail to determine a complete set of worlds, then GR fails to serve up a world at which P even though (by pre-theoretic lights) it is possible that P. Although I will have some cause to deal with the question of consistency (7.2), my main concern is whether GR is complete.

The most natural way of attempting to ensure that GR is complete is simply to add the following axiom:

(C) For every way the world could be there is some world that is that way.

But (C) gives rise to a dilemma. If the notion of a way the world could be is analysed in GR terms, the subsequent ontological identification of such things with worlds, or sets of worlds, renders (C) trivially true whether there are infinitely many worlds or only one. Accordingly, (C) fails to guarantee that all possibilities are realized. Alternatively, if GR treats the notion of a way the world could be as primitive and unanalysed then (C) offers completeness at the price of yielding an analysis of the modal concepts that is not non-modal. Lewis (1986a: 87) acknowledges that GR requires a non-modal expression of the thought that there are no gaps in logical space, and to that end commends a principle of recombination at which, 'patching together parts of different possible worlds yields another possible world'. So, for example, since there exists a horse and there exists a horn, there exists a world which contains a horse with a horn.[5] The principle of recombination has implications about what worlds there are, and so it takes its place in the ontological component as postulate (O12) (see (4.2)). The crucial question of accuracy is whether GR, including the recombination postulate, yields an analysis of possibility that is complete as well as consistent. The theoretical ambitions of GR further require that such accuracy be achieved by an analysing theory that is non-modal. I now turn to the unpacking of that further requirement.

We should distinguish among the claims that an analysis of possibility is conceptually modal, that it is doxastically modal and that it is ontologically modal. Considering specific versions of these broad ways of being modal, I will distinguish those that are objectionable in the context of the analytic ambitions of GR from those that are not and argue that GR analyses are modal in only unobjectionable ways.

(7.2) CONCEPTUALLY MODAL ANALYSIS

In the first instance, whether GR is conceptually modal is a matter of whether any explicitly or overtly modal term – a term that explicitly expresses a modal concept – figures significantly in the statement of GR. It is obvious, and obviously inconsequential, that the explanatory biconditionals of GR feature explicitly modal terms in their explananda – hence the use of 'possible' on the left-hand side of (P).[6] The occurrence of an explicitly modal term is significant for present purposes only if used in the statement of the ontological component of GR or in the explanans of the (basic, non-bridging) explanatory biconditionals. Any analysis of the family of modal concepts afforded by GR on that basis would fail on grounds of circularity.[7]

The question whether GR does so deploy any explicitly modal term promotes the question of which terms in our language are explicitly modal. In response, it seems that a perfectly serviceable distinction exists between those terms that are explicitly modal and those that are not. Competent grasp of this distinction can be manifest by recognizing the overtly modal terms when confronted with them and does not, I will maintain, require that there be any general and precise way of circumscribing the boundaries of the range of explicitly modal terms. Among the explicitly modal terms are 'possibility', 'necessity', 'contingency', 'compatibility' – perhaps even 'consistency', 'actual' – various cognate expressions and, no doubt, many others. But none of these terms appears in the ontological component of GR nor in its ultimate analysans. The (salient) primitive theoretical terms of GR, as noted in Chapter 4, are 'individual', 'set', 'sum', 'part of', 'member of' and 'is spatiotemporally related to', none of which figures in any remotely plausible prior inventory of the overtly modal terms. So if any of the primitive theoretical terms of GR is conceptually modal it is not by being an explicit expression of any modal concept. The next question is whether GR is conceptually modal by way of any such term being an implicit, or

GR: unanalysed modality

covert expression of any modal concept. This is a matter of whether the concept expressed by a term contains an unanalysable modal element or, perhaps, whether the grasp of the concept expressed requires prior grasp of some explicitly modal concept. Were GR to emerge as conceptually modal in either of these implicit ways then, given other reasonable assumptions within which the debate is usually conducted, the GR analysis of possibility would be objectionably modal – the ambition to provide a comprehensive and non-modal analysis of the concept of possibility would be vitiated by circularity.[8,9] However, given that none of the terms in question appears to be implicitly modal in either of the senses indicated, it is reasonable to challenge those who think otherwise to make the case.[10] Such a case has been made in conditional form.

It is open to a critic to accept that the key terms of the GR analysis of possibility are not, as it were, in themselves implicitly modal – each has a perfectly conventional non-modal sense and, as such, a version of GR can be formulated in these terms, with these senses fixed, that is not even implicitly modal. However, the critic proceeds, no such version of GR is accurate and, indeed, any version of GR will be accurate only if its terms are implicitly modal. If this charge can be made to stick, then it appears lethal to the GR ambition to provide an analysis of possibility that is, at once, accurate and non-modal. Lycan has made such a case, focusing initially on the GR term 'world' (1988: 46, 1991a: 224). The specific charge is that the consistency – and so, the accuracy – of the GR analysis of possibility is guaranteed only if 'world' is taken to express the modal concept *possible world*.[11,12] One might meet this allegation immediately, as Miller (1989: 477) does, by observing that GR defines 'world' in terms that are not explicitly or implicitly modal, e.g. 'individual', 'part of' and 'spatiotemporally related' (see postulate (O9) of (4.2)).However, Lycan (1991b) rejoins by reformulating his point in relation to the terms of the *definiens*. Focusing on the case of 'individual' the reformulated argument proceeds as follows.[13] Consistency requires that GR should admit no world which has an impossible individual – e.g. an individual that instantiates an impossible combination of properties – as a part. For otherwise, it remains open that there is a world – *qua* sum of spatiotemporally related individuals – that represents an impossibility by having an impossible individual as a part. So consistency requires the exclusion of impossible worlds via the exclusion of impossible individuals, and that requires, in turn, that 'individual' must be taken to express the concept of *possible individual*.

GR ought to respond to Lycan's argument by admitting the truth of the key premise: consistency requires that GR should admit no world which has an impossible individual as a part. However, the move from that claim to conclusion, that 'individual' must thereby be taken to express the concept of *possible individual*, is a *non sequitur*. The quickest way with the point is this.

Let us grant that since the ontological component of GR, as it stands, contains only existential claims about what worlds there are, it does not rule out the existence of impossible worlds. It is then open to GR to add further axioms explicitly limiting the kinds of possible worlds there are. One way of doing so would be by strengthening the principle of recombination – cf. postulate (O12) of (4.2) – so that the *only* worlds that exist are those that are obtained by recombination of the parts of the actual world. Given that such recombination keeps us within the realm of the possible, GR is in a position to claim that this principle rules out impossible worlds. Of course, by so restricting the domain of worlds, GR risks incompleteness by ruling out some possible worlds. Indeed, Lewis would say so and I will go on to argue that this is so. But the present point is about consistency, and it is this. Just as GR seeks to attain to the expression of completeness by finding a principle that generates all the worlds there could be, so she might seek to express consistency by finding a principle that limits the worlds to only those there could be. Lycan fails to show that any such principle must be implicitly modal.[14]

More generally, I conclude that it has not been shown that GR is conceptually modal in any objectionable way.

(7.3) DOXASTICALLY MODAL ANALYSIS

In distinguishing and evaluating the status of analyses as doxastically modal, it is useful to begin by adapting and generalizing the observation of Lewis (1986a: 154). An analysis cannot be considered objectionably circular just because its construction is guided by prior opinions about its analysanda. Unless a theorist is in the business of stipulating, from scratch as it were, the meaning of a term 'F', then in order to be warranted in asserting a biconditional that purported to articulate an analysis of the concept F, she would have to have some prior beliefs that involved the concept F. For to have warrant to assert a biconditional is having a warrant to assert that its sides have the same truth-value. But that is not a position that can be attained in respect of a biconditional that purports an analysis of the concept F:

(F)   ... F ... iff _____

by one who has no prior F-beliefs. The point as it stands seems unobjectionable, and its application in the present case emerged in our criterion of accuracy and our subsequent account of what it is for GR to underwrite the truth of (P). Someone can have a warrant to assert (or indeed to deny) the GR analytic principle (P), only if she has some prior modal beliefs – beliefs that will allow her to assign a truth-value to the possibility claim that figures on the left-side of an instance of (P). Moreover in constructing GR, a theorist will be guided in her choice of postulates by her legitimate desire to have (P), and other explanatory principles, come out true. For example a prior belief that there are no necessary connections between distinct existences may guide GR choice of one particular version of the principle of recombination rather than another. This is no more objectionable than a philosopher appealing for guidance to his beliefs about who is the nephew of whom in order to construct an analysis of the concept of the nephew relation, or appealing to his beliefs about what the arithmetical truths are in order to construct an analysis of the concept of (natural) number. So GR is doxastically modal in both of the ways indicated: it is constructed so as to conform to prior modal beliefs and it is assertible – especially instances of (P) – only by one who has prior modal beliefs. Yet the doxastic modality of GR is innocuous, and any objection to the adequacy of GR analysis of possibility fails if it shows only that GR is modal in such an unobjectionable way.

One such objection is due to Bigelow and Pargetter (1990: 193–203) who argue that the GR analysis of possibility is circular because: (a) the instances of (P) that articulate analyses of de re modal claims are true only relative to an appropriate selection of counterpart relations; and (b) the process of 'tailoring' the counterpart relations so as to match the truth-values of de re modal claims requires the presupposition that certain properties are essential properties. GR can accept that both claims are true so long as the 'presupposition' that certain properties are essential is understood as no more than an appeal to prior modal beliefs for guidance as to how to construct from conceptually non-modal resources the right analysans for a given analysandum. In light of the present exposition of GR and the argument of the last section, GR is entitled thus far to maintain that she does not require any modal 'presuppositions' in the much stronger sense of having to have implicitly or explicitly modal concepts in her ultimate explanans.

Chihara (1998: 286–7) offers a related objection, albeit an objection that he takes to be 'quite different' from that offered by Bigelow and Pargetter. Chihara's objection attempts to discern a vicious way in which an analysis can be doxastically modal and to pin this feature on the GR analysis of possibility. This allegedly vicious feature of analysis is that pre-analytic modal beliefs are invoked in order to determine what the ontological component of the analysing theory should assert, and not just (benignly) in order to test the accuracy of the analysis. It is manifestly true that GR has this feature. The GR analyst does not begin with two sets of independently generated, pre-analytic opinions, one set modal, the other about the plurality of worlds, and then simply appeal to these in order to test the accuracy of an analytic hypothesis. It is also the case, for example, that GR belief in the existence of the recombinatorially generated set of worlds is not arrived at independently from her belief that there are no necessary connections between distinct existences. But why should these features of an analysis constitute a vice? If the principle is extended to explanations in general, as opposed to conceptual analyses in particular, it looks quite unsupportable. No one thinks it objectionable that the ontology of – say – atomic theory should be postulated, and then adjusted, in light of considerations about the facts of chemical bonding (*inter alia*) that it is invoked to explain. More generally, no one requires for the adequacy of explanations involving entity postulation that the theorist must arrive at her beliefs about the ontology of the explanans whilst she remains behind a veil of ignorance about the subsequent explananda. So why is it vicious in the case where explanation takes the form of conceptual analysis that the ontological postulates of the explanans should be justified in light of (prior) beliefs about the explananda? Is the point not one about conceptual analysis in general, but about the analysis of the modal concepts in particular? Since Chihara does not offer his reader answers to these questions, or resources from which answers can easily be constructed, we still lack grounds for believing that the GR analysis of possibility is doxastically modal in a vicious way.

(7.4) ONTOLOGICALLY MODAL ANALYSIS

Shalkowski (1994) argues that GR reduction of the modal is circular if (in present terminology) accurate, since accuracy requires ontological priority of modal facts over facts about worlds. Strictly speaking, Shalkowski's claim is that the requisite ontological priority

GR: unanalysed modality

renders circular any attempt by the proponent of GR to provide an *ontological* reduction of the modal facts. As I have emphasized from Chapter 3 onwards, ontological reduction of modal facts is an explanatory enterprise that is to be distinguished from that of analysis (analytic reduction) of modal concepts. So Shalkowski's case does not speak directly to the question whether GR offers a successful analysis of the concept of possibility. However, if there is in prospect a new, and distinctively ontological, way for GR to be modal – equally, for GR reduction of the modal to be circular – then it is at least prudent for GR to consider: (i) whether GR is, indeed, ontologically modal (circular); and (ii) whether being ontologically modal would vitiate the GR aim of providing an accurate and appropriately non-modal analysis of the concept of possibility. Since Shalkowski argues that successful non-modal reduction of modal facts is prevented by the accuracy of reduction requiring that the modal facts be *ontologically prior* to the facts about worlds, GR has available three forms of response to that claim.

First, under the heading of point (i) above, GR may rejoin that the element of priority in the notion of ontological priority has not been substantiated. The suggestion is that modal facts are prior to facts about (non-actual) worlds and other individuals because worlds and other individuals have modal features (Shalkowski 1994: 671) or because there are modal constraints on the number and nature of worlds (Shalkowski 1994: 675–6). I have argued that GR ought to accept that worlds have such modal features. In the former case, we have, for example, the de re feature of a world that it might (or might not) have had different laws. In the latter case, we have, for example, as a matter of necessity that the number of worlds is infinite and that worlds have no common parts. Thence the modality, but whence the priority? The admission that individuals have moral features – say – does not plausibly entail a commitment to even the existence of irreducibly moral features of things, far less to any thesis of priority. Nor does the admission that there are numerical constraints on the sets plausibly signal failure of the ontological reduction of numbers to sets.[15] Of course, in characterizing her ontology, and with an eye to the accuracy of reductions, GR allows herself to be constrained by her opinions about the modal facts. But it has already been argued that such doxastic priority is harmless.

Second, and contra the apparent presupposition of Shalkowski (1994: 670 *passim*) the success of the enterprise of ontological reduction does not clearly require: (a) that the notion of ontological priority should be shown to be in good standing nor – if it is – (b) that facts about worlds have such priority over the modal facts. In one conception of the enterprise of ontological reduction success consists in presenting fact identities. In the present case, that amounts to the identification of each modal fact as some fact about the worlds. We are operating with the two characterizations, 'modal fact' and 'worldly fact', but we must do so without prejudice against the ontologically reductive view that these are two characterizations of but one kind of fact. To foist on GR the claim that world facts are ontologically prior to modal facts appears to deprive her arbitrarily of an identity thesis that she might wish to endorse.[16]

Third, assume that the above difficulties can be surmounted and it is (somehow) shown that the adequacy of an ontological reduction of the modal facts to the non-modal facts is vitiated by the ontological priority (in a well-explicated sense) of the modal facts over the non-modal facts. Looking beyond Shalkowski's concerns, it would remain to be shown that such ontological priority vitiates an adequate and comprehensive non-modal analysis of the modal concepts. Grant good sense and truth to some appropriate claim of ontological priority – perhaps the fact of God's existence or the fact of the existence of ontological atoms is ontologically prior to every other (kind of) fact. Still, it is not at all obvious, to put it mildly, that the concept of God (that Being than which none could be greater) or the concept of ontological atom (that which has nothing other than itself as a part) is thereby unsusceptible to adequate – accurate and non-circular – analysis.

I conclude that it has not been shown that GR is, in any clear sense, ontologically modal (circular) and that even if it were, the GR aim of providing an accurate and appropriately non-modal analysis of the concept of possibility would not obviously thereby be vitiated.

(7.5) THE INFINITUDE OF ALIEN PROPERTIES

I will argue, in this section, that there are infinitely many distinct instantiable alien properties and, in the next, that GR is thereby prevented from providing a comprehensive, accurate and non-modal analysis of the concept of possibility.

Recall that GR invokes the principle of recombination with a view to providing a complete analysis of possibility. The ontological component of GR serves up, by way of the actual world postulate (O11), a world to match all of the actualized possibilities. The actual world postulate (O11) along with the recombination postulate (O12) suffices

GR: unanalysed modality

to generate a vast set of worlds at which all sorts of non-actual possibilities are realized – the existence of unicorns, of talking donkeys, of Clinton failing to win the presidency, etc. Yet varied as the plurality of worlds so generated may be, it appears to be the case – and Lewis (1986a: 92) admits as much – that GR including recombination still fails to serve up all the worlds we intuitively think there could be. Following Lewis (1986a: 91), an alien natural property is a natural property that is not instantiated by any individual in α, and is not analysable as a conjunctive or structural property built up from constituents that are all instantiated by parts of α.[17] The principle of recombination will not generate worlds that contain individuals instantiating alien natural properties and the ontological component of GR, as it stands, is quite compatible with there being no worlds in which any such property is instantiated. So given that some alien natural property could have been instantiated, GR is, as it stands, incomplete. There are some modal theorists who deny that any alien natural property could have been instantiated.[18] However, I will shortly indicate why this denial is implausible. Moreover, Lewis (1986a: 159–65) himself admits alien natural properties and seeks to exploit that fact in pressing the advantages of GR over its AR ('ersatzist') rivals. So I will conclude that GR, in its current formulation, is incomplete.

It seems an easy matter to remedy incompleteness by adding a postulate, thus:

(OA1)   There is at least one world in which there is an individual that instantiates a natural property that is α-alien.

(GR) + (OA1), then, has a model in which exactly one alien natural property is instantiated. However, if there are *many* instantiable alien natural properties, the augmented theory still does not determine a complete set of worlds. Moreover, there are available considerations which suggest not only that there are many instantiable alien natural properties but, indeed, that there are *infinitely many*. The infinitude of instantiable alien natural properties is supported by three (related) considerations.

First, anyone who thinks that there *is* such a finite upper bound believes that, for some n, n is the maximum number of alien natural properties that could be instantiated. But a restriction to four, or seventeen or thirty-one possible alien natural properties looks badly ad hoc and arbitrary. There is no natural break amongst the finite numbers that one could reasonably identify as limiting the number of instantiable alien natural properties.[19]

Second, the natural properties that are actually instantiated are given to us by the most fundamental parts of physics. Yet physical facts are contingent. The world could have been Newtonian rather than Einsteinian, it could have been classical rather than quantum, it could have contained quite different fundamental kinds of objects from the ones that actually do exist. Although physics has not yet been completed – although we do not presently possess the list of the fundamental properties – still we believe that there could have been alien natural properties. This is unsurprising. Our belief that there could have been alien natural properties is not underwritten by any discovery that there are merely six, or seven or eight natural properties. No matter how many natural properties our final physics were to postulate, it would still be true that there could have been at least one more. Let L_0 be the (presently unknown) list of all the actually instantiated fundamental properties. Then, by 'alienation' – i.e. (OA1) – and recombination, there exists a possible world w_1 such that the individuals in w_1 variously instantiate all of the properties in L_0 plus some new fundamental property X_1 that is distinct from all the properties in L_0. Call this new list of properties L_1. If the list of actually instantiated fundamental properties had been L_1 then still, the intuition remains, it would be true that some (new) alien fundamental property – say X_2 – that is not in L_1 could have been instantiated. By alienation and recombination, then, there is a world w_2 whose list of fundamental properties is L_2 which consists of the properties in L_1 – i.e. those instantiated in w_1 – plus X_2. Thus, there is more than one α-alien property. Moreover, by repeated application of the argument above, that is by repeated appeal to the persistent intuition that alien properties are possible and the principle of recombination, we generate a sequence of worlds containing more and more alien properties. Since this sequence has no last member, there are infinitely many different instantiable alien properties.

Third, suppose that scientists were to find a collection of particles that, at first sight, appear to be of one and the same kind. After some experimentation it is discovered that some pairs of these particles attract each other with a force inversely proportional to the square of the distance between them, whilst other pairs repel each other with such a force. No other differences in behaviour can be found amongst these particles and, for all the scientists can tell, the particles appear to be structureless. Accordingly, the scientists postulate that the particles instantiate two different fundamental natural properties and hypothesize that it is the instantiation of such properties that is responsible for the particles' lawlike behaviour. The possibility of such particles existing and of their instantiating such properties is, I take it, uncontroversial – indeed, the properties might be our very own positive and negative charges. So by GR lights, there is a world containing two such classes of particle. Nor is there any obvious objection to the possibility of the existence of three such classes of particle. In such a world, as before, any two particles will either repel each other with a force inversely proportional to the square of the distance between them, or they will attract each other with a force of the same strength. But whereas before the maximum number of pairwise repulsing particles was two, in this case the number is three. Such behaviour cannot be explained in terms of two fundamental natural properties, such as positive and negative charge, alone. Again, at this world, the relevant particles are supposed to be structureless, so it is rational to postulate that the particles instantiate *three* different fundamental natural properties in order to explain the particles' lawlike behaviour. There is no need to stop at three. The thought experiment gives us a sequence of worlds containing more and more distinct fundamental natural properties. There is no reason to think that *our* world contains arbitrarily many primitive properties that behave in the way these particles do. So, eventually, at some point in the sequence, we are describing worlds containing fundamental natural properties that are α-alien. Since the sequence can be extended arbitrarily far, there is no finite upper bound to the number of instantiable natural α-alien properties.

(7.6) FROM INFINITUDE TO INCOMPLETENESS

In attempting to encompass the infinity of instantiable natural α-alien properties within a comprehensive theory of possibility, GR will naturally advance the further alien postulate:

> (OAN)   There are worlds such that, for any n, n objects exist across those worlds and n distinct α-alien natural properties are instantiated among those objects.[20]

The crucial question now is whether (GR) + (OAN) closes the gaps in logical space to guarantee a complete analysis of possibility.

One thought, inspired by the emerging dialectic, is that even if the theory is incomplete, the discovery that this is so must point the way to a remedy. Initially, it was argued that GR failed to guarantee the existence of worlds containing individuals that instantiated alien natural properties. Accordingly, a postulate was added – to the effect that there is some world containing some individual that instantiates at least one alien natural property. It was subsequently argued that this resultant theory failed to guarantee the existence of worlds containing individuals that instantiated, among them, many alien natural properties. Accordingly, a postulate was added – to the effect that there are worlds and parts enough to instantiate (among them) infinitely many alien properties. In general, then, it seems that when confronted with some possibility claim, possibly Q, for which the ontological component of her theory has failed to provide, GR can simply add a new postulate asserting the existence of a world at which Q. Thus, any prospective counterexample to completeness points towards a theory that is immune to the counterexample. However, there is an alternative strategy available for establishing incompleteness that does depend on the provision of a counterexample. Thus we have the following reductio of the completeness of GR + (OAN).

(1) Grant for reductio that GR + (OAN) expresses completeness.
(2) Let S be the hypothetically complete set of worlds whose existence GR + (OAN) guarantees. GR + (OAN) entails that there are infinitely many α-alien natural properties instantiated across the worlds of S. So there exists an infinite sequence of α-alien natural properties: P_1, $P_2 \ldots P_n$.
(3) Consider now the set S* which is just like S save that it fails to contain any world in which P_1 is instantiated, it fails to contain any world in which P_3 is instantiated and, indeed, for any odd m, fails to contain any world in which property P_m is instantiated. Then the postulates of GR + (OAN) are true of S* (esp. OAN itself).[21]
(4) If, but only if, there are worlds of S which are not *duplicated* by any world in S*, can S* be said to omit certain possibilities.[22] But duplication is a matter of sharing the same natural properties. So, since S* omits worlds that instantiate the natural property P_1, no possibility where P_1 is instantiated is represented by any world in S*.[23] Accordingly, S* *is* incomplete and since, (by step (3)) S* is a model of GR + (OAN), GR + (OAN) has a model that is, by hypothesis, incomplete.

(5) Thus the assumption (1) that GR + (OAN) is complete allowed us to construct a set of worlds which was incomplete but of which GR + (OAN) was true. In other words, from the assumption that GR + (OAN) is complete, it follows that GR + (OAN) is not complete.[24]
(6) So by reductio on the original assumption (1), GR + (OAN) is not complete.

The first thought in response to the reductio argument is that completeness might be attained by means of specifying further the ontological component of GR so that it is true of S but not of S*. But obvious moves in that direction fail.

First, although S* omits properties instantiated in S the cardinality of natural properties instantiated in the two sets is the same. So no new postulate concerning the number of instantiated alien natural properties is capable of distinguishing between S and S*.

Second, it may be superficially tempting to consider adding a postulate to the effect that there is a world in which there is an individual that instantiates – say – P_1. However, this desperate thought is to no avail. Since we lack the referential resources to specify any alien natural property (Lewis 1986a: 159–65), a fortiori, we lack the referential resources to specify any alien property that is instantiated among the worlds of S but not among those of S*. The terms 'P_1', 'P_2', etc. as they were used in the argument above are actually variables for alien properties instantiated by worlds in the allegedly complete set S – the terms are *not* predicates that designate alien properties. So if the formulation 'There is a world in which there is an individual that instantiates P_2' contains an unbound occurrence of 'P_2', what is formulated is a pseudo-postulate – it expresses no thought. So let us consider quantifying in. We might existentially quantify into such a position:

(7) There is an alien property P_1 such that there is a world in which there is an individual that instantiates P_1

or envisage an infinitary existential generalization of the form:

(8) There is an alien property P_1, there is an alien property P_3, ... there is an alien property P_{2n+1}, there is a world w_1, there is a world w_3 ... there is a world w_{2n+1}, there is an individual x_1, there is an individual x_3, ... there is an

individual x_{2n+1} and (x_1 is in w_1 and x_1 instantiates P_1) and (x_3 is in w_3 and x_3 instantiates P_3) and ... (x_{2n+1} is in w_{2n+1} and x_{2n+1} instantiates P_{2n+1}).

But in neither case is anything added to the postulate (OAN) which already asserts the existence of infinitely many instantiated alien properties. As an alternative strategy we might consider universal quantification and consider the formulation:

(9) For every alien property P_i, there is a world w_i, there is an individual x_i such that (x_i is in w_i and x_i instantiates P_i).

But again we obtain a postulate that is no stronger than (OAN). Thus, the irremediable unnameability of alien properties ensures that GR cannot rescue the completeness of her analysis of possibility by the kind of strategy described.

Third, if there are only finitely many instantiable alien natural properties then – for all that has been argued here – the adequacy of the GR analysis of possibility is undefeated. So GR might pursue this option. But GR does not have the luxury of simply hypothesizing, without further justification, that this is so in order to protect her analytic ambitions. For arguments have been presented for the contrary claim that there are infinitely many instantiable α-alien properties, and the price of resisting that argument is either that of: (i) undermining the persistent intuition of the possibility of alien properties, no matter what the counterfactual circumstances; or (ii) motivating an effective restriction on the principle of recombination.

A fourth and final thought in response to the reductio argument is that it has not been shown that the incompleteness of GR is irremediable. The thought is correct. The argument was that basic GR with recombination, and various 'alienating' extensions of it are incomplete. However, further considerations have been adduced to suggest that incompleteness cannot easily be remedied by means of various strategies that were calculated to preserve the GR ambition to provide analysis of possibility that is non-modal as well as accurate. It was not argued that the incompleteness of GR is irremediable and, indeed completeness can be attained by adding to the ontological component of GR the single postulate:

(OAM) Every way that a part of world could be is a way that a part of some world is.

GR: unanalysed modality

Only if this 'could' is taken as primitively modal does the principle have the bite that it is supposed to have and entail that all the alien properties that could be instantiated *are* instantiated. Then, of course, (OAM) is explicitly conceptually modal and, consequently, any version of GR that incorporates it is incapable of providing an accurate and appropriately *non-modal* analysis of possibility.

In summary, then, so far as local, non-alien possibilities are concerned, I have argued that the GR claim to have provided an accurate and appropriately non-modal analysis of the concept possibility is undefeated. GR with recombination is not conceptually modal, it is doxastically modal, but innocuously so, and it is unclear what it would even be for the GR to be ontologically modal, and that its ambitions of conceptual analysis would be frustrated were it so. The limited claim that GR can provide a successful, accurate and non-modal analysis of non-alien possibility is a fallback position to which GR might choose to retreat without thereby surrendering all of the significant advantages that GR claims over her AR opponent.[25] However, if the reductio argument is sound, GR is not in possession of an analysis of the concept of (absolute) possibility that is comprehensive, accurate (in particular, complete) and non-modal. Nor, a fortiori, is GR in possession of an analysis of the family of modal concepts that is comprehensive, accurate and non-modal. Moreover, responses to the reductio argument have been met by considerations that offer substantial reason for believing that GR cannot escape the analytic predicament that has been described.

CHAPTER 8

Genuine realism: counterparts

Counterpart relations are certain similarity relations between individuals.[1] A counterpart relation is the resultant of similarities (and dissimilarities) in various respects, where similarity in a given respect is a matter of degree and similarities in different respects (to the same degree) may be differently weighted. In GR, counterpart relations are invoked in order to explain how a possible world (or a possible individual) represents, de re, of an individual that it has a given feature – primarily, to explain what it is for it to be the case that at a world, w, a is F – thus: Lewis (1968, 1971, 1973: 39–43, 1983b and 1986a: Chapter 4).[2] In this respect Lewis invokes counterpart relations as an alternative to transworld identity of world constituents (see Chapter 16). As a quite general observation about representation de re, it is clear that an individual may be represented (even in its absence) as having a certain feature by means of simulacra. Thus, for example, Clinton may be represented as sitting by a human lookalike who sits, by a painting of him sitting, by a wax dummy modelled in a sitting pose, etc. As an instance of this sort of representation, Lewis proposes that a world w may represent de re of an individual x (even when x is not part of w) that x has a certain feature F by w having as a part an individual y that is a suitable simulacrum – a counterpart – of x and which is F. Thus, for example, the possibility of Clinton sitting is represented by a world containing a counterpart of Clinton who sits.[3]

Through this role in explicating representation de re, and as we have already seen in Chapter 4 above, counterpart relations figure prominently in the conceptual and semantic applications of the GR interpretation of PW. In the salient cases of basic de re claims of possibility and necessity, the counterpart-theoretic specification of PW truth-conditions for claims of each type are as follows:

GR: counterparts

(CT-P) a is possibly F, just in case there is a world in which a has a (relevant) counterpart which is F.

(CT-N) a is necessarily F, just in case, in every world, every (relevant) counterpart of a is F.

Exactly which counterpart relation is relevant, and so which individuals are relevant counterparts, is a matter that varies from token to token of a given type and is influenced to a large extent by the context in which the token is produced. In particular, it is a matter of context whether similarity in any given respect has any role at all in the selection of relevant counterparts, and where various kinds of similarity have such a role, it is also a matter of context what relative weight should be assigned to each in selecting relevant counterparts. Among such matters of context are the interests and intentions of speaker and audience, background information, spatiotemporal location of utterance and the choice of words used to refer to a relevant individual. Consequently, there is no settled answer, fixed once and for all, to the question of what is true about a given individual at a given world. Representation de re is inconstant, and counterpart theory (CT) reflects this.

Conceptually, GR intends CT as an element in the non-modal analysis of modal concepts. Semantically, GR holds CT essential to capturing the expressive capacity of modal English and CT may serve as a metalanguage that articulates a PW-semantics for QML. Furthermore, GR finds an ontological application for counterpart relations in the articulation of reductive identifications of the essences, accidents and potentialities of individuals. In each case, the attributes in question are identified as complex properties of this or that range of counterparts and hence, following the general GR treatment of properties, as sets of those counterparts. So, for example, the real essence of an individual is the complex property that it shares with all and only its counterparts and so – in turn – is the set of all and only those counterparts.[4]

The original or canonical version of CT is presented in Lewis (1968) as a series of postulates about counterparts followed by a set of principles guiding translation from formulas of QML into formulas of CT. The initial postulates determine that the relata of the counterpart relation are individuals that are 'worldbound', i.e. in exactly one world, thus:

(P1) Nothing is in anything except a world.
(P2) Nothing is in two worlds.

Genuine realism

(P3) Whatever is a counterpart is in a world.
(P4) Whatever has a counterpart is in a world.

Further postulates fix identity as the unique intra-world counterpart relation:

(P5) Nothing is a counterpart of anything else in its world.
(P6) Anything in a world is a counterpart of itself.

Among the theses which Lewis presents as plausible consequences of his account of counterpart relations and the above postulates are:

(P*1) The counterpart relation is not transitive.
(P*2) The counterpart relation is not symmetric.
(P*3) An individual may have distinct counterparts at another world.
(P*4) Distinct individuals that are worldmates may have a common counterpart at another world.
(P*5) An individual may lack a counterpart at another world.

Against this background of canonical CT I will proceed as follows. I begin by discussing the various aspects of the two major, and related, objections of principle against CT – that the facts about counterparts are irrelevant to the truth of the corresponding de re modal claims (8.1) and that the CT truth-conditions assigned to modal claims fail to match our patterns of modal concern (8.2). In (8.3) I evaluate various claims to the effect that canonical CT clashes with, and requires us to revise, pre-theoretical judgments of modal truth and validity. In (8.4), I summarize the various departures from canonical CT that have been licensed (mainly in response to these claims) and consider the implications of such deregulation for the integrity and success of CT.

(8.1) IRRELEVANCE

The most fundamental and persistent objection of principle to Lewis's use of CT is that facts about the counterparts of an individual are, in general, *irrelevant* to the modal truth about that individual. In order to ground a firm discussion of the objection I will state various claims that CT may, and should, make about an ordinary modal claim such as

(1) Humphrey might have won

and its 'translation':

(1*) ∃w[∃x[Pxw & Cxh & Vx]].

First, (1) is a sentence of ordinary modal English (the object language) that is assigned a truth-condition in a CT, non-modal metalanguage. Second, widespread, pre-theoretical intuition has it that (1) is true, and correctly so. Third, (1) is about Humphrey: Humphrey figures in the truth-condition of (1) and (1) is true in virtue of a fact about Humphrey himself. On the basis of such clarification Hazen (1979a) detects various sources of confusion in the versions of the irrelevance objection presented by Kripke (1980) and Plantinga (1974).

Hazen (1979a: 320–2) charges that Kripke (1972: 45 n.13) mischaracterizes CT by attributing to CT the view that in using (1) we are not really claiming that something might have happened to Humphrey but that something might have happened to someone else.[5] As Hazen explains on behalf of CT, in using (1) we are talking about something that might have happened to Humphrey and in specifying the CT truth-condition of (1) we use a non-modal metalanguage in which we do not – indeed cannot – make any explicit modal claim about anything. The confusion suggested by Kripke's characterization of CT could be removed by stipulating that modal vocabulary belongs exclusively to the object language and that the counterpart predicate is an exclusive feature of the metalanguage. The former is a necessary condition of counterpart-theoretic interpretation contributing, in the hands of GR, to a conceptually non-modal analysis of possibility (see Chapter 7). However, the exclusion of counterpart talk from the object language may seem somewhat ad hoc, and may appear even more objectionable since Salmon (1981) has argued that reflection on modalizing about counterparts does sustain a version of the irrelevance objection. Let us consider the Salmon objection.

The modal claim about counterparts implicated in Kripke's version of the objection was:

(2) There might have been a Humphrey counterpart who won.

Salmon (1981: 235) argues that since the modal claim (2) is

Genuine realism

intuitively weaker than (1), and CT interpretation determines that (2) entails (1), such interpretation misrepresents the content of (1).[6]

The claim that (2) entails (1) will be settled in a non-modal first-order metalanguage and, accordingly, we should expect no dispute (in the present context) about what entails what, once interpretations are fixed. Given further that the interpretation of (1) is an entirely straightforward matter, the plausibility of the second premise of the argument depends entirely on how (2) is to be interpreted. If, as the objector envisages, we treat (2) as an ordinary possibility claim, it ought to be interpreted thus:

(2*) $\exists w[\exists x[\exists y[Pxw \& Pyw \& Cyh \& Cxy \& Vx]]]$.

Given postulates (P5) and (P6) of canonical CT, every individual is its own unique counterpart in its own world – i.e. loosely speaking, in (2*), $x = y$ – so (2*) does entail:

(1*) $\exists w[\exists x[Ixw \& Cxh \& Vx]]$.[7]

If we treat (2) as an extraordinary possibility claim – as we are entitled to, given that the counterpart relation is an inter-world relation – it makes no difference. (2) ought then to be interpreted thus:

(2**) $\exists x[Cxh \& Vx]$

and so, since any counterpart of Humphrey is an ordinary, world-bound individual (see (P3) above) (2**) also entails (1*). So the second premise of Salmon's argument is true.[8,9] CT may also allow that (2) is intuitively weaker than (1) and so that the first premise of the argument is true as well. However, concerning the first premise, it may be granted that intuition suggests that (1) is weaker than (2) while resisting that (1) really is weaker than (2), and it is the latter that is required to deliver Salmon's conclusion. The right to insist on that distinction is underlined by considering the unreliability of the following general argument-form: Possibly A is intuitively a weaker claim than Possibly B; according to semantic theory T, Possibly A entails Possibly B, so T misrepresents the content of Possibly B. A compelling counterexample looms in the following case. Consider the possibility claims:

(4) It is possible that it is possible that Humphrey wins.
(5) It is possible that Humphrey wins.

Consider, then, any semantic theory that validates the S4 principle:

(S4*)   If possibly possibly A then possibly A.

(4) is *intuitively* weaker than (5). On any such theory (4) entails (5). But no one is likely to be convinced on this basis that any S4 semantics thereby misrepresents the content of (5). The moral is that pretheoretical modal intuitions, especially in matters of validity, do not invariably deserve to be treated as sacrosanct. This is a theme that looms large in the next attempt to revitalize the irrelevance objection.

Hazen (1979a: 322–4) charges that Plantinga (1974: 117) is misguided in complaining that CT can attain only 'verbal agreement with the rest of us'. Plantinga's complaint is that CT permits agreement about the truth-value of sentence (1), but only by 'using that sentence to express a proposition different from the one the rest of us express by it'. The complaint, says Hazen, is misguided because semantic theorists are (broadly) constrained to reflect communal verdicts on truth-value – a matter of saving the relevant data – but are not constrained to reflect any (other) opinion about which proposition is expressed by use of an object language sentence – a matter of dispute among semantic theorists. In particular, once intuition, or popular opinion, plays its role in serving up truth-values for object language sentences, such sources have no further role to play in determining which account of the propositional content of a sentence such as (1) – which theory – is correct.

Plantinga (1987: 223–4) responds to this criticism by accusing Hazen of subscribing to a 'facile bifurcation', in semantic theorizing, between a sacrosanct body of intuitively endorsed data about truth-values and a thoroughly freewheeling body of theory about truth-conditions. Rejecting this facile bifurcation, Plantinga wishes to hold accountable to 'our firm opinions' not only the truth-values of ordinary modal claims but also (certain) theoretical claims about their truth-conditions. In that spirit he offers that it is clear enough that 'Socrates could have been foolish' expresses a truth and asks (rhetorically, of course) whether it isn't nearly as obvious that the truth that it expresses does not require that Socrates have a foolish counterpart. However, as Plantinga (1987: 223–4) recognizes (of Lewis), CT need not be committed to the facile bifurcation of data and theory.[10] Indeed, in responding on behalf of CT to Salmon's objection, I have already treated as defeasible intuitive data concerning the (in)validity of certain modal inferences. So let CT acknowledge both the principle that variance with pre-theoretical intuition about content is a disadvantage of semantic theory and, indeed, that the CT truth-conditions assigned to modal claims are – in some sense and to some extent – at variance with pre-theoretical opinions about modal content.[11] However, it is one thing to admit that pre-theoretical intuition can count against a semantic theory and another thing to admit that pre-theoretical intuition by itself can count decisively against any semantic theory. It is yet another thing to suggest that pre-theoretical intuition by itself counts decisively against the CT interpretation of modal sentences. Even if CT chooses to defend herself only on this last point, she will be entitled to press the questions of exactly what the nature and the extent of the CT offence against intuition is supposed to be.

In fact there are two distinguishable objections. The first is that CT interpretation varies unacceptably from pre-theoretical opinion about modal content by saying too much; the second is that the unacceptable variation arises from CT saying too little.

In response to the objection from excess, CT might rejoin that any adequate semantic theory is bound to exceed the deliverances of pre-theoretical opinion about modal content because there is no non-trivial pre-theoretical opinion about modal content, or because such opinions as there are fall short of the detail that any effective semantic theory is required to supply. Plantinga (1987) persistently suggests that there is some content that 'we', 'the rest of us', pre-theoretically attach to modal sentences. That is, no doubt, true insofar as we might pre-theoretically say things like the following:

(6) 'Humphrey might have won' means that Humphrey might have won.
(7) Saying, 'Humphrey might have won', is saying something about Humphrey.

Certainly, there is no explicit mention of counterparts in such expressions of pre-theoretical opinion. But, more generally, these expressions of opinion about content lack detail of the kind that we would expect to find in any PW statement of the truth-conditions of such claims. In particular, these expressions of opinion contain no explicit reference to possible worlds, and they certainly contain no explicit reference to the kinds of thing that Plantinga takes possible worlds to be and which he takes to enter into the truth-conditions of modal claims – viz. maximal possible states of affairs.[12]

Any PW account of modality in which the output of interpretation is not simply the homophonic, metalinguistic translation of the object language sentence will be out of line with 'pre-theoretical opinion' about content. If that point benefits anyone, it benefits the kind of abstentionist philosopher who aims to generate truth-conditions for ordinary, unworldly modal claims without recourse to worldly PW talk. The point does not benefit rival, non-abstentionist interpreters of PW such as Plantinga. So much, then, for the objection that CT exceeds pre-theoretical opinion about modal content. But what of the objection from omission – the objection that CT says too little in order to capture pre-theoretical opinion about modal content? In its most obvious specification, the objection from omission has it that the CT truth-conditions for de re modal claims about Humphrey fall short of intuitive requirements by failing to refer explicitly to Humphrey. But that complaint simply gets the facts about CT wrong since the relevant truth-conditions do involve explicit reference to Humphrey – thus e.g. (1*) above.

In light of these responses, one subsequent thought is that the relevance objection might be sharpened by discarding the appeal to pre-theoretical intuitions about content. So let us forget what the folk pre-theoretically think and turn to what educated philosophical opinion ought to discern. Here I will attempt to rebuild the irrelevance objection by attempting: (a) to pin down, among the various philosophically controversial elements of CT interpretation, what the proper and specific target of the irrelevance objection is; and (b) to indicate how such an objection should be prosecuted. I begin by assuming that all, including AR critics of CT such as Kripke and Plantinga, accept the accuracy of the translation from (1) into its neutral, uninterpreted PW rendition:

(1**) There is some possible world w such that at w, Humphrey wins.

Let us consider in turn, then, the CT treatment of the representational clause of (1**), 'There is some possible world w such that at w, _' and then the CT treatment of the complement sentence, 'Humphrey wins'. CT interprets the representational clause of (1**) as stating the existence of a world that has parts of a certain character – thus:

(8) $\exists x[\exists y[[Wy \ \& \ Pxy \ \& \ldots \varphi x \ldots]]]$.

Genuine realism

We ought to distinguish three aspects of this treatment of the representational clause:

(i) The structure contains no explicit modal element of content corresponding to the 'might' of (1) or the 'possible' of (1*).
(ii) Worlds are supposed capable of achieving representation indirectly by standing in a certain kind of relation (whole–part) to things that represent on their behalf.
(iii) The things that do the direct and ultimate representation of individuals are individuals.

The proper target of the irrelevance objection cannot be any of (i)–(iii) as such, or else the relevance objection has been expressed in a thoroughly misleading way. For the GR/CT treatment of representation, as presented at (8), is quite general: it applies to any modal context, de dicto or de re, and makes no appeal to the counterpart relation. Thus, CT will interpret the de dicto claim that there might have been talking donkeys as an instance of (8) – one which goes on to specify that the condition φ is that of being a talking donkey. So let us consider the CT treatment of the sentential complement of the representational clause. CT treats complement sentences by means of open sentences. Thus, 'Humphrey wins', as it occurs in (1**), is treated as:

(9) Cxh & Vx

the role of which is to articulate the condition ('φx') that the representational clause requires individuals in some world to satisfy. Let us distinguish two further different aspects that reside within this element of the interpretation:

(iv) The specified condition involves explicit reference to Humphrey (and to winning).
(v) The possibility of Humphrey winning is construed as a relational state involving similarity relations.

Clearly, (iv) establishes an obvious kind of relevance rather than irrelevance and, indeed, it is aspect (iv) that put paid to the misguided objection from omission that was seen off above. So that leaves (v) as the proper source of the irrelevance objection. But further unpacking is required.

First, we ought to discount presently uncontroversial ways in which the possibility of Humphrey winning is a relational state. We may discount that the possibility in question is related to some world since, it is assumed in the immediate dialectical context (by GR and AR alike), that possibilities in general are related to possible worlds. We may also discount that any state of winning is a state that involves relations between the winner and a contest, and between the winner and her competitors. Moreover, it seems unpromising that it is the specific choice of similarity relations that is objectionable when we consider what other relations might be more apt to sustain relevance. If de re possibilities were construed as a matter of the conditions instantiated by – say – spatiotemporal or causal relata, rather than by simulacra, the intuition of irrelevance would plausibly be augmented rather than diminished. What it seems to come down to is best expressed as follows. If we allow for the moment that identity is not a (genuine) relation,[13] then the point would be that (v) presents de re possibility as generically relational in ways beyond those that have already been discounted. Even when an intuitively non-relational feature is attributed as a possibility, at a world, to an individual – say their being in pain – some other individual, and a relation get in on the (f)act: there is a counterpart who is in pain. It is the very idea that all de re possibility is misconstrued as having gratuitous relational structure – that an n-adic property is misconstrued as an (n + 1)-adic relation – that is ultimately the most plausible target for the irrelevance objection. But if this is the objection properly stated and focused, how should it be prosecuted?

There are various cases in which philosophical interpreters ascribe allegedly erroneous, relational truth-conditions to intuitively non-relational truths. One case is that of naive subjectivist interpretations of various discourses, whereby what appear to be ascriptions to external things of monadic properties of colour, moral value or whatever are construed as attributions of complex relational state involving that thing – thus, for example:

(10) 'The table is yellow' is true as uttered by x at t iff there is some sensation s such that: s is a sensation of x & s is caused by the table & s is yellow.[14]

Another case is where tensed sentences that are not apparently relational are assigned relational, tenseless truth-conditions (and truthmakers) – thus:

(11) 'The Second World War is past' is true as uttered by x at t iff t is later than the Second World War.[15]

Objections to these interpretations do not, typically, rest solely on the grounds that their (allegedly) irrelevant relational dimension is just obviously irrelevant. One can appreciate why this is so. For we have, by way of precedent, plenty of cases in which the attribution of relational truth-conditions turns out to be merited, no matter how contrary to the 'obvious' or 'intuitive' this might have seemed – thus, consider predications of weight, mass, time of day, etc. Rather, it is typically held – and ought to be expected – that the alleged error involved in attributing gratuitously relational truth-conditions to the sentences in question is one that manifests itself in some way other than simply by striking some as an obvious error.

One kind of evidence of error that has already been touched upon, and to which we will return is linguistic evidence. This takes the form of discrepancy between, on one hand, the truth-values for sentences or (in)validity for argument-forms as determined by the CT attribution of truth-conditions and, on the other, the firm consensus of the community of language users in these matters. The other kind of evidence is broadly phenomenological or psychological and takes the form of discrepancy between what our attitudes are and what they ought to be given the CT account of their content. I will consider in some detail the psychological case against CT in the next section. But just before I do so, it is worth emphasizing at this stage of the discussion the distinction between different kinds of application that the CT account of truth-conditions may be supposed to serve.

Even if it were demonstrated that the psychological evidence goes against CT, that might show that CT fails *qua* theory of (psychologically relevant) attitude content. But it would take an argument to show from there that CT truth-conditions fail to meet the requirements of an adequate theory of meaning and further argument yet to show that CT truth-conditions fail to give an adequate account of the structure of the (de re) modal facts (so to speak). The debate about CT often fails to reflect that 'truth-conditions' that are inadequate in some of these respects need not be inadequate in all. Indeed, and more generally, it is often quite unclear which kind of application of CT the irrelevance objection is supposed to undermine. Is it that CT is supposed to be revealed as a failed attempt at conceptual analysis, a failed account of truthmaking or ontological identification, a failure in some other respect that might be counted under the objectives of semantic theorizing, some combination of the above or all of the above? That the relevance objection to CT should be clear on this crucial point is a lesson that ought to be learned from the dispute over the semantics of temporal discourse. In that case, some tenseless theorists of time explicitly aim to provide truth-conditions that present an account of the structure of temporal facts (truthmakers for tensed claims) and are, as such, unmoved by the observation that tenselessly specified truth-conditions do not give a full account of the temporal content of attitudes (whether belief or relief).[16] Is the irrelevance supposed to apply to CT when CT is conceived as having only such resolutely non-psychological aims? Perhaps not. Or at least, once appropriate distinctions are drawn among the different kinds of application that a CT account of truth-conditions might be supposed to serve, it seems that the irrelevance objection might be most effectively pitched against CT *qua* theory of (psychologically relevant) attitude content. Yet even in that most favourable of cases for the objector, I will argue that it is not obvious that the pertinent (i.e. psychological) considerations furnish a strong case against CT.

(8.2) CONCERN

We have cares or concerns that have de re modal and de re counterfactual content, and these concerns are manifest in various practical, moral and emotional responses. Humphrey cares deeply that he might have won – he becomes depressed because he lost, he regrets that he did (or didn't) do certain things that affected the outcome, he gets help in the areas that he thinks would have made a difference to his fate and might make a difference in future, etc. Moreover, in the case of de re modal judgements, as elsewhere, some of the concerns that an agent has are irreducibly egocentric concerns that differ in character from other, non-egocentric concerns that she has. The patterns of concern that one displays in relation to information about x do, in general, vary depending on whether or not one identifies x as oneself. In sum, one may be – let us say – egoconcerned with de re modal and counterfactual truth.

Another kind of complaint that is inspired by Kripke's (1972) expression of the relevance objection (see n.5 above) is that CT is, somehow, at odds with this fact of modal psychology. The discrepancy is supposed to be (somehow) grounded in the following contrast. Humphrey is egoconcerned by his belief that he might have won but is (or would not be, or ought not to be) egoconcerned by learning of the kind of fact which CT construes as giving the content of his egocentric de re modal belief, viz. that someone else won a similar contest. Miller (1992) attempts to formulate, and subsequently, to refute, such an 'argument from concern' against CT which he associates not only with Kripke (1980), but also with Blackburn (1984) and Rosen (1990).[17] I believe that Miller supplies CT with an observation that is most valuable in fashioning a response to the argument from concern – to anticipate, that our de re modal egoconcerns are typically matched by egoconcern about counterparts. However, the issue deserves fuller treatment in three respects. First, if the matter of concern is to be given a genuinely psychological dimension, it is necessary to distinguish between ascriptions of attitudes de re and attitudes de dicto, emphasizing the latter. Second, by deploying Miller's basic observation in that light, CT may make the case that her own account of de re modal attitude content is actually superior to those offered by rival worldly theorists of content. Third, Miller's basic observation does not afford a comprehensive response to the concerns about concern. These points will be developed in what follows.

The Miller (1992) formulation of the argument proceeds from the alleged inconsistency of the triad below, to the rejection of its first proposition (12):

(12) Modal facts are facts about counterparts.
(13) We are egoconcerned with modal facts.
(14) We are not egoconcerned with facts about counterparts.

The first observation that I want to make about this argument echoes a point that I made about the intuitive semantic content of de re modal claims. The argument that is directed against CT is suggestive of a more general form of argument that may be instantiated with respect to any PW account of modal attitude content. In whatever sense Humphrey lacks egoconcern for facts about his counterparts he also lacks egoconcern for the kinds of facts that AR takes to constitute de re modal truth: that there is some maximal possible state of affairs represents Humphrey as winning or that there exists a maximal consistent set of propositions, one of which is the proposition that Humphrey wins, etc. (see Chapter 10). Thus we might construct the following argument:

(15) Modal facts are facts about AR possible worlds.
(13) We are egoconcerned with modal facts.

(16) We are not egoconcerned with facts about AR possible worlds.

In light of the availability of this parallel argument, anyone who thinks that the original argument tells against CT, but not against rival realist accounts of de re modal content, owes us an explanation of why this is so.

The second observation is that in dealing with such an argument against CT we must be clear about exactly how it pinpoints a new, distinctively psychological dimension to the complaint that CT attributed content is irrelevant. To put the point otherwise, if the argument involves no appeal to psychologically relevant aspects of modal attitude content then the worry is that the objector will not have succeeded in showing how the alleged irrelevance of CT is manifested psychologically. To that end, I assume that an adequate specification of the psychologically relevant dimension of modal attitude content requires the ascription of attitudes de dicto and not only attitudes de re.

Putting these two observations together, both of the above arguments from concern – that against CT and that against the rival semantic theory – can be met by reading the key locution 'concerned with' as a de dicto attitude ascription which generates a hyperintensional context.[18] In each case, the triad of propositions can all be true, and indeed true of a perfectly rational 'we' so long as we are unaware that (relevant) modal facts and (appropriate) facts adduced in the explananda are one and the same. The phenomenon is perfectly familiar and is manifest in such cases as when a suitably ignorant subject has certain de dicto attitudes concerning water – she believes that there is water in the glass – but lacks equivalent de dicto attitudes concerning H_2O – she does not believe that there is H_2O in the glass. Unless some other consideration is forthcoming we still have no insight into how either semantic theory is supposed to be in trouble nor – a fortiori – how CT, among PW accounts of de re modal content, is particularly problematic. A suggestion by Rosen provokes one thought about where such considerations may be found.

Rosen (1990: 350–1) suggests that insistence on the consistency of such a triad of propositions is a strategy that comes at some cost in terms of a revision of our modal thought. In fact there are two kinds of revision entwined in Rosen's account. The first kind involves the agent *coming to care* about X's (counterparts, abstract worlds) while the second kind (Rosen 1990: 350 n.31) involves the agent insisting that he has cared about the X's all along. In the first case, one revises

Genuine realism

one's egoconcerns so as to make true what was once false, namely, that one has egoconcern with certain kinds of fact. In the second case, one revises one's beliefs (albeit beliefs about one's concerns) by coming to believe what one did not formerly believe, namely, that one is egoconcerned with certain kinds of fact. The questions that occur, then, are whether either sort of revision is more costly to the CT account of modal content than it is to its rivals and whether either sort of revision is inevitable for the CT account but avoidable for the others?[19] In fact, by drawing on the main insight of Miller (1992), I will suggest, that CT actually has the advantage in this regard.

Imagine that you and I were, until recently, innocent of modal theorizing but egoconcerned in typical ways with certain modal facts – say that each of us, like Humphrey, might have won (whatever). Then you come to accept the identification of modal facts with (appropriate) facts about AR worlds and I come to accept the identification of modal facts with (appropriate) facts about counterparts. Let us consider your position.

You will claim that the following doubly de re ascription of concern was true of you (and of me) in the past:

(17)   x is concerned about facts about AR possible worlds.

Having been then innocent of modal theorizing, you accept that the following (typical), psychologically significant, de dicto concern ascription was not true of you:

(18)   x is concerned that at some AR possible world x wins.

Post-theoretically, (18) is now true of you, assuming that your striving to change your concerns has succeeded, so your modal theorizing is not conservative with respect to your concerns. Moreover, previous innocence of modal theorizing appears to warrant recognition that the following de dicto ascription of belief was not true of pre-theoretical you either:

(19)   x believes that (x is concerned about facts about AR possible worlds).

Since (19) is now true of you, your modal theorizing is not conservative with respect to your set of beliefs (concerning your own psychology) either. Now consider me. In parity with you, I claim that a certain doubly de re ascription of concern was true of both of our pre-theoretical selves – viz.:

(20)   x is concerned about facts about counterparts.

However, we are not in the same position with respect to the past relevant de dicto concerns that we would ascribe to ourselves on the basis of our respectively favoured theories of content. It may be true, at a pinch, that the following, typical, de dicto concern ascription was not true of me:

(21)   x is concerned that a counterpart of x wins.

I say, 'at a pinch', since some case might be made for withholding the de dicto concern ascription simply on the grounds that I, although an English speaker, was not then acquainted with the term 'counterpart'. In any event, as a (*pro tem*) proponent of CT, I can afford to concede that (21) was not true of pre-theoretical me since a safer point is available. The following sort of de dicto concern ascription is and was true of me:

(22)   x is egoconcerned that there is some individual who is similar to x in important respects and who wins.

More generally – and this is how I would articulate Miller's point – we all have egoconcerns de dicto that individuals who are the same as us in respect of family membership, or occupation, or age, or participation in a certain contest, or being sentient etc. are (in certain ways) as they are[20] – e.g.:

(23)   I am egoconcerned whether my colleagues are being paid more or less than I am being paid.

These concerns have de dicto contents that are both egocentric and relational, and they match de re modal egoconcerns (that I might have won, that I am not as well paid as I might, or ought, to be, etc.). The truth of attitude ascriptions such as (22) and (23) is enough to show that a CT theory of content – although perhaps one that does not use the dispensable term 'counterpart' – is not revisionary of my relevant concerns.[21] Nor is CT revisionary of my related beliefs since I also recognize as true of my pre-theoretical and post-theoretical selves the following kind of de dicto belief ascription:

(24) x believes that (x is egoconcerned about individuals who are similar to x in important respects).[22]

So CT is conservative with respect to both concerns de dicto and beliefs de dicto in a way that rival AR theories of content are not, and as such CT emerges as better equipped to cope with an argument from concern than does its rival PW accounts.[23] Better equipped, but perhaps not perfectly so since there are two areas in which concern about concern may reassert itself.

First, it is arguable that the long-standing concern 'for counterparts' for which Miller argues is most plausibly established with respect to cases where we are concerned (de dicto) with individuals whom we represent as actual.[24] There are subtleties here. I may be egoconcerned (de dicto) that there (actually) are colleagues who are being paid more than me even if: (a) I do not quite believe that there are any such colleagues; or (b) there are no such colleagues. However, what seems eminently psychologically possible is that a de re possibility can be an occasion for egoconcern even if the subject is convinced that the possibility is unactualized. When Henrik Larsson muses that he might have scored a goal in every match of a Scottish Premier League season, his musing may sit comfortably with the belief that no one actually has achieved or ever will achieve that feat.[25] But where the subject believes that there is no actual counterpart who achieves the relevant feat, it is implausible to claim that the subject invariably (and pre-theoretically) has a type (23) attitude of concern – that he is concerned that there exists an individual who achieves the feat in question.[26] So our egoconcerns (de dicto) with (de re) possibilities and counterfactuals are not – or at least not obviously – matched perfectly, in extension, by our pre-theoretical egoconcerns (de dicto) with the instantiation of those possibilities by others.

Second, it is arguable that even perfect match in extension between egoconcerns de dicto about counterparts and egoconcerns de dicto about modality de re is insufficient to demonstrate appropriate concern for counterparts. The conversion to CT brings with it various other psychological revisions such as the following. Even if you were egoconcerned that your colleagues were this way or that, and those concerns 'matched' your modal egoconcerns, and such concerns provided causes or even reasons for you to have your egocentric modal concerns, it seems disingenuous to claim that the fates of the others figure in any direct or immediate way in the phenomenology of modal judgment or the understanding of modal claims. So if things are now different in these regards, there has been some non-conservative psychological effect of conversion to CT.

So perhaps CT cannot fully assuage the concern that it is victim to psychological manifestations of irrelevance and that it fails as a theory of psychologically relevant ascription of content to attitudes. But some grounds have been given for thinking that CT may be better off, rather than worse off, than rival PW theories of content in this regard.

(8.3) INTUITIONS OF TRUTH AND VALIDITY

Canonical CT appears to entail the falsehood of certain sorts of ordinary modal claims which, critics allege, we would pre-theoretically judge true, and CT also appears to validate only a relatively weak modal logic. In this section, I will try to pin down exactly where it is, in these respects, that canonical CT clashes with pre-theoretical intuitions. I will also consider where amendment to canonical CT is required in order to accommodate such intuitions and the forms that such amendments should take.

In the first category of cases in which CT is alleged to clash with the intuitively given truth-values of modal claims, similarity relations enter into truth-conditions from two distinct sources: first, and heterophonically, via the CT interpretation of explicitly occurring modal predication and second, homophonically, via the occurrence of (relatively) explicit predications of similarity. Thus we have examples (25)–(27):

(25) I could have been quite unlike the way I, in fact, am.
(26) I could have been more like the way you in fact are than like the way I in fact am, and at the same time, you could have been more like the way I in fact am than like the way you in fact are.
(27) If I were you I would have left immediately.[27]

If, within each case we leave undifferentiated, or otherwise treat univocally, the sort of similarity relation invoked by each relevant expression, an apparently unsatisfiable truth-condition emerges so that what appeared to be a banal truth emerges as an impossibility – e.g. in case (C25):

(C25) At some world, there is someone who is very much like me and who is quite unlike me.

However, a solution to this class of problems is within the means of canonical CT. In all cases the problem is solved by distinguishing between the kind of similarity that is invoked by the de re modal predications (via counterparthood) and the kind(s) of similarity invoked by the relatively explicit predication of (dis)similarity. Thus eminently satisfiable truth-conditions emerge as follows:

(C*25) At some world, there is someone who is very much like me in respect R and who is quite unlike me in respect S.

(C*26) There is a world w in which I have a counterpart x (in virtue of similarity relation R) and x is much more like A (the way you are in α) than like B (the way I am in α) and you have a counterpart y (in virtue of similarity relation R) and y is much more like B (the way I am in α) than like A (the way you are in α).

(C*27) In no selected world is there an x such that x is sufficiently similar to me in respect R and x is relevantly similar to you in respect S and x does not leave immediately.

In (C*25) and (C*26) the counterpart-determining relation R might be construed as match of origin (type) while other likenesses or similarities intimated are post-original.[28] In case (C*27), and other such 'If I were you ...' counterfactuals, the obvious candidates are similarity of thoughts, for being counterpart to me, and similarity of predicament, for being (relevantly like) you. In the above cases, no amendment to canonical CT is required in order to accommodate intuition, but matters stand otherwise with further categories of example.

The second category of cases typically involves the occurrence of multiple de re modal locutions within a sentential context and call for interpretation in terms of a multiplicity of counterpart relations. The 'Cartesian' intuition of the truth of:

(28) I and my body are such that they might not have been identical at time t

is accommodated by the CT truth-condition:

(C28) There is a world at which there is an x that is a personal counterpart of me (a counterpart in virtue of psychological similarity) and there is a y that is a bodily counterpart of my body (a counterpart in virtue of bodily similarity) and such that x and y are not identical (at some counterpart of time t).

A similar story can be told wherever the intuition arises that an entity of a certain kind might have been distinct from an entity that actually constitutes it (a statue and a lump of clay, a dishpan and a parcel of plastic, etc.). However, to equip these possibility claims with satisfiable truth-conditions in this way, as Lewis (1971: 51) admits, is – in a sense – to abandon the referentially transparent treatment of de re modal predication that was intended in canonical CT. Since Lewis takes 'I' and 'my body' (in a given tokening of (28)) to be actually co-referential terms, the success of (C28) depends on two distinct sets of counterparts of one individual being relevant to what is truly modally predicable of that individual. The two distinct sets of counterparts of the one individual are invoked by the presence of two distinct modes of presentation of a single actual individual referent. So, in general, appropriate truth-conditions for de re modal claims may depend – even when sentential context and context of tokening is fixed – not only on the identity of the *res* but on its mode of presentation.[29]

A third category of cases is exemplified by certain intuitively true essentialist claims – e.g.:

(29) Whatever is human is necessarily human.

In order to restrict the interpretation of the claim as is appropriate to its truth, it is required that every counterpart in every world of every actual human is human. More generally, the thought is that, against a background of classification of (unrestrictedly) all individuals into various (overlapping) kinds or sorts – biological kinds, physical kinds, etc. – we may identify the class of (qualitative) same-kind relations as counterpart relations (Hazen 1979a: 332). Such classification admits two limiting cases (Lewis 1983b: 43). In one limiting case, the same-kind relation is identity and each individual stands in that relation to itself and nothing else. In the other limiting case, the same-kind relation is the universal relation on individuals, or to put the point otherwise the individuals form a 'kind', in which case each individual stands in that relation to every other individual. These kind-based counterpart relations appear to correspond to various salient or natural kinds of modality. The universal counterpart

Genuine realism

relation is an anti-essentialist counterpart relation that may seem appropriate when an interpretation of a modality as narrowly logical modality is required. The identity relation as counterpart relation speaks to the claims to truth that some have felt exerted by certain de re modal statements of identity.[30] If it proves viable to say something constructive about the kinds of kinds that are relevant to the determination of the specifically metaphysical modalities (cf. Salmon 1981) then a CT account of metaphysical modality can be constructed on that basis. Suspension of the (P5) requirement that nothing is the counterpart of anything other than itself in the world of which it is part is at least helpful in several cases – thus see claims (2) and (26) above. However suspension of (P5) is mandatory if we are to make available the same-kind counterpart relations mooted in this case. I turn now from the matter of the implications of CT for judgements of truth-value to the matter of the implications of canonical CT for judgements of validity.

If CT is to serve as an adequate applied semantics for QML, we must consider the range of modal principles (*vice* arguments) that it validates.[31] Clearly, it would be a mark of the inadequacy of such a semantic theory were it to validate any patently invalid QML argument or to invalidate any patently valid QML argument. As noted by Lewis (1968) and Hazen (1979a), the following are among the eminent modal principles that are *not* validated by canonical CT:[32]

(i)	$\Box A \rightarrow \Box\Box A$	(the S4 principle / Becker's principle)
(ii)	$A \rightarrow \Box\Diamond A$	(Brouwer's principle)
(iii)	$\Diamond A \rightarrow \Box\Diamond A$	(the S5 principle)
(iv)	$\forall x \Box[Fx] \rightarrow \Box\forall x[Fx]$	(the Barcan formula)
(v)	$(x = y) \rightarrow \Box(x = y)$	(necessity of identity)
(vi)	$\Box Fa \rightarrow \Box\exists x[Fx]$	
(vii)	$\Box\exists x[Fx] \rightarrow \exists x[\Box Fx]$	

Although the converse Barcan formula is validated, the overall picture is one in which canonical CT validates only rather weak modal logics. The first question, then, is whether this outcome puts canonical CT in a special position of conflict with pre-theoretical intuition about validity. Several considerations suggest that it does not.

First, the extent of invalidation is not as bad as it may initially appear. In the cases of the propositional principles (i)–(iii) – i.e. the Becker principle, the Brouwer principle and the S5 principle – invalidity ensues only if we allow, as we may for technical reasons, open sentences as substituends for A.³³ In other words when the substituends of A are restricted to closed sentences, as they are when we regiment arguments proper, the principles are validated. Second, CT will ask us to distinguish the theoretical cost of conflicting with expected results concerning validity for the non-modal fragment of QML (i.e. first-order predicate logic with identity) and conflicting with any expected result concerning validity in the modal fragment. Allegations of the former, more serious, kind are made by Kripke (1972: 45 n.13) and Hazen (1979a) but rebutted by Lewis (1983b: 45–6) on grounds of the inadequacies of QML. It might be argued that certain modal principles are no more negotiable than those of non-modal predicate logic. If we seek an applied semantics for alethic modal logic, two prominent candidates are:

(viii) $\Box A \to A$ (necessity elimination)
(ix) $A \to \Diamond A$ (possibility introduction)

But the validity of these central modal principles is not at risk in CT semantics.³⁴ The principles that are at risk – especially once that list is limited by the first observation about the propositional principles – are all, in various ways, post-theoretically controversial and, arguably, none commands a clear and unqualified pre-theoretical intuition of validity. So it is not clear that the weak modal logic that is validated by CT is any weaker, in its modal or non-modal parts, than that which is given to us, by clear pre-theoretical intuition alone, as the right modal logic. Third, insofar as the validity of these modal principles may be supported by independent argument it is, of course, open to CT to find fault or limitations in those arguments. Thus, e.g., Forbes (1985: 179) on the informal arguments for necessity of identity given in Kripke (1972). It is also open to CT to defend the invalidation of certain formulas of QML as Lewis does in defending certain possibilities that make for (one of the things meant by) 'contingent identity'. Fourth, as we shall see in Chapter 13 the philosophical constraints exerted on semantic theories by just about any AR interpretation of PW result in the invalidation of some of the principles on the foregoing list or others of comparable status. So it is not clear that CT calls for revision of pre-theoretical opinion about modal validity while rival interpretations of PW do not.

Thus far, then, it is unclear that considerations of validity call for any amendment of canonical CT. However, the kinds of amendment of canonical CT that were mooted in response to clashes with intuitions about modal truth also render CT more flexible in its capacity to account for the intuitive validity of certain modal arguments. In particular, and as intimated above, flexibility is increased by the move to suspend the requirement (P5) – that worldmates are never counterparts – in favour of admitting counterpart relations generated by sameness of kind. These kind-based counterpart relations appear to correspond to various salient or natural kinds of modality. One might envisage, for example, a kind of modality in which we are interested only in what is biologically possible for an organism. Reflecting such a modal interest, we might restrict the range of counterpart relations in admissible models to those that are fixed by membership of the same species or membership of the same genus. Reflecting another kind of modal interest that we have, in narrowly logical modality, we might require that models admit only the anti-essentialist, universal relation under which every individual is a counterpart of every other. If such counterpart relations are equivalence relations, and since certain of the negotiable modal principles (e.g. Becker and Brouwer) are (unrestrictedly) validated under the requirement that counterpart relations are equivalence relations, a special logic of these particular modalities is validated under CT interpretation. For CT, as for everyone else, getting the right model structure for the logic of this or that kind of modality is a matter of motivating and effecting suitable constraints on the relations within the models. There is no reason to suppose that this procedure is particularly problematic when the model contains counterpart relations or when (as we might expect) CT construes accessibility relations as counterpart relations of certain kinds.[35]

(8.4) THE CONSEQUENCES OF DEREGULATION

In response to claims about pre-theoretical intuitions concerning modal truth in particular, it has been mooted that two sorts of departure from canonical CT should be licensed. Specifically, deregulated CT treats de re modal predication as referentially opaque and appeals to same-kind counterpart relations that allow worldmates to be counterparts. In this last section I will consider whether CT is in one way or another, devalued, if not fatally compromised, by deregulation. I will discuss three ways in which this objection might be substantiated.

The first thought is that the extensionality of CT (and GR) is compromised by abandoning the canonical treatment of de re modal predication as referentially transparent in favour of a treatment of such predication as opaque. But let us be clear about what the commitments of deregulated CT are in this regard. The thesis to which revised CT is committed is this:

(30)   Object language de re modal predication is referentially opaque.

That is to say that the semantic theory does not always deliver the same truth-conditions for two (de re modal) object language sentence types that differ from one another only with respect to the occurrence of distinct expression types that are actually co-referential. Thus, recall example (28) concerning possible non-identity of me and my body. Furthermore, the referential opacity of object language de re modal predication entails failure of extensionality in the object language, referential opacity being the manifestation of intensionality when the inter-substituted terms are singular terms. However, thesis (30) ought to be distinguished from the further thesis:

(31)   There is referential opacity in the CT metalanguage.

It does not follow from the treatment of object language de re modal predication as referentially opaque that metalinguistic 'counterpart' predication is referentially opaque. We might think here of the primitive vocabulary of the metalanguage as consisting, in this respect, of: (a) different world-relativized counterpart predicates corresponding to each distinguishable counterpart relation ('Cxyw'); and (b) various singular terms that refer to elements in the domain of the object language quantifiers. Then, for each such predicate, the inference from premises 'b = c' and 'C*abw' to 'C*acw' will be (meta-metalinguistically) valid and there is no corresponding referential opacity, or failure of extensionality, in the metalanguage of CT. What we have here is an instance of a general phenomenon that was anticipated in (3.1), namely, that the intensionality of modal object languages is to be regarded as a superficial phenomenon which disappears at the level of interpretation at which the truth-conditional significance of expressions is made clear. As ever, it is the medium of interpretation of PW that is required to be fully extensional in order to achieve that aim.[36]

The second thought is that CT is compromised by seeking to admit as counterpart relations such dubious candidates as the universal relation over (unrestrictedly) all individuals – the relation that each individual bears to every other individual – and the (strict) identity relation that holds only between each individual and itself (Lewis 1983b: 43). The relational credentials of such 'relations' are, by GR lights, impeccable since each is identifiable as a set of ordered pairs drawn from the domain of all individuals. But in what sense are these relations properly to be regarded as qualitative relations or relations of qualitative similarity?[37] Perhaps the most effective response to this question is to show how we can characterize exactly the same relations – i.e. pick out the same sets of ordered pairs – in purely qualitative terms. Grant that the spatiotemporal relations may be presumed to be among the qualitative relations. Recalling, then, that similarity is allowed to be similarity in non-intrinsic respects, the universal relation (on individuals) and the identity relation (on individuals) can then be identified as relations of similarity in certain spatiotemporal respects. The universal relation is, otherwise, the relation of similarity in respect of spatiotemporality – i.e. similarity in respect of being spatiotemporally related to some individual. The identity relation is, otherwise, the relation of exact similarity in respect of spatiotemporal location.

The third thought is that the ground of CT has shifted in a way that has undermined the GR claim to have provided an interpretation of PW that has those methodological virtues that are supposed to be indicative of its truth. It is written on behalf of GR (including CT) that '... [the defenders of GR] have not had to resort to ad hoc hypotheses or convoluted qualifications and disclaimers. Is this not the surest sign of philosophical truth?' (Miller 1992: 133). But is this claim warranted with respect to any version of GR that includes deregulated CT? The appropriate defence of CT is one that distinguishes the unity and simplicity of its underlying philosophical principles from the diversity and complexity of the resources which the theory, so formulated, has at its disposal. As the above discussion indicates, deregulated CT brings in its wake no compromise of GR principle. Humean supervenience (see n.36 above) holds sway and de re modal predication is still explained in terms of quantification over a non-actualist domain and the qualitative features (including similarities) of its elements. So, the defence concludes, there is no compromise or dilution of the general unifying principles that underpin CT – no appeal to primitive or non-qualitative counterpart relations, or to surd de re modal features of things. However, even if that point is accepted the distinct but subsequent complaint that waits in the wings is that deregulated CT is deployed in a thoroughly *ad hoc* manner.

The fourth thought, then, to put this last complaint more firmly, is that deregulated CT admits such a variety of 'counterpart' relations and tolerates, for the purposes of interpretation, such selection and permutation of these within and across 'contexts' that de re modal judgment becomes a free-for-all. Whenever it suits your purposes that a token de re claim should come out true then all you need to do is to pick and choose, mix and match the relations judiciously so as to obtain the desired result. How, then, can deregulated CT embody or reflect the central norms of assent and dissent – the element of discipline over usage – that are essential to the truth-aptitude of the declarative sentences of de re modal discourse?[38] Lewis's general strategy of response to this kind of allegation proceeds from emphasis of two points. First, the capacity of CT to deliver for most de re modal sentence types a truth-condition that is satisfied, is perfectly in keeping with the consideration that for most such types, there is a tokening in a context of a sentence of that type which is true (and would pre-theoretically be allowed to be true). Second, in affording such a variety of distinct interpretations (truth-conditions) over their tokens, de re modal sentence types are far from exceptional.[39] Lewis claims that since our de re modal discourse and de re modal judgments – like many other discourses and related judgments – are marked by a high degree of vagueness, uncertainty, inconstancy and context-relativity, a given type of de re modal claim is apt to express a vast range of different thoughts and it is, for the most part, a highly indeterminate matter exactly which (precise) thought is expressed by a given token of that type. Call that the variety claim. Lewis allies to this variety claim certain general, and highly charitable, principles of pragmatics – in particular, the following charity claim: say something and it is very likely that you thereby create a context in which you speak the truth. The conclusion that Lewis draws from the conjunction of the variety claim and the charitable stance is that the norms of assent and dissent are so weak and localized that in de re modal judgment 'almost anything goes'. However the 'almost' does some work in mandating various assertions and denials. There are, for example, no circumstances in which you speak truly by characterizing the predication of incompatible properties to an individual as possible. So the conjunction of the variety claim and the charity claim is not, and ought not to be construed as, inconsistent with the truth-aptitude of de re modal discourse, even allowing that truth-aptitude requires discipline to be exerted by norms of assent and dissent. However, the further point that I wish to emphasize is that one might endorse CT without agreeing with

Genuine realism

Lewis about either the variety claim or the charity claim. The primary two-fold test of CT *qua* semantic theory is: (a) that it should be capable of generating a sufficient variety of truth-conditions to match (at least) the variety of modal thoughts that are expressible in the object language; and (b) that it associates thoughts with object language sentences after a systematic fashion prescribed by syntax. Assuming, in the absence of outstanding objections, that deregulated CT is well equipped in this regard, it is pointless to complain that CT permits the association with any sentence type, or any token of that type, *more* thoughts than are merited by the facts about how the sentence is actually used. The point of the semantic theory is to allow for the thoughts that *can* be expressed by a sentence type; it is then an empirical and pragmatic matter to decide in interpretation which of these thoughts is expressed by a tokening of that type. Let it be granted that Lewis's variety claim is false so that he typically overestimates the range of thoughts that is permissibly associated with any given sentence type, or with any given token of that type. CT can still plug into the more conservative theory of pragmatics which entails that claim in order to deliver an appropriate (narrower) range of truth-conditions for each sentence type or token. Let it be granted that Lewis's charity claim is false. Then we should be less willing than Lewis is, to allow that a given sentence type or token merits interpretation as having one of the CT generated truth-conditions that are fulfilled. But that too calls for an adjustment in pragmatic outlook, not the rejection of CT.

In summary, then, I have attempted to scrutinize the relevance objection to CT and have concluded that no reasonably precise version of that objection shows CT in a worse light than any other PW account of de re modal content. I have also argued that the transition from canonical CT to deregulated CT is effective and defensible.

CHAPTER 9

Genuine realism: epistemology

The major epistemological complaint against GR is that we cannot know that its characteristic ontological claims are true.[1] In making the positive case for our knowledge of the ontology of GR, Lewis argues that the hypothesis satisfies a general utilitarian condition that is sufficient for knowledge (9.1). This positive case might be resisted by arguing that the condition in question is not sufficient or, even if it is, that the ontological hypothesis of GR does not meet it (9.2). Alternatively, it might be argued, in that context or independently, that the characteristic ontological assertions of GR violate some, perhaps complex, necessary condition of our knowing that they are true (9.3). Having considered both of these strategies I turn finally to the status of claims about modal epistemology and the important comparative question of whether, in light of the discussion, GR stands at any obvious epistemological disadvantage to AR – actualist realism – (9.4). But I will begin by making some preliminary methodological points.

First, the epistemological complaint against GR is sometimes made indirectly via an argument that connects the ontological claims of GR to our modal knowledge. We have modal knowledge but, it is argued, if GR gave the right account of the content of that knowledge, then it could not be known at all, and so GR does not give the right account of modal content.[2] It seems to me that this indirect form of epistemological objection against GR is, arguably, weaker than the direct form of the complaint and, in any case, dependent upon it. The weakness of the indirect complaint consists in its risky play with the notion of content, but I need not pursue that point here.[3] The key point is that the ultimate object of epistemological complaint is that which is conceived as the truthmaker of the modal claim – let us say, the putative worldly fact.[4] Moreover that kind of fact would attract that kind of complaint whether or not it were adduced in that explanatory role. Since the fact in question is exactly of the kind that is characteristically described in the ontological component of GR, facts about other concrete worlds, we do as well as to focus on those facts directly.

Further to this point note that Lewis (1986a: 108–9) claims that the epistemological position of GR 'echoes' the famous dilemma of Benacerraf (1973) for mathematics. The reason why Benacerraf's dilemma is supposed to be a dilemma is that the demands of our supposedly 'best' ideas about how to go about semantics pull us in the direction of Platonism while our supposedly best ideas about how to go about epistemology push us away from Platonism. However, what Benacerraf and Lewis consider to be valuable about the semantic theory that pushes us towards Platonism in the mathematical case is that it is a face-value semantics – a theory that is, *inter alia*, conservative of the syntactic appearances and which does not subject mathematical sentences to any 'devious re-interpretation' aimed at securing the right truth-values while altering substantially the pre-theoretical content. Whatever else might be said about the value of a counterpart-theoretic semantics, or indeed any other possible worlds semantics, for *modal* sentences, it most certainly cannot be said to be a face-value semantics for those sentences. Perhaps a possible worlds semantics for modal discourse will be judged our 'best' semantics in relation to other criteria. But we have a clearer echo of Benacerraf's dilemma in the case of GR if we focus on the discourse PW or, clearer yet, if we focus on the discourse in which the GR interpretation of PW is articulated and treat that discourse, semantically, at face value.[5]

Second, this methodological stance also has the advantage of allowing us to distinguish epistemological challenges that are otherwise in danger of being conflated when certain questions are addressed to GR. Among such questions are how I am to determine whether A is true at some world or other (Richards 1975) and how I can tell whether one of the worlds is a world where Saul Kripke is the son of Rudolf Carnap (Lycan 1979). These are questions of how we know what a possible world represents – they are questions of the epistemology of world-content (as it were) – and they are, in a significant sense, independent from the question of how we know that other possible worlds exist. Questions of the epistemology of world-content seem to persist even if it is granted that I know that the GR worlds exist and what the qualitative character of any relevant world is. The epistemological question of world existence seems to persist even if it is granted that I know what any other GR world would represent (were such a world to exist). The questions of the epistemology of world-content will be discussed in the context of the question of transworld identification (Chapter 16). It is the epistemological question of world-existence – how we know that there are other GR worlds – that will be pursued here.

Third, and finally, it is to be emphasized that the presently intended focus of the epistemological objections to GR is a claim that is de re with respect to us and de dicto with respect to the relevant content. The claim is of the form that we know that P, where P stands for the ontological component of GR (hereafter, GRO) – a de dicto claim that there are many worlds of such-and-such a character.

(9.1) THE UTILITARIAN CASE FOR GR KNOWLEDGE

GRO tells us that there is a vast plurality of spatially temporally disjoined concrete worlds and that in these worlds there are Newtonian spacetimes, talking donkeys, blue swans and – indeed – individuals of every kind that there could possibly be. But how can we know whether such an ontological hypothesis is true? Lewis (1986a: 3–5) argues thus:

(1) If an ontological hypothesis has eminent utility (i.e. sufficient net utility and greater net utility than its rivals) then that gives us good reason to believe that it is true.
(2) Such reason for believing an ontological hypothesis is warranting (i.e. given that the theory is true, having grounds of eminent utility is sufficient for knowing that the theory is true).
(3) GR has eminent utility.

so

(4) We (are in a position to) know that GR is true.

The gross utility of GRO is a matter of what it delivers, in conjunction with the explanatory component of GR, by way of conceptual, ontological and semantic illumination of the modal and the intensional. Net utility is a matter of subtracting its theoretical and methodological costs from the benefits of gross utility. Comparative net utility of the ontological hypothesis is a matter of the difference between the net utility of GR and that of its rivals.[6]

In support of his line of argument, Lewis cites as precedent knowledge of the existence of sets. In that case, it is suggested, the gross utility consists in the capacity of the ontological hypothesis to afford us mathematics via a corresponding explanatory component that 'reduces' the other branches of mathematics (arithmetic, analysis, analytic geometry, etc.) to facts about the ontology of sets. I take it that this gesture towards the set-theoretic precedent is only a gesture. It reminds us that controversial ontological hypotheses are sometimes held to be known on the grounds of their utility. However, I think that it is a mistake to become distracted by the specific precedent that has been cited, and the accompanying gesture towards our knowledge of set theory. The suggestion of an analogy with GR would have to be bolstered, developed and clarified in various ways to be of any serious consequence. For example, there is more than one version of set theory and the argument requires that one of these – the version which has greatest net utility – be specified. No doubt strategies for resisting the argument in the case of sets will prompt and inform parallel moves against the argument in the case of GR. However, the argument for our being in a position to know GRO must stand or fall on its own merits. In particular, the failure of the set-theoretic argument should not automatically signal a refutation of the parallel argument in the case of GRO. One might think that the set-theoretic argument fails because there is a rival, 'nominalistic', hypothesis on the market that secures the utility of mathematics without postulating the existence of anything other than actual *individuals*. But even if so, it is obviously a quite independent matter whether GR has a more economical rival in its own sphere that is equally effective in securing explanations of the modal and the intensional. So, all in all, dialectical clarity is served if we concentrate directly on Lewis's argument in the GR case without having to defend the thesis that set theory is a genuine and successful precedent.

Since I assume that Lewis's argument is valid I consider how its premises might be resisted.

Premise (3) asserts that GR has sufficient net utility. One might dispute this in a number of ways. Here I want to bracket some questions in order to move on to some other, more immediately tractable, points about how a claim of sufficient utility can fail.

First, one might dispute the claim by questioning how calculations of net utility and comparative net utility are to be made and I will return to this question below. Second, one might dispute the claims of gross utility that are made on behalf of GR. In earlier chapters I have discussed, and occasionally endorsed, various complaints to the effect that the GR conceptual, ontological or semantic explanations are not as comprehensive or secure as Lewis takes them to be. Salient among such complaints are that GR does not fund a comprehensive analysis of modal concepts (Chapter 7), that it misrepresents the truth-values of important classes of modal claim (this section *passim*) and that it does not supply sufficiently fine-grained constructs to play various intensional roles (Chapter 5). Having registered these complaints again in the present context, I have nothing to add to them. Third, one might take issue with Lewis over comparative net utility, arguing that a rival theory affords greater net utility. That is a position that will only be evaluable following detailed discussion of the net utility of the species of AR and I postpone such evaluation until the final chapter. The issues that I now turn to address are those concerning the theoretical costs that enter into considerations of net utility.

In calculating the theoretical costs of an ontological hypothesis, among the qualities we are supposed to take into account are (lack of) consistency, coherence, conceptual and ontological conservativeness, conceptual and ontological economy, simplicity of formulation, simplification and unification of explananda. Each of these qualities merits exposition and scrutiny, each, no doubt, is controversial and the list is not intended to be closed. However, for present purposes I need not question the relevance of any of these core qualities to judgments of net theoretical utility. Perhaps some of the qualities listed – notably consistency and (minimal) coherence – ought to be regarded more as prerequisites, rather than as negotiable aspects of theoretical utility. But here I will take it that any such thought can be captured by assigning a special weight to these norms – e.g. demonstrable inconsistency might be taken to set net theoretical utility to the minimum value. In the literature, calls for an increased estimate of the theoretical costs of the GR hypothesis are based on two considerations.

The first consideration emerges from the 'incredulous stare'. The incredulous (or blank) stare characterizes a range of negative reactions – incredulity, bewilderment, professed incomprehension – that are caused in those who are confronted by the ontological claims of GR.[7] Lewis (1986a: 133–5) admits that GR radically outstrips common opinion about what there is and that this is a cost to the theory – more specifically, cost is incurred because GR is ideologically non-conservative. Moreover, Lewis seeks to construe persistent incredulous staring along the lines of a judgement to the effect that, even given gross utility in the form of all of the supposed benefits of GR, this cost is not outweighed by those benefits. Lewis's subsequent attitude is methodologically agnostic, professing that he does not

Genuine realism

know how to judge when such a cost becomes prohibitive or how to argue against someone who takes the view that this cost outweighs the benefits. Bigelow and Pargetter (1990: 183–9) seek to pursue further this line of enquiry, making various attempts to articulate the incredulous stare as a case for assigning prohibitive or irrecoverable cost to GR on grounds of its prima facie incredibility. In this regard many interesting methodological questions are raised. How might we allow a non-zero epistemic probability for a hypothesis that we believe to be impossible if false? Might a hypothesis be set such a low but non-zero epistemic probability that its credibility can increase only infinitesimally in light of incoming evidence? Can we be justified in assigning a zero or otherwise negligible epistemic probability to a hypothesis that is endorsed by an agent whom we believe to be rational and cognitively uninhibited in his deliberations? Bigelow and Pargetter find no rational vindication of incredulous staring in the working out of responses to these questions. Their conclusion is that there is no easily discernible and successful underlying methodological argument for the prima facie incredibility of GR having a decisive effect on net theoretical utility. I agree.[8]

The second consideration that is thought to call for an increased estimate of the theoretical costs is that GR is guilty of ontological extravagance. Despite acknowledging that the ontology of GR is vast and far outstrips what is commonly believed to exist, Lewis (1973: 87) distinguishes two sorts of ontological economy ('parsimony'). Qualitative economy is economy of number of kinds of entity postulated; it is a feature of GR and it is a genuine virtue of philosophical and empirical theories (hypotheses).[9] Quantitative economy is economy in number of postulated instances of a kind; this is not a feature of GR, but no matter since it is not a theoretical virtue. The kind that Lewis presents as crucial to judgements about the economy of GR is that of genuine worlds. GR postulates a vast number of instances of that kind, but is appropriately economical since all that matters is that GR does not thereby postulate the instantiation of a kind that rival theorists take to be uninstantiated.

In response, one might press, first, on Lewis's claim that *no value whatever* should be accorded to quantitative economy (cf. Divers 1994). But this is a difficult claim to evaluate in any case.[10] In any event, it seems that the alleged economy of GR can easily be undercut by focussing on the qualitative claim alone.

If the evaluation of the qualitative economy of GR were confined to the matter of the genuine world kind then, indeed, most metaphysical theories will be on a par with GR in accepting that such a kind is instantiated.[11] However, it has been observed, by Roper (1982) and by Melia (1992), that there are many kinds that GR takes to be instantiated but for which (actualist) rivals do not postulate instances: Newtonian spacetimes, unicorns, dragons, etc. Moreover, as Melia (1992) has emphasized, in construing possible existence as unrestricted existence, GR postulates the (unrestricted) instantiation of every individual kind that *could be* instantiated. So, even by Lewis's own lights, should GR not be reckoned maximally qualitatively uneconomical – as uneconomical as any consistent theory could be?

Melia's complaint is merited in that: (a) Lewis does appear to make the case that GR is qualitatively economical with respect to the range of instantiated kinds of individual that it postulates; and (b) by that measure, GR is, indeed, maximally qualitatively uneconomical. However, a more effective case for Lewis's conclusion can be made in different terms. GR purports to be a comprehensive theory of ontology, and in that light it is plausible that the relevant measure of the qualitative economy of GR ought to be the number of ultimate, fundamental, *sui generis*, ontological kinds that it takes to be instantiated. So what is relevant to the qualitative economy of GR, or any rival comprehensive ontological theory, is not – for example – how many instantiated kinds of individual are postulated. Rather, in matters of fundamental ontology, individuals form one ultimate (instantiated) kind and the relevant question is how many other (non-overlapping) ultimate kinds of entity are postulated. So the claim of GR, *qua* comprehensive ontological theory, to qualitative economy ought to be made in relation to the hypothesis that there are (at most) only two ultimate kinds of entity – that everything is either an individual or a set (postulate (O3), Chapter 4). In that light, GR enjoys greater qualitative economy than rival theories of comprehensive ontology that postulate – in addition to individuals and sets – entities that are neither individuals nor sets but are taken to be of some further *sui generis* kind, e.g. properties, propositions, states of affairs, etc.[12]

Thus, the case may be made that neither the allegations of (prima facie) incredibility nor those of ontological extravagance establish that GR carries theoretical costs that significantly diminish net utility.

(9.2) UTILITY AS WARRANT IN ONTOLOGY

I have nothing to offer by way of a critique of Lewis's argument that would seek to make something of the distinction, reflected in

Genuine realism

premise (2), between non-warranting and warranting utilitarian grounds for believing an ontological hypothesis. In that light I will direct attention onto premise (1), considering whether sufficient utility constitutes good reason for believing an ontological hypothesis. I believe that it is this premise, and not any delicate play with the distinction between knowledge and reasonable belief, that is more likely to incite epistemological suspicions about GR.

The most fundamental reasons that one might have for rejecting (1) concern ontological claims in general. A generalized nonfactualism about ontological postulates has it that such postulates are beyond the pale of truth or falsehood (Carnap 1950). A generalized agnosticism about ontological postulates has it that most, if not all, such postulates, while truth-apt and truth-valued, are beyond the pale of reasonable belief in that we never have good reason to think they are true. I do not propose to engage here with generalized scepticism about ontological hypotheses in either form. In any event, in the local dialectical context, the rivals who confront GR are the AR interpreters of PW, all of whom can be presumed to take ontological questions to be a legitimate subject of rational dispute. Of course, it is another matter, and one that cannot so easily be marginalized, whether GR in particular has certain features – features that are not features of ontological hypotheses in general – that places it beyond the pale of truth or falsehood or rational belief. But more of that soon enough. Following the proposed rejection of generalized scepticism about ontology, however, Lewis's generalized claim – that sufficient utility gives reason to hold ontological hypotheses true – takes on the appearance of a platitude. In one light, acceptance of premise (1) seems a negligible advance on the rejection of generalized scepticism about ontology, so long as we construe liberally enough both the range of things that count towards gross utility and the range of things that count towards theoretical costs. However, it is crucial to the reception of (1) as a platitude that it be distinguished and distanced from the stronger thesis:

(1*) If an ontological hypothesis has sufficient utility then it is true.

One who holds (1), in contrast to one who holds (1*), need not hold that sufficient utility – even liberally construed – is even materially sufficient for truth, and far less need she hold that truth is entailed by sufficient utility, or that truth is supervenient on (degree of) utility. So I take it that allegiance to (1) is compatible with either a broadly

GR: epistemology

realistic attitude, or a broadly antirealistic attitude to ontological hypotheses while allegiance to the far more demanding (1*) is compatible only with the latter.[13]

Having exempted premise (1) from objections based in a generalized scepticism about ontology and having now distanced the thesis from commitment to antirealism about ontology, I am inclined to accept it in principle in the absence of any other objection. If we are to judge that we have reason to hold ontological hypotheses true when philosophizing, how are we to base that judgement if not by weighing conceptual, metaphysical, semantic and other such philosophical benefits against potential costs characterized in terms of the values or benefits of consistency, coherence, conceptual and ontological conservativeness, conceptual and ontological economy, simplicity of formulation, simplification and unification of explananda?

The main problem with premise (1), I believe, is not one of broad principle but rather one about how the key notion of sufficient utility can be pinned down to the extent that we have any basis to judge whether an associated minor premise – e.g. premise (3) concerning GR – is true. Grant Lewis all that he claims in extension, as it were, about the results of GR – that it affords a non-modal analysis of the family of modal and intensional concepts, etc. – and that such results count towards the gross utility of the hypothesis. Grant also that GR has all of those features that are supposed to be theoretically virtuous and that these are, indeed, theoretically virtuous. One might grant all of that, and yet, for all Lewis has told us, reject the claim that GR has sufficient utility to be credible. Such a position might arise in various ways. If the presence of a given theoretical quality is a matter of degree, one might disagree with Lewis about the matter of degree or about how that matter should be judged. One might disagree with Lewis about how theoretical qualities ought to be weighed against each other in calculating the overall qualitative value of the theory. One might disagree with Lewis about the total value that ought to be assigned to those results on the side of gross utility, about the total value that ought to be assigned to that package of theoretical virtues and – hence – about the net value of gross utility against costs. Finally one might even agree right up to the point of evaluation of degree of net utility and disagree about whether this is sufficient to make the theory credible. In the absence of an idea about how disagreements on these points might be addressed or resolved, and especially in the absence of a demonstration of such a resolution in Lewis's favour all down the line, it is difficult to see why the initially agnostic neutral about GR should be moved. That so many escape routes remain open to the neutral leaves the argument for knowledge of the ontological hypothesis of GR far from compelling.

It is unclear how disturbing an outcome this is. In the worst case one might hold that the points of potential disagreement in question are not rationally resolvable and, consequently, that agnosticism is the only defensible attitude. More optimistically, one might take the view that there is no special source or extent of disagreement here that is not also present in any reasonably ambitious theorizing, even when the theorizing is empirical. In that light, one might venture the suggestion that it can be rational to hold one such theory true, and reject its competitors, on broad grounds of comparative net theoretical utility, even if we have no detailed account – far less an algorithm – that deals with matters of how various relevant considerations should be evaluated individually or weighed against one another. In sum, it might be judged that Lewis has produced a defence of his claim to know that the ontological hypothesis of GR is true which is strong enough to be rationally defensible if not strong enough to compel the rational neutral to agree with him. It is eminently reasonable to accept ontological hypotheses on grounds of their (comparative) net utility and it is rationally permissible, but not mandatory, to take the view that GR meets this standard. But another route remains open to the objector.

It might be argued that the major premises of the argument are true only for a restricted class of ontological hypotheses. Perhaps the motivating thought is that these general principles earn their credibility through their application to empirical hypotheses, but cannot be applied to just any ontological hypothesis, however fanciful or remote from our empirical and practical concerns. It would remain then to the objector to produce a criterion of demarcation that appropriately restricts the class of ontological hypotheses and to show that GR falls foul of it. To generalize beyond the context of Lewis's argument, the same kind of substantive points about the GRO hypothesis might be adduced in support of the claim that GRO fails some general necessary condition for being an object of knowledge.

(9.3) OBSTACLES TO A PRIORICITY

The salient question for GR is whether the GRO meets appropriate necessary conditions on a priori knowledge. Here, and henceforth, I characterize as a posteriori any knowledge that requires the existence of some (appropriate) causal connection between the truthmaking fact and any knower. Whatever knowledge requires no such connection is a priori.[14] By GR hypothesis worlds are causally isolated from one another. Accordingly, there is no serious prospect of offering an a posteriori account of our knowledge of GRO and all that remains is for GR to defend the view that such knowledge is a priori. Here, I will not take on the claim that all knowledge is a posteriori.[15] I believe that this claim is false and, accordingly, that there is some domain of knowledge for which, broadly, knowledge does not require causal connection between knower and truthmaking fact. What I am interested in here is the sort of reason that a philosopher might have for accepting that we have some such knowledge, and perhaps even that our modal knowledge is of this character, but that the subject matter of GRO renders it ineligible for membership of that class. In this respect we might be guided by a comparison of our (putative) knowledge of GRO with a certain picture of our (putative) knowledge of the natural numbers. The neo-Fregean and Platonistic picture of our knowledge of the natural numbers has it that the objects in question are abstract, that their existence is necessary and that the relevant existential assertions are analytic. The guiding thought is that if any of these three 'marks' of a priori existential knowledge is a necessary condition then we have a serious threat to the claim that knowledge of GRO is a priori.

The first alleged obstacle to a prioricity is concreteness, for it is claimed that this feature of GRO requires that evidence for the existence of other worlds should be a posteriori (Skyrms 1976: 326). Lewis does not argue against this thesis directly but settles for producing an alternative demarcation principle for a posteriori knowledge which, he claims, produces a stand-off. But an argument is available.

The thesis that existential knowledge of concrete entities entails a posterioricity of evidence is one that appears vulnerable to counterexample. One's mind, for example, would customarily be regarded as concrete given that it stands in either causal, or at least temporal, relations to various things. Yet, even granting that causal connectedness is a necessary condition of any of us having evidence for the existence of other minds, it is simply not obvious – nor even obviously intelligible – that one requires such evidence for the existence of one's own mind. The immediate thought is that we can rescue the general principle from such a counterexample by restricting it to contents that are not indexical in character since it seems to be precisely indexical character that gives rise to a priori existential knowledge of concrete entities in all cases where counterexamples loom – not only 'I exist', but also 'This is now', 'This is here', etc. However, the general and deeper (Fregean) moral that might be drawn, and a moral that is more helpful to GR, is that epistemological status (a posteriori or a priori) does not supervene on facts about reference. It seems that epistemological status does not supervene even on the identities of referents – thus, pairs of identity statements such as:

(5) Hesperus is Hesperus.
(6) Hesperus is Phosphorus.

If so then, a fortiori, epistemological status does not supervene on the metaphysical character (abstract, concrete) of referents. A fallback position is, of course, available in the form of the attenuated principle that epistemological status (a priori, a posteriori) supervenes on metaphysical status when the knowledge claim is explicitly existential in content and non-indexical in character. I have no counterexample to offer to that principle, but there is no argument in its favour on the table either and putative knowledge of GRO has survived the original objection.

The second thought is that the contingent existence of (other) worlds is an obstacle to a priori knowledge of their existence. In this case, the defence of the a prioricity of knowledge of GRO does not require scrutiny of the underlying principle since the appropriate strategy is to deny that the relevant existential claims are contingent. Indeed, the alternative that is offered by Lewis (1986a: 110) to Skyrms' proposed criterion of demarcation is that it is precisely contingency of subject matter and not concreteness that requires that our knowledge be a posteriori, and he subsequently claims that the subject matter of GRO is non-contingent.[16] It does not matter, for present purposes, that Lewis's criterion of demarcation is vulnerable to putative cases of a priori contingency.[17] If there are such cases, then there is, as yet, no feature of subject matter that invariably determines related knowledge as a posteriori, and that is a result that aids resistance to the charge that GRO knowledge could only be a posteriori. If there are no cases of a priori contingency, or no relevant cases then, I assume, Lewis's criterion of demarcation stands by default. But it remains, then, to show that the GRO facts are, indeed, non-contingent facts. In that respect, the key insight is that modal modifications of the existential claims of GRO are modal modifications of unrestricted existential claims which, as such, merit extraordinary interpretation. In general, the subject matter of a claim is non-contingent when its quantificational content is taken to be unrestricted. In particular, the subject matter of GRO is non-contingent. For example, by the extraordinary interpretation proposed in Chapter 4, it is not a contingent truth that there are many worlds and here, I presume, we may infer contingency of fact from contingency of truth. On this approach, the 'subject matter' of a claim is a matter of semantic category rather than a matter of ontological category. When we speak of donkeys or worlds, what matters for the non-contingency of subject matter is not the kind of thing of which we speak, but whether in speaking we quantify unrestrictedly over all that there is.[18] Again, we find that the epistemological status of a claim does not supervene simply on the kind of entity, or even on the identity of the entities, that the claim is about. But more importantly, the objection to a prioricity has been met directly. Even if contingency of subject matter is an obstacle to a priori knowledge, GR is able to make the case that GRO does not fall foul of that condition.

The last of the three potential obstacles to a prioricity is that the existential claims of GRO are not analytic. This obstacle is arguably the least substantial since the analyticity of existential claims is, perhaps, the most widely rejected aspect of Fregean Platonist doctrine. Nonetheless, let us go with the Fregean Platonist thought here and see how it bears on the case of GRO.

Fregean Platonism is epistemologically logicist. It accounts for our knowledge of arithmetical truth as knowledge of the Peano axioms which is obtained by deriving (in second-order logic) those axioms from Hume's Principle:

(HP)   The number of F's = The number of G's iff
       There is a 1–1 correspondence between F's and G's.

Since (HP) is stipulated as an implicit definition of '(natural) number', the Peano axioms, and the further existential assertions about number that they entail, are held to be analytic on the grounds that they are obtained from logic and one primary definitional principle.[19] The appeal to the analyticity of the existential assertions of arithmetic is motivated by a desire to substantiate the claim that our knowledge of these existential claims is a priori. Unsubstantiated claims of a priori knowledge are bound to attract suspicion since the characterization of a prioricity is, here and elsewhere, essentially negative: it is knowledge that does not require causal interaction between knower and fact; it is knowledge that can be attained without (certain kinds of) experience. But what we legitimately expect in epistemology is an account of the means by which knowledge of a given subject matter *can* be acquired – not just an unsubstantiated assertion to the effect that there are certain means by which such knowledge need not be acquired. The account of arithmetical knowledge as knowledge of analytic truth, then, is an attempt to substantiate and improve upon an unqualified claim on a prioricity. It presents a positive account of arithmetical knowledge, one that is consistent with its a priori status, in terms of kinds of knowledge that we are supposed to have already – namely, knowledge of meaning. Moreover, its proponents take this account to acquire some credibility from the weakness of rival accounts of the epistemology of arithmetic. Swiftly, if the claim of analyticity is eschewed the choice seems to be between a kind of neo-Kantian intuitionism, associated with Godel (1947), and the holistic account associated with Quine (1957) and Putnam (1971). In the former case, the worry is that no substantiation has been achieved; we simply have the assertion that there is some pseudo-perceptual intellectual faculty (intuition) that does the job of cognizing arithmetical facts. In the latter case, the worry is that by seeking confirmation of arithmetic through confirmation of the total theory of which it is a part, we ignore or discard precisely those features of the arithmetical case that seem distinctive of it – namely, that arithmetic is non-empirical – and obliterate the distinction between a priori and a posteriori in the process. On this basis, we can put the following challenge to GR. If we are to have a substantive account of how we do know the existential claims of GRO, it seems that there are three prima facie options: some analogue of Kant–Godel intuitionism; some analogue of Quine–Putnam holism; or analyticity. Given the failings of the first two options, it then seems that a substantive account of our a priori knowledge of the truths of GRO must proceed through a claim of analyticity or not at all. So how should GR respond?

First, GR might consider making the case that GRO is analytic in some substantial sense that is comparable to the sense in which Hume's Principle is analytic. This may seem a grossly implausible prospect unless we pay careful attention to what the claim of analyticity in the arithmetical case amounts to. The neo-Fregeans concede that Hume's Principle is not analytic in either Frege's official sense or Kant's – rather the thought is that the principle is analytic in virtue of being determinative of the concept (natural number) that it serves to explain (Hale and Wright 2001: 14). When the claim is so

GR: epistemology

put, it is a natural thought that the body of GR theory which consists in the conjunction of GRO and the relevant postulates that deal with the concept of possibility equally determine the concept of possibility. So a defence of the analyticity of GRO is not immediately out of the question. However, for the sake of argument, let us assume that it is.

Second, GR will not concede that she is out of viable options once the analyticity of GRO has been ruled out. In seeking to account positively and substantially for a priori knowledge of GRO, the analogues of Kant–Godel intuitionism – suggestions that we cognize the existence of other worlds by way of quasi-perceptual faculties or magical instruments – are extremely unattractive.[20] However, as we have seen, the option that Lewis prefers is one which is (explicitly) analogous to the Quine–Putnam option in the mathematical case. Moreover, pursuit of that option in the case of GRO does not appear to be problematic in the ways that it has been thought problematic in the case of mathematics.[21] The 'total' theory that GR offers is not conceived as a theory of all that is actual, it is conceived as a theory of unrestrictedly all that there is; it is not an empirical theory that has contingent subject matter, it is a theory that has non-contingent subject matter; it is not an empirical theory that is answerable to a posteriori information about how the actual part of everything is.[22] So in the case of GRO, appeal to what is, broadly, inference to the best explanation of the explananda (let us not say 'the data') can substantiate the claim to a prioricity and can do so, because of the nature of the explananda, without compromising what is, arguably, the distinctive non-empirical features of our modal knowledge.

There is one final potential obstacle to a prioricity of knowledge of GRO that ought to be considered. McGinn (1981) argues thus: (a) our a priori modal knowledge is conceptual knowledge; (b) the concepts of which we have knowledge are actually existing entities; so (c) our a priori modal knowledge could not be knowledge of non-actual entities. This argument raises many questions but the swiftest route to rebuttal is to follow Yagisawa (1988) in observing that the premise (b) begs the question against GR since GR identifies concepts as non-actual entities, namely transworld sets of individuals (or appropriate refinements thereof). So for GR there is no gap between the concepts and the realm of reality that we come to know by way of our conceptual knowledge.

(9.4) SCEPTICISM ABOUT EPISTEMOLOGICAL OBJECTIONS TO GR

Above I have considered only one kind of epistemological objection to GR, focusing on general issues concerning utilitarian arguments for ontological theses and claims on a prioricity. It is to be acknowledged that there are many other issues that one might raise concerning our knowledge of GRO and our modal knowledge as GR construes it. I have raised some of these in passing and Lewis (1986a: 113–15) raises others. My justification for having dealt so briefly with the epistemological issue that I identified as central and for not discussing the others at all is that there are two very strong general considerations which in conjunction indicate very strongly that epistemological considerations are very unlikely to put GR at a disadvantage to AR.

First, modal epistemology is a radically underdeveloped region of analytic philosophy. I suspect that the following cluster of theses would attract broad support among those who think that we have non-trivial and absolute modal knowledge.[23]

There is no obvious and canonical or salient faculty of modal knowledge or means of forming modal beliefs – nothing strictly analogous to sensory perception in everyday empirical matters or to proof in mathematics. We arrive at our modal opinions by various means that include, centrally, both exercises of the imagination and a priori procedures. The a priori procedures include both non-inferential recognition of certain modal truths and reasoning non-inductively to particular modal conclusions from more general modal principles. Neither the use of imagination nor of a priori procedures are infallible means of acquiring modal knowledge. In particular, imagination is a very weak guide to modal truth since it appears to be the case that some impossibilities are – in some sense – imaginable, and that some possibilities are not imaginable. There are refinements or idealizations of our imaginative capacities that might be invoked so that the exercise of these capacities matches more closely what we take to be the modal truth. However, even if some refined or idealized sort of conceivability proves a reasonably reliable guide to possibility, our (still) modal knowledge of what can or cannot be conceived (by us?) threatens, in various ways, to remain an issue. In sum, there is no very settled or plausible conception of how modal knowledge is required for which conceptions of the metaphysics of modality can be held to account.[24]

GR: epistemology

Second, it is a striking fact about the literature on possible worlds that while GR has been held to account over the epistemology of modality and of other worlds this has rarely been the case with respect to AR.[25] Yet just about every consideration about the ontology of GR that prompts epistemological suspicion is a feature of one or other species of AR (see Chapter 14 below). AR interpretation of modal discourse cannot offer a face-value semantics for modal sentences that motivates us to grasp the epistemological horn of Benacerraf's dilemma. AR worlds (states of affairs, sets, properties) are not entities that would ordinarily be supposed to stand in causal relations to us – especially so when we are dealing with unrealized entities such as non-obtaining states of affairs or uninstantiated properties. But if AR is to defend the a prioricity of our knowledge of other worlds, note that AR worlds are sometimes construed as contingent existents (as in combinatorial realism) and the truth about the existence and variety of AR worlds is not, and does not purport to be, analytic. As far as I am aware, there are no substantial accounts of AR epistemology and no arguments that purport to show that AR is in a superior epistemological position to GR.

In light of the considerations presented in this chapter, two conclusions suggest themselves. The first conclusion is that the best reason that we have, as yet, for thinking that GR ought to be rejected on epistemological grounds is both quite general and radical – namely, that GR relies on a priori knowledge and that a priori knowledge is indefensible. The second conclusion is that GR stands at no demonstrated epistemological disadvantage to AR. However, it is appropriate to register the caveat that the background from which these conclusions emerge is one in which the epistemology of GR, the epistemology of AR and modal epistemology in general are all notably underdeveloped.[26]

Part III

Actualist realism

CHAPTER 10

Actualist realism: exposition

If there has been an orthodoxy in modal philosophy over the last thirty years or so it has been actualist realism – (AR) – about possible worlds.[1] AR is the conjunction of the theses:

(AR1) There exists a plurality of possible worlds.
(AR2) Each possible world actually exists (i.e. for each possible world, there actually exists some entity to which that world is identical).

There are several other theses which, although strictly independent of the conjunction (AR1) & (AR2), are typically held by AR. Thus, I shall assume, AR holds the following:

(AR3) Ontological Actualism: unrestrictedly everything that exists actually exists.[2]
(AR4) The Necessity of Ontological Actualism: whatever entities had existed would, thereby, have been actual.
(AR5) The Existence of One Distinguished Actualized World: among the many possible worlds that actually exist, one possible world is distinguished from the others by being (absolutely) actualized.

The primary motivation for preferring an AR interpretation of PW over a GR interpretation is the desire to lay claim to at least some of the benefits that are associated with straightforward, realistic quantification over possible worlds – benefits of the kind claimed by GR – on the basis of ontological commitments that are more acceptable than those of GR. In Lewis's dialectical terms, AR seeks to offer better value than GR by reducing the (ontological and other) costs that attach to the use of PW. AR will rate her ontological costs lower than those of GR on the grounds that her favoured actualist ontology of possible worlds is philosophically more acceptable than that proposed by GR – or perhaps even because AR ontology is (absolutely) acceptable and that of GR is not. Moreover, AR will typically commend her ontology as conservative by proposing to identify the possible worlds among entities that we are predisposed to recognize, either by our common-sense ways of thinking and talking or by philosophical needs aside from the need to provide a theory of modality. In all, by excluding non-actual things, the ontology of AR purports to be more 'safe and sane' than that of GR (Lewis 1986a: Chapter 3).

On a generic AR interpretation of PW, contested sentences such as:

(1*)   There is a possible world at which there are blue swans

are truth-apt; some such sentences are true and feature existential quantification (over possible worlds) in position of widest scope. Thus ensues the commitment to a plurality of possible worlds that puts the realism into AR. The general form of AR truth-condition for a de dicto modal claim, translated in neutral PW terms as (1*), is:

(A1*) $\exists x[Vx \ \& \ At \ x, \exists y[By \ \& \ Sy]]$.

Here I use 'Vx' to emphasize the presence of a world-concept that differs from that invoked by GR and 'At x' is an operator on the sentential formula within its scope. In a standard de re case – e.g.:

(2)   Humphrey might have been elected

the general form of AR truth-condition is homogeneous with the de dicto case. Thus:

(A2*) $\exists x[Vx \ \& \ At \ x, Eh]$

– there is a world at which Humphrey is elected.

It is crucial to emphasize that the generic AR representation operator 'At x' is to be understood, in general, as a non-factive operator. This point is crucial to the distinction between realism about possible worlds and realism about possible individuals. That distinction, in turn, is crucial since AR is committed to the former, but not the latter. Just as AR identifies 'the non-actual worlds' with actually existing entities, she may – or may not – pursue the option of identifying 'the non-actual individuals' with actually existing entities. In any event, there are many explanatory contexts in which AR will assert constructions of the form:

(A3*) $\exists x[Vx \;\&\; At\; x, \exists y[\varphi y]]$

(as in (A1*) above) thus committing her to the existence of a certain kind of world, but she will not assert the unqualified existential claim:

(A4*) $\exists y(\varphi y)$

(e.g. there are blue swans). It is necessary to be vigilant in this matter since informal AR explanations often suggest a commitment to possible individuals – e.g., to cite a salient case, when talk of transworld identity of individuals is afoot. The point cuts two ways. Sometimes the non-factive 'At x' operator has to be made explicit in order to dispel unwanted ontological commitment. Sometimes making the 'At x' operator explicit dispels the impression that AR can deliver an application that requires commitment to (non-actual) possible individuals.[3]

Generic AR interpretation of PW differs from GR interpretation in three main ways. First, with respect to quantification, AR takes unrestricted quantifiers to range over all and only the actual (actually existing) entities – in particular, AR interpretation is supposed to avoid commitment to the existence of individuals that are non-actual. Second, the worlds over which AR purports to quantify in stating the truth-conditions of typical modal claims are not maximal sums of spatiotemporally related individuals. Third, the AR interpretation of modal claims is homogeneous over the de dicto and de re cases: truth-conditions for the latter do not systematically invoke a kind of element (cf. counterpart relations) that is absent from the former. Each of the above is false with respect to GR.

In contrast with GR, various significantly different species of AR have evolved. The crucial issues over which species of AR differ from one another are these:

(i)   Primitives: the concepts and kinds of entity taken as primitive.
(ii) World-constitution: the kind of thing that a possible world is and how the worlds are constituted, if at all, by worldmaking elements.

Actualist realism

(iii) Representation: how possible worlds represent that such-and-such is the case 'at' them.
(iv) Applications: exactly which kinds of conceptual, ontological and semantic applications the intended interpretation of PW is supposed to serve.

Given that the species of AR may differ from one another in each, or even all, of these respects, it would be reckless to presume that there is little or nothing to choose between the species. It would be no less reckless to presume that the species of AR are (in some important sense) isomorphic to one another, or that if 'possible world' expresses a functional role, it is a role that can be discharged equally well by various kinds of actualia. If we do form any such view, it should be as a result of careful and proper consideration of how each of the species of AR stands on each of the crucial issues and on the various objections that AR elicits. Moreover, since GR takes a clear position on all of the issues that have been identified, proper and fair comparison between GR and AR requires that we compare GR with the species of AR. The species of AR are not only conceived as taking a position on each of the issues individually but as taking a coherent position across the range of issues. If we think of the AR genre in terms of a hybrid of typical positions, we risk forming the picture of either an unattainable ideal – a superficially attractive, but ultimately incoherent doctrine cobbled together from individually successful aspects of the species – or a hopeless caricature – a thoroughly unattractive doctrine vitiated by the conjunction of the failures that attach to different species of AR. For these reasons a proper exposition of AR must identify, and focus directly on, the species.

In the present chapter I will identify four salient species of AR: Plantingan realism (PR); combinatorial realism (CR); nature realism (NR); and book realism (BR). This classification and preliminary exposition will proceed primarily on the issue of world-constitution but also with firm indications on the issues of primitives and representation.[4] I will present exemplary versions of each of the species of AR, and indicate how variation from the exemplar may occur within each. In Chapters 11–13 I will discuss the applications afforded by the species of AR, and in Chapters 14–17 I will discuss various objections that have been leveled at AR in relation to each of the main species. Before proceeding with exposition, some comments and caveats are in order.

First, I have sometimes had to elaborate – with charitable intentions – on ideas that are at best implicit in the primary sources in order to equip a species of AR with the resources required to afford a clear position on each of the crucial issues. This proves necessary since many presentations of AR that figure in the primary literature are only partial. Partial representations of AR are common because presentations are often geared to some specific application of PW, and so only deal with issues relevant to that kind of application, or – less defensibly – because it is simply taken for granted that what is distinctive or novel in a presentation can be accommodated within some (or any) fully developed version of AR. However, such partial presentations do not meet the needs of the more comprehensive comparative project that is attempted here and so a little creativity in exposition is sometimes required. Second, for the latter reason, among others, policy on attribution and acknowledgment should be clarified. While I have sought to acknowledge the philosophers who have contributed to the development or defence of each species of AR, I do not suggest that any is committed to the details of the standard versions that I present. I take this opportunity to acknowledge those philosophers who have been influential advocates or expositors of the AR genre without displaying a firm or settled allegiance to any one of the species to the exclusion of the others.[5] Third, and finally, while I accept that certain authors' particular presentations of AR might have been located within one species rather than another, I have sought to simplify the picture by not associating any author with more than one species.

The hope is that an appropriately comprehensive, fair and useful systematization of the important philosophical issues will be achieved even if it is not the case that every (partial) presentation of AR is addressed directly.

(10.1) PLANTINGAN REALISM (PR)

According to Plantingan realism (PR), possible worlds are states of affairs that are both possible and maximal. In addition to Plantinga (1969, 1970, 1973, 1974, 1976, 1985a, 1985b and 1987), van Inwagen (1980, 1985, 1986) is also at least sympathetic to the PR development of AR.[6]

The salient and basic theoretical terms of PR are: *state of affairs*; *obtaining* (for states of affairs); *property*; *instantiation* (of properties); and (broadly logical) *possibility*.[7] The basic theoretical terms of PR are put to work in the following prominent explanations.

The *possible worlds* are all and only those states of affairs that are both possible and maximal. Maximality for states of affairs is defined in terms of inclusion and preclusion, and then ultimately in terms of possibility and obtaining. For any states of affairs S, S*: S is *maximal* iff for every S*, S includes S* or S precludes S*; S *includes* S* iff it is not possible that (S obtains and S* does not obtain); S *precludes* S* iff it is not possible that (S obtains and S* obtains). The *actualized world* is the (unique) possible world that obtains. For any worlds w, v, for any individual x, for any property F: *at w, v is actualized* iff $w = v$;[8] *at w, an individual x exists* iff necessarily (if w obtains then x exists (*simpliciter*)) – i.e. it is not possible that (w obtains and (it is not the case that x exists (*simpliciter*))); *F is an essence of x* iff: (i) F is an essential property of x and (ii) there is no w such that at w, there exists a y such that $y \neq x$ and y instantiates F; *F is an essential property of x* iff, at every w, if x exists at w then x instantiates F at w; *at w, x instantiates F* iff it is not possible that (w obtains and (it is not the case that x instantiates F (*simpliciter*))).

Among the notable consequences of these analyses and further stipulations is that all of the 'intensional' entities are necessary existents: at every possible world, every state of affairs (including every possible world and every impossible world) exists and every property exists. However, at each possible world only one possible world obtains, not all states of affairs obtain and not all properties are instantiated; impossible states of affairs (including impossible worlds) obtain at no possible worlds and contingent states of affairs obtain at some but not all possible worlds. Individual essences (qua properties) are necessary existents, existing at all worlds; individuals are, typically, contingent existents, existing at some but not at all worlds.

(10.2) COMBINATORIAL REALISM (CR)

According to combinatorial realism (CR), possible worlds are certain constructs out of actually existing individuals and actually instantiated properties – alternatively, constructs out of obtaining simple states of affairs, obtaining particular situations or atomic facts.[9]

In identifying possible worlds with such constructs, CR is to be distinguished from other theories of modality that invoke the constructs in question, or the combinatorial principles that generate them, for other purposes. First, a version of realism about possible worlds may identify the worlds as something other than world-combinations but deploy combinatorial principles in an account of the epistemology of modality, or as comprehension principles that give us some grip on the number or variety of possible worlds that there are – thus Lewis (1983a: 90, 1986a: 113). Second, antirealists about possible worlds may deploy combinatorial principles in their account of the constitution of entities that they distinguish from possible worlds but which are supposed to play some of the same theoretical roles – thus the combinatorial account of situations in Barwise and Perry (1983). Third, there are antirealists about possible worlds who intend to share with CR the concept of a possible world as a certain kind of construct but without commitment to the existence of a plurality of such possible worlds – thus Skyrms (1981), Armstrong (1989), and Hiipakka, Keinanen and Korhonen (1999).[10] Fourth, Bacon (1995) identifies possible worlds with combinatorially generated sets of tropes, and since Baconian tropes are clearly akin to what would normally be conceived as states of affairs rather than as properties, there are obvious affinities between Bacon's realism and CR as presented here. However, Bacon eschews AR in favour of a Meinongian realism about possible worlds and their constituents, in that some Baconian tropes ('alien tropes') do not exist. What is distinctive of CR – as presented, for example, in Quine (1969), Cresswell (1972) and Bigelow (1988b) – is that possible worlds are identified with constructs out of actual existents and the existence of many such worlds is asserted. We will focus on the following exemplary version of CR.

The salient, basic theoretical terms of CR are *property* (including the case of relations); *instantiation* (of properties by individuals); and *conjunction* (as typical of operations that form properties out of properties). The *simple individuals* are those that lack proper parts; the *simple properties* are those that do not have other properties as constituents; *constitution* (for properties) is explained in terms of the property-forming operations. According to CR, there exist (actually or *simpliciter*) simple individuals (a, b, c ...) and the (instantiated) simple n-adic properties and relations ($P^1, Q^1 \ldots P^2, Q^2 \ldots P^n, Q^n \ldots$).[11] Further key terms of CR are explicated as follows. The simple individuals and properties are collected in the *combinatorial base set B*:

(B) $B = \{P^1, Q^1 \ldots P^2, Q^2 \ldots P^i, Q^i \ldots, a, b, c \ldots\}.$

The *combinatorial range set R*, is the set of all and only the (n + 1)-membered sequences from B consisting in any n-adic property followed by n distinct individuals – thus:

Actualist realism

(R) $R = \{<P^1, a>, <P^1, b>, <Q^1, a>, <Q^1, b> \ldots <P^2, a, b>,$
$<P^2, b, a>, <P^2, a, c>, <P^2, c, a>, \ldots <Q^1, a, b>, <Q^2, b,$
$a>, \ldots <P^i, a, b, c \ldots, a_j> \ldots \}.$[12]

Simple states of affairs are all and only the members of R; the *possible worlds* are all and only the subsets of R; *the actualized world* is the subset of R whose members are all and only those simple states of affairs that obtain; *a state of affairs obtains* iff the relevant sequence of individuals instantiates the relevant property.[13] For any possible worlds w, v: *at w, v is actualized* iff v = w; *at w, a simple individual x exists* iff x is a member of a sequence (simple state of affairs) that is a member of w; *at w, a simple property F exists (or is instantiated)* iff F is a member of a sequence (simple state of affairs) that is a member of w; *at w, a simple state of affairs, s, obtains* iff s is a member of w; *at w, a simple state of affairs, s, exists* iff s is a member of the combinatorial range set R_w that is formed when the combinatorial base set is constructed from w; *at w, a possible world v exists* iff v is a subset of the combinatorial range set R_w that is formed from the simple states of affairs that belong to w. Given the standard account of contingent existence as existence at some but not all possible worlds, it follows then from the above definitions (and standard set-theoretic assumptions) that each simple individual, each simple property, each simple states of affairs and each possible world is a contingent existent.[14,15]

In subsequent discussion I will take the foregoing version of CR as exemplary. However, as with other species of AR, a version of CR may differ importantly from the exemplary version in many ways. Indeed, in the case of CR, we ought to advertise an alternative version of the doctrine in which states of affairs are thing-like (see n.6 above) and play a more fundamental role. In this alternative version of CR: (i) states of affairs are a *sui generis* kind (not sets or individuals); (ii) states of affairs are ontologically primitive with individuals and properties being 'abstracted' from them; (iii) possible worlds are conjunctions of simple states of affairs (where conjunction for states of affairs is a constitution relation that is not set-theoretic or mereological). Thus in the case of CR we recognize an exemplary version and an alternative version of the doctrine. However, I will suggest in due course (at (11.2)) that the alternative version does not sustain a viable form of actualist realism about possible worlds.[16]

Among the important questions that any fully developed version of CR ought to address, but which will not figure significantly in

AR: exposition

what follows, are these. Can a viable construction of possible worlds proceed in the absence of the assumption that there are simple (partless) individuals? Can we characterize the simples informatively – relatedly, can we know what the simples are and, if so, how? Which complex first-order states of affairs (e.g. conjunctive, negative, disjunctive, etc.) ought to be recognized as generable from simple states of affairs? To what extent, and under what constraints, may or ought we admit higher-order properties and states of affairs – in particular, totality states of affairs? Should the elements of the combinatorial base set be construed as necessary existents rather than contingent existents? May or ought we include an empty world among the possible worlds?[17]

(10.3) NATURE REALISM (NR)

According to nature realism (NR) possible worlds are world-natures, world-properties, or ways that the world might have been – thus Stalnaker (1976, 1984), Forrest (1986a, 1986b) and Bigelow and Pargetter (1990).[18] In advance of presenting an exemplary version of NR, I want to emphasize that this is the species of AR that is most lacking in detailed development and where, accordingly, most gaps have to be filled.

The salient and basic theoretical terms of NR are *property* (including the case of relations); *instantiation* (of properties by individuals); *conjunction* (or some such terms for operations that form properties of a given order out of properties of the same order) and *completion* (or some such terms for operations that form higher-order properties out of lower-order properties).[19] The *simple properties* are those that do not have other properties as constituents; *constitution* (of properties by properties) is explained in terms of the property-forming operations. The explanations of various non-basic terms proceeds through the notion of a world-nature.

World-natures are a special kind of structural property. The standard example of a structural property is being a methane molecule: this is the property of being exhausted by non-overlapping individual parts a, b, c, d and e such that a is a hydrogen atom and b is a hydrogen atom and c is a hydrogen atom and d is a hydrogen atom and e is a carbon atom and a is bonded to e and b is bonded to e and c is bonded to e and d is bonded to e. World-natures are intended to be special among structural properties by being complete properties of maximal individuals. To say that an individual is maximal is to say that it has all individuals as parts. To say that a property is complete is to say that it is a conjunction that exhausts the properties of a thing – it is the property of having A & B & . . . no other properties.[20] More specifically, a *world-nature* is a structural property of the following type: y is a maximal individual & y is exhausted by simple individual parts $x_1, x_2, \ldots x_n$ & every n-tuple out of its parts $x_1, x_2, \ldots x_n$ instantiates one complete conjunction out of the simple n-adic properties and relations $P_1, P_2, \ldots P_m$.[21]

The *possible worlds* are all and only the world-natures. The *actualized world* is the (unique) world-nature that is instantiated (by the actually existing maximal individual). For any possible worlds w, v: *at w, v is actualized* iff v = w; *at w, an individual x exists* iff the property of having x as a part is a constituent of w. Possible worlds and properties are conceived as necessary existents; each exists at every world since any exists at a world iff it exists *simpliciter*. One notable respect in which a version of NR might differ from the foregoing is by characterizing world-natures in such a way that requires their (potential) instantiators to be Lewisian worlds of spatiotemporally related individuals rather than (more neutrally) maximal individuals.[22]

The most fundamental areas in which one might expect a version of NR to be more fully developed are these. First, there is the question of whether there is anything further to be said – by way of conceptual analysis or ontological identification – about properties, e.g. ought properties, and world-natures in particular, to be construed as tropes, universals, sets or whatever.[23] Second, one might expect a more detailed account of the property-forming operations that figure crucially in the formation of world-natures out of simple properties.[24]

(10.4) BOOK REALISM (BR)

According to book realism (BR) possible worlds are world-books – certain kinds of maximal or complete stories, the elements of which are structured propositions or interpreted sentences of a specified (worldmaking) 'language'.

Philosophers have developed conceptions of world-books for purposes other than identifying them as possible worlds. Thus Hintikka (1962, 1969), Plantinga (1974: Chapter 4) and Roper (1982). As in the case of CR, one motivation for doing so is to get an epistemic grip on the number and variety of possible worlds (*qua* individuals, states of affairs or whatever), or of what is represented by them, by associating the worlds with books that describe them.

AR: exposition

Another such motivation is antirealistic, that is to have world-books do certain theoretical work and thereby avoid commitment to the existence of the possible worlds that they are apt to represent. Then, however, we have the proponents of BR, those who do identify possible worlds with world-books specified in one way or another – thus, notably, Carnap (1947) (state-descriptions), Jeffrey (1965) (complete consistent novels) and Adams (1974) (maximal consistent sets of propositions). I will draw eclectically on these sources to present an exemplary version of BR that is intended to be neutral as to which actual entities are the elements – the words – of the worldmaking language.

According to BR, a possible world is a maximal consistent set of L-sentences (for some 'worldmaking' language L). The lexicon of L consists in elements, all of which actually exist, and these generate sentences of L, all of which actually exist. The lexicon of L consists in a set of names, a set of monadic, dyadic . . . n-adic predicates, a set of variables, and items expressing the semantic operations of sentential negation, sentential conjunction and (in conjunction with the variables) existential quantification respectively. The atomic sentences of L are all and only the sequences of L-symbols consisting in an n-adic predicate followed by exactly n names. It is assumed that a broader set of (closed) sentences of L can subsequently be characterized in relation to the atomic sentences and the recursive elements of the lexicon (the conjunction symbol, the quantifiers, etc.) in line with a standard syntax for first-order predicate logic. Below, relativization of sentences to L is taken as read.

The salient and basic theoretical terms of BR are the lexical concepts of *name*; *predicate*; *sentence*, etc.; *consistency* (for sets of sentences); and *true simpliciter* (for sentences).[25] The further crucial terms of BR are explicated as follows.

The *possible worlds* are all and only the maximal consistent sets of sentences. A set of sentences, S, is *maximal* iff for every atomic sentence, p, S has as a member either p or its negation; a set of sentences, S, *entails* a sentence p iff the conjunction of the members of S ∪ {~p} is inconsistent (not consistent). For any possible worlds, w,v: w, is *actualized* (*simpliciter*) iff all and only the true sentences are entailed by w; at w, any possible world v is actualized iff w is equivalent to v (i.e. w entails v and v entails w); *at w, there exists an individual a* iff w entails that ∃y[y = a]. BR allows that individuals are contingent existents in the, presumed non-empty, case where an appropriate existential sentence, ∃y[y = a], is entailed by some, but not all, possible worlds. We leave open the question of whether possible worlds, properties, etc. are necessary or contingent existents, although actualization (instantiation) for these is contingent – in the latter case, a matter of a certain type of atomic sentence being entailed by some worlds but not others.

The notable or significant ways in which a version of BR might differ from, or further specify, the foregoing are as follows. First, there are several factors that will determine the expressive power of the worldmaking language and which have gone unspecified above: whether the lexicon of L is finite in extent; whether the basic lexical items of L are finite in structure – infinitary predicates, infinitary connectives – and whether in any such case infinity is constrained to countability; whether there are names for every individual and predicates for every actually instantiated property. These are among the factors that bear on the question whether the worldmaking language resembles (to any extent) an actual natural language. For future reference we note the eminent case of a Lagadonian language L* in which, it is stipulated, every individual is a name of itself; every (actually instantiated) property refers to itself; and we have infinitary sentential connectives generating sentences of infinite length.[26] Second, while it is natural to regard the atomic sentences of the worldmaking language as having sub-sentential structure one might consider a worldmaking language in which the atomic sentences were unstructured – in other words the worldmaking language might have the syntactic complexity associated with propositional logic rather than that associated with predicate logic.[27] Third, the exemplary version of BR allows for implicit representation as well as explicit representation, since what a possible world, w, represents (e.g. an individual existing at a world) is characterized in terms of which L-sentences are entailed by w rather than in terms of exactly which sentences are members of w.[28,29] Fourth, the possible worlds have been identified as (certain) sets of sentences, but one might take them to be complexes of these sentences, e.g. (infinitary) conjunctions of atomic sentences. Fifth, if the set of sentences that are entailed by a world w are themselves taken to form a set (the consequence set of w) we can analyse truth at w, for any sentence, as set-membership.

This concludes the exposition of the four species of AR on which subsequent discussion will be based.[30]

CHAPTER 11

Actualist realism: conceptual applications

The primary question of conceptual application for the species of AR is whether any affords a thoroughly non-modal analysis of the family of modal (and intensional) concepts.[1,2] Recall (from Chapter 7) the general constraints on an interpretation of PW in this respect. Focusing on the central and neutral possibility principle:

(P) It is possible that A iff there is a world at which A

we require for an adequate and non-modal analysis of the family of modal concepts that the set of worlds described in the ontological component of the theory should be accurate, and that the characterization of the set of worlds should involve no explicit or implicit appeal to any unanalysed modal concept. Accuracy requires that the set of worlds over which we quantify on the right-side of (P) should be complete (all possibilities are represented across the worlds collectively) and consistent (only possibilities are represented by the worlds individually). In Chapter 17, I will deal with AR difficulties over completeness. But in this chapter I will consider only whether consistency can be achieved by AR without appeal to any unanalysed modal concept. If it cannot, then all AR analyses that quantify over the 'possible worlds' either rely on unanalysed modal concepts or they are inaccurate.

The requirement of consistency looms large for AR since each of its species appears to afford the ontological resources for generating impossible worlds – that is, worlds that are of the same broad kind as those that represent only possibilities but which represent impossibilities in just whatever way they are supposed to represent possibilities. Assume that it is (absolutely) impossible that any particle has both positive and negative charge. Then impossible worlds loom in the following forms: (PR) maximal states of affairs that include *a*

Actualist realism

having positive charge and a having negative charge; (CR) sets of simple states of affairs that have the subset {<N,a>, <P,a>}; (NR) world-natures that have such constituents as having an individual part that has the conjunctive property of being positively charged and being negatively charged; (BR) maximal sets of atomic L-sentences that have both 'Na' and 'Pa' as members. Whether the admission of such impossible worlds is desirable for other reasons, and in other contexts, is presently irrelevant.[3] The present point is that, on pain of inaccuracy, the right-side of (P) should involve no quantification over such things. If the right-side of (P) is made true by a world at which there is something that is both positively and negatively charged, then (P) is false since its left-side (in that instance) is the false claim that it is possible that there is something that is both positively and negatively charged. The subsequent question is whether the species of AR can, without appealing to unanalysed modal concepts, exclude impossible worlds, in the sense of restricting quantification on the right-side of (P) so that it does not range over such things. I will deal swiftly with the case of PR before considering the other species in the detail that they demand.

In PR, the concept of a possible world is analysed as that of a state of affairs that is maximal and possible, with 'possible' accepted as expressing an unanalysable modal concept. Consequently, PR does not purport to interpret PW in a way that affords a non-modal analysis of the family of modal concepts. Naturally, PR will be more at ease with this position for taking the view that no alternative interpretation offers (successful) non-modal analyses either, thus Plantinga (1987). It remains to be seen, for the remaining species of AR, whether this is so given that – like GR and unlike PR – none has been formulated so as to utilize a key theoretical term that is overtly and obviously modal.

(11.1) BR AND PRIMITIVE MODAL CONCEPTS

Lewis (1986a: 150–7) argues that BR must admit primitive modal concepts on pain of inaccuracy. BR has it that a world is a maximal *consistent* set of sentences and a world represents – for example – that A, by *entailing* that A. Each of the terms, 'consistency' and 'entailment', has a legitimate and popular modal definition that renders them interdefinable. Focusing on 'consistency', a set of sentences is consistent just in case it is *possible* that the conjunction of its members is true, and a set of sentences S entails that P just in case the conjunction of the members of S and the negation of P is not consistent. BR may thus adopt an account of consistency (and subsequently entailment) in terms of an unanalysed modal concept, i.e. possibility. But the question is whether BR can offer a non-modal explication of consistency that will secure the accuracy of (P). The cause is abetted by the availability of two accounts of consistency that involve no immediate use of modal vocabulary. The syntactic or proof-theoretic account has it that a set of sentences, S, is consistent just in case no (finite) subset of S is such that the negation of the conjunction of its members is a theorem (assuming a given, syntactically specified set of rules of inference). The semantic or model-theoretic account has it that a sentence is consistent just in case it has a model. Let us focus in the first instance, with Lewis, on the syntactic account.

On the syntactic account of consistency, then, a maximal set of sentences, S, is a world if no (finite) subset of S is such that the negation of the conjunction of its members is a theorem. This will suffice to weed out impossible worlds in (at least some) cases where the impossibility is of a narrowly logical character. Thus consider that our worldmaking language is a standard, first-order language in which every English predicate has a synonym and we have at our disposal standard predicate logic. Then no set of sentences containing both 'Fa' and '~Fa' will be consistent, and there will be no such possible world, since L will have as a theorem:

(1) ~(Fa & ~Fa).

The problem is that, intuitively, not all absolute impossibilities are of this narrowly logical, syntactically detectable, character. Thus, consider that L has two one-place predicates 'R' and 'G' where 'R' denotes the property of being (uniformly and always) red and 'G' denotes the property of being (uniformly and always) green. Since

(2) ~(Ra & Ga)

is not a theorem of predicate logic, we will have syntactically consistent (and maximal) sets of sentences representing explicitly that a is red and a is green – sets that have as a subset {Ra, Ga} – i.e. impossible worlds.

Faced with any putative counterexample to the accuracy of (P), BR has two strategies of response. The strategy of *modal denial* is to resist the putative counterexamples to the accuracy of (P) by denying that the putative impossibility is an absolute impossibility.[4]

Actualist realism

The strategy of *axiom introduction* is to accept that the putative counterexample is a genuine counterexample to (P) and then seek to introduce non-logical axioms that will allow us to weed out the impossibilities syntactically. The strategies are complementary in that some putative counterexamples may be met by modal denial and others by axiom introduction.

Concerning modal denial, it is to be acknowledged that there are many views about the extent of the absolutely necessities (impossibilities). One who takes the extreme view that the only absolute impossibilities are the syntactically specifiable logical falsehoods will deny that axiom introduction is ever required in order to constrain syntactic consistency to match possibility. The extreme view, I suppose, is the view of a small minority of philosophers and the straightforward response to its proponent is to insist, with Lewis (1986a: 153) that she is mistaken about the modal facts. I will not attempt here to improve on that response.[5] I turn instead to the philosopher who acknowledges absolute necessities other than narrowly logical truths and who consequently adverts to axiom introduction at some stage.

Axiom introduction is intended to work by permitting the derivation as theorems of sentences that were not theorems of the set of purely logical axioms. If we add to our predicate logic resources the non-logical axiom:

(3) $\forall x[\sim(Rx \ \& \ Gx)]$

– nothing is both red and green – then we can immediately derive (2) as a theorem and no maximal set of sentences that contains both 'Fa' and 'Ga' will any longer count as consistent. The strategy generalized is to redefine possible worlds more restrictively as those sets of sentences that are maximal, (syntactically) consistent and have as members all of the appropriate non-logical axioms. But which are the appropriate non-logical axioms? It is here that appeal to modality looms.

The negation of any absolute impossibility is an absolute necessity. Consequently, the strategy of axiom introduction aims to ensure that theorem derivation is a sure-fire syntactic test for impossibility by providing axioms that suffice for the derivation of all (absolutely) necessary truths as theorems. The requirement that the theorems be the necessary truths does not in itself defeat the aim of providing a thoroughly non-modal analysis, nor does the related consideration that BR would have to have opinions about what the necessary truths are in order to implement that strategy.⁶ What BR must avoid, if her analyses are to remain appropriately non-modal, is the specification of the axioms in modal terms, e.g.:

(M) If 'p' expresses a necessary truth then 'p' is an axiom.

But Lewis argues that BR cannot do otherwise and secure accuracy.

Recall that our worldmaking language, L, contains a synonym of each English predicate so that it is rich enough to contain both micro-descriptions (e.g. in terms of fundamental particles and fundamental properties) and macro-descriptions (e.g. in terms of molecules and donkeys, their containing carbon and their talking).⁷ Now impossibility is afoot in the form of various micro–macro incompatibilities. Thus consider a maximal set of sentences including micro-descriptive sentences that conjointly describe a talking donkey but also include macro-descriptive sentences that conjointly entail that nothing is a talking donkey. If such impossibility is to be excluded by deriving appropriate theorems, then we will require conditional connecting axioms that articulate all relevant micro–macro necessities. These will be axioms of the form:

(4) If [. . . Micro . . .] then [. . . Macro . . .]

in which – for example – it is laid down that if there is something satisfying such-and-such a micro-description, then there is a talking donkey. In such cases the filler of the Micro-place – perhaps, a disjunctive description of all the fundamental arrangements that would constitute the existence of a talking donkey – would be, even if finite, very long. Also the requisite axioms will be many, if not infinitely so, depending on how we conceive the range of macro-descriptions that might figure in the filler of the Macro-place (talk about atoms, molecules, donkeys, planets . . .). Lewis does not presume that the required axioms would be infinite in both length and number, but he does claim that it is safe to say that nobody could produce the requisite axioms. So the objection is that there is not, and never will be, a theory before us that excludes impossibility by purely syntactic means. The suggested moral is that the cost of dealing accurately with micro–macro incompatibilities is to appeal to the unanalysed and modal (M). BR has available two lines of response.

First, even granting that no one will ever produce the requisite set of axioms – the 'utopian' specification of all micro–macro necessary truths – the case has not been made that the task is, in an absolute sense, incompletable. In other words, it has not been shown that the syntactic account of consistency fails in principle to deliver thoroughly non-modal analyses. The counterclaim, for what it is worth, is correct. But it does nothing to help BR escape the predicament of lacking a non-modal analysis of the modal concepts. BR lacks a theory that is completely stated and which can do the job while her rivals – in particular GR – claim to be in possession of such a theory.[8] Second, there is the more attractive thought that BR might steer a course that avoids both commitment to utopian axiomatization and appeal to primitive modality. The crucial issue here is whether the absolutely necessary truths are exhaustible by non-modally characterizable subclasses. We have, let us allow, the narrowly logical truths. It has also been suggested by Roper (1982: 51–2) – and Lewis is tolerant of the suggestion – that we can capture the subclass of arithmetical truths along the following lines:

(A) If 'p' is part of the arithmetical sub-language and 'p' is true in the standard model(s) of arithmetic, then 'p' is an axiom.

The next subclass that might naturally be identified among the absolutely necessary truths are the analytic truths. The thought that now arises is whether these might be specified generally as the analytic truths:

(B) If 'p' is analytic then 'p' is an axiom.

The question then to be faced is whether the concept of analyticity is implicitly modal. In addressing that question it is natural to consider, in the first instance, the standard account of analytic truth as truth in virtue of meaning alone. On one hand, none of the key terms that figures in this characterization is explicitly modal. On the other hand: (i) it looks a substantial task to provide adequate, non-modal (and actualist) conceptual accounts of 'meaning' and 'truth in virtue of'; and (ii) it is unconvincing simply to insist that these are non-modal conceptual primitives.[9] But what if the subclass of analytic truths could thus be handled successfully? BR would then have two options. If she is prepared to maintain that all of the necessary truths are now covered, the appeal to axiom introduction is exhausted. In the face of any further putative counterexamples, she will either resort to modal denial or argue that they are covered under the cases that have already been covered generically. If she holds that there are residual, non-analytic, necessary truths, the next step is to attempt to cover these in non-modally characterized classes. If there is to be such a further step, the problem of finding appropriate generic classifications now appears even tougher. The residual necessary truths might include the metaphysically necessary truths, but clearly the specification of those truths as such is explicitly modal. So the task would be to get at the truths in question without being forced back into the predicament of brute enumeration that loomed over the cases of micro–macro incompatibility. In the case of the metaphysical necessities, certainly, the process can be started. One might consider identifying, say, necessities of identity – either for individuals or for properties – as a significant subclass. But among the proponents of necessity of identity, it is no part of the orthodoxy that any truth expressed by an identity sentence is necessary – thus consider the standard treatment of definite descriptions in cases such as:

(5)   Blair is the Prime Minister.

So the question then is whether we can pick out – as axioms – all of the right identity statements in a non-modal way. In this regard, note immediately that it is unpromising to appeal to a specification that makes use of the concept of rigid designation, for relevant terms. For the concept of rigid designation, as standardly explicated, is implicitly modal, the explication appealing to counterfactuals about reference, or to sameness of reference across all possible worlds. Even if the case of necessities of identity can be cracked, perhaps other metaphysical necessities remain: exclusive determination of determinables; necessities of constitution; necessities of origin, etc. Clearly enough, the fewer non-modally characterizable classes that one takes to be exhaustive of the necessary truths, the more promising the generic approach to non-modal axiom specification appears. If the range of necessary truths extends only to the analytic truths the approach is not very promising; if the necessary truths range further the approach looks hopeless; and if the range of necessary truths is not circumscribable by means of non-modally specified subclasses the approach must fail.

In the circumstances outlined it is reasonable to judge that, as yet, BR has no promising way out of Lewis's dilemma. The syntactic approach to consistency fails to convince that it can, without appeal to unanalysed modal concepts, weed out all of the impossible worlds as required for the accuracy of (P).

Finally, and briefly, it remains to address the thought that the semantic account of consistency might succeed where the syntactic account has failed. The semantic or model-theoretic account has it that a sentence is consistent just in case it has a model. Such an account renders logical falsehoods such as (2) inconsistent by incorporating constraints on models that ensure, for example, that if the referent of 'a' is assigned to the extension of 'F' then the referent of 'a' is not assigned to the extension of '~F'. Models that are thus congenial to the determination of logical falsehood as inconsistency are often more fully specified as 'admissible' models. Since 'admissible' looks like an explicitly modal term, the suspicion arises that 'consistency' now emerges on the semantic account as an implicitly modal concept (Lycan and Shapiro 1986: 358). But the suspicion is not immediately well grounded. A semantic theory might be formulated by way of non-modal (set-theoretic) axioms, which are intended to capture exactly the (standardly) admissible models and thus to reflect prior modal opinion about what is and what is not admissible or logically possible. Such a theory would be, innocuously, doxastically modal, but the crucial question, so far as non-modal analysis is concerned, is whether the axioms that are intended to capture the admissible models are expressible in terms that are not explicitly or implicitly modal. So far as the inconsistency of logical falsehoods is concerned that is the case – consider, the (informal) non-modal expression above of the constraint that deprives (2) of a model. The problem arises, as on the syntactic approach, with the need to impose non-modal constraints that will exclude models for sentences that express absolute impossibilities that are not narrowly logical – e.g. models that assign extensions to predicates so as to render non-empty the intersection of the extensions of 'R' and 'G', and which also assign to 'a' an extension (referent) that is a member of that intersection. At this point, it seems clear enough that the Lewisian dialectic that emerged in the syntactic case is now apt to be recapitulated in the semantic case. The only difference now is that the strategy of axiom introduction has to be executed at the level of the semantic metalanguage rather than the object-language. But in that case Lewis's objection stands. The only alternatives to a modal specification of the axioms appear to be a specification which is incomplete or which entails the inaccuracy of (P).

(11.2) CR AND PRIMITIVE MODAL CONCEPTS

For CR the possible worlds are collections – either sets or conjunctions – of the simple states of affairs. The challenge to CR is to exclude from these collections without appeal to unanalysed modal concepts, worlds that represent absolute but non-logical impossibilities such as – we shall assume – a being red and a being green. One aspect of this challenge is to show that the appeal to simple properties is both a modally innocent and effective way of ensuring that the possible worlds are collections of compossible states of affairs. Since NR also faces that challenge, I will address it in that context. The other aspect of the challenge, that will be addressed in the present section is the 'implicit representation' problem already familiar from the discussion of BR. For CR, how do worlds that are collections of simple states of affairs represent non-simple possibilities?

One response to the problem of implicit representation is to present CR as a subcase of BR. The simple states of affairs are sentences of a worldmaking language that implicitly represent non-simple possibilities by entailing other, complex sentences of the worldmaking language. This answer is puzzling insofar as we rely on our intuitive picture of what a language, and its lexicon, consists in. However BR is formulated in a way that places no constraints on what the elements of the worldmaking language are, other than that they are of a certain syntactic category and are interpreted accordingly. Consequently, the worldmaking language may be so far removed from our actual natural languages as to be a Lagadonian language – as intimated at (10.4) – in which every actual simple individual is a name, every actual simple property is a predicate and any such element of the language denotes itself.[10] Even though the lexicon of the language may be infinitary, we can complete the finite statement of the syntax and semantics of the language by designating set-theoretic entities to be the sentential operators, quantifiers and variables of the language. The last decision that we have to make concerns the mode of 'concatenation' that forms atomic sentences out of simple lexical items. If – as in exemplary BR – atomic sentences are formed by taking sequences of n-placed predicates followed by n names, then the simple states of affairs of exemplary CR are atomic sentences of the worldmaking language. When CR is so presented as a species of BR, it becomes subject to Lewis's critique of BR with respect to implicit representation. In particular, since the worldmaking language may now be assumed to be a wholly

Actualist realism

micro-descriptive language, macro-descriptive sentences have to be introduced along with suitable connecting axioms in order to facilitate the representation of macro-possibilities by entailment. In the absence of an alternative, non-linguistic response to the problem of implicit representation, CR appears no better off than BR with respect to its capacity to secure accuracy without appeal to unanalysed modal concepts.

A different response to the problem of implicit representation suggests itself if we consider the more robust version of CR in which the simple states of affairs are *sui generis* entities and the possible worlds as conjunctions of these. The thought now is that the conjunctions of simple states of affairs constitute the non-simple states of affairs. A set of simple set-theoretic states of affairs may implicitly represent the existence of any macro-individual, but it does not constitute any such individual. However the obtaining of a conjunction of simple *sui generis* states of affairs is the kind of thing that is supposed to constitute the actual world, and – *en passant*, as it were – the existence of all of the actual individuals and actually instantiated properties. A world constituted by such states of affairs does not represent that a donkey talks by entailing any sentence but by having a talking donkey as a part. So, the thought goes, if CR takes her states of affairs to be sufficiently thing-like there is no problem of implicit representation.

The foregoing response, however, founders on the inconsistency of the following triad:

(i) There are unactualized possible worlds.
(ii) All possible worlds represent non-actualized possibilities by having elements whose existence constitute those possibilities.
(iii) Unrestrictedly everything is actual.

The consequence of asserting (i) and (ii) together is that there exist such things as blue swans and talking donkeys, since the existence of appropriate conjunctions of simple states of affairs (i) is supposed to constitute the existence of blue swans and talking donkeys (ii). But this, we may presume, is inconsistent with (iii). Robust CR – *qua* realist – is committed to (i) and – *qua* actualist – to (iii), and so she is not entitled to invoke the constitutive response to the problem of implicit representation (ii).[11]

What robust CR may wish to claim is that certain conjunctions of simple states of affairs exist such that if these were to obtain there would exist talking donkeys – in other words that the existence of talking donkeys is included in certain non-obtaining states of affairs. She may even offer this claim by way of a primitively modal characterization – if not explanation – of implicit representation by worlds.[12] But then it is clear that the aspiration to provide a constitutive (non-linguistic) and non-modal account of implicit representation has been abandoned.[13]

(11.3) NR AND PRIMITIVE MODAL CONCEPTS

For NR possible worlds are world-natures – higher-order properties of being a maximal individual with such-and-such simple parts having just these simple properties and standing in just those simple relations. Without appeal to simplicity, there is nothing in the account of world-natures to exclude uninstantiable world-natures such as those partly constituted by the property of having an individual part a, which has the property of being red and the property of being green – i.e. impossible worlds. As always, the exclusion problem can be addressed by direct appeal to an unanalysed modal concept: let the possible worlds be the instantiable world-natures, or the world-natures in which individual parts instantiate compatible properties and stand in compatible patterns of relations. The question is whether the exclusion of impossible worlds (qua uninstantiable world-natures) can be achieved, effectively and without recourse to unanalysed modal concepts, by appealing to a non-modal concept of simple properties.[14] Thus an issue outstanding from the discussion of CR re-emerges.

Appeal to simple properties for the purpose of restricting the worlds to the possible worlds can terminate in appeal to an unanalysed modal concept in one of three places. First, there is the issue of ensuring effectiveness. Putative cases of absolute but non-logical impossibility, that arise from unconstrained distributions of properties and relations, include the following: multiple determination of a single determinable (being both red and green, etc.); multiple determination of an extensive quantity (having mass of exactly 1kg and having mass of exactly 2kg); violations of necessary transitivity (a is before b and b is before c and it is not the case that a is before c). The general strategy for dealing with the range of cases will be to argue, case by case, for dismissal of putative counterexamples either on the grounds of absolute possibility (modal denial) or non-simplicity of properties. In our case of necessarily transitive relations, for example, it may be more plausible to opt for modal denial and argue the case down to one of (merely) nomological impossibility. But let us concentrate on the denial of simplicity. In the case of colour incompatibilities, the thought may be that the colour properties are non-simple since each is identical to some complex of primary properties. In the case of extensive quantities the thought may be that quantitative properties of complex individuals (a being of mass 5kg) are complex properties of individuals such as the individual (a) having the (higher-order) property of having (5) distinct individual parts each of which has the unit property (being of mass 1kg).[15] The project of explaining impossibility by discerning complexity is rightly termed a 'research programme' (Armstrong 1989: 78–84) and I will not take a view here on the state of the programme.[16] But the point is that even if the concept of a simple property is not implicitly modal, there is no guarantee that appeal to it is effective in excluding impossible worlds (cf. Shalkowski 1994: 682) and if it is not, then appeal to an unanalysed modal concept may be required. Yet were judicious appeal to property complexity to prove effective in weeding out impossible worlds, the question would remain whether it involves appeal to implicit and unanalysed modal concepts. The suspicion that it does may arise from considerations about the notion of simplicity or from considerations about the notion of property. I consider these in turn.

Second, consider the concept of simplicity for properties which is naturally explained in terms of property constituents: a property is simple just in case it has no (other) property as a constituent.[17] It may well be true that properties have their constituent structures essentially, so that a property that is simple could not have been complex and vice versa (Armstrong 1989, Shalkowski 1994). But to repeat a point now familiar from Chapter 7 above, that there are modal truths about property constitution does not make property constitution a modal concept. As indicated in the exposition of CR and of NR, the concept of property constitution is naturally explained in terms of the property-forming operations. A property is complex just in case it is identical to the output of some property-forming operations and simple otherwise.[18] Among these operations the most widely accepted is conjunction. So let us consider that one way in which a property can turn out to be complex is by being a conjunctive property – as being a man looks like being the conjunctive property of being human and being adult and being male. The question then is how the operation of property-conjunction is to be defined. A natural proposal proceeds along the following lines:

(C) ∀P∀Q [The Conjunction (P + Q) =
The property F such that: ∀x[Fx iff (Px & Qx)]].[19]

The definiens here contains no explicitly modal term, but it is otherwise inadequate. The most serious difficulty is this. Firm modal opinion suggests that the following is an absolute possibility – and a possibility which, for all we know, is actualized: that there are three distinct simple properties M (mass), C (charge) and S (spin) that are instantiated by every (simple) individual. But this scenario is impossible given the explanation of simplicity in terms of property-forming operations and the foregoing definition of conjunction. For M, in our scenario, satisfies the condition for being the conjunction of charge and spin, contrary to the supposition that M is a simple (a fortiori, non-conjunctive) property. What we appear to have here is the predictable failure of a purely extensional analysis of property-complexity to distinguish complex properties from simple properties with which they are co-extensive. In face of this failure, the temptation is to investigate the prospects of a modal definition of property conjunction – e.g.:

(MC) ∀P∀Q [The Conjunction (P + Q) =
The property F such that: □∀x[Fx iff (Px & Qx)]].

Such a definition would, of course, generate a modal account of property complexity and simplicity. So the concept of simplicity, as it applies to properties, remains a potential, if not likely, source of unanalysed modality in the foundations of any otherwise adequate version of NR or PR.[20]

Third, and finally, we must consider the concept of a property itself as a source of unanalysed modality. Here, one view that might be taken is that the concept in question is broadly functional – the property concept is just the concept of playing a certain role or combination of roles. If that complex role is specifiable adequately and non-modally there is no unanalysed modal concept afoot in the notion of property. However, when proponents of AR appeal to properties for the purposes of constructing worlds, what is often intended is not that we should sustain neutrality on the question of what the property-roleplayers (the worldmaking elements) are. Rather the (de re) thought is that there are certain things – say universals or tropes – which are (or play the role of) the properties and of which the possible worlds are composed. Thus, the concept of universal – to take the most prominent example – may figure in the definition of 'possible world'. To make the now customary point, the fact that there are necessary truths about universals – say, that any universal is necessarily a universal, or that no universal could have been an individual – has no immediate bearing on whether the concept of a universal is implicitly modal.[21] The question is whether the concept of a universal can be characterized adequately without appeal to any modal concept. To that end, one might venture that a universal is something that is wholly present in many distinct locations at a time and so forth. However, Lewis (1986c: 104–7) objects that such a characterization is inadequate with respect to uninstantiated universals, for such universals are never present in any location at any time. Now some may choose to persist with the concept of universal so characterized in the knowledge that it is exclusive of the uninstantiated case. But that is no option for NR, for example, who is directly committed to the existence of uninstantiated universals in the construction of possible worlds – indeed that is exactly what she takes the unactualized possible worlds to be. For the theorist who, like NR, appeals to uninstantiated universals in the construction of possible worlds, the question is whether (something like) the earlier, spatial, characterization can be amended to accommodate the case of uninstantiated universals. As usual, we can envisage a modal amendment that solves our problem since both uninstantiated and instantiated (simple) universals appear to be accommodated under a common characterization as that which *could* be wholly present in many distinct locations at a time and so forth. But it is not obvious whether any adequate non-modal characterization of universal behaviour is available. Note also that it is of no avail to seek a non-modal characterization of universals in terms of their intrinsic nature rather than in terms of their actual or potential 'behaviour'. Certainly, structured universals, both instantiated and uninstantiated, can be identified as the products of property-forming operations on instantiated simple universals. Whether such identification, if accurate, would amount to conceptual analysis is one worry here and we are already acquainted with the worry that adequate definition of these operations may invoke modal concepts. The new and crucial worry, however, is that, even if this account covers both instantiated universals and uninstantiated structured universals, it leaves uninstantiated simple universals out of the picture. So if the construction of the possible worlds – by NR or anyone else – relies on a concept of universals that is inclusive of the case of simple uninstantiated universals, it is doubtful whether the construction in question is conceptually non-modal. But what if a construction of possible worlds eschews appeal to uninstantiated simple universals?

Perhaps a version of NR might eschew uninstantiated simple universals and, certainly, CR takes the only universals out of which her worlds are constructed to be instantiated universals. Can such a version of AR proceed on the basis of a non-modal characterization of the range of universals that she requires? Again, it would seem that it cannot. MacBride (1999: 489–90) argues that the earlier characterization is not even adequate for all instantiated universals. Uniquely instantiated simple universals are located, but since they are uniquely instantiated they are not located in distinct places at a time. Of course, it may be the case, for all we know, that the combinatorial base set of CR contains no uniquely instantiated simple universals – that no simple universals are instantiated and so (by CR lights) none exist. But an adequate characterization of the *concept* of a universal cannot be built on this epistemic possibility. Moreover, and more importantly, the epistemic possibility of a uniquely instantiated simple universal is also – by CR lights – a metaphysical possibility, thus: for every simple universal, u, there are many CR worlds (i.e. subsets of the combinatorial range set) which have only one member (i.e. simple state of affairs) of which u is a member. So if the construction of the possible worlds – by CR or anyone else – relies on a concept of universals that is inclusive of the case of simple and uniquely instantiated universals, it is doubtful whether the construction in question is conceptually non-modal.[22]

In sum, any species of AR – notably CR and NR – which relies on appeal to simple properties as an effective and non-modal means of distinguishing the possible worlds from the impossible has substantial work cut out on all three fronts.[23] When we also take account of the respective positions of PR and BR then – even having considered only the requirement to exclude impossible worlds where appropriate – we already have substantial grounds for doubting whether any version of AR can succeed in providing accurate analyses without appeal to unanalysed modal concepts.

CHAPTER 12

Actualist realism: ontological applications

Here I consider the capacity of the species of AR to deliver the two central kinds of ontological applications of PW: identification of entities of various (typically intensional) categories with constructs out of possible worlds (12.1) and an account of the truthmakers for modal claims (12.2).

(12.1) ONTOLOGICAL IDENTIFICATION

Recall (from Chapter 4) the range of identifications offered by GR: the (abundant) properties are the subsets of the set of all individuals; the states of affairs, the propositions, the ways things might have been and the possibilities are all identified with sets of possible worlds; and the possible worlds themselves are sums of individuals that are closed under spatiotemporal relatedness. AR believes in the existence of many possible worlds and so – assuming that she believes in sets and sums at all – she may be assumed to believe in the existence of sets and sums of possible worlds, and in sets and sums of such worldmaking elements as she admits. Thus AR, like GR, has at her disposal a rich array of constructions that she may consider as candidates for identification with various categories of entity. However, two considerations strongly suggest that AR cannot match GR in the range of ontological identifications that it affords. First, the central versions of AR identify the possible worlds as intensional entities of a certain kind (state of affairs, property, etc.) or as constructs out of such entities. So for each of these versions of AR, there is at least one category of intensional entity that is ineligible for identification as a construct out of possible worlds. Second, *qua* ontological actualist, AR does not believe in the existence of non-actual individuals. For AR, unicorns may exist at various worlds, as they do according to various tales, but unicorns do not exist (*simpliciter*) and there is no (non-empty) set of unicorns. Consequently, AR has no recourse to constructs out of (possible but) non-actual individuals for the purposes of ontological identification.[1] The upshot of these two considerations is that AR can offer, at most, intra-intensional ontological identifications wherein certain non-primitive intensions are identified as constructs of the possible worlds, and the possible worlds are either primitive intensions or are identified as constructs of primitive intensions. Thus, for example, propositions might be identified as sets of possible worlds when possible worlds are identified as complex properties.[2] But, comparatively, GR offers ontological identification of every category of intension – including whichever category of intension is taken by any given species of AR as primitive – with some (extensional) construct out of individuals and sets. Since no central version of AR offers the construction of all of the intensions from a basis of only sets and individuals, it is clear that the potential of GR to provide ontological identifications outstrips that of any such version of AR in this respect.

This assessment of the (relatively) limited potential of AR to provide ontological identification may call for marginal qualification. First, AR, generically and *per se*, is not committed to accepting as ontologically primitive any category of entity which GR treats as non-primitive or which is intensional. The ontological primitives of BR are sets and individuals (we presume) and whatever other categories of entity are found in the vocabulary of the worldmaking language. But if all of the words of the worldmaking language are sets or individuals – for example, the predicates might be English predicate tokens rather than properties – there will be no category of ontological primitives other than the sets and individuals. Also, one can envisage deviations from exemplary CR in which the simple properties are identified with sets of individuals – say, sets of those spacetime points at which (we would usually say) the properties are instantiated. Expressive considerations push for the rejection of such fully extensional versions of AR in favour of alternatives that take some intensional entity as primitive. For example, there is – to say the least – no guarantee that constructs out of actual English predicates should suffice to name all of the properties that are actually instantiated, never mind all the properties that could be instantiated. However, the point remains that AR, generically and *per se*, does not require the admission of primitive intensional entities. Second, PR is understood as conceiving of possible worlds – maximal possible states of affairs – as ontological simples (see, e.g., Lewis (1986a: Chapter 3.4) and van Inwagen (1986)). In PR, worlds represent by including (other) states of affairs, but this inclusion is explicated by way of a strict conditional – necessarily if the world in question were to obtain then so would the (represented) state of affairs. It is no part of this account that representation is achieved in virtue of the holding of some categorical relation – whole to part, set to member, set to subset or even conjunction to conjunct – between the PR world and (other) states of affairs that it represents. In that light, it seems open to PR to consider the identification of non-maximal states of affairs, such as Clinton's being president, with the sets of possible worlds (maximal possible states of affairs) that include them. So some states of affairs (the non-maximal) might be identified with constructs out of – abstractions from – possible worlds even if the maximal possible states of affairs that constitute the worlds must be taken as primitive. Third, in the case of alternative CR, the big states of affairs that constitute possible worlds are conceived as genuine complexes (conjunctions) of simple, *sui generis*, states of affairs. To say that states of affairs are *sui generis* is just to express their admission as ontological primitives. However, this admission need not be conceived as admission of an *extra* category of primitive entities over and above the primitive individuals and primitive sets. Rather, it may be held that the individuals, or the sets, are non-primitive entities that can be identified with certain constructions of – abstractions from – the states of affairs. I think that this suggestion of 'abstraction' is murky unless it means, as suggested in the case of PR, identifying entities with equivalence classes of states of affairs.[3] The general point, however, is that AR admission of entities other than sets or individuals as ontological primitives does not immediately entail that the number of primitive ontological categories recognized by AR is greater than that recognized by GR.[4] So while these qualifications allow, at the margins of AR, for a wider range of ontological identifications than that suggested by the general picture, it remains true for the most part, if not always, that the potential of the more central and attractive versions of AR to limit ontological categories by identification with constructs out of primitives is, prima facie, less than that of GR. So in that light, I will assume, if AR is not to concede theoretical advantage to GR, then AR is bound to argue that, despite these initial considerations, GR does not really gain the upper hand over AR. The case that AR does not compare unfavourably to GR in this crucial respect might be made on either an optimistic or a pessimistic basis.

The pessimistic way is for AR to defend a generalized scepticism about, or opposition to, putative non-trivial identifications of

AR: ontological applications

categories of intensional entity regardless of whether the entities in the intended reductive base are intensional (typical AR) or extensional (GR). Plantinga seems to have shifted from agnosticism about whether his own version of AR might afford successful intra-intensional identifications to such a generalized pessimism. Thus, while Plantinga (1974: 45–6) is agnostic about the identification of propositions with states of affairs as mooted by Chisholm (1970, 1971), Plantinga (1976: 257) takes the identification of propositions with states of affairs to be vitiated by a simple 'Leibniz-law' argument against identification and Plantinga (1987: 213–19) wields such an argument against the identification of propositions with any kind of set. The Leibniz-law argument, to exemplify, is that all propositions have truth-values, and no states of affairs (or sets) have truth-values, so – given that identicals have all of their properties in common – no state of affairs (or set) is a proposition. By applying parallel reasoning in obvious ways in order to deal with other putative ontological identifications – properties but not sets are instantiated, states of affairs but not sets of worlds obtain – AR might seek to claim a no score draw with GR on successful ontological identifications. However, as they stand, Plantinga's Leibniz-law arguments are unconvincing. Dialectically, the crucial point in each case is that some justification for the minor premise – sets aren't true, etc. – should be available which is not vitiated by some intensional fallacy. Prior to the hypothesis of identification, we do not ordinarily think of any sets *as* things that have truth-values, just as prior to other hypotheses of identification we do not ordinarily think of any numbers as having members, nor ordinarily think of common salt as being partly composed of metals. But the success of identity hypotheses is often consistent with our lacking such prior opinions, or even requires the revision of contrary prior opinion. So the minor premise in a Leibniz-law argument requires justification and, as far as I am aware, the only justification that Plantinga (1987) has to offer in this respect is an appeal to the obvious – it is obvious that sets are never true, etc. Unfortunately, such an appeal is all too easily met by appeal to the counter-intuition that it is obvious that whether sets are ever true is not the kind of thing that can be obvious, or established solely by appeal to what is obvious.

The optimistic way for AR is to argue that her own putative intra-intensional identifications of intensions succeed where GR's extensional identifications of intensions systematically fail. Recall (from (5.4)) that ontological identifications hypothesized by GR are held to fail by conflating intensional equivalents in cases where

Actualist realism

the relevant concepts impose hyperintensional criteria of identity. Now, one way in which AR might offer to improve on this situation is by postulating as many distinct primitive entities – say, properties – as the role requires, free from the constraint of identifying intensional equivalents. In that case, attention is drawn to the question of whether the envisaged ontology of simple, fine-grained hyperintensional entities is safe and sane (see (17.4) below). But that worry aside it is still extremely doubtful that this strategy would afford an ontological basis for successful intra-intensional identification. The optimistic thought about intra-intensional identification is that one such category of basic hyperintensional entities is available and that the elements of some other category of hyperintensional entities can be identified with constructs out of that basis. For example, the thought might be that given appropriately fine-grained properties from which to construct the worlds, we can identify equally fine-grained propositions as constructs out of the worlds. But that thought is seriously undermined by the following reasoning. By hypothesis, F and G are distinct and necessarily co-extensive properties. On the standard proposal, the set that is apt to be identified with the proposition that there are F's is the set of worlds at which something is F (i.e. the worlds at which F is instantiated). But by hypothesis, F and G are necessarily co-extensive and so the set of worlds at which something is F is identical to the set of worlds at which something is G. So the proposition that there are F's still turns out to be identical to the proposition that there are G's. At this point one might be tempted to consider the alternative identificatory proposal that the proposition that there are F's is identified with the set of worlds at which F exists. But a simple dilemma defeats that proposal. If AR has a conception of properties as contingent existents, as in the case of exemplary CR, the existence of the properties is contingent upon their instantiation and so the set of worlds at which F exists is not distinct from the set of worlds at which something is F. In that case, the alternative proposal has the same outcome as the standard proposal. If AR has a conception of properties as necessary existents, as in the cases of PR and NR, then the set of worlds at which F exists is indeed (typically) distinct from the set of worlds at which F is instantiated. However, in that conception F exists at every world, and so does every other property. The set of worlds at which F exists is identical to the set of worlds at which G exists and is identical to the set of worlds at which any given property exists – in all cases we have the set of all the possible worlds. So the alternative

AR: ontological applications

proposal is worse than the standard proposal since it identifies the proposition that there are F's with the proposition that there are G's and with every other such existential proposition. The foregoing argument suggests that, in general, the optimistic thought is doomed: AR is in no position to claim that she can offer successful, appropriately discriminating intra-intensional identifications of intensions where GR's extensional identifications of intensions systematically fail.

Since, as has been argued, successful AR intra-intensional identifications are not to be had, it seems that the best that AR can do is to salvage a draw on this point by retreating to the pessimistic thought and showing that successful GR intra-intensional identifications are not to be had either. And in that light I emphasize: (a) that it has been indicated how GR resources might be exploited in order to construct relatively fine-grained propositions, etc. (see (5.4) above); and (b) that the only other objection that we have to the success of GR identifications are Plantinga's dubious contentions about what is obvious, e.g. that sets are never true.

(12.2) TRUTHMAKING

In (3.2), I indicated that I would deal with the issue of truthmaking by focusing on the case of non-actualized possibility claims. In (4.4), I argued that even if GR individuals are decent prima facie candidates to afford a fully existential account of truthmaking, all reasonable and familiar theses about truthmaking will hold trivially given the GR conception of the modal status of possibility claims, of matters of unrestricted existence and of the relation between the two. Here, in considering the capacity of the species of AR to deliver truthmakers for non-actualized possibility claims, I will also consider, in turn, the capacity to afford a fully existential account of truthmaking and matters of modal status.[5]

In those versions of AR where there are worldmaking elements, and the worldmaking elements of the possible worlds are characterized by their simplicity or atomicity, it is these simple or atomic worldmaking elements that are the natural candidates to serve as the ultimate truthmakers for modal claims. In that light, the possibility claims that are naturally taken as basic are the possibilitations of atomic sentences in which the names refer to simple individuals and the predicates refer to simple properties (relations).[6] So for an actually existing and simple individual a, and for actually instantiated and simple property G, the true (by hypothesis)

(1) It is possible that a is G

is made true by the existence of: the atomic states of affairs <G,a>, for CR; the higher-order property of having a part which is identical to a and which instantiates G, for NR; or the atomic sentence of the worldmaking language which means that Ga – so perhaps <G,a> again – (for BR). I will comment in due course on the case of PR.

First, then we should consider the knot of issues surrounding the question whether the candidates afford a fully existential explanation of truthmaking for possibility claims. Here, I admit that the form of the worry is vague and that I am unsure of the significance of the various contrasts and comparisons that I will draw. One point of contrast concerns selection of the truthmakers from within an ontological category. In GR the existence of any entity in the general putative truthmaking category – i.e. the existence of an individual – is always (intuitively) sufficient for an appropriate possibility claim to be true. Thus, if there (unrestrictedly) exists a talking donkey thereby it is true that it is possible that there is a talking donkey. In the group of AR cases just considered, it is not the case that the existence of an entity in the general putative truthmaking category is always intuitively sufficient for an appropriate possibility claim to be true. For among the respective general categories there are AR impossibilia – impossible states of affairs, uninstantiable properties and inconsistent sentences – and, say, the property of being green and non-green exists even though it is not true that it is possible that something is green and non-green. I do not claim that it is clear that this contrast is detrimental to the AR cause. In the group of cases considered thus far AR can, as indicated at the outset, identify the truthmakers of possibility claims as the atomic, or least complex, cases among the general category and perhaps that is all that she need do. But notice now, by way of further contrast that PR cannot proceed in exactly that way. In the case of PR, there are no worldmaking elements: the possible worlds are states of affairs and all states of affairs – maximal or non-maximal, possible or impossible – are ontological simples. In PR, the distinction between a possible state of affairs and an impossible state of affairs – and so, we continue to presume, the distinction between the states of affairs that are truthmakers for possibility claims and those that are not – is not marked by a difference of ontological complexity. Were PR to push the claim that she too can identify a sub-kind of the states of affairs as the truthmakers for possibility claims she might claim that the relevant states of affairs are those that are *possible* (i.e. those that

AR: ontological applications

have the property of representing a possibility). Intuitively, it feels as though such a move would signal departure from the spirit of the truthmaking project insofar as the intimated difference does not strike us naturally as an existential difference. But it is unclear to me that there is any more or less of a worry here about the idea that possibility is encoded into a state of affairs than there is about the idea that donkeyhood (for GR) is encoded into an individual. I am unclear, in light of these comparisons and contrasts whether all, some or none of the species of realism that have been considered offer an appropriately existential explanation of the truth of possibility claims.

A second point, conceived as a tentative 'result' rather than an objection, is that even where the AR candidates afford an appropriately existential account of truthmaking for modal claims, it seems that truthmaking for non-modal claims cannot be explained in terms of the existence of entities of the same kind. Consider the case of contingent falsehoods such as – by hypothesis –

(2) a is G.   Say (2) is F.   so $<G,a>$ exists.
               (1) $\Diamond$ a is G is T,

Despite the falsehood of (2), and recalling that the possibilitation of (2), (1), is true: <G,a> exists (CR); the higher-order property of having a part which is identical to a and which instantiates property G exists (NR); an atomic sentence exists which means that Ga (BR) and *a's being G* exists (PR). So, naturally, the existence of such things is not sufficient for the truth of non-modal (2). Now, wherever AR suggests a category of truthmaker for basic possibility claims such as (1), it seems that something has to be added to explain what makes the corresponding non-modal claim (2) true. The obvious additions are, variously, that the relevant state of affairs obtains, that the relevant property is instantiated or that the relevant sentence is true. Among the species of AR, it is palpable that BR reaches a significant explanatory impasse at just this point. For the process of accounting for the truthmaker of an atomic non-modal sentence in one language terminates in the claim that it is sufficient for the truth of such a sentence that there should exist a corresponding (synonymous) sentence of a worldmaking language which is true (*simpliciter*). For the remaining species of AR a question that looms large over truthmaking credentials is whether the neutrally intimated 'account' of truth for non-modal sentences in terms of these additional features is to take the form of a wholly ontological explanation. Such an explanation would consist in the identification of some other entity whose

Actualist realism

existence is at least sufficient for the obtaining of a state of affairs, the instantiation of a property, etc. That no such wholly ontological explanation is readily forthcoming is most easily seen in the case of PR. For PR, the truth of (2) requires, in addition to its existing, that a state of affairs, *a's being G*, obtains. The natural approach to identifying an entity whose existence constitutes fulfilment of that condition is to consider the higher-order states of affairs: *(a's being G)'s obtaining*. It is true that the existence of this state of affairs is materially sufficient for the truth of (2) – the state of affairs exists (according to PR) and (2) is, by hypothesis, true. However, the existence of such a state of affairs is not *in general* materially sufficient for the truth of the corresponding non-modal sentence. For, by PR lights, the higher-order state of affairs – *(b being F)'s obtaining* – exists even if, by hypothesis, we have the falsehood of

(3) b is F.

What might be thought sufficient to 'make (3) true' is the obtaining, not the existence of *(b being F)'s obtaining*. But now it is clear that the appeal to the existence of the higher-order state of affairs has been pointless. For an explanation of truthmaking that took the form of an appeal to a state of affairs obtaining was available on the ground floor by appealing to the obtaining of *b's being F*. If that explanation is adequate then the appeal to the higher-order state of affairs is redundant and if that explanation is, in virtue of its form, inadequate then so is the explanation that appeals to the obtaining of the higher-order state of affairs. We could run a parallel argument against the thought that the existence of a higher-order property is, in general, sufficient for the truth of the possibilitate of a simple possibility claim – for instance that it is sufficient for the truth of (3) that there exist the property of instantiating the property of (having a part that is identical to b and is F). So in general, it seems, whether the additional feature is obtaining or instantiation, there is no higher-order case of either such that, in the AR schemes of things, existence alone is sufficient for the truth of any atomic sentence. Indeed what this consideration suggests is that, in all species of AR, a different category of entity is required to serve as truthmaker for an atomic sentence than is required to serve as truthmaker for its possibilitation.

The next kind of issue that bears on the capacity of AR to provide truthmakers for modal claims is the issue of the modal status – the modal status of modal truth and the modal status of the existence of

AR: ontological applications

the putative truthmakers. With respect to the latter, the fundamental question is whether the worlds or the worldmaking elements of the species of AR are necessary existents. In answer to that question, I will show, the position shared by PR and NR is relatively straightforward and the consequence of that position, I believe, is that these versions of AR are in the same boat as GR on the truthmaking issue. The position of CR is different from that of PR and NR and it is more complicated. BR was presented in such a way that it was left open whether the worldmaking elements were conceived as necessary or as contingent existents and, accordingly, there is no need to treat the case of BR separately and explicitly here. If the worldmaking elements of BR are conceived as necessary existents, the case of PR and NR applies; otherwise the case of CR applies.

Recalling the crucial distinction between existing and obtaining for PR states of affairs, and the distinction between existing and being instantiated for NR properties, PR states of affairs are necessary existents, as are NR properties. In each case, the consequence is that truths about absolute possibility are absolutely necessary. We can articulate that consequence in two different ways. From an external perspective, as it were, the point can be put like this. The truth of possibility claims is a matter of the existence of possible states of affairs (PR) or the existence of instantiable properties (NR). But in neither case could matters have been otherwise. The states of affairs that exist are all and only the states of affairs that could exist and the states of affairs that are possible are all and only those that could be possible (PR). The properties that exist are all and only the properties that could exist and the properties that are instantiable are all and only those that could have been instantiable (NR). From an internal perspective, as it were, the necessity of truths about possibility is represented as the validity of the principle:

(S5) $\Diamond A \to \Box \Diamond A$.

Spelling this out in the case of PR we have the following. The truth-condition of a possibility claim at a world is that there is some accessible possible world at which the related state of affairs is actualized or obtains. But in matters of absolute modality, every world is accessible from every other. So if the truth-condition of a possibility claim at a world is fulfilled, thereby the truth-condition of that possibility claim at each world is fulfilled, for if a world in which the given state of affairs is actualized is accessible from any world, it is accessible from all worlds. Once it is determined that all truths of absolute possibility hold of necessity we have the consequence, already noted in (4.4), that various modal and counterfactual articulations of the truthmaking thesis emerge as trivial truths. Thus: the existence (or non-existence) of anything is modally sufficient for (entails) the truth of any true possibility claim; any counterfactual is true that is of the form, had the truths about possibility been otherwise, then this or that would (not) have existed and the truth about possibility supervenes not only on being, but also on anything else. It is not quite the case with PR and NR, as it is with GR, that all unrestricted matters of being are non-contingent. For PR and NR subscribe to the doctrine of ontological actualism which entails that unrestricted existence is actual existence and so, as we would expect in that light, PR and NR hold that the existence of (most) concrete individuals is contingent. However, that contingency is not a source of any interesting modal or counterfactual variation in the relation between relevant existence and the truth of possibility claims. Indeed on these interpretations, facts about the existence of individuals do not figure in the truth-conditions of basic possibility claims. In PR, the truth-condition of the claim that it is possible that a is G, (1) above, is that two properties, an essence of a and being G, which both exist necessarily, are co-exemplified at some possible world.[7] If there is such a world then there would have been such a world even if the actually existing individual a had not existed, and so the existential facts that are relevant to the truth of possibility claims – the facts about the existence of worlds at which this or that is actualized – are non-contingent. Thus we also have the triviality of the converses of the claims of modal and counterfactual variation that we have already considered. The truth (or otherwise) of any claim is modally sufficient for (entails) the existence of a possible world at which arbitrary P is actualized (given that there is a possible world at which P is actualized). Any counterfactual is true that is of the form, had the totality of possible worlds been otherwise then it would have been true that possibly P. A characterization of the modal relationship between truthmaker and truth will be satisfactory only if it issues in a suitably discriminating matching of truthmakers to truths, and neither PR nor NR offers this. Moreover, even the claim that PR or NR secures the thesis that modal truth supervenes on being would be disingenuous, given the trivialization of the supervenience thesis that has emerged. I conclude, then, that PR and NR are in the same position as GR concerning their entitlement to claim that they offer an account of the truthmakers of modal claims.

In contrast to the other cases that have been considered, the

AR: ontological applications

[margin note: worldly elements are not necessary existents in CR.]

worldmaking elements of CR are not necessary existents. There are two distinct perspectives from which one can trace a route from that position to contingency of the truth of absolute possibility claims. From the external perspective the route opens out as follows. Since the space of possibilities is determined by the simple actual existents and since it is a brute contingent matter what the simple actual existents are, it is a brute contingent matter what the space of possibilities is and so a contingent matter which possibility statements are true. The natural and powerful objection to such a line of thought is that the space of possibilities so characterized cannot be the entire space of *absolute* possibilities – that an adequate account of what *absolutely* could or could not be the case simply fails if it is shaped by constraints that *absolutely* might not have been in place. It is a nice question whether CR is in fact committed to adopting this external perspective and to the subsequent moves that lead to the contingency of truth about absolute possibility. If so, then CR is vulnerable to the ensuing objection. But I will not press that point here. Let us consider instead how the route from the contingent existence of worldmaking elements to the contingency of truth about possibility claims opens out from the internal perspective. The thought now is that the space of absolute possibilities is constrained absolutely, and never mind why, by the actual simple existents. Within that space, there are relatively impoverished or contracted possible worlds such that simple properties that exist at other worlds do not exist there. Consequently, given the account in (10.2) of what it is for one CR world to be accessible from another, an impoverished world is accessible from any world that is at least equally rich in simple properties but any world that is richer in simple properties than the impoverished world will not be accessible from the impoverished worlds. So, [margin: failure of (S,S)] to exemplify this failure of symmetry of accessibility, where w = {<F,a>,<G,a>} and v = {<F,a>}, v is accessible from w but not vice versa, for v exists at w (v is generable from w by recombination) but w does not exist at v (w is not generable from v by recombination). The semantic consequence of this failure of symmetry is the invalidity of the (S5) principle – there are models in which what is possible at one world is not possible at some accessible worlds and so what is possible is contingently possible – and within the space of CR possibilities, that is how the contingency of truth about absolute possibility is represented.[8] Now given that it is not, in general, necessary that a (true) possibility statement is true, the contention that a given possibility statement is true no longer trivializes every entailment claim in which it figures as the consequent. Nor do we have

Actualist realism

trivialization of every counterfactual claim in which the contrary of such a contention figures as the antecedent. Moreover, the simple states of affairs that are candidates for being the truthmakers of basic possibility claims are not necessary existents either. For CR, states of affairs are sequences and CR is entitled to take these sequences as sets and to invoke the following natural principle of set existences: that (necessarily) a set exists if and only if all of its members exist. The upshot is that CR simple states of affairs are contingent existents since their constituent simple properties and simple individuals are contingent existents. Finally, then, it emerges in the case of CR that appropriately discriminating modal variation holds between basic possibility claims and the existence of their putative truthmakers. There is mutual entailment of the truth of an arbitrary basic possibility claim, possibly Fa, and the existence of the related simple state of affairs <F,a>:

(CR1)   For every world w, (*possibly Fa* is true at w iff <F,a> exists at w).[9]

Moreover, we have the desired independence of the truth of *possibly F,a* from the existence of any other simple state of affairs and the desired independence of the existence of <F,a> from the truth of every other simple possibility claim:

(CR2)   For any other simple state of affairs s that is not identical to <F,a> there is some world w such that at w, *possibly Fa* is true and at w, s does not exist.[10]

(CR3)   For any basic possibility claim P other than *possibly Fa*, there is some world w such that at w, <F,a> does not exist and at w P is true.[11]

Finally, if appeal to the claim of supervenience of truth on being is required in order to deal with the truth of logically complex claims, there is no obvious objection to CR making such an appeal. If we adopt the external perspective, the appropriate question would appear to be whether modal truth might have been different given that there was no difference in existence. CR is entitled to answer that question in the negative and so to affirm supervenience on the grounds that the combinatorially determined space of possibilities is, in an obvious and straightforward way, fixed by what exists. The supervenience claim is non-trivial since it may be conjoined with the claim that the totality of being could have been otherwise. If we

AR: ontological applications

adopt the internal perspective, the appropriate question would appear to be whether any two possible worlds differ in what is true at them without differing in base sets. Again, it looks as though CR is entitled to answer that question in the negative and so to affirm supervenience.

At this point it is appropriate to bring into play various constraints and limitations on the significance of this outcome. First, recall that no story has yet been ventured about truthmaking for modal truths other than in the simplest case of atomic possibility claims. Second, recall that it has been argued that the truthmakers adduced in order to account for the modal case will not do for the non-modal case.[12] Third, as we shall see in (17.1) there are questions about the capacity of CR to deal, in matters of truthmaking or otherwise, with the full range of genuine possibility. However, the point remains that when assessed in terms of the capacity to give an account of truthmaking in existential terms along the lines that have been broadly envisaged throughout, CR stands at a significant advantage over both GR and the other species of AR.

In sum, the capacity of AR to afford ontological identifications is very limited, and especially so in relation to the capacity of GR. However, CR is unique among versions of realism in allowing the kind of modal variation between the truth of possibility claims and truthmakers that the standard accounts of truthmaking require.

CHAPTER 13

Actualist realism: semantic applications

Versions of AR are often conceived and presented with the provision of an applied PW-semantics for quantified modal logic (QML) as the immediate aim.[1] Indeed, it is often the case, and especially in the earlier period of the literature, that the conceptual and ontological intentions of AR PW-semanticists are invisible to the reader. I begin this chapter by revisiting the 'intuitive' application that Kripke (1963) suggests for his own semantics.[2] Many hold that, when measured against compelling modal intuitions and other independent sources of modal opinion, the intuitive application does well in outcome – i.e. in the patterns of modal theses that it validates. Yet philosophically, the intuitive application is variously and seriously problematic, if not downright unacceptable, from an AR standpoint. The challenge to AR is to provide an applied semantics for QML that matches the intuitive application in the acceptability of its outcomes for modal validity but which is also, at least from the AR standpoint, philosophically satisfactory. The philosophical problems emerge as follows.

When an interpreter of PW supplies an application of the Kripkean semantics for QML and asserts the applied theory in question, she incurs ontological commitment to the (intended) models of the theory – the sets and, more importantly, their members.[3] In the case of propositional modal logic, the commitment so generated is unproblematic for AR *qua* AR.[4] The models in question are 4-tuples <W, w*, R, V> for which the intuitive application has it that w* is the actual world, W is the set of all possible worlds, R is a relation of accessibility over the possible worlds and V is a function that assigns a truth-value to each sentence at each world. AR can easily adopt an application within this intuitive genre since she already believes in the actual(ized) world and in a set of things that she identifies as the possible worlds. If we have in mind an applied semantics for absolute modality, the default position is that the accessibility relation R should be unrestricted on W (i.e. any world is accessible from any other) in which case the relation becomes a dispensable feature of the models.[5] But the models of QML ask more questions of AR. The QML models are 6-tuples <W, w*, R, D, Q, V>. The intuitive application presents the elements W, w* and R as before, but further presents the additional elements D and Q, and expands the role of V, as follows: D is the universal domain set of all possible individuals; Q is a function that assigns to each possible world w a local domain of possible individuals (a subset of D, D(w)) that exist at that world and V is now a function that assigns to each n-placed predicate at each world an extension – a set of n-tuples from D – as well as assigning a truth-value to each sentence at each world. The intuitive applied semantics for QML poses AR the following problems.

First, there is the D-problem. AR, *qua* ontological actualist, does not believe in the existence of possible but non-actual individuals, so what account will she offer of the members of D?

Second, there is the V-problem. The intuitive application does not require that the extension of an atomic predicate at a world be a subset of the domain of that world. Will AR accept this aspect of the intuitive application with the consequence that an individual can be in the extension of a predicate at a world when the individual does not exist at that world?

Third, there is the Q-problem. The intuitive application allows that the function Q may assign an element of D to the local domains of distinct worlds. Will AR accept this aspect of the intuitive application with the consequence that one individual can exist at different possible worlds?

The Q-problem is an aspect of the issue of transworld identity and as such it will be covered in Chapter 16. In this chapter, I will develop the D-problem and the V-problem, considering both philosophical and logical implications of prospective solutions.

(13.1) THE D-PROBLEM

To solve the D-problem an interpreter must arrive at a conception of the membership of D which she takes to satisfy two conditions: (i) each member of D must exist *simpliciter*; (ii) in each case where a world w is such that an individual x exists at w, there is a member of the domain of w, D(w), and so a member of D, which represents the existence of x at w. GR meets these conditions by construing D as the set of all (actual and non-actual) individuals, with all individuals that represent individual possibilities locally at worlds – either directly or *qua* counterparts – being members of that set. AR, *qua* ontological actualist, must construe the membership of D without incurring commitment to the existence of non-actual individuals. The challenge is to do so while doing justice to our intuitions that certain modal sentences – sentences apt to be construed by GR as claims about non-actual individuals – are true, e.g.:

(1) There might have been an individual other than those that actually exist.
(2) (Actually) childless Richard might have had a son.[6]

In a relatively early discussion of the D-problem Plantinga (1974: 132) makes remarks that are suggestive of a modalist interpretation of talk about possible but non-actual individuals ('non-existent individuals').[7] The core idea of such a modalist interpretation is that assent to (1) – or to its even more existentially loaded variant –

(3) There are possible individuals that do not actually exist

is to assert the proposition that is more perspicuously and explicitly expressed by

(3*) $\Diamond \exists x[\sim(\text{Actually } \exists y[y = x])]$

– the primitively modal expression of the possibility that there exists an x that is distinct from any object that exists at w*. The semantic structure of (3*) is such that the quantifier in x occurs within the scope of a possibility operator which is intended as non-factive. So what emerges is a truth-condition for (3) which, if fulfilled, would not entail the existence of any non-actual individual. Yet, whatever the merits of such an approach may be, it does not provide us with what an applied PW-semantics requires, viz. entities that the (AR) interpreter believes to exist and which she is prepared to identify as the members of the domain D. There are three identifiable strategies through which AR may address the D-problem directly or, to put the matter in Lewisian terms, three conceptions that AR may invoke of ersatz possible individuals. D may be identified with the set of actual individuals, or with the set of actually constructible singular terms or with the set of individual essences. I will now discuss these in turn.

(13.2) D AS THE ACTUAL INDIVIDUALS

The first attempt to solve the D-problem is prominent in various, either relatively early or semantically dominated, discussions of PW-semantics for QML and it consists in the straightforward identification of D with the set of actually existing individuals $D(w^*)$. This identification supports two different conceptions of the function Q that assigns a local domain to each world. The default position is that no further constraint is imposed on Q so that any local world-domain can be any subset of $D(w^*)$. Otherwise Q may be so constrained that the local domain is invariant across worlds whereby all (and only) the actual individuals exist at every world, i.e. for every world w, $D(w) = D(w^*)$. Either way, the threat looms of the validation of various modal theses that are at odds with prior modal opinion.[8]

The natural implications of models in which world-domains are invariant include the validation of the Barcan Formula (BF), the converse Barcan Formula (CBF) and the principle of the Necessity of Existence (NE):

(BF) $\quad \forall x[\Box Fx] \rightarrow \Box \forall x[Fx]$
(CBF) $\quad \Box \forall x[Fx] \rightarrow \forall x[\Box Fx]$
(NE) $\quad \forall x[\Box \exists y[y = x]]$.

The intuitive groundings of these principles in models of invariant world-domains are as follows.[9] In the case of (BF), the antecedent holds when each individual that exists at w* has a given feature F at every world v. This means that at every world v, every individual that exists at w* has F. But since world-domains do not vary, this means that at every world v, every individual that exists at v has F. Thus the consequent holds. For (CBF), convert the foregoing. In the case of (NE), take any individual x that exists at w*. By invariant domains, at every world w, x exists and so any x exists necessarily.

(BF) appears to conflate certain de dicto possibilities with de re relatives, and conversely so for (CBF). (NE), obviously enough, conflicts with the intuition that some individuals exist contingently. In the case of (BF), we appear to have conflict with the intuition that there are possibilities de dicto that are not possibilities de re for any actual individual – e.g.

(4) It could have been that (actually childless) Richard had a son even though no actual individual is such that it could have been the son of Richard.[10]

If we drop the requirement of invariant domains and require only that every world-domain is a subset of the set of actual individuals (= $D(w^*)$) then none of the problematic theses is validated. In the case of (NE), counterexamples of contingent existence are constructible within models since we can have world-domains that are *proper* subsets of the set of actual individuals. In the case of (BF), we have a counterexample in a model where there is a world w, at which nothing exists that could be the son of John, but at w^* there exists something that is (and a fortiori, could be) the son of John. However, even though (BF) is not validated – it is false at some worlds on some models – there remains the particular problem of assigning intuitively adequate (i.e. satisfiable) truth-conditions to actual-world counterexamples such as (4). For the truth of (4), on the standard PW-semantic account of truth-conditions, requires the existence at some world of an individual that is not identical with any individual that exists at w^* (on pain of falsifying the second, de re, conjunct).

In a recent and intriguing variant on the standard solution to the D-problem, Linsky and Zalta (1994, 1996) – hereafter, LZ – construe the actual individuals as having an unfamiliar nature that is calculated to render acceptable to AR the validity of (BF), (CBF) and (NE). The actual individuals are construed as including both the familiar concrete individuals and also some non-concrete (abstract) objects but crucially – and herewith the unfamiliarity – the (non-)concreteness of each of these things, concrete individual or non-concrete object, is a contingent matter.[11] When we add to this conception of the actual individuals, the invariant conception of world-domains – at every w, $D(w) = D(w^*)$ – the various problematic theses are still validated. However, the thought is that the significance of this commitment is deflated when modal existence claims are contrasted with modal claims about concreteness. Thus consider (NE) and (BF). (NE) is valid – and our intuitively true (1) is false – since every actual individual exists at every world. But not to worry since our intuitions of contingent existence about individuals – say, Socrates – are matched by the contingent concreteness of individuals. Socrates exists at every world but that is not as bad as you think since there are many worlds at which he does none of the things that you would associate with his existence: come into existence at a time; occupy space; have a career, etc. (BF) is valid. But not to worry, since the possibility that there exists a son of Richard implies the existence (not the concreteness) at w^* of an individual which, at another world, is concrete and is the son of Richard. In the latter case, our true consequent is the intuitively true (2). Finally, and swiftly, for an individual to have a property essentially is for it to have that property at every world at which it is concrete rather than, as per the standard account, for it to have that property at every world at which it exists.

One advantageous inferential consequence of the LZ proposal is that the model theory, with invariant domains, validates the simplest version of QML. But the philosophical consequences are extremely unattractive. Manifestly, the idea that there is a category of entities for which concreteness is contingent is metaphysically queer. Perhaps some contingencies are just brute – that is to say it is contingent that P even if there is nothing *upon which* P is contingent. But contingently non-concrete individuals, and individuals that have no substantive identity conditions, are not the stuff of safe and sane ontology. However, it cannot be said of the LZ proposal that it is any more representationally queer than the Lagadonian variant of BR. For presumably, given such entities, we are in a position to stipulate that each represents itself at every world. I will not argue further against the LZ proposal, although I will note that even if it is semantically successful and ontologically sane no case has been made for such a version of AR affording any of the conceptual or ontological benefits that are associated with the use of PW.

Before leaving the standard solution there is another difficulty associated with the conception of world-domains as varying subsets of $D(w^*)$ which was intimated at (12.2) and which I will address here. The CR principle that all possibilities are recombinations of actually existing entities is naturally understood so that it allows the existence of certain 'contracted' worlds at which only a proper subset of the actual individuals (those in $D(w^*)$) exist. However, a problem ensues if it is then maintained that accessibility of a world v from a world w is construed as existence of v at w as explained at (10.2), i.e. when accessibility of v from w is understood as v being generable-by-recombination from the simple states of affairs that obtain at w. To see this, suppose that the property of being an electron is a simple property. At w^*, there are (individual) electrons, but at some worlds at which there exist only some of the individuals that exist at w^*, there are no electrons. Allow then that at some such world v, the property of being an electron does not exist, since – in CR – property existence is contingent on the existence of individuals that instantiate the property. The combinatorial domain set of v does not include the property of being an electron and so the set of worlds generable from the combinatorial domain set of v does not include w^*. If the identification of the accessibility relation R with this *generable-from*

Actualist realism

relation is maintained, then R is restricted over the set of worlds W, for some worlds are not accessible from others (e.g. w* is not accessible from v). In particular, R so understood is not a symmetrical relation – v is generable from w* but not vice versa – and consequently the models are not strong enough to validate certain theses which are naturally held valid concerning absolute possibility and necessity. Notable among these are the Brouwerian thesis and the characteristic (S5) thesis:

(B) $A \to \Box \Diamond A$
(S5) $\Diamond A \to \Box \Diamond A$.[12]

However, there is a principled way in which this consequence can be avoided. Consider the CR slogan that all possibilities are recombinations out of actually existing elements in light of the, now standardly observed, ambiguity of 'actually'.[13] In the shifting, non-rigid, sense of 'actually', the disambiguation of the slogan is that what is possible at each world w is a matter of what can be generated out of what exists at w. That, indeed, is how combinatorialists tend to understand the principle and why they subsequently accept the intimated weakening of modal logic (cf. Armstrong 1989: 62–3). But in the unshifting, rigid sense of 'actually', the disambiguation of the slogan is that what is possible at each world w is a matter of what can be generated out of what exists at w*. Incorporating the latter, rather than the former, into the definition of accessibility, for all worlds v and w, v is accessible from w just in case v is generable-from w*. Thus we see that the real source of the suggested consequences for validity is not actual-world chauvinism. Indeed 'actual-world chauvinism' is most obviously and naturally understood as expressing the metaphysical stance that is reflected in the new, unshifty definition of accessibility. The real source of the suggested consequences for validity is the (tendentious and unacknowledged) shifty understanding of what it means to be an actual-world chauvinist and what it means to have possibility fixed by what actually exists.

(13.3) D AS THE ACTUAL SINGULAR TERMS

A clue as to how an ontologically actualist solution to the D-problem might be formulated is given by the second general condition on the interpreter's conception of D that was specified in (13.1), i.e.: (ii) in each case where a world w is such that an individual x exists at w, there is a member of the domain of w, D(w), and so a member of D, which represents x's existence at w. The thought is that since AR requires a set whose members correspond to the individuals represented at each world, she should just take D to be the set of all of the actually existing individual-representations – that is, those ersatz individuals, whether themselves individuals or not, whose role is to represent the existence of an individual at a world. In the case of BR, the specific expression of the natural and general form of AR response to the D-problem is that D is the set of the (actually existing) singular terms of the worldmaking language.

Let us assume, then, that we have, in extended Lagadonian fashion, *all* actual individuals as names of themselves. In addition to these individual-representations, BR will need expressions that do not apply to any actual individual but which represent 'possible individuals' such as talking donkeys, blue swans, etc. Thus, BR requires complex predicates that represent, implicitly or explicitly, such conditions as being a talking donkey. Such complex representation, when we build on the Lagadonian language, would appear to require complex entities that have as elements not only the actual simple properties (and maybe actual simple individuals), but also whatever set-theoretic entities are deployed in the roles of the logical operators – presumably, at least one sentential operator, one quantifier and attendant variables. So it would seem that BR has good reason to construe D, *qua* set of singular terms, as a heterogeneous set that includes the actual individuals and actual non-individuals – the actual individuals, at least in the simple case, representing themselves, and certain actual non-individuals, representing non-actual individuals.[14] One would expect that there should be a non-accidental relationship between the set of actual individuals and the set of singular terms of the worldmaking language (as recently presented). If we take all of the singular terms, then the set of their simple individual urelements, as it were – the simple individuals that are such terms, or are constituents of sets that are such terms, or that instantiate any simple property that is the constituent of any such term – is the set of all actual simple individuals. What this shows is that, in a fairly natural sense, the universal domain D so conceived will be supervenient upon, but distinct from, the set of actual individuals. I will assume that CR incorporates a linguistic solution to the implicit representation problem and so is a subcase of BR in this respect.[15]

On this strategy no immediate problem looms concerning (NE), (BF) or (CBF) since we have countermodels of the kind afforded by the standard solution with varying world-domains. It would also seem that the truth of (4) can be accommodated by the existence in the domain of some world of an individual-representation – an ersatz individual that is not identical with any actual individual – that represents the existence of a son of Richard. However, such a solution to the D-problem threatens to determine as false on every model a class of claims involving iterated modalities that are intuitively true. Thus consider the following variant on our (2):

> (5) (Actually childless) Richard might have had a son who was contingently famous.

(5) has the natural QML form:

> (5*) $\Diamond \exists x[Fx \ \& \ \Diamond Gx]$

where the first occurrence of bound 'x' is purely de dicto and the second occurrence of bound 'x' is de re with respect to the second possibility operator.[16] The BR specification of the standard PW truth-condition of (5) is as follows:

> (5**) There is some world w such that (w entails that there is an x such that x is a son of Richard and x is famous and (there is a world v at which x exists and is not famous)).

On the present solution to the D-problem, the only generalizable way we have of representing the existence at v of the very x that is represented as existing at w, is by having as a member of D(v) an individual-representation which has the character of the description:

> (I1) The unique x such that x is a son of Richard & x is famous & . . . .

But then for the truth-condition (5**) to be fulfilled, v is to entail that the individual in question is not famous, which is to say that v is to entail

> (I2) (The unique x such that x is a son of Richard & x is famous & . . .) is not famous.

Thus, type (5) claims are determined false.[17,18] There is no obvious way of saving the intuition that some such sentences are true while maintaining the conception of D as the set of singular terms that is constructed from the subvenient base of actual individuals and actually instantiated properties.

Certainly, there are other ways of manufacturing singular terms out of the actual individuals. One way is by exploiting more fully the representational resources of the actual individuals when they are taken to form an infinite set. If there are infinitely many actual individuals we can map the set of individuals onto itself in such a way that each actual individual has a name among the actual individuals (as in Lagadonian representation) but there are still individuals 'left over' to represent non-actual individuals. To see how this would work, consider that we could exploit the 1–1 correlation between the natural numbers, N, and the even numbers, E, in the following way. Let each member of E name its correlate in N, so that 2 names 0, 4 names 1, 6 names 2, etc. Then we have left over, among the elements of N, the odds 1, 3, 5 ... to function as names of things other than the natural numbers. Another, rather more straightforward, way is to adduce as additional singular terms in the worldmaking language singleton sets of the individuals. But all such constructions give rise to a dilemma. The singular terms in question have to have meanings that make them apt to represent individuals that do not actually exist. If they do so because they are disguised definite descriptions, never mind how, the type (5) problem recurs. If the singular terms in question are to be taken as semantically unstructured singular terms, i.e. proper names or unstructured demonstratives, how could such a term, in the context of an appropriate worldmaking sentence, come to represent (de dicto) the existence of a son of Richard rather than anything else?

In face of this latest difficulty, it seems that two options remain. As usual, there is the option of modal denial. In the present case, this requires that systematic falsehood must be accepted, or meaninglessness stipulated, for the likes of (5), and the intuition of truth explained away (cf. Lycan and Shapiro 1986: 372). Otherwise, D must be reconceived as a set of non-linguistic individual-representations.

(13.4) D AS THE INDIVIDUAL ESSENCES

The most prominent non-linguistic conception of individual-representations is Plantinga's conception of individual essences. In PR, possible worlds have no proper ontological structure and so, a fortiori, there is no kind of worldmaking element that is a candidate to play the role of individual-representation (ersatz individual). However, in each case where a world represents the existence of an individual that is different from any actual individual, PR has it that at that world there exists a property – even though such a thing is no worldmaking element – that corresponds uniquely to that individual. Thus the settled and favoured PR solution to the D-problem (Plantinga 1976) is to construe D as the set of individual essences – exemplified essences representing the existence of actual individuals, and unexemplified essences representing the existence of non-actual individuals.[19] The general PR specification of individual essence is as follows:

(E) An essence (of x) is a property E, such that: (i) if there is a world w such that at w, there is an x that exemplifies E, then at every world v if x exists at v then x exemplifies E at v and (ii) at every world v such that at v, there exists a y that exemplifies E, then y = x.

As with all PR properties, essences are necessary existents – each exists at every world, although many are unexemplified at many worlds. In the case of NR, the appeal to unexemplified essences as semantic surrogates for possible individuals is even more natural. For in NR, the possible worlds are conceived as ontological complexes, higher-order structured properties that have as constituents properties of the kind that are typically construed as essences, e.g. the property of being identical to a. So I will assume that NR like PR articulates an application of PW-semantics on that basis.[20]

Consequently, PR assigns to the intuitively true modal claims such as (1) and (2) the respective, and fulfilled, truth-conditions:

(P1) At some world w there is an essence E such that E is exemplified at w and E is not exemplified at w*.
(P2) At some world w there is an essence E such that E is co-exemplified at w with the property (relation) of being a son of Richard and E is not exemplified at w*.

The previously problematic (5) also falls to such a treatment by way of the truth-condition:

(P5) At some world w there is an essence E such that E is co-exemplified at w with the property (relation) of being a son of Richard and E is co-exemplified with the prop-

erty of being famous and E is not exemplified at w*
and (at some world v, E is co-exemplified at v with
the property (relation) of being a son of Richard and
E is not co-exemplified with the property of being
famous).

(NE) is invalidated since the thesis of necessary existence is interpreted as meaning that every essence should be exemplified (instantiated) at every world. Yet the PR/NR claim about essences is, at strongest, that each essence exists at every world but – in the case of contingent existents – exemplified at only some. (BF) is thereby invalidated by models such as the following. In some w there is an essence E that is co-exemplified with F, thus we have a true (BF*) antecedent:

(BF*1) $\Diamond \exists x[Fx]$.

However, it is not the case that at w* there is an exemplified essence E such that at some w, E is co-exemplified with F, thus we have a false (BF*) consequent:

(BF*2) $\exists x[\Diamond Fx]$.[21]

The appeal to individual essences generates problematic commitments about the truth-values of certain modal claims when combined with the thesis of existentialism. That matter will be considered in due course. But I turn now to consider the threat posed to the individual essence solution to the D-problem by two objections that Linsky and Zalta (1994) lodge against Plantinga's treatment of exemplification and co-exemplification.

The first complaint is that PR semantics disrupts our ordinary ways of non-modal thinking by leaving us with no way to express that an individual exemplifies a property. What is correct about this complaint is that no object-language QML formula that looks like a simple property ascription to an individual is interpreted in terms of exemplification *simpliciter* rather than co-exemplification. The kind of formula that might naturally be taken as expressing as much, '$\exists x[Px]$', is interpreted as meaning that some essence and P are (actually) co-exemplified. Yet it is not clear why, from a semantic standpoint, this should matter. It would be a problem if some intuitively meaningful QML formula went uninterpreted or was assigned an interpretation that enforced the ascription to a QML formula of an intuitively incorrect truth-value. The LZ point here seems to echo the kind of misconception which Hazen (1979a) diagnosed in the critics of counterpart-theoretic semantics.[22] For it seems as though the complainants are demanding, inappropriately, that one semantic theorist should reach metalinguistic agreement with a rival semantic theorist. 'Exemplification' etc. are theoretical terms of the metalanguage for which we would not expect to find object language analogues. It is one thing to hold PR accountable over data about the use of object language data, but quite another to require her to find object-language expressions to express truth-conditions that a rival theorist would associate with those sentences.

The second LZ complaint can be taken as having both philosophical and semantic dimensions. The philosophical dimension is that 'co-exemplification' cannot be associated with its intuitive analysis in terms of exemplification, i.e.:

(CE) At every world w, ((P and Q are co-exemplified at w) iff (at w, there is an individual x such that x exemplifies P at w and x exemplifies Q at w)).

For in PR, the above analysans is a condition that must be analysed – on pain of reintroducing a domain of non-actual individuals for worlds – in terms of co-exemplification of properties, and not vice versa. Again, the observation is correct. But again the question is why this should matter. Let it be true that, intuitively, exemplification of properties by individuals is – conceptually or ontologically – more fundamental than a relation of co-exemplification between properties. Perhaps there is some cost associated with adopting a non-intuitive order of explanation. But is there any more to the matter than that? The more substantial aspect of the second complaint is that the coherence of metalinguistic talk of essences and co-exemplification is dubious. Consider the definitions of 'essence' ((E) above) and 'co-exemplification' as follows:

(CE*) For all w, P and Q are co-exemplified at w iff (if w had been actualised then the state of affairs that something has both P and Q would have been actualised).[23]

The claim is that the availability of these definitions presupposes a metalanguage in which there are variables ranging over individuals – as in 'for any x if x exemplifies E' (essences) and 'something has both P and Q' (co-exemplification). This is supposed to be 'confusing, to say the least' (Linsky and Zalta 1994: 442 n.33) since no individuals are postulated in the PR semantics.

It is true that no individuals are postulated in the PR semantics in the sense that the semantics does not interpret any object language quantifiers as ranging over individuals. Equally, it is manifestly false that the proponent of such an interpretation of those object language quantifiers is committed, in general, to denying the existence of individuals or to eschewing metalinguistic talk of such things. So there appears to be no more confusion afoot in the PR semantics in this respect than there is in a semantic theory that deploys metalinguistic talk of sets but does not construe object language quantifiers as quantifiers over sets. Note also, that the apparent quantification over individuals that is identified never occurs in wide-scope position and, indeed, always occurs inside the representational and non-factive context, 'at $w\_$'. In this respect, the proper focus of worry about what is going on in PR semantics may be the workings of this operator, but that is a matter to which I will return in Chapter 16.

The third source of philosophical difficulty for PR lies with a dilemma posed by McMichael (1983a) to those who would solve the D-problem by appealing to individual essences. In outline the dilemma is this. Either essences must be construed as purely qualitative properties or as (at least partially) non-qualitative properties. If essences are purely qualitative, then AR faces serious problems with respect to issues of transworld identity and the adequacy of the range of possibilities that she is able to represent. If essences are (partially) non-qualitative then the alleged safety and sanity of AR ontology is in doubt. PR has no intention of occupying the first horn of the dilemma but the issues that McMichael raises for others in that respect will be discussed in Chapter 16 and Chapter 17. I discuss the safety and sanity of PR ontology, in respect of McMichael's worries and others, in Chapter 14.

(13.5) THE V-PROBLEM AND ITS EXISTENTIALIST SOLUTION

The V-problem is how to account for the function V in a way that avoids the representationally and metaphysically queer consequences of the intuitive application. On the intuitive application, the only constraint on V is that the extension that it assigns to any atomic predicate at any world should be a subset of the universal domain D. Consequently, statements about individuals turn out to be true at

Actualist realism

worlds at which those individuals do not exist. Thus, Nixon can be assigned to the extension of 'human' at a world w, thereby making it the case that 'Nixon is human' is true at w, even though: (i) it is not the case that 'Nixon exists' is true at w (since Nixon is not a member of D(w)); and (ii) 'there are no humans' is true at w (no member of D(w) is assigned to the extension of 'human'). Representational queerness is afoot here in that a world can represent that an individual has a certain atomic property without representing that the individual exists. It is as if a book or a painting could represent that hobbits are furry without representing that there are hobbits. Metaphysical queerness resides with the apparent violation of the thesis of serious actualism:

(SA) Necessarily, if an object has some property then the object exists.

I will not attempt to elaborate upon these allegations of queerness.

The straightforward and natural solution to the V-problem is to impose on V the 'existentialist' constraint that for any world w, and for any atomic predicate 'F' the extension of 'F' at w is a subset of the local domain D(w).

As an immediate, and seemingly favourable, consequence of this constraint we have the validity of the non-modal thesis:

(EI) $Fa \to \exists x[Fx]$.

In the absence of the existentialist constraint, or at least on the intuitive application, the principle is not validated and so (for completeness) we require a free-logic even for the non-modal quantificational fragment of the language.[24] However, in PW-semantics a favourable outcome for validity in the non-modal fragment of QML often turns out to be a mixed blessing. In this case of EI the price of validation is some complication of the interpretation of the necessity operator. On the strong (and simple) interpretation of the operator (Kripke 1963) a necessitation is true (at a world) just in case the necessitated formula is true at all worlds. In the absence of the existentialist constraint, then, one can consistently conjoin claims of absolute necessity and contingent existence – e.g.:

(7) It is necessary that Nixon is human.
(8) Nixon might not have existed.

(7) can be true since Nixon is assigned to the extension of '_ is human' at every world while (8) is also true since Nixon is not assigned to the local domain at every world. If we maintain the strong interpretation of the necessity operator along with the existentialist constraint on extensions, all such conjunctions will be inconsistent since contingency of existence ensures that there will be worlds at which Nixon is not available in the local domain for assignment to the extension of 'x is human'. So if the existentialist constraint remains in place, the natural move is to opt for a weak rather than a strong interpretation of the necessity operator. The general principle behind a weak interpretation is that necessary truth is truth at all worlds at which relevant individuals exist, so that – for example – (7) is true because there is no world at which Nixon exists and is not human. The thought is that whatever complication this might bring by way of stating precisely the truth-conditions of modal claims is a price worth paying for the preservation of standard principles of non-modal validity, and metaphysical and representational sobriety. However the matter does not end there since reliance on a weak interpretation of the necessity operator brings difficulties of its own. The first difficulty is that of avoiding commitment to the necessary existence of all individuals in virtue of the fact that every individual exists at every relevant world – i.e. every world at which it exists. The second and related difficulty is that of subsequently avoiding throwing the baby out with the bath water by depriving oneself of the means of stating truly that certain objects – perhaps numbers – do exist necessarily. Perhaps the solution is to discern that two related but distinct sorts of necessity – weak and strong – are expressed in the object language and to complicate the syntax of QML accordingly by introducing two corresponding sorts of modal operator. The issue is complicated and unfolds along many different dimensions. Suffice to say, in any event, that endorsing the existentialist solution to the V-problem seems certain to enforce on the semantics some series of complications that do not arise on the intuitive application.[25]

Finally in this regard, it should be emphasized that while the existentialist constraint on V is a natural semantic reflection of the metaphysical thesis of serious actualism, the relationship between the two is complex. The former is (expressed as) a thesis about predicates, the latter is a thesis about properties. The relationship between these two categories is complex because: (a) it is a matter of controversy which properties there are; and (b) it is a matter of controversy how predicate complexity relates to property complexity. On the former, the plausibility of the thesis of serious actualism depends greatly on whether existence is a property, on whether the set of properties is closed under complementation (so that if existence is a property then so is non-existence) and on how world-indexed properties (humanity-in-w, etc.) are treated. Related to these questions is the perennial question of whether the (putative) property of existence can or should be expressed by a predicate. Consequently, and most notably, the metaphysical thesis (SA) and the existentialist semantic principle may both be troubled by potential counterexamples in the form of claims such as:

(9) There is a world w, at which Socrates is non-existent.

So, depending on further views that are taken about properties and predication, acceptance of the existentialist solution to the V-problem may cause other semantic complications. But I will not explore these detailed developments here.[26]

In summary, as far as our familiar species of AR are concerned, the capacity to deliver an adequate applied PW-semantics may be judged as follows. The D-solution associated with BR/CR threatens unacceptable consequences by determining falsehood in the case of an interesting, but arguably peripheral, class of claims of iterated modality. The D-solution associated with PR/NR threatens no immediate and unacceptable modal consequences. However, problematic consequences loom whether AR accepts or rejects the existentialist solution to the V-problem. But, arguably, if these consequences are confined to matters of validity in the modal fragment of QML, all are negotiable. So, no version of AR should be judged incapable, on grounds of its modal consequences alone, of providing an adequate applied PW-semantics for QML. What remains to be weighed, however, are the further philosophical consequences of accepting the solutions that have been outlined.

CHAPTER 14

Actualist realism: safe and sane ontology?

Having considered which benefits an AR interpretation of PW can deliver, I turn now to consider the associated ontological costs. Even if AR cannot compete with GR on benefits (applications) she may compete on ontological costs by arguing that her actualist ontology of possible worlds is philosophically more acceptable – safer and more sane – than the non-actualist ontology of GR. What the safety and sanity of AR ontology amount to is its being conservative in some or all of the following respects: (a) the possible worlds and worldmaking elements are identified among entities that we are predisposed to recognize, either by our common sense ways of thinking and talking or by our philosophical needs aside from the need to provide a theory of modality; (b) it respects the common-sense ontological principle that everything is actual; (c) the ontology of concrete individuals is not extended either qualitatively, by admitting new kinds (unicorns, dragons, etc.) or quantitatively, by admitting infinitely many more individuals of the kinds that we already recognize (universes, planets, humans, etc.). Considerations (b) and (c) seem straightforwardly true of AR and the question then is how heavily they ought to be weighed as advantages over GR. But there is more to the innocuous-looking (a) than meets the eye.

It may well be the case that AR identifies worlds or worldmaking elements with kinds of entity that are described under familiar names that invoke familiar theoretical roles – 'states of affairs', 'properties' or even 'propositions'. Yet it remains to be seen whether the metaphysical account offered by AR of the nature of the entities in question preserves confidence in the safety and sanity of the ontology on offer. It is one thing to admit believing already that there are states of affairs, for example. It is another thing to believe in the kinds of thing that AR takes the states of affairs to be and another thing again to believe that such things are the states of affairs. What may seem safe and sane in advance may not seem so safe and sane once we are presented with an account of its nature or when we are asked to do without such an account. Finally, and perhaps most seriously, even if it is the case that AR presents us with an ontology of safe and sane worldmaking elements, paradox is threatened by various accounts of how these elements are collected to form a possible world. In the worst case scenario, such a paradox may be read as a demonstration that there can be no such thing as a possible world (so conceived). I will devote the next chapter to the paradoxes, developing here the other considerations that threaten to compromise the safety and sanity of AR ontology.

I will begin by outlining and evaluating in general terms four generic challenges to the safety and sanity of AR ontology. These concern: the nature of the actual world (14.1); abstractness (14.2); unrealized existence (14.3); and the absence of criteria of identity (14.4). I will then consider how these generic challenges bear on the different species of AR via the two basic categories of property (14.5) and state of affairs (14.6).

(14.1) THE ACTUAL WORLD

It has been observed that the AR conception of the actual world is, in various ways, at odds with our conception of ourselves and our world as concrete. Such observations arise from the juxtaposition of certain intuitive characterizations of the actual world – it is our world, it is us and all our surroundings – with the theoretical characterization offered by AR – it is one of the possible worlds and the possible worlds are abstract. The upshot of the juxtaposition is then supposed to be the absurdity that we and all our surroundings are abstract (Lewis 1973: 86) or that we cannot validly infer what is true of our world from what is true of all of the possible worlds (McGinn 1981: 159). However, there is no real difficulty here. Confusion can be dispelled if we take care to distinguish two sortal concepts (cf. van Inwagen 1986) and to distinguish the notion of an entity being actual (actually existing) from an entity being actualized (Lewis 1986a: 137).[1]

The concept of a C-world is that of a maximal individual – that individual of which every individual is a part. It is, plausibly, analytic that there is one such individual, call it 'C*', and AR and GR can agree that this is so. AR and GR disagree about the nature and extent of C*. GR asserts that C* has non-actual individuals as parts and AR denies this. GR asserts C* has parts that are spatiotemporally isolated from us while AR (typically) refuses to assert that this is so. Neither GR nor AR identifies C* with any possible world. GR identifies the possible worlds as certain proper parts of C*. AR identifies the possible worlds as the A-worlds. For (standard versions of) AR no individual – not C* or any of its parts – is an A-world. The species of AR offer their respective, positive characterizations of the concept of an A-world. Here let us take as our example that the conception of a (possible) A-world is that of a maximal consistent set of propositions – an abstract entity. For AR, all A-worlds are actual (existents) but among these one A-world is actualized. The actualized A-world, A*, is that which entails all and only the true (non-modal) propositions. C* differs in category from A* and from all A-worlds since C* is a concrete individual and a non-set while each A-world is an abstract entity and a set (of propositions). For AR, if anything is to be identified with us and all our surroundings, it is C*. AR denies that A* is to be identified with C* or with us and all our surroundings, although A* does stand in an important, distinguishing relation of representation of, or selection by, C* (us and all our surroundings). While GR may speak unambiguously of 'our world' – us and all our surroundings – AR is well advised to eschew the term since it threatens equivocation between C* (us and all our surroundings) and A*. In terms of the AR applied PW-semantics for QML the set of worlds, W, is the homogeneous set of all A-worlds, the actualized world, w*, in W is A* and C* does not figure in any theoretical role. We properly infer truths about A* from truths about all members of W. In turn, we properly infer truths about C* from truths about A* since A* represents, or is selected by, C*.

The accounts of the actualized world offered by the species of AR may threaten paradox (see Chapter 15) and other difficulties may be afoot.[2] However AR, properly understood, does not threaten to 'deconcretize' us and all our surroundings nor to render irrelevant to us and all our surroundings what is the case at all possible worlds.

(14.2) ABSTRACTNESS

The ontological difference between GR and AR is sometimes represented as that between a conception of worlds as concrete objects and a conception of worlds as abstract objects. The subsequent thought is that this contrast renders AR ontology relatively problematic. However, the representation, although broadly accurate, is unhelpful and the subsequent thought is not illuminating. The representation is unhelpful because there are many different accounts of the distinction between abstract and concrete.³ The subsequent thought is not illuminating because it gives no insight into why abstractness, in any sense, is problematic. One might seek to improve on the initial representation by conducting a thorough investigation of the various ways of drawing the distinction, the problems to which abstractness (in each sense) gives rise and whether each species of AR countenances ontology that is (in each sense) abstract. But I will seek swifter justice for AR.

The worlds of AR are naturally counted as being abstract – and AR typically and justifiably accepts that characterization – since the possible worlds of AR are (typically) not conceived as individuals, nor as being spatiotemporally located nor as standing in causal relations to anything. Equally, the non-actual worlds, and other non-actual individuals, of GR are naturally counted as being concrete since they are not sets, they are particulars rather than universals, they and their parts are spatiotemporally located, they have parts that (typically) enter into causal relations and they are not abstractions 'from' anything (cf. Lewis 1986a: 81–6).⁴ Because the possible worlds of AR are so conceived, they attract the salient complaints that abstract entities typically attract – in general, that we cannot stand in the kinds of relation to these things that would (normally) be required for knowledge of them, (singular) thought about them or (singular) reference to them. So, let us grant, AR worlds are abstract but GR worlds are not. Moreover, it is true that the salient complaints that are made about abstract entities are made on grounds that apply to AR worlds. Swiftly, AR ontology is not safe and sane because its causal isolation from us renders it semantically and epistemologically queer – we do not stand in the kinds of relations to AR worlds that are (normally) considered necessary for us to be able to refer to things and to know about them. However, although the non-actual worlds of GR are not abstract, the suspicion of semantic and epistemological queerness falls upon them for exactly the same reason – causal isolation from us – as it falls on the worlds of AR.⁵ So what is revealed by the consideration of abstractness is a common predicament for GR and AR. Moreover, it is not obvious that GR is any better placed than AR to deal with this common predicament. Certainly, reference to the non-actual individuals of GR is, as intimated in (5.6), highly problematic and it has even been suggested (see (9.3)) that the combination of the concreteness of non-actual worlds is a special obstacle to vindicating our knowledge of them. So, the significance of the abstractness of AR worlds is that they face (semantic and epistemological) difficulties that are of the same broad

AR: safe and sane ontology?

character as those that face GR worlds, and which are not obviously more severe than they are in the GR case. And this suggests that abstractness *as such* has no obvious bearing on the relative safety and sanity of AR ontology. What may have a bearing on that question, however, is that a general strategy for providing semantic and epistemological vindication of abstract ontology in general is not applicable in the case of some particular category, or categories, of abstract entity postulated by a species of AR. I will return to that point in (14.4).

(14.3) UNREALIZED EXISTENCE

A different complaint has it that AR ontology is neither safe nor sane insofar as it includes various unrealized existents. Here, I use 'realized' as a generic term for the ontological features of actualization, instantiation and obtaining that AR typically invokes in order to distinguish, either directly or indirectly, the actualized world from the others.

Let us note immediately that BR is atypical in this respect – and advantageously so, if trouble ensues from unrealized existence. For BR explicates actualization in terms of the familiar notion of truth and makes no appeal to being instantiated or obtaining. No doubt truth presents its own metaphysical challenges. But the postulation of sentences that are not true is, prima facie, much safer and saner than the postulation of uninstantiated properties or non-obtaining states of affairs. However, the other versions of AR are committed to unrealized existents and there are two aspects to the worry that such a commitment prompts.

One aspect of the worry is that the unrealized existents themselves are queer. It is to be anticipated, for example, that the unrealized existents will be, if anything, more problematic – epistemologically and semantically – than their equally abstract but realized kin. Thus, it seems far more plausible that our putative knowledge of universals is vindicated by our standing in appropriate causal relations to them in cases where the universals are instantiated than it is in cases where the universals are uninstantiated. It also seems more plausible that our putative reference to states of affairs, say, is vindicated by our standing in appropriate causal relations to them in cases where the states of affairs obtain than it is in cases where the states of affairs do not obtain. The second aspect of the worry concerns the 'selection' relations that underlie the property of realization. One AR world is realized because it (alone) is selected by – obtains in virtue of, is instantiated by – the (one) concrete world that exists. We shall see, in (17.4) below, that Lewis despairs of the intelligibility of the unrealized existents when the selection relation is supposed to be internal, and despairs of the intelligibility of the selection relation itself when it is supposed to be external. So there are grounds aside from aggravated semantic and epistemological queerness for the claim that the safety and sanity of AR ontology is undermined by inclusion of unrealized existents.

(14.4) CRITERIA OF IDENTITY

I continue to assume that all hands accept the existence of individuals and sets. AR typically believes that there are kinds of entity, such as states of affairs or properties, that do not fall under the categories of set or individual. The question then arises whether criteria of identity are available to vindicate acceptance of these further categories of entity. I will consider below whether there are such criteria in various cases. But more than half of the philosophical battle here is fought over the questions of the work that such criteria of identity are supposed to do, what is at stake if none are available and in which cases it is appropriate to demand that they be provided. I will address each of these points generally and briefly.[6]

The first sort of motivation for the demand for criteria of identity is semantic. One thought here is that a criterion of identity can vindicate the meaningfulness of our F-talk and, in particular, our purported quantification over F's. Another such thought is that even granting that there are F's, and that we can coherently say so, the availability of an appropriate criterion of identity for the F's may allow us to refer to (and think about) the various single F's. The second sort of motivation is epistemological. The thought is that a criterion of identity for the F's may figure in the explanation of how we know that there are F's and how we know various other important things about F's. The third sort of motivation is immediately ontological. The thought is that, where the F's are supposed to be a sort of thing, a criterion of identity captures or articulates what it is to be one F rather than another F. The kind of fact in question is something in virtue of which identity or difference in the F-case would not be bare identity or difference. All of these motivating views are controversial, and I will not attempt to defend any of them in detail here. But here is the general and crucial point that puts the issue of criteria of identity to the heart of considerations about the safety and sanity of AR ontology.

As presented, the status of the availability of a criterion of identity for a sort, F, is that of a *sufficient* condition of semantic, epistemological or ontological vindication. Moreover, there is reason for suspecting that the availability of a full-blown criterion of identity is not, everywhere, necessary for vindication in each of these respects. In the case where we are dealing with entities that are putatively concrete, and which are supposed to be causally related to us, there might well be reason to think that semantic and epistemological vindication – at least – can be secured by other means. I will not attempt to spell out this thought in detail. But it is based on the conviction that, where we stand in causal relations to a given kind of entity, our capacity to talk and know about such things can be secured by our having a certain kind of primitive intellectual contact with them, and it is not the case that all of the work of identifying thought or talk has to be done by our own internal conceptual resources. For that sort of reason, and skipping over a host of other difficult questions, one can at least see the case for claiming that in the case of – certain, actual – concrete entities, the availability of a criterion of identity is not a *necessary* condition for the semantic or epistemological vindication of controversial ontology. With abstract entities, however, the question that will not go away is the question of how we can talk about and know about the entities in question given that, in the nature of the case, our capacity to do so is not underpinned by our standing in any causal relations to them. One response to that question, as we have seen, is that provision of an adequate criterion of identity is sufficient to supply such vindication. Thus consider the role played in the neo-Fregean defence of arithmetical Platonism by Hume's Principle:

(HP) The number of F's = The number of G's iff
There is a 1–1 correspondence between F's and G's.[7]

Arithmetical Platonism (in this context) is the ontological doctrine that the natural numbers exist and that they are abstract objects. Hume's Principle is naturally viewed as a criterion of identity for the natural numbers. The neo-Fregean response to the epistemological challenge that is put to the arithmetical Platonist by Benacerraf (1973) rests upon the a priori and analytic status of (HP). The neo-Fregean response to the semantic and ontological challenge that is put to the arithmetical Platonist by Benacerraf (1965) also rests upon appeal to (HP) and to a certain reading of the context principle of Frege (1884). I do not, of course, claim either that this defence of

Actualist realism

arithmetical Platonism is unproblematic, or that I have yet given reason for holding that the availability of an appropriate criterion of identity is necessary for the semantic and epistemological vindication of all controversial abstract ontology. But given that we stand in no causal relations to the controversial entities of AR, then it looks as though a substantial burden of explanation is there to be discharged by one who further accepts that she has no criterion of identity to hand. For in that case, I think it is fair to say, the most obvious and most promising route to semantic, epistemological and other vindication is closed off. One might put the point by holding that, for this reason, the availability of a suitable criterion of identity is *presumptively necessary* for the vindication of the controversial entities of AR. Perhaps the presumption can be overturned. One consideration is that AR might seek to join GR in seeking epistemological vindication for her controversial ontology by adducing the argument from theoretical utility (see Chapter 9). But that course is far from straightforward. For one thing, it has been argued here that the range of theoretical applications offered by GR is greater than that offered by any version of AR. So given that comparative utility is a factor in credibility, why not opt for GR rather than AR? And, of course, it is no good AR appealing to the lower cost of her ontology at this point in the dialectic since the safety and sanity of AR ontology is what is presently under scrutiny. So, I maintain, the availability of a suitable criterion of identity is *presumptively necessary* for the vindication of the controversial entities of AR, and that that presumption cannot easily be overturned. To draw together, then, two important aspects of the case that has been made, neither abstractness nor the absence of a criterion of identity would, individually, be a damning feature of a controversial ontological hypothesis, but the combination of these features generates a substantial presumption against safety and sanity.[8]

Before turning to a substantial challenge to the view that has emerged, I will deal more quickly with two other general considerations that might be thought capable of demotivating the call for a criterion of identity for the (various) controversial entities of AR. First, it might be allowed that any of the motives for providing a criterion of identity directly for a sortal concept F might be undercut by the provision of a criterion of identity for some other sortal concept G if the F's fall under G. But that fallback position does not apply when we are dealing with a *sui generis* category of F's as is the intended case when AR postulates the existence of properties, states of affairs, etc. For GR such things are sets (of individuals) but for

AR: safe and sane ontology?

AR each is an ontologically primitive category. Second, the demand for a criterion of identity is appropriate only for concepts that are sortal, and one might acknowledge that it can be a controversial or indeterminate matter whether a predicate expresses a (fully-fledged) sortal concept – perhaps 'wave' or 'photon' are cases in point. But again, there is no obvious basis for excusing predicates such as 'property' and 'state of affairs' (as used by AR) on those grounds.

It has been argued that doubt would be cast on the safety and sanity of AR ontology by the absence of a criterion of identity covering entities that AR takes as primitive. This line of argument faces a serious challenge in the observation that the demand for criteria for identity is unfair in the case of the distinctive ontology of AR if it cannot be met in the cases of other ontological categories that we accept and presume to be in order. In order to evaluate the force of this response let us consider the problems that the demand for criteria of identity poses in the relevant other cases, namely those of individuals and sets. Indeed, in order to do so, let us consider the cases together. In the case of the sets there is a standard criterion of identity: sets are identical just in case they have identical members. Granting that the notion of set-membership is in order,[9] the next question raised by this criterion is that of the category of the members of sets. If we are in the realm of pure set theory then the only things that are set members are sets. But in that case, one might wonder how the criterion of identity improves the standing of sets if all that it succeeds in doing is telling us that certain sets are identical just in case other sets are identical. If we are in the realm of impure set theory, and wishing to stay within the bounds of safe and sane ontology, we may construe any series of applications of the standard criterion of set identity as terminating in the case where the only members of the sets are individuals. Then sets are identical when exactly the same individuals are members of both. So we must now face the question of the identity of individuals upon which the question of the identity of sets is seen to turn. But then the going gets tougher. Certainly, we can appeal to a *lateral* criterion after the fashion of the standard criterion of set identity as it applies when restricted to pure sets – a criterion that states identity conditions for some entities in the category in terms of the identity of entities in the same category. Thus, we can say that individuals are the same when they have exactly the same parts. But given that all individuals have only individuals as parts, we are back in the predicament of shifting sideways from the question of the identity of some individuals to the question of the identity of other individuals. What might we say

235

about the case of individuals if not that? We might appeal to Leibniz's law and hold individuals identical when they have all of their properties in common, but the safety and sanity of *sui generis* properties is *sub judice*. But where else is there to turn if not to individuals, not to sets and not to any other *sui generis* category whose safety and sanity is in doubt? One might abandon the idea that the concept of an individual is a sortal concept. One development of that thought is that we can then take refuge in the prospect that each of the things that we want to count as individuals falls under some genuine, non-categorical, sortal concept for which adequate criteria of identity can be supplied – horse, water molecule, ship, etc. That course is problematic at least to the extent that, notoriously, logically necessary and sufficient conditions for falling under such concepts are not in the offing. Another development of the thought is that we can analyse the non-sortal concept of individual by defining individuality explicitly as non-sethood or as being of the lowest logical type. But that course is problematic, at least because it appears to close the circle which began with pursuit of a criterion of identity in order to vindicate the concept of a set. So, in light of all of these serious and interrelated difficulties concerning the provision of criteria of identity for sets and individuals, is it not unfair to charge that the distinctive entities of AR are dubious for want of adequate criteria of identity? In defence of the view that it is not unfair to do so, one might argue as follows.

What the foregoing considerations suggest, perhaps, is that there is no question of providing adequate criteria of identity for all of the *sui generis* sortal categories of entity in one's ontology that are not, at least in part, lateral in some cases and interdependent across cases. Yet, the positive moves intimated above in the cases of sets and individuals might be construed as showing that there is enough to say about the cases separately and collectively to sustain the view that an ontology of individuals and sets is safe and sane. One way in which to draw upon and expand upon those moves would be to build up a picture as follows. We might begin with the view that the concept of an individual is a sortal concept, venturing that the individuals are the occupants of spacetime and that they are the same when they are spatiotemporally coincident. Then take the bottom level, impure sets to be sets with only individuals as members and appeal to the standard criterion of set identity as sameness of members. It would be acknowledged that the criterion of set-membership is lateral, but it need not be conceded that the criterion is vacuous or 'viciously circular' in virtue of that consideration. It would also be

AR: safe and sane ontology?

admitted that there is a large degree of vagueness, uncertainty and indeterminacy about the semantic question of which underlying individuals are invoked when we speak of the temporally persistent 'macro-individuals' – horses, water molecules, ships, etc. I believe that this is a story which supports the safety and sanity of individuals and sets, and that no comparable story can be told in defence of the additional categories postulated by AR.[10] But there are other dialectical moves available to one who would maintain the pressure on AR. First, perhaps identity and difference for some category has to be taken as unexplicated and perhaps the category of individuals is a strong candidate for having that status since there is no obvious alternative to admitting such things. Second, since, by hypothesis, we all believe in individuals and sets anyway, these categories have a certain default status which allows us, at least *pro tem*, to ask more by way of vindication of any further categories that are postulated than we do of the accepted cases. Third, and as a last resort, even if my assessment is quite wrong and considerations concerning criteria of identity cannot show the ontological categories of AR to be any less safe or sane than those of GR, the upshot would be that considerations of criteria of identity produce, as it were, a no score draw between GR and AR. But in view of the deficit in applications afforded, one might think that AR needs to register victories over GR, not draws, in matters of comparative safety and sanity of ontology. However, I do not think it necessary to retreat to that last resort. So, on balance, and while acknowledging that the issues raised by appeal to criteria of identity are deep and difficult, I take it that the absence of adequate criteria of identity for the distinctive categories of AR ontology would cast doubt on the safety and sanity of that ontology.

I turn now to consider in application to each of our species of AR the generic issues that have been raised concerning AR ontology. All species of AR, as I will present matters, take properties as primitive while PR is distinctive in taking states of affairs as primitive as well.[11] So worries about primitive properties apply in some form or other to all species of AR while worries about *sui generis* (PR) states of affairs apply to PR alone.

(14.5) PROPERTIES

All salient species of AR admit (actually) instantiated properties. The instantiated properties offer the prospect of a distinctive response to the allegation that our knowledge of, thought about and

Actualist realism

reference to such things is suspect since we do not stand in causal relations to them. In stating the allegation in the present case we cannot but attend to the question of what the relata of the causal relation are supposed to be. If one has in mind, as the objector to GR appears to, that it is appropriate to speak truly – even if indirectly – of individuals being causally related, or not, to one another then it might be argued that we stand in (cognitively or semantically) appropriate relations to instantiated properties when we stand in appropriate causal relations to individual instances of those properties. We stand in appropriate relations to donkeyhood in virtue of standing in appropriate causal relations to donkeys and, one might add, the donkeyhood of those things being causally efficacious in the production of our thoughts and sayings about donkeys. The instantiated properties are also susceptible to various sorts of account of their criteria of identity. It is standardly held that co-extensiveness of actual instances is necessary but insufficient for property identity. However – ignoring for the moment the impact on explanatory potential in the modal sphere – properties are associated with various theoretical roles that suggest related criteria. If we envisage properties in the role of causal agents, sameness of causal powers is one candidate to be the criterion of identity. If we envisage properties in the role of semantic values of predicates, necessary co-extension is another. Perhaps the putative criteria conflict and perhaps none is beyond suspicion, but at least there are decent prima facie candidates.

All salient species of AR also admit actually uninstantiated properties. The crucial issue is whether each admits uninstantiated simple properties. If the uninstantiated properties are invariably the products of complex property-forming operations on instantiated properties, perhaps the burden of establishing the causal credentials and criteria of identity for uninstantiated properties can be borne by their instantiated elements. If simple uninstantiated properties are admitted, no such recourse is available and the safety and sanity of the ontology of properties may thereby be compromised. Simple uninstantiated properties are eschewed by BR, as presently envisaged, and by CR, but embraced by PR and NR. In eschewing simple uninstantiated properties BR and CR court representational inadequacy (see Chapter 17) but at least they avoid the associated ontological suspicion. It also merits emphasis that even within the realm of simple uninstantiated properties, not all are equally safe and sane. Among the uninstantiated simple properties admitted by PR and NR are uninstantiated (non-qualitative) essences – the

AR: safe and sane ontology?

uninstantiated and perhaps essentially unnameable analogues of being (identical to) Socrates.[12] In line with the ontological actualism of AR, such entities actually exist and their theoretical roles require precisely that they should exist necessarily (exist at every world) – in particular, individual essences exist uninstantiated when the 'corresponding' individual does not exist. It is this theoretical role that exerts the pressure to treat the properties in question as simple, for to treat them as complex in the obvious way, so that Socrates is a constituent of the property, would appear to ensure that the existence of such properties is contingent upon the existence of the individual Socrates. But for many, to treat the property of being identical to Socrates, or any other essence of Socrates, as a simple entity whose existence is not contingent on the existence of Socrates is simply to misrepresent the nature of the property in question and to distort its conditions of existence in the process.[13] So even those who are prepared to admit the existence of uninstantiated simple properties may find it less safe and sane to admit uninstantiated non-qualitative essences under that heading.

(14.6) STATES OF AFFAIRS

The distinctive ontological commitment of PR is to *sui generis* states of affairs (of a certain sort). The independent credentials of PR states of affairs are not impressive. The loose notion of a state of affairs is, of course, one that is familiar from our ordinary ways of speaking. But that should give us no more confidence in states of affairs as a fundamental category of ontology than it does in scenarios, circumstances or predicaments. In contrast to properties, and even propositions, there is a somewhat limited range of theoretical roles that are associated with 'states of affairs'. The relata of the causal relation is one such role and truthmakers for non-modal sentences is another. But the states of affairs *of PR* are not apt to play either of these roles. In the former case, the states of affairs, insofar as their variety is intimated to us, are far too abundant to be, generically, the kind of things that are causes or effects – consider negative states of affairs, disjunctive states of affairs, states of affairs that are 'about' numbers or pure sets, impossible states of affairs, etc. But there is no (intrinsic) ontological difference between these 'causation-unfriendly' PR states of affairs and the others. Nor, for reasons that have been rehearsed in (12.2), are the states of affairs of PR apt to serve, in general, as truthmakers for non-modal sentences.[14] So the states of affairs of PR have the air of a newly postulated kind of entity rather than that of a familiar kind of entity that is adduced in a new, and further, role. What, then, do we know of this novel kind?

It would seem that states of affairs are abstract, although it is unclear by which of the common criteria they qualify. It would seem that states of affairs are *sui generis* since their identification with other categories of abstracta is precluded by the Leibniz law arguments reported in (12.1) above.[15] It would seem that states of affairs are unstructured, and certainly they do not have individuals or properties as parts – since they are not individuals or properties – nor as members – since they are not sets. Thus whatever problems states of affairs encounter in virtue of being abstract, these problems cannot be addressed by way of any familiar category of entity with which they may be identified or by devolving the problem to their elements. We are offered nothing by way of criteria of identity for states of affairs and it is hard to see how we could be. We have canonical singular terms that are supposed to refer to states of affairs – the now familiar gerundival terms that we form intuitively from sentences – and can frame statements of identity accordingly, e.g.:

(S1)   *Socrates' being human* is identical with *Socrates' being a featherless biped*.

But consider what might be said about the truth-conditions of such identity statements – even in the restricted case where our singular terms for states of affairs are formed out of atomic sentences, thus:

(S)   *a's being F* is identical to *b's being G* iff . . .

One might think that one could fill out the right side by stating that a is identical to b and F is identical to G. But what would justify such an approach? Since states of affairs are not complex entities, why should we appeal here to any familiar model on which identity for complex entities is determined by equivalence of elements of another kind – sets by identity of individual members, directions by parallelism of lines, numbers by one–one correspondence between concepts? Moreover, the simplicity factor also appears to rule out any role here for the kind of non-vacuous but lateral criteria of identity that were pinpointed in other cases. When such criteria are mooted in the case of individuals and that of sets, they have certain uses which, arguably, contribute to the elucidation – from within, as it were – of the concepts of set and of individual. The identity of sets

AR: safe and sane ontology?

is partly explicated in terms of identity of members where some members of sets are sets. The identity of individuals is partly explicated as a matter of identity of parts where the parts of individuals are individuals. There is no analogue in the case of PR states of affairs. Arguably, the most promising criterion of identity for PR states of affairs is mutual inclusion – that the obtaining of one state of affairs entails and is entailed by the obtaining of the other. But, for familiar reasons, that criterion might be thought too coarse-grained and conflationary. As ever, the worry is that modal (intensional) equivalents will wrongly be deemed identical – *Socrates being human* or *Socrates' being non-human* and *2's being even*, etc.[16] Finally, note that all that has been said thus far concerns *obtaining* states of affairs and recall that on top of these we have the *non-obtaining* states of affairs to consider. It seems unlikely – to put the point mildly – that consideration of that further case is likely to improve the case for PR being a haven of safe and sane ontology, but I will not rehearse the earlier worries anew for this class of unrealized existents.

I believe that there is no normal standard of safety and sanity in ontology which PR states of affairs have been shown to meet. I do not believe that anything like so harsh a judgement is merited in the case of properties. For that reason alone I judge that all of the other species of AR offer an ontology that is safer and saner than that offered by PR. BR comes off best since there is no problem about unrealized BR worlds and there need be no dubious simple uninstantiated properties. CR is slightly worse off for needing a notion of realization (instantiation) to do some work. NR is worse off again for needing a notion of realization and invoking dubious simple uninstantiated properties. PR properties enjoy the union of these vices, and PR further offers states of affairs whose safety and sanity is more dubious than that of its properties.[17]

In comparison with GR, I note the following. It is acknowledged that GR stands at a relative disadvantage to all species of AR in rejecting the common-sense ontological principle that everything is actual, and in extending the ontology of concrete individuals both qualitatively and quantitatively beyond what common sense and science admit. In the matter of the conception of the actual world, AR was exonerated and GR has no case to answer. In the matter of abstractness, the relevant comparative judgement is that there is nothing to choose between GR and AR on susceptibility to the problems to which abstractness is famously supposed to give rise. In the matter of unrealized existence, one might think that the commitment

Actualist realism

to such things is a non-conservative extension of ontology that counts just as much against AR as the commitment to non-actual individuals counts against GR. Moreover, AR has substantial outstanding problems in that respect while GR has no case to answer.[18] In the matter of criteria of identity, AR is especially troubled by the claim that the availability of adequate criteria is a presumptively necessary condition of semantic and epistemological vindication of controversial abstract ontology. While GR is not free of difficulties over semantic and epistemological vindication of its controversial ontology, and while there are some difficult questions hanging over the availability of adequate criteria of identity in the cases of individuals and sets, I have argued that the ontology of GR emerges looking safer and more sane than that of AR in this respect. Thus, my overall assessment is that AR emerges as having no clear advantage over GR on the point of safety and sanity of ontology.

CHAPTER 15

Actualist realism: paradox

It would be one thing for a species of AR to be ontologically problematic in any, or even all, of the ways discussed in Chapter 14, but it would be quite another matter for its ontological claims to be inconsistent. Yet commitment to various claims about sets threatens to show that such inconsistency is afoot in some, or perhaps even all, species of AR. The PW-paradoxes are a family of arguments to this effect. The PW-paradoxes depend on Cantor's theorem which will be stated here as follows:

(CT)   For any set S, every subset of S is smaller than P(S).[1]

Here, 'P(S)' stands for the power set of S, i.e. the set of all of the subsets of S which, in the elaboration of the theorem, is of cardinality (size) 2^k if S is of cardinality k. In the PW-paradoxes, (CT) is invoked to yield a reductio of the hypothesis that there is a set of a certain kind S. The negation of (CT), that S has a subset that is not smaller than P(S), is standardly established in an instance by showing that there is a one–one or a many–one mapping of the members of a subset of S onto the members of P(S).

I will begin, in (15.1), by giving a broad overview of the PW-paradoxes, their significance and the strategies for escaping them. I will consider the impact of the paradoxes on the different species of AR in some detail (15.3) and then expand on the various strategies of escape (15.4–15.6).

(15.1) PW-PARADOXES

To begin, I will sketch one PW-paradox to exemplify the kind:

(1) For all S, S is a maximal consistent set of propositions iff S is a set of propositions such that:
  (i) for every proposition p, (p ∈ S) or (~p ∈ S)
  (ii) the conjunction of the members of S is consistent [Definition of mcsp]
(2) There is a maximal consistent set of propositions S* [Hyp]
(3) For each set that is a member of P(S*) there is a corresponding proposition, q*, that is about that set and the propositions about the distinct sets are distinct propositions.[2] [Prem]
(4) For each such q*, (q ∈ S*) or (~q ∈ S*). [From (1)]
(5) There are at least as many propositions in S* as there are elements in P(S*) [From (3), (4)]
(6) S* is a subset of S* [Set Axiom]
(7) S* has a subset that is at least as large as P(S*) [From (5) and (6)]
(8) S* has no subset that is at least as large as P(S*) [From (CT)]
(9) There is no maximal consistent set of propositions S* [Reductio of (2) from conjunction of (7) and (8)]

The foregoing can be deployed most straightforwardly as an argument for the non-existence of possible worlds by adding to it a definition of possible worlds as maximal consistent sets of propositions. But there is another way. If we add a further premise:

(A) For every possible world, there is a corresponding maximal consistent set of propositions

it will follow from (A) and the non-existence of such sets that there are no possible worlds. Thus, our exemplary PW-paradox threatens directly the existence of a kind of set but also threatens indirectly the existence of whatever entities are appropriately correlated with such sets. Such PW-paradoxes have been construed as direct or indirect demonstrations of the non-existence of: the set of all possible worlds (Davies 1981); the set of all true propositions (Grim 1984);[3] maximal sets of states of affairs (Bringsjord 1985); the set of all possible states of affairs (Chihara 1998: 126–7); and the set of all possible essences (Chihara 1998: 130–1).

The negative existential consequences of a PW-paradox can impact on an interpreter of PW in two quite distinct ways. Such an argument can bring refutation: there are no possible worlds as the interpreter intends. Otherwise, and with various degrees of significance, such an argument can deprive an interpreter of an application of PW by depriving her of sets whose existence the application requires. In either event, the salient strategies for resisting the conclusion are these.

First, the restriction strategy: replace the hypothesis that there are sets of the problematic kind with the more modest hypothesis that there are sets of entities of that kind of a given rank or order. Second, the class strategy: maintain the hypothesis that there exist set-like collections of the kind hypothesized but declare that these set-like collections are proper classes, i.e. non-members, and not sets. Third, the non-maximal strategy: where the paradox is generated from the hypothesized existence of a certain kind of maximal set, try and apply PW by appealing only to non-maximal sets that can achieve what the maximal sets are supposed to achieve.[4]

This sets the scene for the main discussion, but in advance of that discussion, I will comment briefly on the case of Kaplan paradoxes.

(15.2) KAPLAN PARADOXES

The most accessible example of the kind is that presented in Davies (1981: 262).[5] The example is a Cantorian paradox that is taken by some – Bringsjord (1985) and Grim (1986: 191 n.5) as an argument to the conclusion that there is no set of all possible worlds. The argument, in outline is as follows.

The power set of the possible worlds is the set of all thinkable propositions, given that every subset of the set of all possible worlds is a thinkable proposition. But for each proposition, there must be a possible world corresponding to the possibility that only that proposition is thought (by a at t). So, contra Cantor's theorem, the set of possible worlds is at least as big as its own power set.

In that version, the conclusion can be blocked by denying the 'correspondence premise' – that every subset of worlds corresponds to a thinkable proposition – whilst maintaining that there is a set of

Actualist realism

all the possible worlds and that each thinkable proposition can be identified with some subset of that set.[6] However Kaplan (1995) expands the general theme of this most accessible of paradoxes in various ways – for example, by indicating how a possible world version of the Liar paradox can be constructed by describing a formula that appears to denote a possible property but which the standard semantics determines to be an impossible property. Perhaps the straightforward reply to the simple Kaplan paradox will do or perhaps some other effective response is available.[7] In any event, I will not pursue Kaplan paradoxes any further here. Apart from the level of technicality involved in doing so, I believe that they are marginal to my concerns over AR for the following reasons.

First, the paradoxes are general. They appear not to depend on any particular account of what a possible world is, not even at the level of GR versus AR; they apply to all applications in which propositions are correlated with the subsets of the possible worlds and in which the semantic theory is supposed to handle uniformly all iterations of intensional, non-logical operators. Second, even if a Kaplan paradox bites, any interpreter of PW might respond by simply relinquishing the rather specific applications of PW that are culpable, i.e. the construction of an adequate model theory for a certain class of intensional languages. So, I am inclined to think that even if some Kaplan paradox proves inescapable, this will tell us little about competition among the rival interpretations of PW. Certainly, the Kaplan paradoxes do not appear to threaten the ontological foundations of any version of realism about PW that we have considered. Since others do so, and also threaten philosophically central applications, I will concentrate on those.

(15.3) PW-PARADOX AND THE SPECIES OF AR

There is varying opinion about how PR is susceptible to PW-paradox. Bringsjord (1985: 64) thinks so on the grounds that Plantinga 'champions' a set-theoretic construal of possible worlds. But as we know neither Plantinga, nor PR as represented here, holds that the possible worlds are sets. Grim (1984: 207) is closer to the mark when he holds Plantinga (PR) vulnerable by association with the view that possible worlds are 'some sort of fleshed-out correlates' to maximal consistent sets of propositions. Menzel (1986: 68) hits this nail on the head in observing that PR – cf. Plantinga (1974: 44–6) – is rendered vulnerable by asserting that for every possible world W, there exists a corresponding book on W, i.e. a maximal consistent set of propositions. So the PW-paradox that threatens the existence of maximal consistent sets of propositions threatens the world-books of PR and, by correlation, the worlds themselves. One can envisage a version of PR in which the correlation of (possible) world-books to possible worlds is rejected so that the immediate threat to the existence of possible worlds is removed. Such a rejection promises to carry some cost to PR in terms of using PW as a means to theorize about propositions. But in any event, PR faces more serious and direct threats that are independent of her doctrine on propositions.

One such threat is a prospective demonstration that there is no set of all states of affairs. The general principle here is that wherever we have quantification we have, in our best and standard semantic accounts of quantification, commitment to a corresponding set of entities over which the relevant quantifiers range. Thus, the PR definition of 'possible world' in terms of states of affairs brings commitment – via the quantifier, 'for any state of affairs S', that figures in the maximality clause – to a set of all states of affairs (Grim 1986: 191).

Another threat is a prospective demonstration that there is no set of all of the possible states of affairs that obtain.[8] Chihara (1998: 126–7) argues that there is no such set. The crucial 'correspondence premise' (cf. (3) in our exemplary paradox) is that for each set of state of affairs S there exists another state of affairs S* which is the obtaining of all and only the members of S. The denial that there are such states of affairs, Chihara suggests, comes at the epistemological cost of undermining the only safe proof that we have of the existence of any PR possible worlds and at the ontological cost of giving up an intuitive principle – 'a sort of Abstraction Axiom' – that gives us a grip on how the existence of various higher-order states of affairs are generated out of more basic states of affairs.

The most serious threat of all, however, is a prospective demonstration that there is no set of the kind that PR identifies as the universal domain set D in her applied PW-semantics (Chihara 1998: 130ff.). As characterized by Chihara, the set in question is the set of all possible essences, and the crucial correspondence premise is this: for every x that is a member of the power set of the set of IESAO's (identity essences of the states of affairs that obtain) there corresponds the state of affairs of x's being an IESAO. This argument is crucial. Since the PR interpretation of PW offers no substantial conceptual application (see Chapter 11) or ontological application (see Chapter 12), its utility lies in its putative capacity to provide an applied PW-semantics for QML. In that light, a demonstration that there is no set of all possible essences now threatens the thorough demotivation of PR as we know it.

Thus, PW-paradox has no fewer than four potential routes into PR: world-books; the definition of possible worlds by means of quantification over states of affairs; the 'Abstraction Axiom' for states of affairs' existence; and the account of the universal domain D that figures in the favoured applied PW-semantics for QML.[9]

In the case of NR we face the customary difficulty of having less detail of exposition and application to go on. One parallel source of vulnerability might be the admission of the set of all properties, either through unrestricted quantification over properties or otherwise.[10] Another source of vulnerability, that NR shares with PR, is the NR account of the set D as the set of all possible essences. I take it that this is enough to show that NR is threatened by PW-paradox, but note that detailed development of the position in the context of a full theory of properties with 'abstraction axioms' may prove to be a further source of vulnerability.

Both BR and CR are more immediately vulnerable to PW paradox than are PR and NR since the former pair, but not the latter, construe possible worlds as sets. BR is even more immediately vulnerable than CR since BR construes possible worlds directly as maximal sets. Indeed, if we replace 'proposition' with 'L-sentence' throughout the exemplary paradox, we have before us an argument that threatens to show that BR possible worlds, *qua* maximal consistent sets of L-sentences, do not exist. More specifically yet, that there is no actualized world, as defined in BR, is an immediate corollary of the thesis that there is no set of all truths (Grim 1984). To see whether BR or CR are otherwise vulnerable to PW-paradox, consider the inroads that were uncovered in the case of PR.

First, BR possible worlds are correlated with world-books in the strongest possible sense – they *are* world-books. Whether CR correlates, or identifies, possible worlds with world-books is a matter of whether and how CR proposes to theorize about propositions.

Second, as with NR, the CR definition of a possible world involves quantification over properties. BR may also be vulnerable in this way if properties play the role of the L-predicates or, indeed, if that role is played by actual entities of any of the kinds for which PW paradox threatens the non-existence of a totality set.

Third, to pursue the parallel of the PR abstraction axiom for states of affairs, BR and CR may both also be vulnerable if they incorporate principles that generate either complex or higher-order instances of the canonical worldmaking elements, e.g. higher-order states of affairs or propositions about propositions (L-sentences about L-sentences).

Fourth, since both BR and CR have been envisaged as accounting for the set D in their applied PW-semantics as a set of actual individuals (see (13.2) above), no immediate problem beckons on that front. However, there is another problem that threatens both BR and CR that has no analogue in PR, for one PW-paradox has it that there is no set of all atomic propositions.[11] This claim may impinge on BR directly and may have implications for the CR commitment to the existence of the combinatorial range set of all atomic states of affairs.

All species of AR have now been presented with difficulties that are sufficiently many and serious to urge investigation of the various strategies of response to PW-paradoxes.

(15.4) RESTRICTION SOLUTIONS

The restriction strategy is inspired by a familiar kind of attempt to deal with the paradoxes of naive set theory. The idea in the latter case is that rather than attempt to quantify, all at once, over all sets, the interpretation of quantifiers over sets should always be restricted to sets of a certain rank or type or position in the hierarchy – sets at rank 0 whose only members are non-sets, sets at rank 1 whose only members are non-sets or sets of rank 0, etc. The point of implementing such a strategy in the case of the PW-paradoxes is to block the argument at stage (1) where we are offered, as it were, the notion of a maximal consistent and unrestricted set of propositions. It is because the notion of a maximal consistent set of propositions is (otherwise) unrestricted that propositions that are about sets of propositions 'get back in' at stages (3) and (4) of the argument. However, the thought goes, we might begin with a restricted maximal consistent set of propositions such as a maximal consistent set of propositions of rank 1 – propositions that are about non-propositions – or maximal consistent sets of those propositions expressible in a certain limited vocabulary. Then, the propositions at stage (3) would not get back into the postulated sets at stage (4).[12]

It should go without saying that substantial work will be involved in fleshing out such proposals in adequate detail. But these important matters of detail aside, the generic danger with the restriction strategy is that it will secure the consistency of AR, if at all, by compromising significantly the range of possibilities that an AR interpretation of PW is capable of addressing in its (conceptual,

Actualist realism

ontological or semantic) applications. The range of possibilities is squeezed – as it were – both vertically and horizontally. The vertical range is a matter of whether AR can deal with possibilities other than 'ground level' possibilities about individuals, the horizontal range is a matter of whether AR can address all possibilities at that level.

If AR pursues the broadly semantic approach to restriction that was intimated above, so that possible worlds are maximal consistent sets of only those propositions that are about non-propositions, we get the problem of vertical range. The problem is that the possible worlds correlated with such sets of propositions do not offer us any immediate way of representing possibilities about the propositions. It may be true at w that Socrates is a philosopher, since the proposition that Socrates is a philosopher is a member of w. But, by the restriction (as intended) it is not the case that any proposition that is intuitively about the proposition that Socrates is a philosopher is a member of w. So how is the possibility of the existence of such a proposition to be represented and how, in general, are we to understand modalizing about propositions?

One way forward, and perhaps the natural way suggested by this kind of solution, is to postulate a hierarchy of possible worlds and have possibilities for non-propositions represented at rank-0 worlds, have possibilities for rank-1 propositions represented at rank-1 worlds, etc. One pressing problem for that kind of approach would be that of adequately characterizing the ranks of possible worlds. If the worldmaking elements are – say – states of affairs, are we to have possibilities about all things other than states of affairs (properties, propositions, sets) represented at rank-0 by rank-0 states of affairs? Or should we be sensitive to the consideration that *all* such kinds may have to be stratified if paradox is avoided and seek to represent at a given rank of possible world only possibilities that are 'about' entities that are all at that rank? Clearly, it is a research programme rather than an immediate solution that is intimated here and there is some way to go before a consistent theory of even rank-0 possibilities, via an adequate characterization of rank-0 possible worlds, has been secured.

If AR imposes the broadly syntactic approach to restriction, so that possible worlds are the maximal consistent sets of those sentences of a restricted language L, then we get the problem of horizontal range. The persistent worry is that restrictions that are required in order to guarantee consistency will curtail the expressive power of the worldmaking language so that even at the level of ordinary ground-level possibilities, not all possibilities can be represented by the worlds. One way in which this worry is substantiated is if the worldmaking language is restricted so that all of its sentences are finite in length and drawn from a finite vocabulary. In that case, AR is exposed to the cardinality argument of Lewis (1973: 90) according to which such a worldmaking language is inadequate because: (a) a set of worlds constructed from such a language is no bigger than the set of real numbers; and (b) if the set of possible worlds is to represent all of the distinguishable possibilities then it must be as large as the power set of the real numbers.[13] The crucial question is whether we have any metalogical results showing that there are languages for which we can construct maximal (syntactically) consistent sets of sentences which are as many as the subsets of the real numbers. In the absence of such results, syntactic restriction carries with it the threat of expressive limitation.[14]

Having made these very general points about the risks entailed by pursuing the strategy of restriction, I will indicate one case in which the pursuit of the strategy may prove reasonably tolerable and effective.

Recall Chihara's claim to have shown that there is no set of the kind that PR construes as the universal domain D of her applied semantics. Chihara advertises his argument as demonstrating the inconsistency of the hypothesis that there exists a set of all possible essences (all essences exemplified in at least one world), claiming further that Plantinga's applied semantics for QML identifies D as that set. The argument on offer construes the set of all possible essences as including the identity essences of all possible states of affairs. The set for which the equinumerosity result is proved directly – the analogue of our step (5) above – is the set of all OSAIE's (the set of all obtaining states of affairs' identity essences). However, the conception of D that is naturally adopted by PR (and NR) is that of the set of identity essences of individuals and not the set of identity essences of all things. I do not dispute that Plantinga believes in the larger set, or even that he ought to believe in such a set given other things that he believes. The claim is simply that, for all we have been shown, PR (and even more obviously NR) can have an applied semantics in which D is construed as the 'restricted' set of essences of (possible) individuals.

(15.5) PROPER CLASS SOLUTIONS

The proper class strategy, like the restriction strategy, is inspired by consideration of the paradoxes of naive set theory. The leading idea

Actualist realism

is that where trouble ensues from the hypothesis that a big collection forms a set, we should step back from that position and assert only that the collection in question forms a proper class. The crucial point, for our purposes, about proper classes is that they are, definitively, non-members – i.e. they are not members of any other more inclusive collections. The general move to deal in classes rather than sets is highly controversial.[15] Yet aside from general considerations that are internal to the foundations of set theory, the appeal to proper classes as a means of responding to the PW-paradoxes in particular prompts two kinds of local objection.[16]

The first objection is that the move will not be available because the collections that cause the trouble in the PW case fall on the set side of the set/proper class divide (Menzel 1986). The two-fold thought is: (a) that what makes for a proper class is – *inter alia* – members that are of arbitrarily high rank; so that (b) maximal consistent 'sets' of propositions are indeed sets, if anything, since all are of the first set-theoretic rank by virtue of having no sets (but only propositions) as members.[17]

The second objection, echoing the case of the restriction strategy, is that the appeal to proper classes will significantly curtail the applications that an interpretation of PW will afford. Indeed, if we interpret PW as talk about proper classes, the threat to applications strikes at a quite fundamental level. Ontological applications of PW, as we have often seen, often take the form of identifying certain sorts of entity with collections (sets) of possible worlds. But if the possible worlds are taken as proper classes, then they are not available to be the members of such a collection. Perhaps the effect of that observation is mitigated by the limited ontological ambitions of AR, but note that some such identifications were considered available to both CR and NR.[18] Ontological applications aside, however, we have seen that applied PW-semantics, as we know it, requires a set of possible worlds W, and so the ineligibility of possible worlds to be so collected would appear to count decisively against the provision of such an application.[19]

(15.6) NON-MAXIMALITY SOLUTIONS

Where PW-paradox is generated from the hypothesis that a certain kind of maximal set exists, the present idea is that we should seek to deliver the same applications by appealing to surrogate, non-maximal entities. One thought behind the hypothesis of maximal consistent sets of propositions is that the representational content of a possible world is characterized by a set of entities in which all that is the case at the world is explicitly represented. On an alternative, non-maximal, approach the representational content of a possible world is characterized by a non-maximal entity in which much that is the case at the world is implicitly represented. The notion of implicit representation might be glossed in terms of entailment or supervenience. All that is true at a world supervenes on its basic worldmaking elements, or what is explicitly represented as true at a world entails all that is true at that world. To generalize then, the thought is that if possible worlds *qua* non-maximal entities can fix complete representational content, that will be enough to ensure that we can have all of the applications associated with possible worlds *qua* maximal entities.

As the strategy has been proposed in the literature it involves the further assumption that non-maximal worlds will be non-maximal sets of entities (Menzel 1986, Hazen 1996a). Under that assumption, the strategy is already embodied in both CR and BR as presented here. For in each case possible worlds are conceived as sets (of simple states of affairs, and atomic sentences respectively) that represent various more complex matters implicitly, if at all, rather than by having corresponding complex members.[20] Since PR and NR conceive worlds as (different kinds of) maximal non-sets, the present strategy is not directly available to them. But I do not see why, in principle, a version of AR – perhaps even a recognizable variant of PR and NR – should not take the form of attempting to construe representationally complete worlds as non-maximal non-sets, such as non-maximal properties or non-maximal states of affairs.

Grim (1997) has three kinds of objection to this strategy. The objections are aimed directly at the account of non-maximal possible worlds in Hazen (1996a) but I will attempt to deal with them here in a general form.

The first objection to the present strategy is that no satisfactory account is available of the notion of supervenient content (or entailed content) that figures in the gloss of the idea of implicit representation by a possible world. The objection might be fleshed out as a dilemma. The only satisfactory accounts of such notions either invoke maximal sets of the type that the account seeks to avoid, or they invoke possible worlds, the very entities that are now being explicated in terms of supervenience and entailment. The first horn of the dilemma is powerful and instructive. We cannot have any account of the concepts of supervenience and entailment that involves treating either of these as relations between non-maximal worlds, on one hand, and the propositions true at those worlds, on the other. The relation in question might be presented as that between a non-maximal set of formulas and the set of their proof-theoretic consequences. The relation in question might be presented simply in extension, as a set of ordered <world, proposition> pairs. But either way, commitment ensues to maximal sets of the kind that it was intended to avoid – sets of all formulas derivable from T, sets of all propositions true at a world, etc. The second horn of the dilemma is less sharp. What, I think, is clear enough is that the specification of the non-maximal worlds must, for reasons given in Chapter 11, invoke some unanalysed modal concept. In CR, the species of AR to which Hazen's specific proposal belongs, it is necessary to specify as possible worlds, sets of worldmaking elements upon which all that is true at a world will supervene. Recall from Chapter 11 that in order to specify such worlds, CR need not invoke the concept of entailment (or supervenience). But it was argued there that if CR is to succeed in her broader aims, she is bound to specify the worlds in implicitly modal terms – in terms of simple properties, on the exemplary version of CR, or in terms of sets of 'independent' properties on Hazen's version. Thus, it may be true that the specification of possible worlds that are capable of adequate implicit representation may involve appeal to an unanalysed modal concept. But I presume that AR already lives with that outcome, and to be reminded of it in the context of appeal to non-maximal possible worlds is not to present a new objection.

The second objection is that if the representational content of a possible world is not given explicitly as a set of representations, then AR is not entitled to the elegant set-theoretic account of what is true at a world – thus: P is true at W iff P is a member of W. The objection does not apply to all species of AR but only to certain versions of BR and CR to whom such an account of representation is available.[21]

The third objection is *ad hominem* to those who prosecute the non-maximality strategy by holding that non-maximal possible worlds containing set-many elements can represent implicitly the truth of more than set-many propositions.[22] The charge is that if we are prepared to countenance the idea of totalities of more-than-set size then, by default, we should countenance the possibility that there should co-exist more than set-many of the worldmaking elements (independent properties or whatever). Yet the non-maximal possible worlds are constrained to have set-many independent elements and so cannot represent (even implicitly) such manifold possibilities. I do not intend to defend on this point, or any other, the view that non-maximal possible worlds represent implicitly the truth of more than set-many propositions. As in the case of the proper class solutions, I would rather point the discussion away from the territory of the foundations of set theory. In this case the question that I want to raise, but cannot attempt to settle, is whether the non-maximality strategy might be pursued without commitment to the idea that the implicit representational content of a possible world is inevitably correlated with, and brings commitment to, a collection of propositional entities that outstrips the basic worldmaking entities. That matters should be otherwise is a thought that might be motivated in at least two ways. One thought is that the representational content of a world need not be reified at all. Briefly, that one can truly say that at some world w there are talking donkeys without being committed to a corresponding representational entity such as the proposition that there are talking donkeys. Another thought would be that the only genuinely representational entities are atomic propositions, which are collectable in sets, while what is implicitly represented by those sets is not apt to be represented explicitly by any collection of entities – the objection here being not that such a collection would be 'too big' but, as it were, a kind of antirealism about non-atomic propositions. It is worth considering how such antirealism about all or some propositions would sit on top of an actualist realism about possible worlds. But, in any event, the general dilemma that looms for the non-maximality strategy is this. If implicit representation is to be explained relationally, then it looks as if the second term of the relation must be a set-like non-set of propositions. If implicit representation is not to be explained relationally, how is it to be explained?[23]

I draw a line here under the discussion of this difficult issue and summarize as follows.

It is clear that there is much work to be done if any species of AR is to demonstrate, in the face of the PW-paradoxes, that her proposed interpretation of PW is consistent and that her intended applications are, subsequently, secure. In comparison, the position of GR seems far more comfortable. It was indicated in (Chapter 6) how the GR principle of recombination threatens paradox but I argued that the price of escape – commitment to the claim that there is a maximal possible size for spacetime – was low. It is difficult to imagine how AR could reasonably disagree with that characterization of the cost that GR must pay as she confronts, in her own case, the prospect of having to execute successfully the strategies outlined in order to escape the PW-paradoxes. In sum, paradox would appear to be a substantial and unresolved difficulty for AR, but not for GR.[24]

CHAPTER 16

Actualist realism: transworld identity and transworld identification

The problem of transworld identity, due to Chisholm (1967), is a non-epistemic problem. It covers questions about the conditions, if any, under which an individual that relates to one possible world in a certain non-epistemic way is identical to an individual that relates to another possible world in that same kind of way. The problem of transworld identification due to Kaplan (1967) is an epistemic problem. It covers questions about how, if at all, we can reliably or successfully tell whether we have a case of transworld identity. Sometimes the problems are conflated, and conflation is abetted by unqualified talk of how we 'individuate' possible individuals or by unexplicated talk of 'criteria of identity'. Even when the problems are not conflated, it often seems that the (alleged) intractability of the problem of transworld identification is supposed to have one or more of the following consequences for transworld identity: that claims of transworld identity are semantically deficient; that we do not understand claims of transworld identity; or that there are no facts of the matter about transworld identity.[1] It is easy to gather from the literature the impression that transworld identity, at least, is a problem for AR but not for GR, since AR asserts the transworld identity of individuals while GR rejects this thesis in favour of the worldboundedness of individuals. I will argue, however, that this impression is highly misleading. The substantive issues generated by the problem of transworld identity do not render the position of AR obviously more problematic than that of GR. On the other hand, it is mistaken to think that the standard AR solution to the problem of transworld identification – the 'stipulation solution' – also provides a solution to the real epistemological problem set for AR by considerations of transworld identity.

I begin by distinguishing various types of transworld identity thesis (16.1). I discuss the problem of transworld identity (16.2)–(16.5) and then that of transworld identification (16.6) before linking these to each other and to the GR/AR debate (16.7).

(16.1) DISTINGUISHING TRANSWORLD IDENTITY THESES

Having distinguished the problem of transworld identity from the problem of transworld identification, the former requires us to distinguish three types of thesis about identity across possible worlds, viz.: identity across possible worlds of represented individuals; the identity across possible worlds of (individual) world-constituents; and the identity of (individual) members across world-domains.

The thesis of the transworld identity of represented individuals is:

(TW1) There is an individual x such that there is a world w and a world v and w ≠ v and at w, x exists and at v, x exists.

(TW1), as Lewis (1986a: 194) remarks, is an uncontroversial thesis which both GR and AR accept under their respective preferred interpretations.[2] Humphrey, say, exists at more than one world, winning in some and losing in others. The cost of denying (TW1), while maintaining the standard neutral PW account of truth-conditions for de re modal claims about individuals, is commitment to the hyper-essentialist thesis that all individuals have all of their (non-modal) properties essentially. Essential properties of any individual are those it has at every world at which it exists. But if 'every world' here picks out (at most) the only world at which an individual exists, then all properties had by that individual at that world are essential properties of that individual. The commitment to hyper-essentialism is obviously undesirable and may even be construed as providing a reductio of the neutral PW approach to the truth-conditions of de re modal claims. So the falsehood of (TW1) would pose a serious problem for GR and AR alike.

The next pair of theses concern transworld identity of world constituents. The weaker thesis of the pair is:

(TW2) There is an element x such that there is a world w and a world v and w ≠ v and x is a constituent of w and x is a constituent of v.

(TW2) is controversial. It is denied by GR on the grounds that there is no individual that is wholly part of more than one world. (TW2) is accepted by those species of AR who hold that worlds have constituents. Thus one atomic state of affairs is a member of many worlds (CR); one simple property is a constituent of many worlds (NR); and one atomic sentence is a member of many worlds (BR). It is uncomfortable to attribute (TW2) to PR for the familiar reason that PR worlds do not (properly) have constituents although, for the record, any given state of affairs is typically *included in* many worlds. Our initial thesis of transworld identity of world constituents can be strengthened to require that the constituents of worlds are individuals, thus:

(TW3)   There is an individual x such that there is a world w and a world v and w ≠ v and x is a constituent of w and x is a constituent of v.

At this stage a certain ambiguity in the notion of a world constituent becomes relevant. In no salient version of AR are the salient constituents of worlds individuals, they are *sui generis* states of affairs (PR), properties (NR) or sets (CR and, let us assume, BR).³ However, in these cases where the salient constituents are sets, some of the ultimate constituents of the worlds, i.e. the ur-elements of the sets, are individuals. CR does, and BR may, conceive of worlds as sets and admit distinct worlds that have common individual ur-elements; there is one legitimate interpretation of (TW3) on which it is endorsed by these species of AR. No other species of realist endorses (TW3) under either interpretation.⁴

Recall that all who proffer an applied PW-semantics accept that associated with each world w there is a set of things D(w) that represent the individuals that exist at that world. The associated Q-problem was whether models should allow common members across world-domains. The next pair of theses speak to that problem since they are theses of identity across the world-domains of PW-semantics, or theses of transworld identity of individual-representers. The weaker thesis of the pair is:

(TW4)   There is an element x, a world w and a world v such that w ≠ v and x is a member of D(w) and x is a member of D(v).

(TW4) is controversial. GR rejects (TW4) since she identifies each world-domain with the set of constituents of the world, and since different worlds have no common constituents, contra (TW2), different world-domains have no common elements. However, (TW4) is, (typically) endorsed by all species of AR. PR and NR allow the same individual essence to be a member of many world-domains and, indeed, may have every individual essence as a member of every world-domain. We have already seen in Chapter 13 various conceptions of world-domains – e.g. as various subsets of the actual individuals – that will allow CR and BR also to endorse the transworld identity of representers. A stronger thesis of identity across world-domains requires that the members of world-domains, the individual-representations, are individuals, thus:

(TW5) There is an individual x, a world w and a world v such that $w \neq v$ and x is a member of D(w) and x is a member of D(v).

Among those who allow overlapping world-domains, *à la* (TW4), only CR and BR endorse (TW5) since only they take the elements of the domains to be individuals. Before proceeding to the main business of the chapter, and by way of demonstrating the utility of the foregoing distinctions, I will put them to work in resisting one attempt to turn to the advantage of AR (over GR) considerations about individuals 'persisting from world to world'.

Lycan (1991a) claims that AR has no problem about individuals persisting from world to world while GR has to reject that 'strongly intuitive view' in favour of counterpart theory. Lycan contends in this respect that such 'persistence' is most obvious when AR worlds are sets of elements achieved by recombination of actual entities so that actual individuals are present – with different features – at a variety of worlds. In this positive claim on behalf of AR – *de facto* CR – any or all of three different kinds of transworld identity claim might be intended: identity of individuals represented; identity of individual constituents; or identity across world-domains. But no matter since CR endorses transworld identity of individuals in all respects. However, the failure to distinguish these theses does matter when GR is alleged to reject 'this strongly intuitive view' in favour of counterpart theory. For what is a strongly intuitive view is a view that GR does not reject, namely that there is identity of the individuals represented across worlds (TW1). What GR rejects, in favour of counterpart theory, are the theoretical views about how possible worlds (TW2) are constituted and how the world-domains of PW-semantics are comprised (TW3). But these views are not strongly

AR: transworld identity and identification

intuitive. One might argue that counterpart-theoretic representation is counter-intuitive. That is another story (see Chapter 8). But Lycan's claim about what GR rejects, rather than about what GR accepts, is undermined on distinguishing the different types of transworld identity claim.

(16.2) THE DISCERNIBILITY ARGUMENT AGAINST TRANSWORLD IDENTITY

Chisholm (1967) is most plausibly interpreted as intending scepticism about the thesis of transworld identity of represented individuals (TW1) and may be construed as offering two arguments against that thesis.[5] The first argument proceeds from discernibility, via the indiscernibility of identicals, to failure of identity. The second argument is a dilemma against (TW1) that can be constructed out of the Adam–Noah example. I will discuss these arguments in turn. I reiterate, however, that both GR and AR owe us responses to these arguments since both endorse the transworld identity of represented individuals.

The discernibility argument proceeds as follows. By hypothesis any two distinct possible worlds w and v differ in some respect. Let us say, as an arbitrary instance of difference, that at w there are swans but at v there are no swans. It follows that for any x that exists at w, x differs in some respect from any y that exists at v, in that x co-exists with swans and y does not. Then, by the indiscernibility of identicals, any x that exists at any w is non-identical to each y that exists at any v that is distinct from w, contra (TW1).

The success of the discernibility argument against (TW1) requires an example of a genuine property such that the individual represented at w by x has that property and no individual represented at v by y has that property. So what is the property? Note that the kind of property that is taken to distinguish worlds in the argument is a representational property. World w differs from world v in that at w something holds about some x which at v does not hold about anything. The crucial thought to bear in mind here is that we would not, in general, expect it to follow from the fact that representations (here worlds) are distinct that they represent discernible things. Two different newspaper stories, say, can differ in what they represent as being true without being about truly discernible (distinct) individuals. We can spell out the point about worlds in this respect with reference to the different accounts of what it is for a world to represent. The crucial point throughout is that none of our protagonists is

261

Actualist realism

compelled to admit that there is some property such that – say – Adam need have that property in order to be represented by w as co-existing with swans and which anything must lack in order to be represented by v as being otherwise.

GR accounts for the representation-relevant features of the worlds as follows. w has the property of having as a part something – say Adam – that co-exists with swans and v has the property of having no parts that co-exist with swans. What follows from this about the properties of relevant individuals is that one, Adam, has the relational feature of co-existing with swans and none – including Adam – has the distinct relational feature of having a counterpart that is a part of v and co-exists with swans. PR/NR treat the relevant different representational features of the worlds as follows. w has the property of being such that if it were actualized Adam and swans would co-exist while v lacks the property of being such that if it were actualized something would co-exist with swans. CR/BR treat the relevant different representational features of worlds as follows: w has the property entailing that Adam and swans would co-exist while v lacks the property of entailing that there is something that co-exists with swans.

One might resist the idea that there is a basis in any facts about Adam-representations for the ascription of any genuine relation to Adam. But if there is such a relation afoot then it is a relation that has a place for the representing item. Taking the first PR case as example, Adam has the property of co-existing-with-swans-were-w-to-be-actualized and nothing has the property of co-existing-with-swans-were-v-to-be-actualized. Or as the point is sometimes put, the relevant representational properties of represented individuals, if any, will be world-indexed properties (see Plantinga (1974: 91–2) and Loux (1979: 42)). Adam has the property of co-existing-with-swans-at-w and nothing has the property of co-existing-with-swans-at-v.[6,7]

Although GR and AR will take this common approach to the discernibility argument against (TW1), divergence of approach is required if the argument is construed against the identity of world-constituents (TW2) – a thesis which GR rejects and AR accepts. For GR, Adam is represented by w as co-existing with swans by being a constituent of w and co-existing with swans, but since there are no swans at v, no constituent of v co-exists with swans. So Adam is discernible from, and hence non-identical with, each constituent of v and, generalizing, no x that is a constituent of a world w is a constituent of any v(≠ w). Thus, GR can derive from Chisholm a sound discernibility argument against (TW2) or (TW3), the theses of

262

transworld identity of world-constituents. Indeed, since (for GR) world-constitution determines world-domains, we thereby have sound arguments against the theses of identity across world-domains (TW4) and (TW5). In contrast with GR, it does not follow from the accounts of representation favoured by AR that worlds that so differ representationally have no common constituents. What follows (at most) is that the worlds do not have exactly the same constituents. In the NR case, there is some property that is a constituent of w and which is not a constituent of v. In the CR/BR case, there is some sequence that is a member of w (or of the consequence class of w) but is not a member of v (or the consequence class of v). However, that is manifestly insufficient to show that the worlds have no common salient constituents (properties, sets), and far less that the worlds have no common ultimate individual constituents.

(16.3) THE ADAM–NOAH EXAMPLE

A second argument against (TW1) emerges from Chisholm's Adam–Noah example.[8] At the actual(ized) world W_1 Adam exists, Noah exists and Adam is not identical to Noah. By hypothesis, there is a non-actualized world W_2 at which Adam exists and Noah exists and they 'exchange' some property that they have at W_1 – say that at W_2, the maximum height of Adam is 1.9m (1.9m is the maximum height of Noah at W_1) and the maximum height of Noah is 1.89m (1.89m is the maximum height of Adam at W_1). By further hypothesis there is a sequence of such worlds $W_1 \ldots W_n$ through which Adam and Noah continue to 'exchange' their W_1 properties so that at W_n we have two individuals as follows: there is an individual, a, which is continuous with, or constructed from Adam at W_1, and which has all of those properties that Noah had at W_1; there is also an individual, n which is continuous with, or constructed from Noah at W_1, and which has all of those properties that Adam had at W_1. The ensuing argument is a dilemma concerning essential properties proceeding from:

(T) At W_n, Adam = a.

On the first horn of the dilemma, if (T) is held true then we get a clean account of the extent of the essential properties of individuals but a mystery about representation de re. What is exemplified here about essential properties is that individuals don't have any – except, perhaps, those logically necessary properties that are essential properties of all individuals.[9] What is exemplified about representation is haecceitistic representation of individuals by worlds: that one possible world can represent of an individual (Adam) that he occupies a complete individual-role while another possible world represents of a distinct individual (Noah) that he occupies exactly the same individual-role.[10] Here I digress briefly in order to spell out one approach to the characterization of individual-roles.

We start with a representation, by means of atomic sentences and their negations, of all of the qualitative features that an individual, named by 'a', has at a world w:

(1)   Fa & Ga & ~Ha & Rab & Sac & . . .

If we subsequently quantify into name-places uniformly as follows:

(2) $\exists x[\exists y[\exists z \ldots [Fx \& Gx \& {\sim}Hx \& Rxy \& Sxz \ldots]]]$

then any corresponding sentence with all occurrences of one variable unbound is (or expresses) an individual role – e.g. for unbound 'x':

(3) $\exists y[\exists z[\ldots [Fx \& Gx \& {\sim}Hx \& Rxy \& Sxz \ldots]]]$.

In this light we see that one who endorses (T) is committed to it being the case at W_n that Adam occupies the Noah-role. But that is in addition to the manifest commitment to it being the case at W_1 that it is Noah, not Adam, who occupies the Noah-role. So on the first horn of the dilemma we have commitment to haecceitistic, and so non-qualitative, representation of individuals by worlds.

On the second horn of the dilemma, where (T) is held false, then there need be no immediate mystery about representation de re but we face the burden of meeting the challenges – primarily epistemological challenges – that face non-trivial essentialism. According to non-trivial essentialism, there are some properties such that identity of Adam can tolerate the loss of that property (perhaps being of maximum height 1.9m) but other properties for which this is not so. Thus, in our example, there is at least one property that is essential to Adam and such that when we come to consider at the next world a subsequent individual who lacks that property, we 'leave Adam behind' and pick out some distinct individual. But how do we know that a given individual has non-trivial essential properties and how do we find out which properties these are? Chisholm further suggests that the absence of adequate responses to these questions casts doubt on the metaphysical claim that individuals have (appropriate, non-trivial) essential properties.

The way to avoid both horns of the dilemma, of course, is to reject all transworld identity of represented individuals. Thus one would deny that even the first non-actual world W_2 is one at which Adam exists and then either embrace hyper-essentialism or reject the PW account of truth-conditions for de re modal claims.[11] Let us immediately rule out that either GR or AR find that course acceptable, so that the question for both is which horn of the dilemma is to be grasped. Since the ensuing dialectic is subtle, I offer an overview in advance of the detail.

The connection between the respective horns of the dilemma and the respective positions of GR and AR is not entirely straightforward. Consequently the dilemma does not present any straightforward opportunity for GR to score an advantage over AR or vice versa. While GR is driven onto the non-trivial essentialist horn of the dilemma and AR is not, the advocates of AR will naturally choose to occupy that position anyway. The question then is whether non-trivial essentialism is better defended from the haecceitistic standpoint, to which AR is entitled but GR is not, or from the non-haecceitistic standpoint. I do not think that either defence is so obviously flawed that it disqualifies its proponent from maintaining non-trivial essentialism in order to block Chisholm's argument against (TW1). However, as I will go on to show, the problem that hangs over the haecceitistic AR defence of non-trivial essentialism is not solved by the standard AR ('stipulation') response to the problem of transworld identification. I will expand on these claims and then relate the issues that emerge to the problem of transworld identification.

(16.4) GR, HAECCEITISM AND NON-TRIVIAL ESSENTIALISM

On the neutral PW account, essential properties of an individual are all of those features that it has at every world at which it exists, and an essence of an individual is an essential feature of that individual such that, at any world, anything that has that feature is identical to that individual. So via the neutral account, facts about representation (i.e. facts about what is the case at a world) and how these are fixed, have an obvious bearing on questions of essential properties and essences. The GR specification of the neutral account proceeds as follows.

All facts about de re representation of individuals are facts about counterparts and ultimately facts about relations of qualitative similarity. Thus, all essences are purely qualitative in the sense that an essence of an individual is determined as such by the qualitative features that an individual has and the similarity relations to other individuals that are thereby instantiated. This purely qualitative account of representation and essence is inconsistent with the haecceitistic representation of individuals by worlds as explicated above. So GR must eschew the first horn of Chisholm's dilemma on pain of abandoning the grand Humean project of showing that all, including facts about representation and essence, supervenes on qualitative character.[12] GR is thus propelled onto the other horn of the dilemma and is committed to the defence, on a purely qualitative basis, of non-trivial essentialism. The defence proceeds as follows.

Being an essential property of Adam is always a matter of being a property of all of Adam's counterparts, and being one of Adam's counterparts is always a matter of standing in some relation of qualitative similarity to Adam. However, there are many respects and many degrees of qualitative similarity, correspondingly many counterpart relations and correspondingly many essences of Adam. It is misleading to speak of 'the' essence of Adam as if there is a unique feature that is picked out determinately and uniformly across all cases when we speak or think, de re and modally, of Adam. If it is a determinate matter at all which features of Adam are essential, that can only be so relative to a context in which an appropriate thought or sentence about Adam is tokened. It is a matter of which kind of similarity is salient in that context and that is fixed, if at all, by aspects of conversational implicature (intentions, expectations, interests of speaker and hearer, etc.)[13] and the connotation of the term that is used to refer to Adam. Ascription of essential properties is thus, typically, vague and non-extensional.[14]

That ascriptions of essential properties have this character answers well to the datum that we (communally) have a lack of hard, fast, unqualified and context-independent agreement about the truth-values of many essentialist claims – that Socrates could have been female or that there is some donkey that could have talked. The GR explanation of this datum has it that the primary source of underdetermination of opinion is semantic rather than epistemic. Assuming that we have knowledge of the existence of a plurality of worlds, as characterized by the principle of recombination, then the kinds of facts that make for de re (and de dicto) modal truth are, a priori, within our grasp. We know, for example, that there are series of worlds with individual constituents and series of small qualitative (atom by atom) differences over which Adam is continuous with *a*, Socrates is continuous with something that is female and some actual donkey is continuous with something that talks. Crucially, we also know that these worlds are possible worlds since we know that there are no impossible worlds. For we know to be false what the existence of such a world would require to be true, i.e. that there is a true contradiction. What remains unclear, in the absence of knowledge of context, and perhaps even irremediably, is whether the given facts about the possible worlds fulfil the truth-conditions for a given de re modal claim – that Adam could be identical to *a*, or that Socrates could have been female or that this donkey could talk. What remains unclear in the absence of context are the semantic questions of whether *a* represents Adam, whether some other-worldly female represents Socrates and whether some other-worldly talker represents this actual donkey.[15] What is clear, in general, is that since even very minimal qualitative similarities generate counterpart relations, and generous counterpart relations generate widespread de re representation of individuals by others, the purely qualitative account is highly permissive with respect to the extent of de re modal truth. That is, for just about any de re modal claim (type) there is some context in which a token of that type would be true; 'Adam could have been Noah', 'Socrates could have been female', 'some donkey could have talked', 'Russell could have been a poached egg'. The worry then is that we have an account of de re essentialist claims on which anything goes. The most fundamental form of the worry would be that our de re modal discourse is, on this account, deprived of truth-aptitude, since it is not adequately disciplined by norms of assent and dissent.[16] That worry will be met by the response that the discourse is governed by norms of mandatory assent and dissent in the limiting cases. Thus, for example, dissent is mandated in cases of attribution of contradictory or anti-analytic features as de re possibilities. These limiting cases aside, the response continues, very little in the way of assent or dissent is mandatory in every context of utterance. But such permissiveness is a feature of our discourse in general and where truth-aptitude is not in doubt.[17] A related worry is that consistency is threatened on the grounds that for many an essentialist claim such that there is a truth-making context of utterance, there will also be a truth-making context for its negation. In response, it will be conceded that there will indeed be such contexts. But what is no part of the account and what inconsistency in this respect requires is that a (scope) distinct thesis should hold, namely:

that there is some context which is a truth-making context for the tokening of the conjunction of an essentialist claim with its negation. So it is not that just anything goes. However, the worry may persist in the weaker, but still substantial form that the account of the truth-conditions of essentialist claims is too permissive. Certainly, the truth-values of de re modal claims turn out, on the GR account, to be context-sensitive to an extent that those of firm essentialist intuitions would not recognize. Their thought is that there is no context in which (with present actual English meanings fixed) I utter, 'Russell could have been a poached egg', 'this pain might have existed unfelt' or 'Water might have been hydrogen-free' and utter an absolute alethic modal truth. So the purely qualitative account of representation and essence is erroneous for saying otherwise.

(16.5) AR, HAECCEITISM AND NON-TRIVIAL ESSENTIALISM

On the face of things AR has more options than GR. GR is forced onto the second, non-trivial essentialist horn of Chisholm's dilemma by adopting a purely qualitative account of representation de re and essence. Since no species of AR is committed to such a purely qualitative account, none is forced onto the second horn of Chisholm's dilemma by that route. Indeed, this is to understate the point, since an alternative approach to representation and essence is not only consistent with each of our versions of AR, but most advocates of AR find such an approach at least congenial.[18] Moreover, although AR is not forced to occupy the non-trivial essentialist horn of Chisholm's dilemma that, again, is the position which, *de facto*, most advocates of AR find congenial. Thus, the preferred option for AR will be to combine the defence of non-trivial essentialism with an account of representation that is not purely qualitative and I will further assume that such an account incorporates haecceitism.

Many have endorsed haecceitism – e.g. Kaplan (1975), Lycan and Shapiro (1986), Adams (1981) – and there are examples other than the Adam–Noah case that promote the intuition that worlds (and possibilities) can differ in such ways.[19] In fact the strongest adverse consideration that is based on anything other than intuitions about sameness of possibilities is a rather indirect argument. Lewis (1986a: 220–48) rejects haecceitistic differences between worlds on balance of theoretical advantage. Haecceitism is more trouble than it is worth since the versions of realism that are congenial to it are in trouble on other grounds and those that are not congenial have cheap substitutes to hand. Yet this argument raises no new objection to the haecceitistic versions of the species of AR that are not already objections to the species per se.

In the case of those versions of AR that offer a linguistic explanation of how worlds represent (typically CR and BR) the worldmaking language can support haecceitistic differences by including proper names or constants for which reference is stipulated. Then worlds can represent appropriate differences by predicating different individual-roles of different (non-co-referential) names. The objection here is not that such an account of representation de re is illegitimate, but rather that it is limited in certain ways because the worldmaking language is limited to actually existing elements (see Chapter 17 below).[20] In the case of those 'magical' versions of AR which are judged to offer no substantive explanation of how, in general, representation is achieved by worlds (typically NR and PR) there is – a fortiori – no substantive explanation that is consistent with representational haecceitism. But if 'magical ersatzism' incorporates or even entails haecceitistic representation, Lewis tells us nothing that would make it, thereby, any worse than magical. So far, then, there is no objection the haecceitistic account of representation. But let us now consider its implications for the account of essence.

By embracing haecceitism AR appears to have earned the right to assert once and for all, in appropriate cases, certain plausible essentialist claims that GR cannot assert once and for all.[21] One world represents (by naming) that Russell exists and another world represents the existence of all sorts of things that are similar to Russell in ever so many respects. But the second world might explicitly represent (by name) that Russell does not exist, and so none of the properties had by any of the 'Russell-counterparts' at the second world are represented as potentialities of Russell. Thus, by judiciously stipulating, by name, what is true of Russell, we can ensure that every world that represents Russell as existing represents him as human, that no world represents Russell as being a poached egg, etc.

The question that hangs over this haecceitistic AR account of representation and essence is the epistemological question of how we know that a world of a given representational content is possible. I will expand on this point when it emerges again in discussion of the problem of transworld identification.

(16.6) THE TRANSWORLD IDENTIFICATION PROBLEM

There is broad agreement that the foregoing problems of representation and essence – i.e. problems bequeathed by Chisholm's problematic of transworld identity – are genuine, serious and difficult (Plantinga 1974, Lewis 1986a, van Inwagen 1985). However it is widely alleged that Kaplan's problem of transworld identification bequeaths us only pseudo-problems (Kripke 1972, 1980 and Plantinga 1974).

The Kaplan (1967) problem of transworld identification is how we are to tell which of the individuals among the constituents of one possible world is the representative (the 'transworld heir') of an individual that is a constituent of another world. We are to imagine that we have a Jules-Verne-o-scope through which we observe the goings on in some non-actual(ized) world. We then carefully conduct empirical investigation of the individuals that we so observe, examining fingerprints, etc., with the aim of 'locating Dylan', proceeding just as we would if we were set the problem of identifying Dylan in the actual world. The problem of identification, so posed, appears intractable because at any number of worlds there are many individuals who resemble Dylan in various respects and which have, as it were, competing claims to be Dylan. At one world, there is an individual whose fingerprints are indiscernible from those of Dylan but who never picked up a guitar or wrote a song, and another with a Dylanesque career, but who has an origin of a type that differs from that of (our) Dylan. So how can we tell in such worlds which individual, if any, is to be identified as Dylan?

Kaplan subsequently outlines three responses to the problem. The 'sceptical' response has it that the problem cannot be solved and so we should abandon PW-semantics as a means of assigning truth-conditions to de re modal claims. Thus compare the escape from Chisholm's dilemma. The 'relativistic response', which Kaplan favours, is to allow that an individual has at a world various transworld heirs as determined by detectable similarity in various different respects. The affinity of the relativistic response to the GR account is underscored when Kaplan calls the various transworld heirs 'counterparts' and draws the conclusion that an individual has various essences that vary in salience from one de re modal claim to another. The 'metaphysical' response has it that facts about transworld identity of represented individuals are bare facts. The affinity of the metaphysical response to the haecceitistic account of representation de re is established when Kaplan emphasizes that the relevant claim about 'bare' facts is supposed to rule out that facts about transworld identity of represented individuals are facts that obtain in virtue of qualitative similarity.

The challenge that emerges for the proponents of the haecceitistic or metaphysical position is to defend the possibility of such bare representation. To that end, and in any event, the proponents of the haecceitistic position have often sought to respond to Kaplan by showing that the challenge is the product of various misconceptions and errors. Some of the alleged misconceptions and errors may quickly be put aside. Certainly, it is true that AR may resist the supposition that the constituents of other possible worlds (and the elements of other world-domains) are individuals, or that they resemble individuals or that other worlds can be objects of empirical inspection (cf. Chihara 1998: 58–9). But the challenge can be (re)formulated in less pejorative terms as follows. How are we to identify an individual-representer that is specified in qualitative terms as the representative at a world of Dylan? Even when the question is so put, the thought is that various further misconceptions, illicit presuppositions and errors are afoot.

One such thought is that it is mistaken to hold that the properties that are epistemically salient or important in the process of identification of an individual in the actual world are, at another world, necessary or sufficient for being identical with that individual (Kripke 1972: 49–50). It may be epistemically salient that Dylan is the writer of certain songs even if it is contingent that he is the writer of those songs and so at another possible world did not write those songs. It may be essential to Dylan that he is the great-grandson of x even though his having that property is epistemically marginal.[22] But once that point is taken, there are two further related, and potentially more significant, deflationary thoughts on offer.

The next thought is that while some of the representational content of a world can be presented to us in qualitative terms, the content of a world need not be so presented and that no privileged status attaches to content so presented (Kripke 1972: 49–50, Plantinga 1974: 95). Perhaps something turns on the availability of a correct answer to the question of which individual at w is Dylan, or on there being a fact of the matter as to which individual at w is Dylan. If so, such answers can be provided, invariably, if uninformatively, by answering that at any world w, any individual y is identical to Dylan iff y is Dylan (or y has the property of being identical to Dylan). We can also do so informatively in a variety of different ways over a variety of different types of individual, e.g.:

(4) For any world w, for any y, y is identical to Dylan iff y is the propagule of gametes e and f.

What we cannot do is to provide such conditions in general and when constrained to consider only qualitative properties, thus:

(5) For every world w and every individual x, there is a set of empirically manifest, empirically detectable or qualitative properties Q such that at w, for any y, y is identical with x iff y has Q.

But no argument has been put forward to show that it matters that we cannot do so. So the demand to provide a purely qualitative identification of every individual represented is unmotivated. The related thought is that Kaplan makes a mistake in holding that facts about transworld identity must be discovered rather than stipulated (Kripke 1972: 49–50). The associated examples are intuitively compelling. There is something amiss when a claim of the type 'Suppose that Socrates had never gone into philosophy ...' is met with the challenge to demonstrate how you know that it is Socrates that is the object of your supposition. The same might be said of the question how you know that the subject of the proposition that Socrates is a philosopher is the same as the subject of the proposition that Socrates was married (Chihara 1998: 59).

The theme that unites the last two deflationary thoughts is that one can 'give' a possible world or a representational content in a non-qualitative way by relying on stipulation. Thus, the received view is that the definitive AR solution to the problems of transworld identification or identity is to recognize them as pseudo-problems that can be solved by means of stipulation. I will now argue that this received view, even if it adequately deals with the problem of transworld identification, does not deal adequately with the problem of transworld identity. Appeal to stipulation disguises the important epistemological questions about essence that hang over the haecceitistic AR response to the latter.

(16.7) SEMANTIC STIPULATION AND MODAL EPISTEMOLOGY

Among the specific claims associated with stipulation in this context are:

(6) Questions of identity of represented individuals can be settled by stipulation.
(7) Stipulation can give epistemic access to other possible worlds.[23]

If there is anything legitimate and correct in the appeal to stipulation it is captured by (6). I believe, however, that (7) is, at best, extremely misleading and is apt to promote a serious misunderstanding about what stipulation can achieve.

What one might successfully stipulate, in the present context, and at most, is what one is talking about. One might perhaps stipulate the sense of one's words, but not that the words refer, or what the nature of the referent (if any) is. Thus I might preface my remarks by the somewhat gratuitous stipulation: 'Hereafter, when I use the word "Socrates" I thereby speak of Socrates.' From an AR standpoint one might even stretch this point to claim that I can stipulate the following. When I use the word 'Socrates' inside an explicitly worldly context, 'at w', or inside an implicitly worldly (modal or counterfactual) context ('Suppose that Socrates . . .', 'Socrates could have . . .', 'If Socrates had not . . .', etc.) I thereby speak of some world at which Socrates exists, and of some world that represents the existence of Socrates. But this much is only plausible, or even sane, so long as the precise content and effect of stipulation is construed modestly. I do not thereby make it the case, nor do I come to know, that such a world is a *possible* world. It is this crucial point that underlies the complaint against (7). Although the point is quite general, it can be made most clearly in the context of BR. Perhaps I can construct a worldmaking language and worldmaking sentences and even worlds which represent de re – as a result of a stipulation about the referent of a given name of the language – Nixon losing the election. But in whatever sense I can legitimately do that, I can equally 'stipulate' that there is a world at which Nixon is a poached egg. What is not in the gift of my stipulation, in the latter case or in the former, is that such a world is a *possible* world. It is one question how we know which objects are the objects of our de re modal thought and talk, and perhaps there stipulation has a legitimate role. It is another question altogether how we know what is modally true of those objects, and there stipulation has no legitimate role to play.[24]

The question that hangs over this haecceitistic AR account of representation and essence is the epistemological question of how we know that a world with a given representational content is a *possible* world. What the discussion of the last section is intended to show is that even if semantic indeterminacy is obliterated by stipulation, neither the modal status of the world nor our knowledge of that status is thereby guaranteed. It may be intimated that we have such knowledge by a priori reflection on, say, the nature of pain or on the nature of water – or, indeed, by such reflection on the relevant concepts. Such reflection may be supposed to yield opinion about what is absolutely and context-independently possible or necessary about pain or about water, and thereby yield opinion about whether a world at which there is hydrogen-free water or a world at which there is unfelt pain is a *possible* world.[25] Perhaps so, but that is the form of an account, and the form of a partial account at that.[26] Moreover, the need to fill out the account should not be obscured by appeal to 'stipulating possible worlds'.

In sum, then, there is a choice about how the essentialist horn of Chisholm's dilemma, and so the transworld identity of represented individuals (TW1), is better defended. With GR, the claim is that it is in the nature of all of the worlds that they are *possible* worlds – they represent only possibilities – but it is a soft matter which possibilities they represent. With haecceitistic AR, the claim is that we often have hard, once-and-for-all, facts about what the worlds represent, facts established by stipulation, but that does not yet settle the question of how we know which worlds are possible. I will not attempt to adjudicate here between these defences of non-trivial essentialism. But herein lies the real significance of questions about transworld identity or transworld identification for the competition between GR and AR.

CHAPTER 17

Actualist realism: representation

The two main issues about representation that confront any interpreter of PW are how her worlds represent possibilities – how something is true at a world – and which possibilities her worlds are apt to represent – what is true at the worlds. In this penultimate chapter I examine Lewis's famous (1986a: Chapter 3) critique of AR representation, according to which each species proves inadequate in one of two respects.[1] On the approach of Lewis's 'linguistic ersatzist', associated here with BR and CR, representation by worlds is linguistic. The linguistic doctrines are alleged to misrepresent the range of possibilities by failing to distinguish indiscernible possible individuals and alien properties that differ from one another haecceitistically. On the approach of Lewis's 'magical ersatzist', associated here with our PR and NR, representation by worlds requires no explanation. The magical doctrines do not give us reason to believe that they represent the range of possibilities inaccurately, but that is only because they afford no grounds on which a judgement about accuracy or inaccuracy in that respect might be based. I will consider how these allegations of misrepresentation and magicalism might be resisted by AR and how they might be turned on GR.

(17.1) MISREPRESENTATION BY LINGUISTIC AR

The issue of whether linguistic AR accurately represents the range of possibilities can be articulated as the issue of whether the relevant worldmaking language has adequate expressive power – the power to represent all possibilities and to discriminate appropriately one from another. It is prima facie plausible that the chances of expressive adequacy are maximized when it is assumed that the worldmaking language L is a (broadly) Lagadonian language in which: every actually existing individual is its own name; every actually instantiated property is its own predicate; we have pure set-theoretic entities to be the variables and logical expressions; there are infinitely many names, predicates and sentences; and sentences may be infinite in length.[2]

The first allegation is that L cannot give us indiscernible (distinct, non-actual) possible individuals, e.g. distinct individuals that play the same role as in a world of eternal recurrence or in an appropriately symmetrical spacetime. The allegation here is not that L-worlds fail to represent the existence of indiscernible possible individuals. That can be achieved by an L-world entailing a sentence that can be formulated in the language and which expresses that (at a world) there are distinct individuals that play the same individual role – thus:

(1) $\exists x[\exists y[\Phi x \ \& \ \Phi y \ \& \ y \neq x]]$.

The thought is that we need the possible individuals themselves for certain applications (e.g. to populate the universal domain D in an applied PW-semantics and to represent certain egocentric and other individual possibilities). In that respect, however, what we require from L is not a sentence expressing that there are distinct but indiscernible individuals, but distinct and indiscernible ersatz possible individuals – i.e. two singular terms of L that are apt to refer to distinct but indiscernible individuals. That might be achieved in the case of actual individuals since we can exploit appropriately context-dependent means of reference in order to distinguish indiscernibles. Even if our world is perfectly symmetrical or exhibits two-way eternal recurrence, appropriate terms – 'me', 'here', 'next', 'last' – allow one to refer to oneself rather than to one's doppelgangers or vice versa. Yet when we attempt to contrive two singular terms *for* distinct but indiscernible individuals that do not actually exist, we appear condemned to toil with purely descriptive resources.[3] The problem then is that when we seek terms for indiscernible individuals, purely descriptive terms that are terms for indiscernible individuals would thereby appear incapable of being terms for only one such individual. To put the point contrapositively, if purely descriptive singular terms are terms for distinct possible individuals it must be in virtue of the discernibility of those individuals.

The second allegation is that L is bound to conflate certain possibilities that differ only haecceitistically. We have already encountered the idea of an individual-role and the thesis of individual haecceitism. According to individual haecceitism, two worlds may differ by one representing that a certain individual-role is played by one individual and the other world representing that the same role is played by another individual (see Chapter 16). A property role can similarly be abstracted from a conjunctive sentence of L that gives us a maximal description of a world. To simplify, from the pretend maximal description:

(2) Fa & Gb & Gc

(where all terms are presumed to have distinct referents) we abstract the property role played by F as the open (in 'X') sentence:

(3) $\exists Y[\exists x[\exists y[\exists z[Xx\ \&\ Yy\ \&\ Yz\ \&\ x \neq y\ \&\ x \neq z\ \&\ y \neq z\ \&\ X \neq Y]]]].$[4]

Property (or second-order) haecceitism, then, is the thesis that worlds may differ by one representing that a certain property role is played by one property and the other world representing that the same role is played by another property. The difficult cases for AR are haecceitism concerning non-actual individuals and haecceitism concerning alien properties (i.e. instantiable properties other than the properties constructible from those that are actually instantiated). Here, I will follow Lewis by concentrating on the latter.[5]

The case for property haecceitism in general proceeds thus. Grant that there could be simple properties other than those that are actually instantiated — perhaps other primary colours. We cannot introduce names for these properties either through ostension or description.[6] Yet there are sentences of L which express the possibility of there being such properties. Just as we can use first-order quantification to express the possibility that there are non-actual individuals — thus:

(4) $\exists x[\exists y[(x \neq a)\ \&\ (x \neq b)\ \&\ \ldots\ (y \neq a)\ \&\ (y \neq b)\ \ldots\ \&\ (y \neq x)]]$

— we can use second-order quantification to express the possibility that there are colours (properties) alien to us and which are variously distributed over individuals — thus:

(5) $\exists X[\exists Y[(X \neq F)\ \&\ (X \neq G)\ \&\ \ldots\ (Y \neq F)\ \&\ (Y \neq G)\ \ldots\ \&\ (Y \neq X)\ \ldots\ \&\ \exists x[\exists y[Xx\ \&\ Yy\ \&\ \ldots\ ]]]].$[7]

In (5) we specify that there are alien properties that play property roles of the kind specified by (3). However, note that the role expressed by (3) could be played by different properties at different worlds. In one world it is red that plays the F-role of being the colour of exactly one individual while blue plays the G-role of being the colour of the other two individuals. In another world, the roles are reversed since we have one blue thing and two red things. We can express these haecceitistically distinct possibilities in the case of actual properties precisely because we can name the actual colours – thus:

(6) $\exists w[At\ w, (Fa\ \&\ Gb\ \&\ Gc)]$
(7) $\exists v[At\ v, (Ga\ \&\ Fb\ \&\ Fc)]$.

Pre-theoretical modal opinion would strongly suggest that possibilities can differ in just this way in the case of alien properties also. That one thing can have one alien property and two other things another alien property is a distinct possibility from one thing having 'the second' alien property and the other two things having 'the first'. But in L this haecceitistic difference between alien properties cannot be expressed. So what appears to be our best worldmaking language appears doomed to conflate distinct alien properties as well as conflating indiscernible possible individuals.

(17.2) LINGUISTIC AR REVITALIZED

The direction of argument that we have encountered is from the irremediable referential incompleteness of L – re. singular terms for indiscernible non-actual individuals and predicates for alien properties – to the inevitable conflation of possibilities. Melia (2001) argues, primarily for the case of property haecceitism, that the former does not entail the latter since difference of role-occupiers can be expressed without singular reference to role-occupiers. In our case of colour roles the whole story about sameness and distinctness of role-occupancy is the following: (i) that the property that b and c instantiate at w is not identical to the property that a instantiates at w but is identical to the property that a instantiates at v; and (ii) the property that a instantiates at w is identical to the property that b and c instantiate at v. Thus the expression of haecceitistic difference indeed requires the expression of transworld identity (and difference) of represented properties. But to see that information of this calibre does not require singular reference for its articulation consider the following analogy.

An art gallery catalogue deploys only shades of grey in its mini-pictorial representations of a collection of paintings in a (prospective) exhibition. Yet the catalogue can thereby represent that different colours 'switch roles' across paintings without employing a key which assigns any particular shade of grey to any particular colour – without each shade of grey being a representer for a particular colour. That is achievable under the general stipulation (convention) that shades in the catalogue (or even across a series of catalogues) are one–one representers for colours in paintings. If we have geometrically similar exhibits in which a circle appears against the background of a square, one can pick up a catalogue and learn that the foreground circle in exhibit 12 is the same colour as the background square in exhibit 17 but a different colour from the foreground circle in exhibit 27. The catalogue can convey such information about sameness and difference of colour without letting us in on the secret of which colour is represented by each shade. Equally, a child who looks at two scenarios in which she is invited to 'colour by numbers' is in a position to know that the dog is supposed to be the same colour as the barn, even if the page of the book in which colours are associated with numbers is missing and just so long as she is familiar with the convention that there is – as we would say – some one–one correspondence between number and represented colour. Thus all relevant information about transpainting identity and transpainting difference of colours can be expressed in the absence of a convention that specifies any particular representer as the representer for any particular colour.

Analogously, Melia continues, in a worldmaking language we can deploy as 'pixels' entities such as actual-property/empty set pairs. Here let capitalized asterisked letters stand for property-pixels. The interpretation of the key sentences containing pixels is given as follows:

(P1) For all w, at w <A*,a> is true iff at w, there is some alien property that is instantiated by a.[8]

(P2) Pixel tokens represent (*à la* P1) the same property iff they are of the same type.

Then property-haecceitistic differences between two worlds w and v – differences such as that expressed by the pair (6) and (7) above – can be expressed in the case of alien properties as follows:

(8) ∃w[At w, {<A*,a>, <A*,b>, <B*,c>}] &
∃v[At v, {<B*,a>, <B*,b>, <A*,b>}].⁹

As in the case of the gallery catalogue and the children's picture book, we can get more representational content – information about transrepresentational identity and difference – when we consider two representations as a pair than when we consider one and then the other in isolation.

Before proceeding to further discussion of Melia's proposal let us note that these new expressive resources promise to aid AR in other important cases. Recall (from Chapter 13) the problem of providing adequate truth-conditions for those claims of iterated modality in which it appears that we make de re modal claims about non-actual individuals, as in:

(9) Actually childless Richard might have had a child who was contingently famous.

In a sense the expressive problem here is the mirror-image of that which arises over individual haecceitism. For, in general terms, what the present kind of case requires is expression of the idea that at different worlds one and the same individual plays different individual roles. We achieve this easily enough under the present proposal, all being well, by introducing individual pixels to represent non-actual individuals in a way analogous to that in which property pixels represented alien properties – thus:

(P3) For all w, at w <F,a*> is true iff at w, there is some non-actual individual that instantiates F.

So for our case (9) we have:

(10) ∃w[At w, {<Rr_,a*>, <F,a*>}] & ∃v[At v, {<Rr_,a*>, <~F,a*>}].

This move incorporates the following approach to the problem (for AR) of expressing the transworld identity of represented non-actual individuals:

(11) ∃w[At w, {<∃x[x = _],a*>}] & ∃v[At v, {<∃x[x = _],a*>}].¹⁰

The present proposal does not appear to afford us distinct indiscernible ersatz non-actual individuals. At least that is so, assuming that such individuals would have to be singular terms of the world-making language. For individual pixels, as I will explain shortly, are not singular terms. However, from what we have seen, Melia's proposal appears to enhance the expressive power of the BR/CR worldmaking language considerably and to provide all that is required for the worlds to represent all relevant possibilities with due discrimination. The expressive range of Melia's proposed extension to the worldmaking language is impressive. But is the proposed extension legitimate?

Lewis (1986a: 144) allows that anything can count as the worldmaking language so long as it constitutes a system of structures that can be parsed and interpreted. The major question, then, is whether we can provide an adequate account of parsing (syntax) and interpretation (semantics) for a system of pixel structures that have the features indicated. Melia does not purport to offer a full account of these matters but the following points might be developed from his paper. On syntax, we add to L two classes of pixel: individual pixels (which are the pairs of the actual individuals with the empty set) and property pixels (which are the pairs of the actually instantiated properties and the empty set). Individual pixels behave like singular terms in that inter-substitution of individual pixels for singular terms of L preserves wff-hood. Similarly for property pixels and predicates. I leave it open at the moment whether pixelated wffs are closed sentences of L. Semantically, pixels are not names – not even empty names. If the semantic function of pixels were to name individuals or properties, then they would be expressions that were not apt to do the job of increasing the expressive power of L in the ways mooted. This is the force of the objection by Melia (2001) to a proposal by Roy (1995) – a proposal to the effect that we can, for the purpose of solving the iterated modality problem, extend the expressive power of L by adding new constants to the language. The constants are envisaged as being the very set-theoretic entities that Melia deploys as pixels, but *qua* constants they are of no use. For an adequate interpretation of constants requires that we specify their referents, and since we cannot (in general) do this in the case of names for non-actual individuals or alien properties all that is left to do by way of interpreting the constants is to state that they are empty. But adding new empty names – considered as semantically unstructured constants – does not increase the expressive power of the language. Our best Lagadonian language is referentially incomplete and no improvement on its expressive power is attainable by adding new expressions that have a referential function.[11] Thus we must look to expressions that have a different semantic function, and that is where pixels come in.[12]

There may well be more to be said in defence of pixels by way of citation of precedent for the intelligibility of expressions that have such a combined syntactic and semantic character. Individual pixels have to be broadly of the syntactic category of singular terms but are to be interpreted as something other than referring expressions (even in the broad sense that would include definite descriptions). Syntactically, we might seek clues about the more detailed workings of individual pixels in two more refined syntactic categories within the broad class of singular expressions – the categories of first-order variables and of arbitrary names respectively. An account of pixels as variables looks unpromising. If the 'atomic' wffs in which the pixels figure – e.g. <F,a*> – are open sentences, as they would be were 'a*' a variable and in the absence of binding, it is hard to see how wffs such as:

(12) $\exists w[At\ w\ \{<F,a*>\}]$

could be anything other than open sentences. In that case the canonical statement of truth-conditions for sentences containing individual pixels, (P3), would itself – quite inappropriately – be an open sentence, since it would be a biconditional linking an open sentence on the left with a closed sentence on the right. The thought that pixels are of the category of arbitrary names offers more room for manoeuvre. The idea here, familiar from a popular approach to the quantifier elimination rules in natural deduction, is that in order to derive something from an existential generalization, we proceed by deriving it from a wff containing an arbitrary name that 'represents' the existential generalization – thus:

{1}	1.	$\exists x[Fx]$	Premise
{2}	2.	Fm	Assumption of typical case re. 1
.	.	.	.
.	.	.	.
{2}	n.	X	....
{1}	n+1.	X	Existential elimination 1, 2, n

The arbitrary names of the language are not interpreted explicitly by being assigned a referent. Rather the understanding that we have of their meaning can be given, roughly and implicitly, in terms of their inferential role as follows:

(A1) If (certain restrictions obtain then if) X is a consequence of Fm then X is a consequence of $\exists x[Fx]$.

Compare, then, the implicit interpretation of pixels that is given in the canonical truth-condition (P3). I am not asserting that pixels are arbitrary names for non-actuals. Although such a characterization is now tempting there are, of course, any number of disanalogies between pixels and the arbitrary names of predicate logic. But the thought is that with the case of the arbitrary names of predicate logic we have a precedent for a language and a class of expressions for which (a) the expressions are of the broad syntactic class of singular expressions; (b) the terms in question are not treated semantically as genuine singular terms or as variables; (c) the meanings of such expressions can be given implicitly; and (d) the language is thereby adequately parsed and interpreted. This makes a prima facie case, at least, that the proposed parsing and interpreting of the pixel extension of L is in good order.[13]

Finally, however, it is worth reflecting on the kinds of application that the expressively enriched worldmaking language would afford. Certainly, there is the conceptual advantage that more, and duly discriminated, possibilities can be represented at worlds, thus removing various previously appropriate restrictions on the accuracy of the neutral PW possibility principle:

(P) Possibly A iff there is a world w such that at w, A.

But the mooted expansion in expressive power appears to be independent of the capacity to provide a PW-semantics for QML. The proposal extends the expressive power of the worldmaking language in a way that does not, in itself, call for an expansion of ontology beyond that already accepted.[14] So while pixels can be deployed in order that a world represent, say, the possibility that some non-actual individual exists, the expanded language does not provide us with (ersatz) non-actual individuals with which to populate the universal domain. Of course linguistic AR need not make any claim on a PW-semantics that requires ersatz non-actual individuals. But the capacity of a worldmaking language to express certain non-actual possibilities is not to be confused with the capacity to provide a PW-semantics, in the standard sense, that deals adequately with the possibility claims so expressed.

(17.3) MISREPRESENTATION BY GR

So it would seem that the linguistic AR account of representation misrepresents the range of possibilities by getting wrong the case of indiscernible non-actual individuals at least. But failure to represent accurately the possibility that I might have been an inhabitant of one region rather than another in a world of two-way eternal recurrence or a world of symmetrical spacetime may not strike AR as devastating, and especially so if this is the only proven case of misrepresentation. Moreover AR is entitled to have her failings in this respect measured against those of GR. So we now turn to the question of how GR misrepresents the range of possibilities.[15] There are various modal claims over which misrepresentation by GR might be alleged. I will begin by dealing with relatively easy cases, some of which have already been discussed, and then proceed to new cases.

First, it is tempting to think that GR misrepresents extraordinary possibilities by conflating them with ordinary impossibilities.[16] Thus, for example, the possibility that there exists a plurality of worlds ought not to be conflated with the impossibility that some world should have many worlds as parts. But I have shown in Chapter 4 how GR can avoid such misrepresentation through the redundancy interpretation of advanced possibilities. Second, insofar as GR relies on an account of identity and difference of worlds in terms of spatiotemporal relatedness, it attracts the charge that it misconstrues certain claims concerning the co-existence of spatiotemporally unrelated individuals. I have argued (Chapter 6) that the damage here is limited by the observation that GR does allow us to represent the possibility that there are spatiotemporally unrelated individuals, and is vulnerable only to the less serious charge concerning the possibility of actual co-existence, or ordinary compossibility, of spatiotemporally unrelated individuals. Third, GR is liable to attract the complaint that it is incapable of representing individual possibilities that differ only haecceitistically. Here Lewis (1986a: 230ff.) admits that GR cannot represent such possibilities by means of different worlds representing that a common individual role is played by distinct individuals, but counters that the distinctness of such possibilities can be represented by means of distinct intra-world counterparts. Fourth, and to introduce a new consideration, GR is incapable of representing the possibility that nothing (concrete) exists. For the

AR: representation

GR account of representation de dicto is such that such representation is always achieved by means of the existence of a world and the existence of a world is sufficient to represent that something concrete exists. Here the closest surrogate available is the representation that only empty spacetime should exist, but that is unsatisfactory and the bullet has to be bitten.[17]

Thus far, it seems that the representational deficiencies of GR are not serious. However, it might be held that the case for GR misrepresentation can be strengthened by taking into account cases other than the representation of possibility.

We have seen (in Chapter 5) that GR has a case to answer over impossibilities. GR standardly represents that P is impossible (in an ordinary case) as the non-existence of a world at which P. The subsequent complaint is that GR thereby represents as one the many distinct impossibilities that we pre-theoretically distinguish – something being red and green, the existence of a vixen that is not a fox, etc. It seems that this charge cannot be levelled at linguistic AR since the removal of the constraints of consistency (BR) or simplicity (CR) on the generation of worlds promises worlds – impossible worlds – that are capable of representing the existence of red and green things without representing the existence of vixens that are not foxes, etc.[18] However, the positive claims on behalf of the representational capacities of linguistic AR need not immediately be granted. Certainly, taking BR as our example, there may well be a set of L-sentences that has as a member a sentence that means that there are things that are red and green but does not have as a member a sentence that means that there are vixens that are not foxes. But if worlds represent by entailing what is true at them, rather than just by representing explicitly (by membership) what is true at them then there is a problem. For according to the classical account of entailment, any set of sentences that contains an inconsistent sentence will entail every sentence and so, a fortiori, any world that is impossible will entail that every impossibility (specifiable in the worldmaking language) is true at it.[19] So even if the case can be made that impossibilities ought to be discriminated, it is not obvious that this requirement can be met by a version of linguistic AR that is otherwise adequate.

In sum, there are few proven cases of misrepresentation of possibilities by linguistic AR or by GR and consideration of the representation of impossibilities – to put the point cautiously – does not present linguistic AR at an obvious disadvantage to GR. So GR does not have any clear advantage over linguistic AR with respect to accurate representation of (im)possibility.

(17.4) MAGICAL REPRESENTATION BY AR

Lewis (1986a: 174–5) presents GR and certain species of AR (in particular our BR) as offering an account of how representation works. In the case of GR, the notion of something being true at a world is supposed to be analysed exhaustively in terms of the worlds having individual parts with various qualitative features. In the case of BR, the notion of something being true at a world might be analysed in different ways depending on the details of the version at hand – if we think of AR worlds as sets of Lagadonian sentences, we have the analysis of various linguistic concepts in set-theoretic and logical terms. Thus, sentences are construed as sequences, reference for simple elements of the vocabulary is construed as identity, truth-at-w for atomic sentences is set-membership and truth-at-w for non-atomic sentences is defined in terms of truth-at-w for atomic sentences. But it is not the case that all species of AR offer a substantive account of representation. What each version of AR has, Lewis suggests, is commitment to at least a minimal account of representation. The form of the minimal account is to present how things are non-modally, p, at a representing element, E, as a matter of the necessity of p being the case if the representing element (E) is selected by whichever (unique) concrete world, w*, exists – thus:

(M) At E, p iff necessarily (if E is selected by w* then p).

In the species of AR identified here, the elements are *sui generis* states of affairs, certain sets or sentences, or certain properties: selection by whichever unique concrete world exists is a matter of such an element – respectively – obtaining, being true *simpliciter* or being instantiated. The charge of a magical conception of representation against a species of AR is a charge of unintelligibility made on the basis of a dilemma concerning the classification of the selection relation which emerges from the acceptance of the nominated selection concept as primitive. The outline of the dilemma is as follows. The selection relation picked out by an (*ex hypothesi*) primitive selection concept will be either an internal relation or an external relation. If the relation so picked out is an internal relation, then our capacity to pick out that relation, in thought or talk, is unintelligible. If the relation so picked out is external, then it is the (*ex hypothesi*) necessary connection between concrete world and selected element that is unintelligible. So either way, unintelligibility ensues from commitment to an unanalysed concept of selection of an element by the concrete world. Of our remaining species of AR, it is PR that seems most liable to face the charge of magicalism since PR offers no substantive account of selection (obtaining) and conceives of representing elements (states of affairs) as ontological simples.[20] I will now expand the horns of Lewis's dilemma for PR.

Let us assume that the PR selection relation, x is actualized at w, is internal. Then if a state of affairs x stands in that relation to a concrete world w, it does so (necessarily) and in virtue of the intrinsic nature of x and the intrinsic nature of w – any duplicate of x and any duplicate of y would also stand in the selection relation. So what is the intrinsic property that a state of affairs must have in virtue of which it is actualized at w iff w has (say) the intrinsic property of having a donkey as a part? Which intrinsic property of a state of affairs constitutes this specific disposition to obtain or to be actualized? A sub-dilemma then opens up when we attempt to fix on one of these representational properties either by analysis (description) or by acquaintance. On the first horn of the sub-dilemma we go for analysis and proceed as follows:

(R) R is the property of representing that a donkey talks iff necessarily (if E has R and E is actualized then a donkey talks).

Then there are two problems. First, there is no question of pinning down *all* representational properties in this way since, we may presume, not all of the possibilities that the elements must represent (as required by completeness), including the alien possibilities, seem apt to be expressible in any actual language. But in any event, (R) is trivial. For what we need here is an informative specification of that intrinsic representational property that a state of affairs has necessarily iff it is actualized if a donkey talks. At the parallel point of theory construction, GR specifies mereological properties as the representational properties and BR specifies semantic properties – perhaps concocted out of identity (in place of reference) and set-theoretic relations. But, manifestly, (R) does not give us any substantial specification. On the second horn of the dilemma we appeal to acquaintance – we can succeed in thinking about or referring to such a representational property by being causally connected to one of its instances. Then there are two problems. When we consider those instances of the intrinsic representational properties that directly concern us, the states of affairs, we find that they are abstract and presumed to stand in no causal relations to us. So if we are acquainted with instances of these intrinsic representational properties it can only be because some actual concrete things are also instances of those properties and we are acquainted with those things. But of the representational properties with which we might thus be acquainted, Lewis writes:

> There are not very many candidates, since they must be properties capable of being instantiated by simples. Properties of charge, mass, quark flavour and colour and the like might perhaps do. (If somehow they could be shared by abstract simples. But I don't see why they couldn't be.) But there are not nearly enough of those properties to make all the differences we need. So at least the great majority of the 'representational properties' must lie entirely outside our acquaintance.
> Lewis (1986a: 178)[21]

So the hypothesis that selection is an internal relation gives rise to a predicament in which AR relies, in constructing her theory, on a capacity to think and talk about a family of intrinsic representation relations which is not explicated by analysis, by acquaintance or otherwise.

If the PR selection relation, x is actualized at w, is external, then it is *not* required that if a state of affairs x stands in that relation to a concrete world w, then it does so (necessarily) in virtue of the intrinsic nature of x and the intrinsic nature of w – there may be a duplicate of x and a duplicate of w that do not stand in that relation. Now free from the constraint that grasp of the selection relation should be explicated via intrinsic properties of the relata, attention naturally turns away from the nature of the relata and towards the relation itself. The objection then is that the selection relation is unintelligible since the holding of such a relation would constitute the existence of a repugnant kind of necessary connection. That a given concrete world selects a given state of affairs is a necessity. But then given that the selection relation is not constrained to hold in virtue of the intrinsic natures of its relata, whence the necessary connection between the distinct existences? Here we have our concrete donkeys, there (so to speak) we have the state of affairs which is selected by our world having such parts. But why are these 'distinct existences' not connected only contingently, so that the state of affairs can obtain or not whether there are donkeys or not? We are told only that it is not so. Thus what is postulated is an external relation which holds of necessity, if at all, despite the fact that there is no postulate of any underlying constitutive association between the relevant entities of the kind that would usually be held to ensure that the existences are not wholly distinct after all.[22] So underlying the complaint against necessary connections between distinct existences is a deeper complaint of unintelligibility against the idea that the intrinsic nature of a thing should constrain the external relations in which it stands.

So one way or another, PR relies on magic in order to maintain that the states of affairs represent possibilities and that we understand what it is for them to do so. On the internal horn of the dilemma it is our alleged grasp of the actualized-at relation that is magical; on the external horn it is the relation itself.

(17.5) *TU QUOQUE*

Van Inwagen (1986: 207–10) rejoins that the foregoing argument is too powerful for Lewis's own good since a parallel argument will show that the set-membership relation – upon which, of course, GR is variously reliant – or our grasp of it, is also magical. The *tu quoque* argument is not straightforward since it is demonstrable that set-membership is not an internal relation. It is possible that we have duplicate but distinct individuals a and a*, in which case a is a member of {a} but a* is not a member of {a}. But given that duplication is reflexive {a} is a duplicate of {a} and so we have a counterexample to the internality of set-membership. For the failure of a* to be a member of {a} is a failure of a duplicate of a to be a member of a duplicate of {a}. However, it is an open question whether the set-membership relation is *range-internal*. The idea is that it is sufficient for a relation to be range-internal that, necessarily, if we hold fixed the first relatum of a relation then, necessarily, the relation holds between that thing and any duplicate of the second relatum. Whether set-membership is a range-internal relation now depends squarely on what we take the intrinsic properties of sets to be. To that end, van Inwagen offers two kinds of candidates which issue in four permutations and two relevant cases. Aside from the property of being a set, the candidates are of Type A and of Type B. Type A properties are, we might say, membership-identity properties, as when {a} has the property of having-a-as-a-member and has the property of having exactly one member. Type B properties are, we might say, membership-property properties. So if a is spherical then in this category there is {a} having-a-spherical-member and {a} having no square members.[23] The four permutations of these candidates give all of the prima facie possibilities for drawing the boundaries around the intrinsic properties of sets – thus: (i) all and only the intrinsic properties of sets are those entailed by both A-type properties and B-type properties; (ii) all and only the intrinsic properties of sets are those entailed by A-type properties alone; (iii) all and only the intrinsic properties of sets are those entailed by B-type properties alone; or (iv) sets have no intrinsic properties except that of being a set. These possibilities determine two relevant cases as follows. If the intrinsic properties of sets are as specified in possibilities (i) or (ii) then set-membership is range-internal. Given (i) or (ii), sameness of intrinsic properties entails sameness of membership and sameness of membership entails identity of sets. Thus duplicate sets are identical sets, whatever is a member of a given set is a member of any duplicate of that set and so set-membership is range-internal. If the intrinsic properties of sets are as specified in possibilities (iii) or (iv) then set-membership is external.[24] Given that set-membership is not internal, van Inwagen's *tu quoque* proceeds from the two remaining options for classification – range-internality or externality. The argument then is that if set-membership is range-internal then our capacity to think of the relation is magical and if set-membership is external then it is the relation itself that is magical.[25]

Lewis (1991: 35–8) responds to van Inwagen with respect to the case of the relation between a singleton set and its unique member. The *tu quoque* is incomplete on its external horn since the set-membership relation is not an instance of an unintelligible necessary connection between distinct existences. The question whether it is necessary that Lewis stands in the set-membership relation to {Lewis} is, for GR, a question about counterparts. It is the question whether every counterpart of Lewis is a member of every counterpart of {Lewis}. The natural principle governing counterparthood is that the counterparts of {Lewis} are those singleton sets that have a member that is a counterpart of Lewis. And so the upshot is this:

(X) Lewis is necessarily a member of {Lewis} iff every counterpart of Lewis is a member of a singleton set that has as a member a counterpart of Lewis.

If we have a univocal interpretation of the 'counterpart' predicate, so that the same counterpart relation is invoked by both occurrences of that predicate, then the connection between Lewis and {Lewis} is necessary. But not inexplicably so, given (X), and it is not a necessary connection between *distinct* existences. However, that point aside

Lewis is extremely concessive to van Inwagen's argument allowing: (a) that the internal horn of van Inwagen's *tu quoque* is complete and (b) that even though the external horn does not sustain the charge of a mysterious necessary connection between singleton and member, that leaves untouched the worry that we have no independent, or informative, way of pinning down the relation in analysis or description. In light of that assessment of the situation, GR and PR are presented as sharing the predicament of claiming that their (respective) primitive concepts are intelligible while admitting that no account is available of how these concepts could be understood. Lewis, of course, cannot characterize the predicament as one that visits refutation on both GR and PR, and so the predicament of being stuck with such a primitive is classified as a formidable difficulty.[26] Thus, commitment to magic becomes a tradable and negotiable 'cost' of a theoretical position rather than an absolutely unacceptable feature. Moreover, commitment to magic comes in relevantly distinguishable forms and Lewis has things to say about why commitment to magic in the PR case is worse than commitment to magic in the GR case. For example, PR asks us to accept a double-dose of magic, once in the case of the selection relation and (presuming she has no alternative) once in the case of the set-membership relation, while GR asks us to accept only a single dose. Moreover, and relatedly, GR will charge that acceptance of the magic of selection is a heavier price to pay than it would otherwise be given that, in the case of possibility, non-magical accounts of representation are available.

It is not easy to assess Lewis's assessment of the *tu quoque*. In particular, it is not clear why, given the limitations of the external horn, Lewis did not pursue more vigorously on behalf of GR the option of classifying set-membership as an external relation. Here are some tentative suggestions along those lines as to how that option might be pursued. First, it seems that it may be possible to escape the internal horn of the dilemma altogether by discarding the relation x is a member of y in favour of its inverse x has as a member y. For the having-as-a-member relation is not even range-internal. It is possible that there are distinct duplicate individuals a and a* so that {a} bears the has-as-a-member relation to an individual a but does not bear that relation to every duplicate of a (e.g. a*). So if we can do set theory with the has-as-a-member relation, what force remains in the internal horn of the *tu quoque*? Second, Lewis is not entirely happy with his response to the external horn of the *tu quoque* because, he claims, it leaves untouched the complaint that we have no

Actualist realism

account of our grasp of the set-membership relation. Now that complaint figured in the development of the internal horn, rather than the external horn, of the original dilemma. But, in any event, it would be of interest to see spelled out in the case of set-membership the sub-dilemma that was supposed to show that selection could not be grasped either by analysis (description) or acquaintance. On the sub-horn of acquaintance, one thought is that the things that are supposed to have the property that determines membership of this or that singleton set are not abstract simples but concrete individuals. What then is the objection to our being acquainted with the property by acquaintance with its instances? On the sub-horn of analysis, we have seen from Chapter 7 that allegations of circularity and lack of independence of analysans from analysandum have to be treated very carefully, and so one might pay careful attention to the claim that attempts to analyse the selection concept are, in that respect, on a par with attempts to analyse the set-membership concept.

The Lewis–van Inwagen dialectic is subtle and difficult. And despite inclinations to pursue further how GR might resist the *tu quoque* more vigorously, I believe that van Inwagen's *tu quoque* should be regarded as doing enough to convince us – as it appears to have convinced Lewis – that the critique of magical ersatzism does not amount, in its present form, to a lethal objection to PR.

I conclude that neither aspect of the Lewis (1986a) critique of AR is decisive. It has not been shown beyond reasonable doubt that linguistic AR is condemned to misrepresent possibilities by conflation or that non-linguistic AR is condemned to resort to an absolutely unacceptable kind of magic.

Part IV

Conclusion

CHAPTER 18

Summary and evaluation

Possible-world discourse promises to illuminate the modal and intensional by articulating conceptual, ontological and semantic explanations.

Explanations of all of these sorts are offered by GR, and I have argued that these explanations are, for the most part, successful. As far as non-alien possibilities are concerned, the GR claim to have provided an accurate and appropriately non-modal analysis of the concept possibility is undefeated. The argument of Chapter 7 sought to show that the boundary between non-alien and alien possibility marks the analytic limit of GR. But if that argument succeeds, it shows that in failing to provide an analysis of the family of modal concepts that is accurate, non-modal, and absolutely comprehensive, GR analysis is limited in a way that any analysis of the modal concepts must be. I have defended GR against the objections concerning quantification over non-actuals. There, I paused only to note that if legitimate first-order quantification is constrained by the possibility of singular reference to the objects of the domain, then the limits that Lewis discerns on the expressive power of AR worldmaking languages will also constrain GR. I have been sanguine about the primary GR spatiotemporal criterion of identity for worlds, arguing that its modal consequences are more palatable than the critics suggest. For the most part, the troublesome consequences of the criterion are theoretical and negotiable claims about which possibilities might have been co-actual or compossible – not intuitive claims about what is possible *per se*. Retreat to the secondary criterion of identity for worlds, and so to analogically spatiotemporal relations may be merited in face of uncertainty about how far the meaning of our term 'spatiotemporal relation' is constrained by the facts about its actual extension. If the secondary criterion proves inadequate, then GR has a problem about certain *alien* possibilities. But in light

Conclusion

of the argument of Chapter 7 that may be no additional problem. In Chapter 8, I attempted to get to the bottom of the relevance objection to counterpart theory and concluded that no reasonably precise version of that objection shows counterpart theory in any worse light than any other PW account of de re modal content. In Chapter 9, the conclusion was that, despite the underdevelopment of the epistemology of GR, a comparable underdevelopment of modal epistemology in general, and of the epistemology of AR in particular, left GR free from any decisive absolute epistemological objection and at no demonstrated epistemological disadvantage to AR. This is not a very satisfactory outcome and epistemology may yet prove to be the field on which GR will fall. For that reason, and others, work on modal epistemology is urgently needed.

I found that the two kinds of complaint against AR which are most prominent in the literature – problems of transworld identity and identification, and Lewis's critique of AR representation – are not the most compelling. But what we learn from the former is that a fuller assessment of AR, like GR, awaits work in modal epistemology. This leaves us to weigh, in the case of AR, the acceptability of the ontology, the threat of paradox and the range of applications delivered. I argued, in Chapter 15, that the threat of paradox runs far deeper for all species of AR than it does for GR. It is some kind of defence of AR in that respect to point out that all who rely on set theory are no less troubled since no obvious and compelling solution is available to the threat of paradox on that front either. So perhaps it would be unwise to rest a critique of AR on that point alone. I have argued, in Chapter 14, that the ontology of most species of AR is not obviously more safe and sane than that of GR, and that the ontology of PR is eminently dubious in all respects other than its respect for ontological actualism. Indeed, I would be inclined to claim that GR has advantages over AR in the matter of ontological costs. But even if I am wrong about that, there are still the questions of application to be considered. I argued, in Chapter 13, that in seeking to provide an adequate applied PW-semantics, all versions of AR are troubled to some extent, but not to their enormous detriment, by either the D-problem or the V-problem. The modal consequences of the solutions on offer seem no more worrying than those entailed by counterpart-theoretic semantics of GR and all such consequences might reasonably be treated as negotiable. Thus, I see no clear difference between GR and AR with respect to the range or quality of semantic applications that each provides. I argued in Chapters 4 and 12 that GR and most species of AR were prevented

Summary and evaluation

from providing a possible-worlds account of truthmaking for modal claims. Here, the crucial and general consideration was that all of these versions of realism shared a conception of the modal status of modal truth and of the existence of various worldmaking elements that combined to prevent a suitably discriminating association of truth with truthmaker (either locally or globally). Since, I argued, a CR claim to provide a possible-world account of truthmaking for modal truth is not undermined by that consideration, here we may have one kind of ontological application of PW that is afforded by a species of AR but not by GR. With respect to ontological identifications, it was argued across Chapters 4 and 12 that GR offers a more impressive range of applications than that offered by any species of AR. Thus I argue that, on balance, GR wins over all versions of AR other than CR on the point of the range and quality of ontological applications that it offers. Finally, I argued in Chapter 11 that no version of AR can offer non-modal analyses of the modal and intensional concepts, having argued previously, in Chapter 7, that GR succeeds in that respect over the sphere of non-alien possibility at least. Thus, I argue that GR stands at a clear advantage over AR with respect to the conceptual applications that it affords.

Overall, I claim that the beneficial applications afforded by GR are greater than those afforded by AR and the ontological costs of GR are (at worst) not clearly greater than those of AR. Thus, I claim (with Lewis) that the balance of benefits to costs afforded by GR is greater than that afforded by AR and that this makes GR the superior option. Perhaps I have misconstrued the kinds of benefit that are relevant. Perhaps by considering conceptual, ontological and semantic applications I have been too restrictive or, more worryingly, perhaps I have counted pseudo-explanations as benefits. Perhaps there is something wrong with judging competing philosophical theories on a cost/benefit basis. In all of these respects I echo the methodological remarks made by Lewis (1986a: 4–5) just before he advised us to consider whether AR might offer better value than GR. But I believe that we have now reached a stage at which those who would persist in the use of possible-world talk and avoid commitment to genuine realism should look beyond actualist realism to the antirealist options.

Notes

1 WHERE POSSIBLE-WORLD TALK IS USED

1 In this chapter I am presenting a maximal picture of where possible-world talk is used and of what it is supposed to elucidate. I do not mean to endorse all of the claims that will be made and I do not suppose that anyone else does.
2 Equally, given two different M-specifications of collections of possible worlds – say, as the analytically possible worlds and the metaphysically possible worlds – it is often controversial whether the collections are co-extensive (i.e. whether the analytically possible worlds are all and only the metaphysically possible worlds).
3 This concentration on the alethic modalities reflects the balance within the philosophical literature on modality at large. The obvious explanation of this balance of interest is that metaphysical, epistemological, conceptual and (broadly) logical concerns are fundamental and ubiquitous philosophical concerns.
4 Since discussion of propositional attitudes as such will not figure very much or very directly in what follows I will take this opportunity to make a number of related points. First, it is widely acknowledged that the pioneering work on the possible worlds approach to the elucidation of propositional attitudes was done by Hintikka (1957, 1962, 1963, 1969 and 1975). For a general survey of the topic of the logic and semantics of propositional attitudes and the relationship between those topics and the modalities I recommend Aho (1994). Second, it is well known that various connections have been mooted between certain kinds of propositional attitude and certain kinds of speech act and, in turn, between certain kinds of speech act and certain syntactic types of sentence. Thus, we have the intuitive connections between belief and assertion and then between assertion and declarative sentences. Accordingly, the idea of elucidating certain types of propositional attitudes by reference to possible worlds is closely related to the linguistic projects of elucidating the related kinds of speech act or sentence. So the project of elucidating the propositional attitude of wondering whether, for example, brings in train the prospect of a theory of meaning or 'logic' of questions. Much of the work that has been done on the

propositional attitudes and associated speech acts involves a degree of detail and ingenuity that far surpasses the very basic account sketched above. Here, in outline, is an example of how work in this territory proceeds. One strategy for elucidating the meaning of (yes/no-answerable) questions in terms of possible worlds begins by treating questions as disguised commands to make known. Once questions are thus revealed as a bimodal phenomenon, talk in terms of possible worlds is available to elucidate each of the component modal elements, the deontic modality and the epistemic modality, and their interrelation (see Fine and Schurz 1996). Third, it ought to be acknowledged that the treatment of propositional attitudes is one of the salient grounds on which it is held that we need to extend the discourse of possible worlds to encompass impossible worlds (see Yagisawa 1988, Lycan 1991a and (5.4) below).

5 Two comments on this point. First, if, as envisaged, the project is to elucidate the modal in terms of non-modal truth at a world, a law of nature is best conceived here as being, or being represented by, a non-modal truth. Second, there is scope for variation here on exactly how nomological modality is to be characterized in terms of laws holding at worlds. In one such variation, a world might be considered nomologically possible relative to the actual world so long as everything that happens at that world is consistent with the nomological truths that hold at the actual world.

6 The reflexivity of the accessibility relation is another worldly mark of the alethic modalities. The features of the accessibility relation are placed in the context of a semantic theory in (3.4) below.

7 The concentration, within the realm of alethic modalities, on the absolute again reflects a balance in the philosophical literature on modalities at large. The absolute modalities are naturally thought fundamental precisely because relative or restricted modalities are characterized in terms of relations to, or restrictions upon, the absolute.

8 For more on intension and extension see (3.1) below.

9 The classical possible world treatments of counterfactuals are those of Stalnaker (1968) and Lewis (1973). For further discussion of PW treatments of conditionals see Sanford (1989).

10 The notion of a maximal property is a technical one but the general idea, as the term suggests, is to allow characterization of how the complete base state (say, the physical state) of a thing relates to a complete associated state (say, the mental state) of that thing.

11 For the seminal work on the taxonomy and expression of supervenience theses see Kim (1993). For further discussion of the modal issues raised by the formulation of supervenience theses, and references to the recent literature on the topic, see Divers (1998).

12 Among the further prominent territories of philosophical interest in which possible-world talk has been invoked are (along with preliminary references): the epistemic and non-epistemic probabilities (Bigelow and Pargetter 1990: 147–58); truth in fiction (Lewis 1978); rigid designation (Kripke 1972); and verisimilitude (Lewis 1986a: 24–7).

Notes

2 WHAT POSSIBLE-WORLD TALK MEANS

1 In this chapter, I apply to the case of possible worlds a general approach to the taxonomy of realist and antirealist positions in ontological disputes which I associate with Wright (1983, 1987 and 1992).

2 Of course such commitment may lie only a little further down the line. One might attempt to show that an interpreter assumes certain substantial philosophical commitments as a consequence of other claims that she makes about the sentences, or as a consequence of particular uses she makes of the sentences. For example, commitment to a certain kind of account of logical form for the sentences might be imposed by insistence that certain inferences are valid (and absence of an alternative account that underwrites validity). But use alone is not enough to establish substantial philosophical commitments, for, as we shall see below, philosophers have too many ways of backing up the claim that their apparently committing claims don't mean what they appear to mean, that they don't hold their claims to be true, etc.

3 Consider that a sentence may be held true because it is believed to be in one of the following categories: the negation of a false sentence; the disjunction of any sentence with its own negation (and other cases of logical truth); a conditional with a false antecedent, a universal generalization for which nothing satisfies the antecedent predication.

4 Perhaps (2) and (4) are not the safest examples of contested sentences since the presumption that the actual world does not satisfy the relevant conditions is vulnerable to defeat. But I will persist with (4) and its ilk since these are familiar and graphic examples of non-actuality.

5 Some genuine realists, e.g. Lewis (1986a: Chapter 3), hold that they alone are truly The Realists with the actualist 'realists' cast as mere 'ersatzers'. Some actualist realists, e.g. Plantinga (1987), hold that they alone are truly The Realists with the genuine 'realists' being cast as 'reductionists' or worse. My ecumenical usage respects the positive claim made by each camp on the term 'realism'.

6 To save space I use initial titles (e.g. 'GR') throughout to name both a certain philosophical thesis (genuine realism) and the proponent of that thesis (the genuine realist) allowing context to settle which is intended.

7 At this stage I aim for a broad, generic formulation of GR, but I will focus on David Lewis's further specified version of GR from Chapter 4 onwards.

8 I say the worlds of GR are 'concrete' since most who operate with a notion of concreteness would so classify them. However, the champion of GR is disinclined to call genuine worlds 'concrete' since he has misgivings about the utility of the term (Lewis 1986a: 81–6).

9 I intend under this heading interpretations that deny truth-(in-an-ontologically-significant-sense)-evaluability to PW sentences. I do so in order to accommodate the quasi-realism of Blackburn (see references below).

10 Among (what are usually read as) prominent sources of such nonfactualist views are Hume (1759) and Ayer (1936) on the moral;

Notes

Wittgenstein (1953) on certain mental states (*inter alia*); the Wittgenstein of Kripke (1982) on meaning and instrumentalist construals of scientific discourse about unobservables (as characterized by Nagel (1950)). For a nice general discussion of the various manifestations of non-factualism ('expressivism') see Blackburn (1984: 167–71).

11 Thus, among (what are usually read as) prominent sources of error-theoretic factualist antirealism we have: Mackie (1977) on morals; the Locke of Mackie (1976) on colours; Prior (1970) on the past and the future; Churchland (1981) on the propositional attitudes; and Field (1980, 1989) on mathematics.

12 The pre-eminent example of an agnostic factualist antirealism is that of van Fraassen (1980) on the unobservables postulated in physical theories.

13 A construction, or more specifically and directly to our purpose, a sentential operator 'O' is non-factive just in case the inference from O(p) to p is not valid.

14 Strictly speaking, to allow for an agnostic version of structure-based antirealism, the essential feature is more properly the refusal to assert that the operator in question is factive rather than the assertion that it is non-factive. But I ignore that fine distinction here.

15 Thus the 'if-thenism', deductivism or postulationism attacked by Russell and Whitehead (1910).

16 For a critique of the fictionalist interpretation of PW see Divers and Hagen (forthcoming).

17 The precise and explicit origin of Prior's modalism is not easy to pin down but might be traced back from Prior and Fine (1977), Fine (1977) and Copeland (1996). For modalist interpretations with the worldly turn see Fine (1982, 1985) and Forbes (1985, 1989). I must emphasize that the simple example given here does not do justice to the sophistication and complexity of the modalist position – or to the difficulty of the modalist task. The modalist aim is to provide primitively modal reinterpretation ('paraphrases') of sentences that present realistic interpretations of PW, and that requires much more than, as it were, sticking a single simple possibility operator on the front in each case (see references above). In this respect, fictionalist interpretation appears to score an advantage of simplicity over modalist interpretation precisely because it does appear to make do with one simple, non-factive operator 'According to GR'. For further discussion of this point see Divers (1999c).

18 Thus modal structuralism – cf. Putnam (1967) and Hellman (1989) – treats the existential sentences of arithmetic as assertions of the existence of infinitely many (concrete) objects which occur within the scope of a (primitive) possibility operator.

3 WHY POSSIBLE-WORLD TALK IS USED

1 It is a difficult and extremely controversial question how exactly conceptual analysis relates to giving the meanings of expressions and how

that in turn relates to specification of their senses. Some of these general issues will emerge in the course of subsequent discussion (see e.g. Chapter 7 and (8.2) below) but I hope that I will be forgiven for glossing over both the general and the specific issues at this stage.
2 I ignore here presently irrelevant complications that arise when an infinitary analysans is envisaged.
3 One way in which interpreted PW might be envisaged as affording implicit analyses is by articulating criteria of identity for intensional entities. Famously, Hume's Principle:

(HP) The Number of F's = The Number of G's iff
the F's correspond 1–1 with the G's

has been mooted as offering an implicit analysis of the concept of natural number – thus: Frege (1884), Hale and Wright (2001). Similarly, then, PW might afford implicit analysis by supplying an appropriate right-side for the likes of the following biconditional:

(PP) Property F = Property G iff A(F, G)

in which a truth-condition of the left-side identity statement in given in terms of possible worlds. The prospect of an interpretation of PW affording such implicit analyses of (putatively sortal) intensional concepts is intriguing, for it would appear to be independent of the capacity to afford either an explicit analysis of the concepts in question or an ontological identification (see below) of the entities that fall under those concepts.
4 For further discussion of this point see (7.2).
5 See Chapters 4 and 14, and see n.7 below.
6 Here I draw a simple distinction between the extensional and the intensional. But I will be concerned occasionally with the distinction among non-extensional operators between the intensional and the hyperintensional (e.g. see (5.4) below).
7 Quine (see refs in text) emphasizes the case where inter-substitution of (apparently) co-referential singular terms fails to preserve truth-value, thus arguing for the referential opacity of modal contexts. Referential opacity, I take it, is a matter of failure of substitutivity in the special case where the substituted expression is in the syntactic category of singular term and the associated semantic value is an object. Thus, referential opacity is sufficient but not necessary for the intensionality, in the presently intended sense, of modal operators. I have exemplified the intensionality of the modal operators in what I take to be the simpler case where the substituted expression is in the syntactic category of sentence and the associated semantic value is a truth-value.
8 There is no doubt that the desire to provide a compositional account of the truth-conditions of modal sentences, and the conviction that a substantial element of Quine's critique of modality would thereby be defused, motivated the development of the kind of semantic theory (a

possible-worlds semantic theory) that will come to the fore in (3.4) below. On this point see Linsky (1971). The reaction of Quine (1976) to the development of such 'extensional' semantic theories was to shift emphasis back to his original complaints about 'intensional' ontology, centring on the absence of satisfactory identity conditions for the entities postulated by the theories. As indicated, these ontological issues are addressed in Chapters 4 and 14.

9 One general point of contrast between principles of conceptual analysis and principles of ontological identification is modal status. Having offered a functional analysis of a given concept – pain, belief, goodness, etc. – in terms of a certain role, R, one might take the view that it is actually, but not necessarily, the case that the players of role R are the F's. So, the thought goes, what actually plays the role of pain in humans are brain states of type B, so to that extent we endorse the ontological identification of human pain with B-states. But that very role, what conceptual analysis presents to us as what is essential to pain, might have been played in humans by some other brain state B*. So any such 'identification' of human pain with B-states is intended as contingent identification. However, in the kinds of case that concern us – cases like property, proposition, state of affairs, etc. – it is unlikely that anyone would envisage the analytically given role actually being played by one sort of entity and possibly (counterfactually) by another. Relatedly, the identification of role-players in the cases of these intensional concepts appears to be a wholly a priori matter in contrast with concepts such as pain or redness where candidates to be players of the relevant roles are established a posteriori.

10 I return to this point in n.13 below.

11 The claim is made explicitly by Bigelow and Pargetter (1990: 165).

12 A selection of views on the second and third points can be found in the following discussions of truthmaking: Armstrong (1989, 1997), Fox (1987), Hochberg (1994), Mulligan, Simons and Smith (1984), Simons (1993) and Smith (1999).

13 The antirealist might maintain the realist's identificatory principles, e.g. that the propositions are all and only the subsets of the worlds, and then assert that there are exactly two propositions (or one), on the grounds that there is exactly one world (or none). But I take it that these degenerate identifications would only be invoked in service of a reductio of something or other, rather than in service of a serious attempt to identify the role-players of some bona fide theoretical role. Hence the comment on numerical constraints on proper ontological identification located in the text preceding n.10 above.

14 I think it is reasonable to venture that worries about whether these explanatory aims can be met in the modal case are traceable to aspects of the substitutivity problems raised by Quine (see (3.1) above). But that is not to say that Quine would have recognized the legitimacy of all of these explanatory aims.

15 That there are good philosophical reasons for distinguishing these styles of semantic theory is a theme that emerged strongly from the

Notes

highly influential work on theories of meaning and truth by Davidson (1982).

16 It is widely acknowledged that around the time of Kripke's key publications – viz. his (1959) and (1963) – many other authors treated the semantics or 'logic' of modal or intensional object languages in ways that directly invoke, or strongly suggest, the idea of a possible world – thus see Meredith and Prior (1956), Kanger (1957), Hintikka (1957 and 1961), Montague (1960) and the many other fascinating contributions to Acta Philosophica Fennica 16 in which Kripke's (1963) paper was published. For views on precedence, patterns of influence, etc. see Hintikka (1969) and Copeland (1996).

17 Equally, in the dispute between our realists the issue of which interpretation of PW best matches the expressive resources of modal English does not loom very large. But that issue does loom large in the debate between realists, on one hand, and antirealists and abstentionists on the other. See e.g. Hazen (1976), Hodes (1984), Lewis (1986a: 8–17), Forbes (1989) and Divers (1996).

18 My exposition is broadly in the style of Hughes and Cresswell (1996). The main difference is that the models described here have a distinguished element w^*, a feature that is not required if all we want from the theory is an account of validity. Aside from Kripke (1963) and Hughes and Cresswell (1996) the reader will find other more careful, but still philosophically motivated, presentations of Kripkean semantic theories in Forbes (1989) and Chihara (1998).

19 The distinction between pure and applied semantics is due to Plantinga (1974: 126–8).

20 Here it is presumed that the variables $x, y_1 \ldots y_n$ are the only variables free in the formula $A(x, y_1 \ldots y_n)$ and that a value in $\{0, 1\}$ has been assigned to the pair $<A(x, y_1 \ldots y_n), w>$ for each assignment, I_i, of D-members to $x, y_1 \ldots y_{n-1}$. In the basic case where $A(x, y_1 \ldots y_n)$ is an atomic predication, $F^{n+1}x, y_1 \ldots y_n$, that assignment is achieved as follows. For any $(n + 1)$-adic predicate F^{n+1}, for any assignment I_i of D-members to $x, y_1 \ldots y_{n-1}$ and for any w, we have: $V<F^{n+1}(x, y_1 \ldots y_{n-1}), I_i, w> = 1$ iff the n-tuple $< a_1 \ldots a_{n+1} >$ is a member of $V< F^{n+1}, w>$ where I_i assigns a_1 to x, and ... I_i assigns a_{n+1} to y_n; otherwise $V<F^{n+1}(x, y_1 \ldots y_n), I_i, w> = 0$. In cases where the formula $A(x, y_1 \ldots y_n)$ is complex, we need to appeal to recursive principles that assign a value in $\{0, 1\}$ to the pair $<A(x, y_1 \ldots y_n), w>$ for each assignment, I_j, of D-members to $x, y_1 \ldots y_n$ on the basis of such assignments for the atomic sub-formulas of $A(x, y_1 \ldots y_n)$. Again, the reader who wishes to see how this is done in detail should consult the sources cited at n.18 above.

21 To give a flavour, and some examples, of the most familiar results the (antecedently) familiar modal logics B, S4 and S5 are demonstrably sound and complete when the relation R of the models is constrained to symmetry (B), symmetry and transitivity (S4), and equivalence (S5).

22 Since I am not immediately concerned with realism about sets I ignore the sophisticated thought that it may be possible, ultimately, to avoid

Notes

the commitment to sets that appears to come along with acceptance of the pure semantic theory.
23 For example, and roughly, facts about the usage of 'It is possible that' in English, patterns of assent and dissent, etc. dictate that it does not mean the same as 'there is a city at which' or 'there is a set of real numbers in which . . .'. So to the extent that we are interested in what the sentences of the modal fragment of English actually mean, what their truth-conditions are, what makes them true, etc., we are not interested in a semantic theory that leaves models so unconstrained that these unwanted interpretations of the modal expressions are left in play.
24 Indeed, we shall see in Chapter 9 that realist interpreters of PW face particular epistemological challenges.

4 GENUINE REALISM: EXPOSITION AND APPLICATIONS

1 Henceforth, then, GR is classical, standard Lewisian GR unless some departure is indicated. I will consider various departures from the Lewisian version that are consistent with the broad, generic conception of GR that was introduced in (2.5). But, I will argue, in each case where such a departure is mooted, that the cause of GR is better served by maintaining the classical doctrine. I will further argue that global considerations about GR – specifically, epistemological considerations – militate in general against the acceptance of locally motivated departures from the classical Lewisian doctrine (see Chapter 9 n.6).
2 The de re/de dicto distinction figures prominently in the history of the philosophy of the modalities and of the propositional attitudes. The intuitive idea is that modalizing de re is modalizing *about* a specific thing or things while modalizing de dicto is modalizing about (the truth of) a proposition. But beyond that it is unclear precisely how, or even in which terms – ontological, syntactic, semantic, etc. – the distinction should definitively be drawn. To illustrate the syntactic approach, and focusing on the syntax of quantified modal logic, we might say that a sentence is de dicto if it contains no proper name and no modal operator in it governs a formula that contains a variable that is free in that formula; otherwise the sentence is (in some respect) de re. To illustrate the distinction in the absence of proper names, antecedent instances of the Barcan Principle present paradigm cases of de re modal contexts:

(DR)   Everything is necessarily material
(DR*) $\forall x \Box Mx$

while the corresponding consequent instances present paradigm cases of de dicto modal contexts:

(DD)   It is necessary that everything is material
(DD*) $\Box \forall x Mx$.

Notes

To see how the de re/de dicto distinction feeds into various other issues, the reader might consult in the first instance Linsky (1971) and Fine (1978). But I trust that the combination of the intuitive idea with the above illustration of the syntactic approach will suffice to render the de re/de dicto distinction serviceable for the purposes of this book.

3   I emphasize that talk of what is the case 'at' a possible world is intended as neutral and awaits explanation by all non-abstentionist interpreters of PW.

4   Why does a world represent Carnap vicariously, by means of a counterpart of Carnap rather than by means of Carnap himself? This is a complex question that speaks to issues at many levels. The immediate answer to the question is two-fold: (i) in GR worlds represent individuals by having individuals as parts; and (ii) every individual that is part of any world is part of exactly one world, so when many worlds each represent possibilities of Carnap, it cannot be as a result of Carnap being part of each world. GR cleaves to (i) since thereby representation can be accounted for directly by one of the conceptual primitives of the theory, viz. parthood (see (4.2)). GR cleaves to (ii) because, given (i), an adequate account of the modal phenomenon of accidental intrinsic properties forces one's hand (Lewis 1986a: 198–209). Swiftly, having a certain number of fingers is an intrinsic property of Carnap. But how can the individual Carnap have ten fingers at w and have only nine fingers at v, if Carnap having a certain number of fingers at a world is (a) a matter of one individual (Carnap) being part of a world and (b) that one individual having different numbers of fingers at the different worlds? It seems that something has to give, and Lewis holds that it should be tolerance of individuals that are wholly present in more than one world. Consequently, de re representation of individuals is achieved (in general) vicariously, by counterparts, rather than directly. I have no comment to make on Lewis's discussion of accidental intrinsic properties. The adequacy of the counterpart-theoretic account of de re representation is the subject of Chapter 8 and transworld identity is discussed extensively in Chapter 16.

5   In presenting the 'indexical theory of actuality' I have, like many other commentators, concentrated on the primary sense attributed to the expressions. However, I emphasize that Lewis insists in all of his essays on the topic that expressions of actuality are ambiguous and must sometimes be read as having a secondary, shifting sense if appropriately charitable interpretation is to ensue (see Lewis (1970: 18–20, 1983a: 22, 1986a: 92–101). For further discussion of the ambiguity, context-dependence and shiftiness of expressions of actuality see Hazen (1979b), Davies and Humberstone (1980), van Inwagen (1980), Davies (1983), Forbes (1983) and Hodes (1984).

6   The GR handling of case (2*) does not quite entail realism since our very own world, as opposed to a non-actual possible world, might be taken as one that represents the possibility of Carnap having been a footballer by its containing a Carnap counterpart who is a footballer. See Chapter 8 below.

Notes

7   In the ensuing exposition of GR I draw substantially on material from section I of Divers and Melia (2002).
8   The postulates (O1)–(O3) are strictly neutral on the question of whether the sets are non-individuals. That question is pursued in Lewis (1991). However, in this book I will present GR, for the most part and unless indicated otherwise, as though she holds that the individuals and the sets are primitive and distinct categories of entity and, consequently, that nothing is both an individual and a set.
9   No more than a very basic familiarity with the notions of mereology (sum, part, overlap) will be assumed. For a basic sketch of the mereological concepts in the context of GR and further references see Lewis (1986a: 69 n.51, 1991: 1–3, 72–80). For a comprehensive study of mereology see Simons (1989).
10 The foregoing list of postulates is supposed to capture the ontological position of GR accurately, perspicuously and naturally, but I do not claim that it is the most economical formulation of the ontological component of GR. Indeed, an anonymous referee has shown me that postulate (O10) is redundant, given (O9) and standard mereology. The argument is as follows. Suppose for reductio that individual x is in distinct worlds w and v. Then one of these worlds, say w, has a part, y, that is not part of the other world, v. Since x and y are both parts of w, then by (O9), x and y are spatiotemporally related. But then by (O9) v does not count as a world, for v has a part, namely x, that is spatiotemporally related to something, namely y, that is not part of v. This is contrary to the hypothesis that v is a world. So no individual x is in distinct worlds w and v.
11 I talk of 'proper' concepts here and elsewhere to contrast with logical concepts. I presume, and allow, that the conceptual basis of any medium of interpretation of PW will include those of first-order logic with identity (although a primitive concept of identity may be eschewed by some).
12 For the GR treatment of more specific intensional roles associated with propositions and properties see Lewis (1986a: 50–69).
13 Bridging postulates (see below) reflecting the standard definitions will deal with the related cases of modality – i.e. impossibility, contingency and necessity.
14 In what follows I recapitulate the justification and development of this GR treatment of extraordinary (or advanced) modal claims given in Divers (1999a). That treatment follows a remark by Lewis (1986a: 6) on exceptional uses of expressions that typically function as restricting modifiers. The need for GR to consider a special treatment for modal claims about the plurality of worlds, in particular, and the remark by Lewis to which I have just referred, have been noted – but not much developed – in the literature on modal fictionalism. See Menzies and Pettit (1994), Noonan (1994) and Rosen (1995).
15 For further discussion of the latter point see (6.1) below.
16 'It is contingent *that* A' is intended, here, as contingency in the factive sense, i.e. A follows from it being contingent that A. Its being

contingent that A is a matter of A being the case and possibly not-A being the case: hence, (AC) from (A). Contrast contingency in the non-factive sense – it is contingent *whether* A – which is a matter of being neither necessary nor impossible.

17 On this analysis anything can be the counterpart of anything else, the real issue is how context contributes to the selection of an appropriate counterpart relation or relations. See Chapter 8 below.

18 I emphasize that we have here a case in which an ontological application of GR depends on realism about possible individuals in addition to realism about possible worlds. A further example is that of the uniform identification of propositional attitude contents with sets of possible individuals. At the level of neutral elucidation, the doxastic modalities – what could or must be true given my beliefs – were treated in terms of sets of doxastically accessible worlds. Such an account may do whenever the contents of propositional attitudes can be treated as attitudes about the world and so can be characterized by means of worlds. However, it is a now familiar point that there is a class of attitude contents that are irreducibly egocentric – I am cold, etc. – and that such representation de se cannot be equated to any combination of representation de dicto or de re. The proposal of Lewis (1986a: 28–41) – and see further references there – is that what is necessary for the characterization of these egocentric contents is sufficient for the characterization of all egocentric and non-egocentric contents alike. In the case of the doxastic modalities, the class of my doxastic *alternatives* consists in all of those individuals, across all the worlds, such that what I believe does not rule out my identifying such an individual as myself – for all I believe about myself, any such individual could be me. Moreover, although belief de se is not a special case of belief (de re or de dicto) about the world, the latter is a special case of the former. For my non-modal belief that *the* world is such that there is intelligent life on many planets amounts to the same thing as my egocentric belief that *my* world is such a world. Thus, it appears that it is only by embracing realism about possible individuals, and not just possible worlds, that GR affords a uniform ontological reduction of attitude contents whether attitudes de re, de dicto or de se.

19 On propositions, see Lewis (1986a: 27–50), on properties, Lewis (1986a: 51–69), on states of affairs and possibilities, Lewis (1986a: 187), on events, Lewis (1986b), and on the empty set, and subsequently on number, see Lewis (1991).

20 To put the point the other way round, among the constructs that GR has available for such identificatory purposes are ordered pairs of individuals and worlds, sets of sets of individuals, n-tuples of individuals, etc.

21 We arrive at this number by taking the recombination postulate (O12) to entail that there are worlds corresponding to every possible distribution of the values (empty, full) over the actual spacetime points and assuming that there are continuum many such points. See Lewis (1973: 89–90). The reasoning is vulnerable in at least two ways. There may not

Notes

be continuum many actual spacetime points. In any case, it looks as though some of these distributions of values over points will turn out to be duplicates of each other so that there will not be as many indiscernible worlds (see (5.6) below) as there are recombinations.

22 See, again, the discussion of indiscernible worlds in (5.6) below.
23 See (5.5) below.
24 As throughout GR is, by default, classical Lewisian GR. Thus, I take it that GR excludes universals from her ontology (see Lewis 1986c). GR, of course, admits properties and identifies these as sets. For GR, we may truly say, and for certain semantic purposes we may have to say, that the property of being green exists (it is a set of individuals) and that a certain individual, a, has that property (that it is a member of that set). But the consideration that the individual in question is a member of the set in question is not a fact that offers any legitimate explanation of the truth that a is green.
25 The attempt to characterize the modal relationship between truth and truthmakers as one of global supervenience – see e.g. Bigelow (1988a) – is motivated to a large extent by the earlier problem case of negative existential truths. The hope is that we can account for each such truth globally – in terms of all that there is – even if we cannot do so locally – in terms of an entity whose existence corresponds to each such truth.
26 Lewis's scepticism about QML emerges thus. We have at one level, the English sentences themselves and, at another, a direct translation of each of these in counterpart-theoretically interpreted PW. In most cases the intermediate translation from English into QML is simply redundant, but in others no such translation is available since various locutions of modal English outrun the expressive power of QML. So for the purposes of 'regimenting' modal English QML is either redundant or inadequate. See Lewis (1986a: 8–14, esp. 12–13).
27 For the case of AR see Chapter 13.
28 Lewis (1968) clearly thinks that the availability of a broadly Kripkean semantics is crucial to the project of providing truth-conditions for modal sentences and that the correct way in which to ascribe such truth-conditions is in line with the counterpart theory he proposes. Lewis does not go so far as to spell out directly a counterpart-theoretic version of a Kripkean semantics for modal logic but others have shown how to do so. See Hazen (1979a) and Hughes and Cresswell (1996: 354). There are various options in this respect. For example, the C element in each model could be taken as a set of counterpart relations and – as has been suggested by both Bigelow (1990) and Yagisawa (1992) – one might dispense with the R element on the supposition that the counterpart relation can do the work of accessibility relation.
29 Lewis does, of course, offer reasons for prosecuting the metaphysical details of GR as he does – endorsing isolation, worldboundedness of individuals, etc. – that make appeal to general desiderata of theory construction (maximizing simplicity and coherence). So there may be reasons that are not directly to do with applications for fleshing out the hypothesis of a plurality of worlds one way rather than another. But

the point that is being made here is that it is only considerations of application that offer any reason for believing some fleshing out of the hypothesis rather than none.

30 The passage that is usually quoted is this: 'If an argument is wanted, it is this. It is uncontroversially true that things might have been otherwise than they are. I believe and so do you that things could have been different in countless ways. But what does that mean? Ordinary language permits the paraphrase: there are many ways that things could have been, besides the way they actually are. On the face of it, this sentence is an existential quantification. It says that there exist many entities of a certain description, to wit "ways things might have been". I believe things could have been different in countless ways; I believe permissible paraphrases of what I believe; taking the paraphrase at its face value, I therefore believe in the existence of entities that might be called "ways things might have been". I prefer to call them "possible worlds"' (Lewis 1973: 84). In the less widely quoted, but crucial qualification of the foregoing Lewis writes: 'I do not make it as an inviolable principle to take seeming existential quantifications of ordinary language at face value. But I do recognize a presumption in favor of taking sentences at their face value unless (1) taking them at face value is known to lead to trouble and (2) taking them some other way is known not to' (Lewis 1973: 90). Lewis proceeds to argue that the presumption is undefeated in the case of ways things might have been when these are identified as genuine possible worlds.

5 GENUINE REALISM: QUANTIFICATION OVER NON-ACTUALS

1 The most frequently cited source of the allegedly Meinongian doctrines is Meinong (1910). There are Meinongian realists about possible worlds – e.g. Parsons (1980) and Bacon (1995) – who assert explicitly that possible worlds are non-existent entities over which we properly quantify. An exhaustive account of the varieties of realism would consider Meinongian realism about possible worlds in light of – for example – the vigorous critique by Lycan (1979), the spirited clarification and defence of Meinongian quantification by Routley (1980) and Lewis's (1990) discussion of the relationship between his own conception of quantification and properly Meinongian alternatives. I have chosen not to deal with properly Meinongian realism directly since the programme is already crowded by more familiar, more popular and – frankly – more promising interpretations of PW. Finally, it should be noted that GR is sometimes characterized as Meinongian simply on the (uncontestable) grounds that GR quantification, like Meinongian quantification, purports to range over non-actual possibilia as in Loux (1979: 46–7).

2 For example, '... possible beings will be included in our domain of discourse. The idioms of quantification, therefore, will be understood as ranging over all the beings we wish to talk about, *whether existent or nonexistent*' Lewis (1970: 11, my emphasis).

Notes

3   Lycan (1991a: 218) admits that his (1979) conception of Lewis as a Meinongian resulted from overlooking the availability of the mature account (my term) of GR quantification over possibilia that is presented in Lewis (1986a). Since the emergence of that account it has been more common to counter GR with the claim that its controversial existential claims are intelligible and logically consistent but false or not knowably true (see e.g. van Inwagen 1986).
4   We shall see in Chapter 13 how AR deals with this domain problem.
5   Thus Lewis's critics van Inwagen (1986), Armstrong (1989), Bigelow and Pargetter (1990) who oppose the element in GR that identifies other island universes as possible worlds.
6   Of course the denial need not be flat denial. In the case of analytic actualism, the opponent may allow that it is prima facie analytic that everything is actual, but insist that prima facie grounds for analyticity are defeasible and that the intelligibility of GR is such a defeating consideration in this case.
7   This is not a very hard datum. My own experience is that many hear 'actual' as connoting what philosophers might recognize as concreteness. Compare the German 'wirklich' which is often translated as 'actual' and which Frege uses in contrasting the metaphysical nature of numbers with that of physical objects – thus 'I distinguish what I call objective from what I call handleable, spatial or actual [wirklich]' (Frege 1884: 35).
8   The foregoing assessment of the objection from analyticity is fairly conservative, but clearly more radical courses of response on behalf of GR might be entertained. First, it is clear enough that one might resist any objection from analyticity by attacking the credentials of the concept of analyticity. But I will not pursue that course here. Apart from the general issue of how attractive a course that is, it will not be easy for GR to pursue it while remaining faithful to two of her central motivating ideas: that the enterprise of conceptual analysis is legitimate; and that the realm of the intensional can be rendered philosophically respectable. Second, an altogether more promising course for GR might begin by simply conceding that her concept of actuality is distinct from that which is implicit in the usage of the folk. GR might further observe that such an outcome is not uncommon when we use a folk term ('number', 'weight', etc.) as a way in to our metaphysical enquiries. Moreover, the concession does not amount immediately to abandoning the goal of giving an analysis of the modal and intensional concepts of the folk since there is the prospect that these might be explicated in terms of, but without identification with, the concepts expressed in the GR theory.
9   As McGinn formulates the objection it is that Lewisian worlds are not 'genuine individuals'. I have written 'proper individuals' to avoid a clash with my use of 'genuine'. On a more substantive point, it is worth noting that the present objection is perhaps stronger than initially meets the eye in that it is poised to tell against not only GR but also to check the antirealist who would count even one genuine possible world (the actual world) among the actual individuals.

Notes

10 That GR should treat the modal features of worlds in the same way as those of other genuine individuals is a suggestion put to work for different purposes by Bigelow (1990).

11 Aside from the consideration that it is perfectly natural and plausible to allow that genuine worlds stand in counterpart relations – relations of various kinds and degrees of similarity – to other things, recall (cf. (4.5) n.16) that the recognition of counterpart relations among worlds promises the theoretical advantage of allowing GR to do without a special class of accessibility relations in his adaptation of the Kripke semantics.

12 The immediate defence of GR need go no further but other aspects of McGinn's objection merit comment. First, in articulating the deficiencies of genuine worlds McGinn claims further: (a) that what transpires in a world is essential to its identity; and (b) that the identity of a world is fixed by its content. But neither claim is plausible concerning the worlds of GR. (a) seems false if we read 'transpiring in a world' as a matter of what is represented by a world (what holds at a world) and construe what is essential to the identity of a world as what is the case for all of its counterparts. For the counterpart of a world need not represent all that the world itself represents, so that it would be possible for this world to have existed without representing (as it actually does) that Carnap is a philosopher. (b) seems false insofar as GR does not rule out the existence of distinct but indiscernible worlds. Such worlds would be, *ex hypothesi*, distinct, but exactly the same in respect of representational content given the supervenience of representation on qualitative character (see Chapter 16). Fine (1977: 158) makes claims (a) and (b) about possible worlds conceived as propositions. In citing Fine's claims in support of his own claim about the essential properties of genuine worlds, McGinn (1981: 152) appears to have (unwarrantedly) construed Fine's claim about a certain species of AR world as one that applies to possible worlds however conceived, or at least to GR worlds in particular. For the record the objection from essential properties is an objection to proper individuality and as such would be powerless against AR worlds insofar as these are conceived as non-individuals (sets, states of affairs, properties, etc.).

13 Hudson (1999) argues that we can defend the principle of sufficient reason by adopting a version of GR which (a) characterizes transworld individuals as impossible individuals and (b) abandons the identification of propositions with sets of worlds in order to assert (c) that there are true necessary falsehoods. I have indicated that GR ought to regard move (a) as gratuitous. Moreover, one might think that GR would regard admission of true necessary falsehoods as something that she would strive to avoid at most costs – not as something that she would seek to secure at the cost of abandoning her ontological account of propositions. So I take the version of GR that Hudson presents to be manifestly less attractive than the version that is defended here. Iconoclasm aside, Hudson does give grounds for thinking that the admission of propositions about transworld individuals – whether those indi-

viduals are characterized as impossible individuals or not – calls for some modification of the general GR account of *which* set of worlds it is, in general, with which a proposition is to be identified. But since I see no threat in that consideration to GR as presented here, I will not pursue the point.

14 See Chapter 4, n.29.
15 That such a specification is available to GR is noted in the Sharlow (1988) response to the paraphrase argument of Naylor (1986). This form of truth-condition mirrors exactly what we would expect from any broadly Kripkean semantics given: (a) the intuitive equivalence of 'It is impossible that A' and 'It is not possible that A'; and (b) the standard recursion clauses for negation and possibility operators.
16 Yagisawa's further argument presents a challenge to GR which is different from, and more substantial than, the paraphrase argument for impossible worlds. So it is misleading of Miller to claim repeatedly – see his (1989: 476, 1990: 453, 1991: 50) – that the arguments of Yagisawa (1988), as well as those due to Naylor (1986), are refuted by the Sharlow (1988) response to the paraphrase argument.
17 Here I project an ontological distinction among entities corresponding to the semantic distinction between intensional and hyperintensional contexts. A hyperintensional (sentential) context is one inside which substitution of sentences that have the same strict truth-conditions – interpreted sentences that are necessarily equivalent in truth-value – may fail to preserve truth-value. This condition does not hold of all intensional contexts (see Davies (1981: 47–8)).
18 Lycan (1991a) also takes it that Lewis's GR fails to discriminate adequately among the intensions by failing to admit impossible worlds but, in contrast to Yagisawa, Lycan construes this point as promoting the cause of AR (see (11.1)). Both Yagisawa (1988) and Lycan (1991a) cite non-material conditionals as a further case in which adequate discrimination calls for acceptance of impossible worlds. But here, and in line with the initial treatment of conditionals as relations between intensions (propositions) I will treat it as a subcase of the general case of intensions.
19 It is interesting to speculate how PGR might be guided, in exploring the representational capacities of her ontology, by those AR accounts of representation that she deems acceptable (see Chapter 12 below). PGR may acknowledge that distinct impossibilities may be represented by distinct books or stories (cf. Lewis 1986a: 7 n.5). Moreover, PGR contains the resources for constructing books *qua* sets of propositions (Lewis 1986a: 185). Books, *qua* sets of propositions, are sets of sets of genuine worlds, and inconsistent books, *qua* sets of inconsistent propositions, are sets of mutually disjoint sets of genuine worlds. Inconsistent books, *qua* sets of propositions, are distinguished by their membership. Now let us consider the intuitively distinct impossibilities, P & ~P and Q & ~Q, where P and Q are distinct contingent propositions (say that donkeys talk and that there are blue swans). Consider now a simplified model in which: the set of all genuine worlds is the set {u,v,w};

the proposition P is the set {u,w}, the proposition Q is the set {u,v} and the negation of each proposition is identified with its complement in {u,v,w} so that ~P = {v} and ~Q = {w}. The book at which P & ~ P is the inconsistent set of propositions {P, ~P} which is, in turn, the set of sets of worlds, S = {{u,w}, {v}}. The book at which Q & ~Q is the inconsistent set of propositions {Q, ~Q} which is, in turn, the set of sets of worlds S* = {{u,v}, {w}}. Manifestly, S ≠ S*. Thus PGR has resources that permit the representation of impossibilities, and with some due discrimination, without admitting impossible genuine worlds.

20 Yagisawa (1988: 191–4) makes the point that even if PGR is as effective as IGR in providing sufficiently various constructs to match the variety of intensions, the other theoretical virtues may favour the latter.
21 Here I recapitulate part of section V of Divers (1999a).
22 If we take the occurrence of 'actually' as making a genuine semantic contribution to (7), then from the PGR standpoint the claim is nonsensical since it invites us to restrict quantification to within some world although no such world is specified by the antecedent clauses of (7). So letting 'actually' go redundant is the charitable option. Allowing 'actually' to function as an indexical that refers to a logical space, as Yagisawa (1992: 202) advises, the semantic effect is equivalent to redundancy since, from the PGR standpoint, it thereby 'restricts' quantification to within the maximal, unrestricted domain.
23 Here I indulge the pretence that we can refer to other PGR worlds, to which we stand in no causal or spatiotemporal relation, by means of what appear to be locative indexicals like 'there' and by means of proper names.
24 To put the point otherwise, I am taking the challenge to be, more generally, that of expressing that what is absolutely necessary might not have been absolutely necessary.
25 In light of these remarks, I think that there is far more at stake than Miller (1989: 477) suggests in judging that a commitment to genuine impossibilia would prove at most a 'mere embarrassment' by showing that Lewis's (PGR) ontology is incomplete.
26 The classical source of the doctrine that objects are the possible referents of singular terms is Frege (1884). The doctrine is discussed by Dummett (1981: 234) and figures in the recent, neo-Fregean defence of arithmetical Platonism (see Wright 1983: 53 and Hale 1987: 9).
27 By way of indicating independent motivation, I will mention, rather than endorse, a further, and by no means Fregean, thought that might motivate enquiry into the possibility of singular reference to non-actual possibilia. The thought is that the impossibility of singular reference to the contested individuals threatens to render unmanifestable our purported understanding of quantification over them. The obvious and natural way in which to manifest understanding of purported quantification over a range of controversial objects would be to present correct applications of the introduction and elimination rules governing the quantifiers with respect to such objects. However, the application of any

Notes

such rules presupposes the availability of appropriate singular referring expressions to change places with bound variables. If there can be no singular terms that effect reference to the contested objects then the obvious means, at least, of manifesting understanding of quantification over possibilia is unavailable.

28 So the present objection is not properly subject to the kind of complaint that Lewis (1986a: 82) levels against Dummett (1973: Chapter 14). Lewis's complaint is that we ought not to draw inferences about the intrinsic natures of things (e.g. abstractness) from considerations about how we refer to them.

29 Perhaps this assumption needs argument but given no obvious source of dissent, I will not attempt to argue for it here.

30 Two comments. First, this brief argument for the impossibility of ostensively grounded singular reference to possibilia echoes an older concern of sceptics about possibilia who complain that since possibilia are not 'there', they are not 'there to be referred to', cf. Black (1960) and Marcus (1985: 205). The concern so expressed appears to involve an equivocation on 'there' between its locative sense and its neutral existential sense – at least it suggests the presumption that we cannot refer to that with which we are spatially unrelated. The present argument does not place so much weight on (the possibility of) spatial relations between speaker and referent and I take it to be stronger for that. Second, I do not deny that once successful reference is – somehow – taken to be secured, it may be possible for a speaker to refer by broadly ostensive means to an individual to which she stands in no causal relation. For example, even an arithmetical Platonist need not rule out the cogency of referring to a natural number in an appropriate context by means of phrases such as 'that number' – for example when the utterance is accompanied by pointing to a numeral, or to a collection of objects where a sortal concept is distinguished by context as salient. But here we are trying to understand how singular reference to possibilia could, as it were, get started.

31 Here a peculiarity of the dialectic becomes particularly explicit. It is necessary for the objector to buy into the prima facie intelligibility of the controversial quantification in order to demonstrate its deeper failings.

32 The reasons I will give for the failure of the foregoing modal response also undermine the modal response that I previously commended (in Divers 1994) to GR as a means of resisting the allegation that non-actual possibilia could not be adequately individuated.

33 This is not just a point about the world, α, that is actual from our standpoint. The possibility of reference to non-actuals is, from the standpoint of any world, a matter of inter-world reference. Note also that the present rejection of the ordinary treatment of transworld reference claims would appear to have authoritative precedent when Lewis characterizes actual reference to alien properties as impossible, thus: 'I do not see how we could have words for alien properties' (Lewis 1986a: 159).

34 McGinn (1981: 151) may have overlooked this point in claiming that 'a world has not been *uniquely* specified *until* all of its properties have been listed' (first emphasis in original, second emphasis mine).

35 If the argument is successful it meets the complaint of Armstrong (1989: 22–3) that the existence or otherwise of indiscernible worlds is an important matter on which GR ought not to remain agnostic. Towards resolving agnosticism, I have suggested elsewhere (Divers 1994) that GR might rule out indiscernible worlds on grounds of simple quantitative economy. If considerations of economy are to count at all in matters of a priori theorizing, it might be thought arbitrary to let quantitative economy count for absolutely nothing – especially in a case such as the present, where a version of GR that includes indiscernible worlds does no more work than a version of GR that rules them out.

36 I note two lines of resistance to the present response. First, Maudlin (1996) argues that GR agnosticism about indiscernible worlds is not sustainable since indiscernible worlds are an inescapable commitment of genuine modal realism – he argues further that this commitment generates inconsistency. Lewis (1996) responds by rejecting (in its various disambiguations) the principle that makes the trouble in both respects, viz.: that what does not result in the impossible is possible. Clearly the principle is no part of GR as it has been presented here. Second, as an anonymous referee has impressed upon me, there may well be a cost to be reckoned for insisting on a totality of non-replicated worlds. If (unrestrictedly) there are no duplicate worlds then, by the extraordinary possibility principle, there could be no duplicate worlds. We are supposed to be comfortable with GR worlds because they are of the category of individuals, but now we find that unlike any other non-worldly individuals, these are constrained – as if by magic – to lack duplicates.

37 McGinn (1981: 152) takes it to be significant that there is only one way – exhaustive description – in which any non-actual world could be specified since it follows that we could not form any informative identity statements involving worldly singular terms. However, even if there were an irremediable absence of such worldly identity statements, the significance of this fact – from the Fregean standpoint – would not be obvious. GR provides an explicit definition of 'world' as a maximal sum of spatiotemporal relata (see postulate (O9) in (4.2)). So there is no need for an implicit definition of 'world' of the kind that neo-Fregeans typically attempt to formulate in the absence of such a definition – that is, a stipulation of truth-conditions for canonical identity statements of the kind that are familiar from the cases of number and direction (the number of F's = the number of G's iff . . ., the direction of a = the direction of b iff . . .). Moreover, if – for whatever purpose – informative worldly identity statements are required, GR is now in a position to supply them. Wherever there is more than one way of specifying a part of the actual world – say by means of the terms 'a' and 'b' – this presents the possibility of formulating worldly identity statements and supplying them with truth-conditions as follows: the world that is the

Notes

duplicate of a = the world that is the duplicate of b iff all and only the parts of the world that is the duplicate of a are all and only the parts of the world that is the duplicate of b. The question of whether, or how, we could be in a position to judge whether, on any occasion, the truth-condition is satisfied is a distinct, epistemological question, the broader significance of which is unclear.

38 Although it is difficult to see how the referential potential of an unusable language might be thought to have any bearing on the senses of the quantifiers of the languages that we actually do use.
39 For the moment, and in order to maximize *ad hominem* value, Lewis's critique of the limits of linguistic ersatzism will go unchallenged. For discussion see Chapter 17 below.
40 Of course in the event that a remedy is available, it may be presumed to be available to the linguistic ersatzist also, and thereby a significant part of Lewis's (1986a: Chapter 3) critique of linguistic ersatzism would go by the board.
41 We would have, in effect, an ambitious version of GR in competition with a modest version. From the standpoint of modest GR, ambitious GR intends to extend first-order quantification to a contested domain (that of alien non-actual individuals) that fails the weaker Fregean requirement (S2) – there is no individual in the intended domain to which singular reference is possible.
42 As far as I can see no GR application of PW depends directly on the availability of singular reference to non-actuals.

6 GENUINE REALISM: WORLDS

1 As Rosenberg (1989) has emphasized it is not a serious option for GR to leave the concept of a worldmate unanalysed since to do so would be to invite the charge that the relation is either unintelligible or intelligible only as the notion of compossibility by another name, thus leaving all GR analyses involving the 'world' predicate implicitly conceptually modal (see Chapter 7) below.
2 (GRW1) makes precise the ontological postulate (O9) of Chapter 4 above.
3 A temporal account of the worldmaking relation is thought more desirable than a spatial account since, it is widely held, there are at least some minimally plausible examples of absolutely compossible individuals that are temporally but not spatially related, e.g. a Cartesian ego and a body, one Cartesian ego and another (see Lewis 1986a: 73).
4 In Field (1989) we have an example of a philosopher who holds that the non-existence of certain non-individual entities – Platonistic numbers – is contingent.
5 As presented here the problem concerns the de dicto possibility that (some) sets exist. But I intend this formulation to do duty for both the de dicto and de re cases. The de re possibility that any given set exists – say, your singleton – presents essentially the same problem as the de dicto possibility since it too requires that some set – a counterpart of

the given set – be part of a world. Or at least that is the case so long as we presume, as I shall, that only a set can be a counterpart of a set.

6   As I have presented the problem here it concerns non-individuals but, as is now evident, it effects extraordinary individuals as well. The problem of the possible existence of extraordinary individuals is potentially significant. For while an earlier Lewis (1983b: 39–40, 1986a: 96) thinks that such individuals are oddities that do no work, a later Lewis (1991) considers identifying the empty set with such an individual, namely the great individual that has all individuals as parts.

7   This move is prefigured by the brief provision made for 'abstract entities' in Lewis (1973: 39–40) and Davidson and Pargetter (1980: 390–1). Yagisawa (1992: 89–90) makes a precisely analogous move in order to 'localize' non-individual possibilia in the individuals that he proposes as surrogates for worlds (see (6.7) below).

8   Contrast on all fronts the notion of being partly in a world.

9   As several readers have pointed out to me, the ellipsis of clause (ii) of (D) cannot accurately be cashed out (finitely) since individuals can be embedded at arbitrary depth within the sets. I am unsure of the significance of this consideration, but it inhibits me from calling (D) a 'definition' of the 'x is in w' predicate.

10 Recall here Frege's assertion of the existence of certain abstract objects (numbers) and denial that their existence is actual ('wirklich'). See Chapter 5 n.7.

11 We shall shortly encounter the contrary view in the dual existence example of King (1995). GR may seek to ground an explanation of this (supposed) modal fact about us in the more general consideration that no individual stands in any perceptual relation to disjoint times. But I will not attempt to unpack such an explanation here.

12 As Rosenberg notes, GR need not let the Kantian have this point so easily. For Lewis's scepticism about inference from conceivability to possibility see his (1986a: 90).

13 Taylor (1998) argues that the time travel doctrine of Lewis (1976) furnishes such an explanation.

14 Rosenberg (1989: 421 n.9) credits this use of the chaotic worlds example to Lewis.

15 Conjoining this third consideration with the first and with the primary account of worlds, we can see why GR is likely to regard causal connectedness as sufficient but not necessary for individuals to be worldmates.

16 See Chapter 4 above.

17 Especially so when she is by no means at a loss for an alternative explanation of the imaginative data that have been produced (see n.13 above).

18 In addition to the (epistemologically) crucial matters of utility, the revisions that King moots threaten the very metaphysical integrity and identity of GR. If worlds are collections of causal relata, what kinds of things are these relata and what kinds of collections (sets, sums) constitute the worlds? The (missing) answers to these questions carry massive

Notes

19 This Lewis adopts a familiar strategy for countering prima facie counterexamples to modal claims. Compare the Kripke (1972: Chapter 3) explanation of the intuition that there could be molecular motion in the absence of heat by offering worlds in which there is molecular motion in the absence of *sensations* of heat. See also Miller's contrast (in 6.2) of the impossibility of the existence of disconnected times with the impossibility of the actual existence of disconnected times.

20 Given the primary account of worlds, GR takes the actual co-existence of disconnected times to be impossible and so inconsistent with general relativity or, indeed, anything else.

21 To underline the last point, it would not normally be thought *arbitrary* to apply certain treatment to murderers and not to apply it to those for whom there is an unrealized non-zero objective chance of having murdered.

22 This defence depends on unpacking a single modal word 'contingent' into a complex form that involves multivocal – ordinary and extraordinary – modal operators and so multivocal – restricted and unrestricted – quantification over individuals. There is precedent for the move. In the case where GR seeks to interpret the claim that there could be no A-differences without B-differences as *weak* supervenience, initial quantifiers have to range unrestrictedly over all individuals while subsequent quantifiers are world-restricted (see Divers 1999a: 232). Moreover, to clarify the status of the response, all that has been claimed is that there is a legitimate interpretation of the contingency claim under which, and given the primary account of worlds, the claim is true. I do not claim that this interpretation is mandatory. In particular, one could easily make the case for the legitimacy of an extraordinary interpretation of the first conjunct of (C) on the grounds that a and b are, by hypothesis, not parts of one world. It seems to me that it is a moot point how the first conjunct should be treated precisely because, in this context, the primary account of worlds is moot. The proponent of the account may take the claim of temporal relatedness as an intra-world claim on grounds of content (truth-conditions) whether or not a and b are (by hypothesis) temporally related. When the proponent of the primary account considers a temporal-relatedness proposition (content), she construes that as an intra-world proposition (content) – and as long as she may, then she has the right to endorse the contingency claim. That is all that is claimed and all that is required in order to meet the objection.

23 In the example as written, the antecedent clause is, 'If we had not met Jane ...'. I have reformulated to give 'met' its broadest, and surely intended, sense.

24 It would seem that syntactic considerations offered the GR interpreter more room for manoeuvre in the preceding example of contingency. In that case the key modal claim unfolded into a formula involving two modal operators and as such was syntactically susceptible to four

Notes

distinct permutations of interpretation of its operators – two univocal and two multivocal. In the present case, there is only one modal operator involved and so only two distinct interpretations are syntactically permissible.

25 Of course the classical principle is debatable, but there is no obvious reason why it should be optional for some kinds of modal realist but not others.

26 Plantingan realism and nature realism are among the species of actualist realism that are presented in Chapter 10.

27 There may be an even more fundamental kind of ontological difference between other worlds and our own if false accounts of actual spatiotemporal ontology are true of other worlds (see Lewis 1986a: 76 n.55). But I will not pursue the point here.

28 Lewis does not explicitly say that the point concerns alien relations – as opposed to relations that are actually uninstantiated but constructible in standard ways from spatiotemporal relations that are. But clearly, this is the intention since one way in which he thinks that the primary account would encompass the Newtonian world is if the two sorts of distance relation in such a world were a matter of the unique relativistic distance relation playing both roles (i.e. 'doubling up', cf. Lewis 1986a: 74).

29 We might also note, in connection with the present objection, that the term 'spatiotemporal relations' also figures in the recombination postulate (O12) of GR. However this is no separate difficulty since the occurrence of the term there is derivative from and subordinate to its occurrence in the account of worlds. The relations that should be invoked in the recombination postulate are just whatever the world-unifying relations are supposed to be.

30 On the contingent existence of our spatiotemporal relations, note the caution of Miller (1990: 455–6) who qualifies his 'B-series' explication of the GR conception of time with the phrase, '... but in all possible worlds that have time ...'.

31 A certain kind of semantic optimist, inspired by the kinds of considerations made famous by Putnam (1975), might hold that we can make our good baptismal intentions do enough work so that the spelling out is avoidable. On one way of construing the problem, it is that of attempting to refer to a genus of relations when we are causally connected to only one of the species of that genus. So why not say, 'By "worldmaking relations", let us mean that kind of relation of which these, our actual spatiotemporal relations, are a species'? Of course the natural thought is that this stab is hopelessly indeterminate and that we need to introduce some further discriminating conceptual resources to home in one such genus rather than another. But another thought is that we can rely on a principle of charity, rather than conceptual articulation, to do the trick. In the case of an element that actually has only one kind of isotope or a compound that has only one kind of isomer we can *now* invoke the appropriate generic concepts ('the element X', 'the compound Y') in order to make clear that it is a given genus rather than

Notes

the species to which our terms 'X' and 'Y' are intended to refer. But it was not always so, and when it was not so did those who were causally related to mono-isotopic elements or mono-isomeric compounds refer to species or genus when they introduced undifferentiated kind terms by saying things like, 'Let X be anything that is of the same kind as This'? One response may be that what they referred to is a matter constrained by charity. If we make them more intelligible, and that includes being more truthful, under the hypothesis that they referred to the species, they referred to the species and so – *mutatis mutandis* – for a given genus. So can we appeal to self-charity in order to avoid spelling out the nature of the intended genus to which our spatiotemporal relations belong? Since I am no such semantic optimist I note, but will not pursue, this line of thought.

32 Thus: '[The relations] are *discriminating*: it is at least possible, whether or not it happens at every world where the relations are present, that there be a great many interrelated things, no two of which are alike with respect to their place in the structure of relations' (Lewis 1986a: 76).

33 Lewis (1986a: 76) cites only messiness, rather than looming counterexample or modal error, as a reason for seeking to characterize worldmates without appeal to the notion of analogically spatiotemporal relations.

34 For a detailed explanation of this point see Chapter 7.

35 Here I make explicit what is usually understood implicitly in discussions of this topic, namely, that the principle of recombination applies only to worldbound or ordinary individuals, all parts of which are worldmates. Unrestricted summing gives rise to extraordinary individuals that have parts that stand in no spatiotemporal relation, but recombination does not require – *per impossibile*, by the lights of GR – that any world should contain any duplicates of these individuals. Hereafter I take the restriction to worldbound individuals as read.

36 The strategy of appealing to proper classes in order to avoid set-theoretic paradoxes is discussed a little further with respect to AR in (15.5).

37 The admission of universals is motivated by considerations about second-order properties. Properties of properties are naturally identified in GR as sets of sets of individuals. But if the first-order property of being an individual, say, is not to be identified with the set of all individuals it must be identified otherwise so as to be available as a member of the second-order properties. The identification of the first-order property as a class (a non-member) does not permit this, hence the hypothesis that the first-order property is something other than a set, or a class (or an individual), viz. a universal.

38 Armstrong (1989: 32) takes it to be an advantage of AR ('non-natural actualism') over GR that the latter has difficulty, over recombination, in sustaining a fully iterative account of which worlds there are while 'there seems to be no reason why the non-Naturalist Actualist should not accept an iterative account of how certain maximally consistent sets of propositions are formed'. Certainly neither the Forrest–Armstrong

Notes

argument nor the Nolan argument applies directly to any species of AR. Nonetheless, Armstrong's claim is well wide of the mark given that other, directly appropriate, paradoxes await any attempt to provide a fully iterative account of AR worlds. Chapter 15 is dedicated to the discussion of these paradoxes.

39 To put the point less mildly, why is UGR exempt from the critique of genuine realism with overlap presented by Lewis (1986a: 198–209) (see also Chapter 4 n.3)? Or if it is not exempt, what response should be made to that critique?

40 For more on the importance of this point see Chapter 7 below.

41 Behind the present point there is a notable general principle. If aggregates of individuals in general are relatively functionally inept when compared with Lewis worlds it can only be because the aggregates are too indiscriminate – too many or varied – to play the required roles (e.g. *loci* of laws of nature). It cannot be that aggregates in general are too few since all Lewis worlds are among the aggregates.

42 Van Fraassen (1995) argues more generally, and not just within the confines of modal metaphysics or GR in particular, that there is no good reason to treat 'world' as – in effect – a sortal predicate and that it should be treated in a broadly non-cognitivist fashion (my characterization) as a means of expressing that a certain domain of quantification is appropriate to the interpretation of utterances in which it features. We have just seen that GR, at least, ought not to treat 'world' so lightly.

7 GENUINE REALISM: UNANALYSED MODALITY

1 As throughout (P) is intended to deal only with ordinary possibility claims but clearly it is necessary for GR to deal adequately with this salient case in order to deal adequately with the entire family of modal and intensional concepts. The companion principle (A) (see (4.3)) deals with extraordinary possibilities, and other modalities, by taking the modal words in such contexts to express no semantic content and so, a fortiori, no irreducibly modal semantic content.

2 This chapter draws substantially on Divers and Melia (2002).

3 The 'by and large' in clause (ii) is significant, since there are cases, as Lewis admits, where GR fails to serve up worlds to match pre-theoretical beliefs about possibility – e.g. there are no worlds representing that nothing (concrete) exists (Lewis 1986a: 73) and – although I have recently downplayed the case – there are no worlds representing the co-actuality of disjoint spacetimes. I do not think that it is reasonable to require in the name of accuracy that GR should confirm all and only 'our' pre-theoretical modal beliefs and propose to allow instead for a certain degree of reflective equilibrium between the success of the theory and our pre-theoretical modal beliefs. However should GR disconfirm too many of our pre-theoretical modal beliefs, or if it disconfirms beliefs that are central to or constitutive of our modal concepts, then the analysis ought to be condemned as inaccurate. So

Notes

prior modal beliefs do and should exert a substantial constraint on the accuracy of the GR analysis of possibility, lest the analysis be left open to the charge of attaining accuracy trivially by having (arbitrarily) redefined its subject matter.

4   Two points on the notion of completeness. First, completeness is intended as an articulation of the requirement that there be no gaps in logical space. The term 'completeness' is preferred to Lewis's 'plenitude' because the latter may suggest that GR is required to determine the existence of some maximal number of worlds. That the set of worlds should be of exactly a given size is something that can easily be determined by means of an explicit postulate to that effect. But that the set of worlds is of exactly a given size is neither necessary nor sufficient for completeness if – along with Lewis – we do not rule out indiscernible worlds (1986a: 224). That there are exactly k worlds is a postulate that is modelled by a set containing the actual world and $(k-1)$ distinct duplicates of it, but such a set of worlds is incomplete for failing to represent all the possibilities. On the other hand if, by hypothesis, there is a set of worlds that is of size k and complete, then we can generate from that set by replication of its members a set that is of a size greater than k but still complete. So completeness (and consistency) is a matter of the range of types of worlds that is determined to exist by GR. Second, completeness, as understood here is – of course – very different from the metalogical notion of completeness. It is not required, or expected, that every single modal truth is provable from GR.

5   The plausibility of this principle stands or falls with that of the Humean denial of (absolutely) necessary connections between distinct existences.

6   If GR analyses were articulated metalinguistically, as in:

(P*)   'It is possible that P' is true iff there is a world at which P

the point would simply be that GR is conceptually modal if it involves the use, as opposed to the mention, of explicitly modal terms. But the metalinguistic approach brings specific complications that we do best to avoid. For example (P*) appears apt to articulate the analysis of only such possibilities as can be expressed in the sentences of some specific actual language, and that does not obviously amount to an exhaustive analysis of the concept of possibility.

7   Modalist interpretations of PW (see (2.6)) afford analyses that are, in this way, explicitly conceptually modal and are invariably acknowledged by their proponents to be so.

8   The qualification – 'given other reasonable assumptions within which the debate is usually conducted' – speaks to the following consideration. We might entertain the prospect of taking the high road here, seeking a grand transcendental argument for the vast claim that the very capacity to grasp any concept whatsoever – and a fortiori, any concept that is expressed in GR – requires the possession of modal

Notes

concepts. However, even were that conclusion to be demonstrated, it is not clear that it would drain all interest from the ambition to provide a non-modal analysis of possibility. For even if there could be no grasp of concepts without grasp of modal concepts, it would be something else to show that the salient concepts expressed in GR are, as it were, covertly and locally modal. That would be to say that some of the theoretical terms of GR express concepts that were properly analysable only in irreducibly modal terms. The enduring idea that colour concepts are so locally modal (dispositional) while shape concepts are not – see, e.g., McGinn (1983: Chapter 2) – provides one familiar example of an attempt to substantiate this distinction.

9   It is in this way that AR analyses of modality tend to be modal. See Chapter 11.
10 We note, by way of an appeal to authority, that Quine, the arch-enemy of all things modal, is happy with all of the terms that feature on the GR list of primitives.
11 Recapitulating his objection, Lycan (1991b: 212) writes: '[Lewis] is forced to stipulate the non-existence of impossible worlds in order to distribute truth-values correctly over modal sentences, "world" for him means "possible world" and to mean "possible" as opposed to "impossible" is to be a modal term.'
12 Lycan (1979) argued that the intelligibility of GR quantification depended on assigning existential locutions (e.g. 'there is') a modal sense (there could be). That claim is subsequently and correctly withdrawn (Lycan 1991a) on the grounds that GR is entitled to claim the ordinary sense for her quantificational locutions and then define quantifications over actuality, non-modally, as a restricted case of such quantification. There is a more general point here. It will not do to claim that GR is implicitly modal on the grounds that existential quantification, as it figures in the theory, is intended as ranging over possible individuals. It is true that GR so conceives the domain of quantification, but that is not at all to say that the concept expressed by GR use of the idioms of existential quantification is different from the concept that is expressed by the ontological actualist's use of the same symbols. Indeed, were GR to be regarded as operating with a concept of existential quantification that is different from that of her actualist opponent, then there would be no substance left to the idea that these two parties are engaged in a genuine ontological dispute. If different concepts are afoot in the claims of the protagonists, then when GR says 'there are many worlds' and the actualist says 'there is at most one world', their claims stand in no conflict. The two philosophers merely talk past one another (Divers 1997: 149–50).
13 The term of the definiens on which Lycan (1991b) actually focuses is 'spatiotemporal relation' but that does not effect the general point.
14 Perhaps this response grants Lycan too much. Even if the ontological component of GR were limited to a collection of existential axioms still it would be wrong to say that, unless 'individual' means 'possible individual', the theory permits the existence of impossible worlds. For GR

entails that there are no impossible individuals. The hypothesis of the existence of impossible individuals is an inconsistent proposition and so the existence of impossible individuals is inconsistent with the ontological postulates of GR. Lycan's further claim, in effect, is that such entailment has to be analytic entailment – entailment that is directly underwritten by the meaning of the term 'individual' that figures in the GR postulates. Yet Lycan offers no argument for that further claim, and such argument is certainly required in face of the widely held view that there are cases of absolute non-analytic entailment – e.g. that the theory consisting in the single postulate 'all molecules are water molecules' entails that all molecules are H_2O molecules even though 'water' doesn't mean the same as 'H_2O'. In the absence of argument for the crucial claim of analytic entailment – that GR admits no impossibilia only if GR analytically entails that there are no impossibilia – Lycan has failed to make the case that GR is implicitly conceptually modal. For some further criticisms of Lycan see Miller (1993).

15 Despite such striking counterexamples, the general principle – that an analysis of possibility might be, at least, compromised by this kind of consideration – is no mere straw man. Armstrong appears to object to any analysis of the concept of possibility in terms of sets precisely on the grounds that sets have a modal feature that is defined in terms of possibility – thus: 'It seems that sets supervene on their members, that is, ultimately, things that are not sets. Supervenience, however, is a notion to be defined ... in terms of possibility. It seems undesirable, therefore, to make use of sets in defining possibility' Armstrong (1989: 47).

16 At least, this is so given that facts – as Shalkowski (1994: 671) intends – are to be construed as language-independent and mind-independent entities.

17 Strictly this is what it is for a property to be alien to α, but in the present context the relativization is taken as read.

18 See combinatorial realism, Chapter 10 below.

19 This point has special *ad hominem* force against Lewis who invokes such reasoning in order to resist the suggestion that the possible size of spacetime is restricted to any specific finite number of dimensions (1986a: 103). I have resisted the force of the reasoning in precisely that context (see (6.7) above) and would not want to rely on it here.

20 Note that it is not thereby required here that there is a world in which all instantiable α-alien properties are instantiated.

21 Postulates (O1)–(O10) are easily seen to be true of S*. Moreover, since only worlds containing α-alien natural properties have been deleted from S, it follows that α is a member of S* (and is, of course, still the unique world of which we are parts). Accordingly, (O11) is true in S*. The principle of recombination, (O12), is also true in S*. For the only α-alien natural properties omitted by S* (P_1, P_3 . . .) are all – indeed – *natural* properties, there is no way of constructing these from the properties instantiated in S*. Accordingly, applying the principle of

recombination to any collection of worlds in S* only results in another world that omits all these natural properties. Since S* contains *all* worlds in S that omit these properties, and since S is (by hypothesis) itself closed under recombination, it follows that S* too is closed under recombination. Finally, (OAN) is also true of S*. This is because, for any n, there are n distinct alien properties $P_2, P_4 \ldots P_{2k}$ instantiated by objects existing in S*.

22 Although S* is a proper subset of S, it does not *immediately* follow that S* is incomplete. Two indiscernible worlds represent the same possibilities. Accordingly, if S contained indiscernible worlds then there exists a proper subset of S containing no indiscernible worlds which nevertheless deserves to be called complete if S did.

23 This is the reason why the argument has to be put in terms of alien properties rather than non-actual individuals. If we try to run the argument for individuals then we have no way of constructing a set S* that demonstrably represents fewer possibilities than does S.

24 Recall that, as the term is used here, the theory is complete iff it guarantees that the set of possible worlds is complete (that there are no gaps in logical space).

25 Two areas in which GR would maintain her claim of advantage over AR would be in representing the relevant range of possibilities non-magically and with appropriate discrimination; see Chapter 17.

8 GENUINE REALISM: COUNTERPARTS

1 Lewis suggests that sets have counterparts in his (1973: 39) where each of the abstract entities that exist from the standpoint of all worlds is stipulated to be its own unique counterpart in each world and in his (1991: 37) where singleton sets are held to be counterparts just in case their members are counterparts. I have already discussed how GR might otherwise accommodate modalizing about non-individuals in Chapter 6 and I will be concerned here only with counterpart relations between individuals.

2 Several commentators allude to the idea that a counterpart-theoretic treatment of modality and possible worlds is anticipated by Leibniz – e.g. Kripke (1972: 45 n.17). Lewis (1968: 26 n.1) reports that Geach communicated to Prior (in 1964) a treatment of de re modality which is similar to that of Lewis (1968). That counterpart relations may be invoked for various purposes – notably, in order to resolve various modal and analogous temporal paradoxes – has been suggested by various philosophers who do not embrace GR, see e.g. Kripke (1972: 51 n.18), Forbes (1985: Chapter 7), McMichael (1983a, 1983b).

3 Here I follow Bigelow and Pargetter (1990: 167–70) in presenting counterpart-theoretic representation as an example of a broader genre of representation by simulacra (they say, 'replicas'). But it is important to emphasize at the outset that the similarity that makes for counterparts can be similarity in extrinsic respects as well as similarity in intrinsic respects (see n.27 below).

Notes

4 To fill out the picture, we have two categories of essence in addition to the category of real essence. The nominal essence of x under the kind predication 'F' is the complex property that is instantiated by all F's. The intermediate essence of x under the kind predication 'F' is the complex property instantiated by all those counterparts of x that are F's (Lewis 1971: 54).

5 Here I will quote Kripke's brief but highly influential comment on Lewis's CT since various aspects of this comment will come into play in the course of our discussion: 'The counterpart of something in another possible world is *never* identical with the thing itself. Thus, if we say, "Humphrey might have won the election (if only he had done such and such)", we are not talking about something that might have happened to *Humphrey* but to someone else, a "counterpart". Probably, however, Humphrey could not care less whether someone *else*, no matter how much resembling him, would have been victorious in another possible world' (Kripke 1972: 45 n.13, all emphases in the original).

6 Strictly speaking, Salmon's objection does not concern directly the English claims (1) and (2) but their natural regimentations in QML. The difference is irrelevant to what follows.

7 I note here that the entailment can be blocked by freeing CT from the (P5) constraint and thereby allowing that an individual can have (distinct) worldmates as counterparts. There is independent motivation (see (8.3) below) for so relaxing CT. However, I will argue that even canonical CT – including (P5) – can be defended against Salmon's objection.

8 In addressing a related aspect of the irrelevance objection (and acknowledging Mondadori (1983)) Lewis (1986a: 196) claims that (3):

   (3) A Humphrey-like counterpart might have won

and (1) are both made true by the fact that there is a Humphrey counterpart who wins, and that (1) and (3) express the same possibility. Now (3) may be heard as expressing a distinct possibility from that expressed by (2) since (3), but not (2), invites a de re reading – of this thing that is a Humphrey-like counterpart, it might have won – and the subsequent interpretation (3*):

   (3*) $\exists x[Ix \ \& \ Cxh \ \& \ \exists w[\exists y[Pyw \ \& \ Cyx \ \& \ Vy]]]$

However, nothing turns on the choice of the de dicto claim (2) rather than the de re claim (3) for present purposes. For (3*) is also equivalent to (1*) and so to (2*), given the assumption that Humphrey is his own counterpart in α.

9 Forbes (1985: 178) observes that the entailment holds only if we 'legitimise' the translation of the object language counterpart predicate into the metalanguage counterpart predicate by treating the former like a logical constant, interpreting it constantly across every model. I take it

Notes

that this is an objection to the entailment claim. But Forbes does not quite say so, nor does he explain why he thinks that translation cannot be so legitimized.

10 I should add that I see no evidence of Hazen (1979a) having held either that there is a sacrosanct body of data or that theory is unconstrained by anything except assigning the right truth-values to sentences.

11 Lewis (1986a: 196) accepts that it might be a point in favour of an interpretation of PW that it represents Humphrey winning by postulating that Humphrey himself is a winning part of another possible world. But in the same breath Lewis insists that his AR rivals are no more in a position to claim this advantage than CT is, for none takes a possible world to be the kind of thing that has individuals as parts. See Chapter 10 for the various AR accounts of the nature of worlds.

12 See (10.1) below. In order to enhance the '*tu quoque*' to Plantinga, one might also emphasize that it is not the individual Humphrey but a property, an essence of Humphrey, that figures in the PR truth-conditions of the relevant modal sentences. See (13.2) below and c.f. Lewis (1986a: 196).

13 One need not deny that identity is a relation in order to make the point. The point, strictly speaking is that counterpart relations in general, and most other relations, belong to a subclass of relations from which identity is excluded, namely the subclass of relations such that it is possible for something to stand in such a relation to something other than itself.

14 I owe the term 'naive subjectivism' and some of the subsequent observations about that class of philosophical positions to Blackburn (1984: Chapter 5). The points that I am about to make apply to many other reductive interpretations that are not subjectivist.

15 See Mellor (1981).

16 As indicated above Mellor (1981) is such a tenseless theorist. The classical objection, on psychological grounds, to the tenseless interpretation of tensed sentences – an objection which I take to foreshadow the argument from concern against CT – is due to Prior (1959). For a full range of references on the topic of tenseless truth-conditions and attitude contents see LePoidevin and MacBeath (eds) (1993: 2–4, 223–4).

17 Both Miller (1992: 134) and Rosen (1990: 353 n.34) take Blackburn (1984: 213–16) to be making an objection from concern against CT. However, what Blackburn is criticizing directly in those pages is not CT, but rather that aspect of the Lewis (1973) account of truth-conditions for counterfactuals in which global similarity is the criterion for selecting among the possible worlds those that are to figure in the truth-conditions of a given counterfactual conditional claim. The objection is that such an account leaves unexplained how bizarre or idiosyncratic opinions about the relative overall similarity of other worlds to our own would lead – via counterfactual judgments so formed – to incapacity in dealing with the actual world. That objection may, indeed, be suggestive of an objection against CT since, for GR, both world accessibility rela-

Notes

tions and counterpart relations are relations of comparative similarity (see Lewis (1986a: 234), Yagisawa (1992)). However, Blackburn's objection is more general – it applies to any accounts of counterfactuals that invoke comparative similarity of worlds as the criterion of selection (the measure of proximity) even if those accounts do not buy into either GR or, in particular, a CT account of de re counterfactual or modal claims. Indeed, Blackburn's broader intentions are more general still since, as indicated at (2.6) his ultimate target is any realistic construal of the truth-conditions of modal claims.

18 Hyperintensional contexts are those in which the substitution of even intensional equivalents is not guaranteed to preserve truth. Intuitively, and on many semantic accounts, de dicto propositional attitude contexts are distinguished from modal contexts by having this character. See Davies (1981: 48) and Chapter 5 n.17 above.

19 Rosen understands Lewis to accept that CT entails some (justifiable) cost in terms of revision of our modal thought. However, it is notable that in response to various other similar objections, Lewis (1986a: 115–33) invariably denies that GR has the revisionary implications for our attitudes and practices that critics allege. I am about to suggest that the proponent of CT has that option here. Since I will not be discussing these other objections to which I have alluded, I point the interested reader to their sources. Concerning our practices and standards of non-deductive inference see Forrest (1982) and Schlesinger (1984); concerning our attitudes to this-worldly goods and evils see Adams (1974); concerning our appreciation of arbitrariness see Unger (1984), Schlesinger (1984) and – for discussion of Lewis's response – Beadle (1997).

20 There is implicit appeal here to the idea that distinct worldmates may be counterparts in violation of canonical CT postulate (P5). This and other departures from the canonical theory will be discussed in (8.3).

21 Recall from (4.2) that 'counterpart' is not intended as a conceptually primitive theoretical term of GR or of CT and is in fact subject to explicit, if messy and variously hedged, analysis in terms of similarity. The messiness of such an explicit analysis can harmlessly be glossed over in this context if we idealize and envisage replacing generic locutions of the type 'x is a counterpart of y' with those of the type, 'x is similar to y in important respects' and ultimately, in context, by specifications of appropriate species of such relation e.g. 'x is similar to y in respect of occupation'. So what (22) represents is, at worst, a merely verbal reformulation of CT.

22 One might have the same worries about 'egoconcerned' occurring in the content-ascribing sentence as arose concerning 'counterparts' but I trust that such worries will prove superficial.

23 I presume here that rival, PW but non-CT, accounts of modal content are not susceptible to merely verbal reformulation in ways that would ground a parallel defence of their non-revisionary status.

24 See n.20 above.

25 Perhaps beliefs of this nature are more rationally grounded when not subject to future contingency, but that is variously beside the point.
26 Of course it need not be the case that possibilities are unaffecting, or remote to our concerns because we believe them to be unactualized. You might be tortured by the regret that you did not help the person now gone, and all the more so if your belief that you might have helped is combined with belief that no one actually did so.
27 Cases of type (25) and (26) are due to Feldman (1971) and discussed by Plantinga (1974: 108–14). Case (27) is presented and resolved by Lewis (1973: 43).
28 Since it was never required that counterparthood obtain in virtue of intrinsic similarity alone – see n.1 above – CT is entitled to count similarity in extrinsic respects, including match of origin type in particular, as constituting counterparthood in certain cases and contexts (see Forbes (1985: 177–8) and Lewis (1986a: 255)). Lewis (1983b: 43) appeals to this option as a means of addressing the complaints that CT cannot allow for an individual having its most important properties contingently (Kripke 1972: 77) and that match of origin ought to figure *as well as* similarity relations in determining counterparts (Hintikka 1975: 127–9).
29 Gibbard (1975) proposes a referentially opaque CT treatment of modalizing about constitution and identity. For points of contrast with Lewis's treatment see Lewis (1986a: 245).
30 Plantinga (1974: 108–14) objects that CT is 'semantically inadequate' since it underwrites the truth of (the doubly de re reading of) the obviously false:

(8) Socrates could have been distinct from Socrates.

A related objection, Plantinga (1973: 157–62), has it that by underwriting the truth of:

(9) Socrates is essentially self-identical

but the falsehood of:

(10) Socrates is essentially identical with Socrates

CT enforces the coming apart of the property of necessary self-identity and its instances. A direct response to both objections would provide for the falsehood of (8) and the truth of (10). The problem in both cases is that the truth-value comes out 'wrong' because there are counterparts of Socrates – any other than Socrates himself – who are distinct from Socrates and who lack the property of identity-with-Socrates. CT is now able to remedy this defect by providing identity as a counterpart relation and envisaging a context in which that is the only counterpart relation that merits consideration.

Notes

31 It is Hazen (1979a) rather than Lewis (1968) who makes explicit this application of CT (GR).
32 Here I elide the distinction between rules of inference and conditional sentences of the object language that encode or reflect them.
33 Lewis (1968: 36) makes this point explicitly concerning Becker's principle and Brouwer's principle.
34 The motivation to extend CT semantics to deal with extraordinary modal claims arises, in part, from the desire to preserve the unrestricted validity of these principles (see Divers (1999a: 217–27) and (4.3)).
35 Lewis (1986a: 246–8) is hostile to relations of world accessibility or merely relative possibility that are non-qualitative or unexplicated, but he is not hostile to accessibility relations *per se*. Appeal to accessibility relations is required to deal with restricted de dicto modalities – such as, say, nomological necessity – where we are not concerned with all the worlds and restriction is not achieved, as it is in de re cases, by selection of only the worlds in which relevant individuals have counterparts. For further detail on the semantic options opened up by the advertised amendments to canonical CT see Hazen (1979a: 325–38).
36 This is perhaps the place to emphasize that commitment to (30) does not entail in any interesting sense that de re modality is mind-dependent. Whatever facts constitute the de re modal facts are mind-independent facts about similarity. Which of these facts enter into the truth-conditions of a given utterance depends, in part, on how we think of a referent. But what that makes 'mind-dependent', if anything, is the semantic fact about which non-semantic facts (about counterparthood and the counterparts, etc.) are truthmakers, not the non-semantic facts in question. Here, of course, I use the terms 'facts' and 'truthmakers' loosely.
37 The question is motivated by the desire to keep CT in line with the grand project of defending the Humean thesis according to which all supervenes on qualitative character (see Lewis 1986d: ix–xvii).
38 That such discipline is a minimally demanding but necessary condition of truth-aptitude is a prominent theme of Wright (1992).
39 The claims of Lewis (1986a: Chapter 4) concerning the interpretation of de re modal claims are to be understood in the context of the more general conception of methodology in linguistics that is developed in Lewis (1972, 1979).

9 GENUINE REALISM: EPISTEMOLOGY

1 The minor epistemological complaint, which I will not discuss here, is whether acceptance of GR undermines our knowledge claims concerning the actual world. See Schlesinger (1984), Forrest (1982) and – in reply – Lewis (1986a: 115–23).
2 Lewis (1986a: 108) almost puts the argument in this way but stops short of stating the conclusion in the terms, explicitly concerning modal content, that the premises invite.

Notes

3 The general point is better appreciated when we consider certain versions of AR. If, *qua* proponent of AR, I take PW truth-conditions to serve my semantic objectives, but not to articulate a non-modal analysis of modal claims, nor to present an account of the truthmakers of modal claims, have I thereby given an account of 'content' that falls foul of appropriate constraints on knowledge?

4 Here and throughout this chapter I speak in terms of the truthmaking facts for modal claims in spite of the GR reservations, expressed in Chapter 4, about facts and about truthmaking. I hope that this general way of discussing the matter is harmless and that it may be construed here as signalling no more than the existence of those other-worldly individuals that GR distinctively believes in.

5 The idea that we may use a discourse that has the syntactic appearance of quantifying over worlds, but which is then subject to devious reinterpretation which dispels this appearance is the stock-in-trade of certain antirealist interpretations of PW (see Chapter 2 above).

6 The fact that the justification for believing GR has this utilitarian character gives a global reason for resisting the various departures from official Lewisian GR that have been suggested by way of strengthening the GR position. We have now seen that versions of GR have been envisaged in which, respectively: impossible worlds are admitted (Chapter 5); worlds are taken to be unified causally rather than spatio-temporally (Chapter 6); the worldmate relation is taken as primitive (Chapter 6); and we dispense with worlds (Chapter 6). These moves are mooted when official Lewisian GR comes under local pressure from this or that objection. Apart from the specific and local reasons that one might have for resisting these amendments, the general and global complaint against them is that they are epistemologically reckless. The case for believing GR relies on the economy of its primitive ontological categories, the claim that it does not lead to serious trouble, and hierarchies of concepts and entities in which each concept and entity has its place. The worry about these deviant versions of GR is that even if they avoid the problem caused by the local objection, they do so at the price of undermining, in one or more of these ways, the utilitarian justification for believing GR as a whole. What I maintain about each of the deviant versions of GR that we have encountered is either that its gross utility is less than that of official Lewisian GR or that insufficient consideration has been given to the question of gross utility to allow us to rule out that this is the case.

7 Although recently Chihara (1998: 1) directs his incredulity at the epistemological claim that the existence of many marvellous things has been discovered.

8 Another thought about the low credibility of GR might arise from reflection on the sheer range of objections to the theory. It is a striking feature of GR that it appears to have attracted every kind of objection that has ever been lodged against any philosophical position – everything from incoherent quantification to the promotion of moral corruption, from irrelevance to out-and-out inconsistency, etc. So even if

Notes

not defeated decisively by any one objection, the thought goes, GR is undermined to a sufficient extent at sufficiently many points to depress its credibility. In response, I am agnostic about whether we would be justified in inferring that some philosophical fire must underlie so much smoke and about how, if so, that consideration should be factored into a judgment of net utility.

9 'A doctrine is qualitatively parsimonious if it keeps down the number of fundamentally different *kinds* of entity: if it posits sets alone rather than sets and unreduced numbers, or particles alone rather than particles and fields, or bodies alone rather than both bodies and spirits' (Lewis 1973: 87).

10 The example that Lewis (1973: 87) gives of (valueless) quantitative parsimony is an example which has an empirical and contingent subject matter, namely that one theory might postulate 10^{29} electrons and a rival theory postulate 10^{37}. This raises the worry that what goes for the contingent may not go for the non-contingent. In particular, in contingent matters, as opposed to non-contingent matters, it is not easy to envisage how two theories could differ only quantitatively. It is a natural thought that such theories must differ otherwise in some other way. Won't the bigger theory have causally inert electrons, or a complicated story about how the net observable effect of their behaviour is zero? Or won't the smaller theory explain a smaller range of phenomena? Perhaps Lewis's thought is that whatever negative value we are inclined to associate with quantity of ontology *per se* can always be assigned, in such cases, under some other relevant heading.

11 Recall our unworldly metaphysicians Yagisawa (1988) and van Fraassen (1995).

12 Perhaps this is an appropriate point at which to comment on Lewis's presentation of GR as delivering utility with respect to 'total theory, the whole of what we take to be true' (Lewis 1986a: 4). I assume that GR is intended as a total theory in the following, reasonable senses: (a) ontologically, GR is to be taken as an attempt to characterize (unrestrictedly) everything that there is; (b) the explanatory component of GR addresses the whole of what we take to be true at a certain general level of characterization by combining with the ontological component in various ways to pinpoint what it is – semantically and ontologically – for any sentence, modal or non-modal, intensional or non-intensional, to be true; and (c) GR might even reasonably be held to account for entailing, in some interesting sense, all of the facts. It is unreasonable, however, to expect that GR should address *qua* 'total theory' every fact under every description or, relatedly, any thought that I might formulate in the terms that it is formulated. It is equally unreasonable to expect GR to come equipped with a 'complete' proof procedure from which it is provable as a theorem that – for example – there is actually a country in which there is a city in which there is a donkey that wears a blue hat. I find that the reading which Chihara (1998: 99–100) imposes on Lewis's talk of 'total theory' or 'the theory of everything' is unreasonable in many of these sorts of ways. The unreasonable (and

psychologistic) reading then leads Chihara to make a number of points that are irrelevant to GR as formulated here in Chapter 4 – e.g. that we don't know whether total theory can be axiomatized, that we don't know what the primitives of total theory are, that some of what we think can't be sententially represented, that the sum of what anyone thinks about everything is likely to be inconsistent, that an individual's beliefs stand in relations to each other that cannot be charted fully by the deductive relations presented in a theory, etc.

13 We can apply here the general characterization of typical realist thought as involving both presumptive and modest elements (cf. Wright 1992: 1–2). (1) expresses the presumptive thought about ontological hypotheses that, in favourable circumstances, we may come non-accidentally to detect the truth and rightly to believe that we have done so. The option of asserting (1) and rejecting (1*) points up the possibility of adopting, in the case of ontological hypotheses, the modest thought that truth is not guaranteed by the epistemic virtues of (sufficient) theoretical utility. Certainly, one way of arguing for (1) would be via (1*), arguing for the latter by adopting a general antirealistic conception of truth along the lines of semantic antirealism (Dummett 1978), internal realism (Putnam 1978) or construal of truth in terms of superassertibility (Wright 1992: Chapter 2). These antirealist conceptions of truth are all broadly verificationist whilst a conception of truth as entailed by, or supervenient upon, theoretical utility is suggestive of a conception of truth which is at least partially pragmatic. Perhaps there is no ultimate contrast between verificationist and pragmatist conceptions of truth if verification and pragmatic value are both counted as grounds of assertion. I am not ruling out a defence of (1*) on such antirealist grounds but I also want to distance the defence of (1) from a commitment to any such antirealism.

14 Such a causal characterization of a posteriori knowledge is derived from a causal characterization of a posteriori warrant. Here I follow (*inter alia*) McGinn (1976).

15 Note: (a) that once we spell out the a posterioricity thesis in causal terms it is a thesis that is explicitly about causation and, arguably, implicitly about entities such as facts (truthmakers) or propositions (knowledge-contents); and (b) that these are among the categories that possible worlds are invoked to explain, ontologically and conceptually. One can imagine, broadly, that a realist about possible worlds might attempt to exploit this 'priority' in seeking to exempt knowledge of other worlds from the a posterioricity thesis. But I will not attempt to develop the thought here.

16 Swiftly, the rationale is that precisely where our knowledge requires that we investigate (directly or indirectly) parts of our world, we have causal dependence between one contingent fact (our cognitive states) and another (the fact known) and this in turn requires the non-trivial truth of counterfactuals of the form, 'If Cygnus A did not exist, we wouldn't believe that it did'. Since such counterfactuals are non-trivially true only if they have contingent antecedents, it is contingency of truth that

Notes

emerges as the correlate of knowledge that requires causal acquaintance between knower and subject matter (Lewis 1986a: 111–12).

17 Among the alleged cases of contingent a prioricity we have the above-mentioned claims involving indexicals and others governed by certain 'reference-fixing' stipulations or conventions – e.g. the standard metre rod S is one metre in length (Kripke 1972: 54–7). Presumably, we ought to count also the logical consequences of any successful cases. For further references to a range of literature on the question see Divers (1999b).

18 To be clear, the claim is that if content is unrestricted then it is non-contingent. But the converse does not hold. Talk of 'our world' and what is 'actualized' exerts world-restriction on quantification, and Lewis (1986a: 111–12) claims that it is a contingent matter what exists at our world and which possibilities are actualized at our world. That is so typically and for the most part. However, not all world-restricted claims of existence are contingent. It is necessary that there is a world. That claim comes out true when the modally modified content – that there is a world – is interpreted as a world-restricted claim and, as we would expect, the necessitation is subsequently subject to ordinary interpretation. The relevant truth-condition is fulfilled since every world has a part that is a world. So the 'demarcation' thought that emerges is that it is sufficient, but not necessary, that a content should be unrestricted for it to be exempt from the requirement that knowledge can only be a posteriori.

19 I here report in the swiftest of terms the position of Hale and Wright (2001: 11–23, 117–52).

20 The prospect of a quasi-perceptual epistemology is usually ridiculed by way of the suggestion that other worlds might be detected by means of a special 'telescope' (Kripke 1972: 44) and any such prospect is ruled out by causal isolation of worlds (Lewis 1986a: 80). Appeal to a faculty of 'mental vision', even if exempt from that problem, is troubled by the extent of the existential knowledge of worlds we are required to account for – thus see Richards (1975: 114–15), McGinn (1981: 154) and Lewis (1986a: 114).

21 In the mathematical case, the Quine–Putnam position is apt to be articulated as involving the claim that quantification over mathematical entities is an indispensable part of best total theory but Lewis (1986a: 5) explicitly renounces the claim that quantification over genuine possibilia is so indispensable. Dialectically, however, just as the Quine–Putnam epistemology of mathematics is vulnerable to the prospect of a demonstration of the dispensability of quantification over mathematical entities (as mooted by Field (1980, 1989)), so Lewis's epistemology of GR is vulnerable to the prospect of a demonstration that a rival theory of all there is which does not involve quantification over non-actual things should have greater net utility than GR. Thus Lewis's (1986a: 5, Chapter 3) challenge to AR to make that case.

22 GR does not aim directly to provide an informative account of which things are actual or of how the actual world is; however, it is reasonable to require that GR be 'actualistically' adequate in at least the following

limited sense. If we have an independently warranted belief to the effect that there actually are F's, then GR is constrained to provide from its ontological resources adequate candidates to be the F's (cf. Lewis 1986a: 112). But arguably, even if the information that there unrestrictedly are F's (i.e. that there could be F's) comes to us through learning, by a posteriori means, that there actually are F's, it is the kind of knowledge that could have been acquired by a priori means alone. The issue is delicate and difficult because: (a) a priori knowledge is usually regarded as knowledge that we can obtain after we have had whatever causal interactions and experiences that we need in order to acquire relevant concepts; and (b) a plausible kind of externalism about content has it that we could not acquire the concept donkey unless we had appropriate causal interactions with donkeys. That does not obviously compromise the claim that our knowledge that there could be donkeys is a priori. But it seems to have the consequence that had there actually been no donkeys we could not have formed the thought that there could have been donkeys nor, a fortiori, known that to be the case.

23 I count as trivial modal knowledge, modal knowledge that is deduced from knowledge that (non-modal) P by way of uncontroversial modal (and other principles) – e.g. knowing that Possibly P by inference from knowing that (non-modal) P. By absolute modal knowledge I mean that the content of the knowledge is absolute modality rather than merely relative modality. Hereafter I take the 'non-trivial' and 'absolute' qualifiers as read.

24 By way of an initial foray into the sparse literature on modal epistemology the reader might consult – in addition to Lewis (1986a: 108–15) – McGinn (1981), Blackburn (1986), Yablo (1993) and van Inwagen (1998). I do not mean to suggest that all of these authors are party to even the minimal picture of modal epistemology that I have sketched.

25 By way of notable exceptions, McGinn (1981) and Armstrong (1989) both remark that AR and GR violate naturalistic or causal requirements on knowledge.

26 I remind the reader at this point that my overall aim is strictly limited to the consideration of the relative merits of the two realist accounts of PW. One might conclude that this common epistemological failing of both versions of realism about PW provides strong motivation – as it has in other cases – for the pursuit of an antirealist interpretation of the discourse. Although I cannot argue the case here, I register my conviction that appeal to antirealist interpretations of PW will not provide an escape from the commitment to construe modal knowledge (or an antirealist surrogate) as a priori. Indeed, I am tempted by the view that the point will hold no matter what specific account of modal 'facts' is in the offing.

10 ACTUALIST REALISM: EXPOSITION

1 Since this is a region in which terminology proliferates I will explain why I choose 'actualist realism' over nearby alternatives. I have in mind

Notes

the family of views that Lewis (1986a: Chapter 3) calls 'ersatz realism' and Stalnaker (1976) calls 'moderate realism' but my term is less pejorative and more informative. The family of actualist realist interpretations is strictly broader than any which could rightly be called 'abstractionist' interpretations (cf. Lycan 1979 and van Inwagen 1986) views or 'non-natural actualist' interpretations (cf. Armstrong 1989). In particular, these other terms leave no room for versions of realism that conceive possible worlds as actual concrete, natural individuals (cf. Lewis 1986a: 148). The case of MR, see n.30, is another where a version of actualist realism is not abstractionist and not obviously non-naturalistic. I also resist the characterization of actualist realist interpretations as 'one world' or simply 'actualist' interpretations since both terms invite the conflation of interpretations of PW that are realist and actualist with those that are antirealist and actualist.

2 Consequently, if there exist any individuals that stand in no spatiotemporal relations to us these too (*pace* GR) actually exist.

3 This crucial point will re-emerge in Chapters 13, 16 and 17 below.

4 One might proceed differently. Both Lewis (1986a: Chapter 3) and Bigelow and Pargetter (1990: Chapter 4) distinguish versions of AR primarily with reference to issues of representation. But I take my preference to be a matter of presentation and not of substance.

5 Two philosophers come to mind in this respect and for quite different reasons. Kripke is widely acknowledged as a most influential advocate of generic AR, especially in virtue of remarks in Kripke (1980: 15–20). Lycan tends to defend a generic version of AR whilst indicating preferences for some species over others (see e.g. Lycan 1979).

6 Although van Inwagen is inclined, on occasion, to use the term 'proposition' in place of 'state of affairs', there is no doubt that his conception of propositions is in all essential respects the same as Plantinga's conception of states of affairs – see especially van Inwagen (1986). There are good terminological reasons for preferring 'proposition' here to 'state of affairs' – unfortunately there are good reasons for the opposite preference as well, and I take the latter route. However, reflecting the former considerations, the use of 'states of affairs' terminology in the present exposition of AR – both in the present case of PR and in the case of CR below – comes with the following caveat. Neither the things that are called 'states of affairs' by PR nor the (different) things that are called 'states of affairs' by exemplary CR are the thing-like things of the kind that Armstrong (1997) calls 'states of affairs'. Nor is it the case that the things that are called 'states of affairs' by PR, or the (different) things that are called 'states of affairs' by exemplary CR, are apt to play the salient roles that are associated with Armstrongian thing-like states of affairs. By way of swift elucidation, there is the red cup and that – the cup being there and being red – is supposed to be (constituted by) the existence of a thing-like state of affairs. I will have more to say about thing-like states of affairs at (10.2) and (11.2) and I will have more to say about the capacity of PR states of affairs and CR states of affairs to play the roles of thing-like states of affairs at (12.2) and (14.6).

Notes

7   Here and throughout I assume, and grant, that the various proponents of AR also utilize standard logical, set-theoretic and mereological terminology.
8   Here and throughout the exposition of AR I use the term 'actualized' to characterize the distinguished possible world that represents actuality – the world that we would naturally call 'actual'. The term allows us to distinguish that world against the theoretical background in which AR asserts that every possible world actually exists.
9   The most commonly cited historical source of such an approach is Wittgenstein (1921).
10 The antirealistic intentions of Skyrms (1981) are not explicit but have subsequently been reported by Armstrong (1989: 46).
11 Neither the number of entities in each category nor the 'adicity' of properties is constrained to be countable.
12 We need sequences rather than sets here since an adequate means of representation of simple states of affairs must be capable of reflecting the different ways in which individuals can bear a given n-adic relation to one another. It is not the case in general, to take the dyadic case, that Fab is the same state of affairs as Fba – say, a being heavier than b and b being heavier than a – but ground-level sets such as {F,a,b} are incapable of representing such a difference. Sequences, which may standardly be taken as sets of higher levels, are capable of representing such a difference, thus the distinct sequences <F,a,b> and <F,b,a> which may be identified with distinct higher-level sets, e.g. {F,{a},{{b}}} and {F,{b},{{a}}} respectively.
13 The intention here is that the *members* of the sequence (sequentially) instantiate the property or relation, e.g. <being the brother of, John, Mary> obtains iff John takes the first place in the relation of being the brother of and Mary takes the second place.
14 By way of illustration, consider two arbitrary simple states of affairs <F,a> and <G,b> and the possible worlds S1 = {<F,a>} and S2 = {<F,a>, <G,b>}. It is easily verified that individual b, property G, simple state of affairs <G,b>, and world S2 – for example – are all contingent existents since all exist at S2 and none exists at S1.
15 This may be an appropriate point at which to refer the reader back to the caveat concerning 'states of affairs' terminology that was issued at n.6 above. A further source of potential terminological confusion across the literature that I now make explicit is that the exemplary CR states of affairs (i.e. sets) that have been introduced here might well be construed as representations of Armstrongian, thing-like states of affairs.
16 There is a further version of CR that ought to be noted since it is probably the best example of a non-abstractionist version of AR. Assume that there is some fundamental subvenient quality such that all supervenes on the instantiation or otherwise of that quality by each simple individual. The most familiar model for this assumption is a Democritean world in which the simple individuals are the spacetime points and the fundamental quality is occupation (by matter). Let each point then represent the simple state of affairs of that point being

occupied and then each collection of such points may be construed as a possible world that represents exactly those points being occupied (and the others vacant). The sort of collection in question may be taken to be a set (Cresswell 1972) but it might be taken to be a sum (Lewis 1986a: 148) in which case we have a conception of possible worlds as actually existing individuals that are the sums of actually existing simple individuals. In that case the combinatorial base would be the individual that is the sum of all simple individuals and the possible worlds would be the parts of that sum. Of course, the success of the proposal depends on the existence of an appropriate subvenient and bivalent quality. If, as a posteriori investigation of the actual world suggests, the subvenient facts involve many non-bivalent qualities then it looks as though set-theoretic construction – cf. Quine (1969), Bigelow and Pargetter (1990: 207–10) – rather than mereological construction of possible worlds is required.

17 For extensive discussion of these issues, in the context of a combinatorial antirealism based on thing-like states of affairs, and references to further relevant sources see Armstrong (1989).

18 Forrest (1986a: 15) suggests that such an account of possibility is anticipated historically ('hinted at') in Leibniz and Husserl.

19 The crucial thing here, as we shall see, is that NR should be able to appeal to such properties as the property of having no other first-order properties.

20 This conclusion is justified by the uncontroversial combinatorial consideration that if (simple, non-relational, first-order) F can be instantiated by a solitary spacetime point, then it can be instantiated by such a point which co-exists with other such points so that F would then be instantiated by something that was a proper part of, and so distinct from, the maximal individual that existed in that scenario.

21 A property P is maximal with respect of a set of properties S iff P is a conjunctive property such that for every member of S, Q, exactly one of Q or the complement of Q is a conjunct in P.

22 Stalnaker (1976) adopts Lewis's earlier and informal notion given by 'I and all my surroundings' in characterizing the things that could instantiate total ways, while Forrest (1986a) presents world-natures informally as properties that Lewisian worlds would instantiate. However, in taking this approach one risks contracting controversial consequences of GR such as the non-compossibility of disjoined spatiotemporal regions. For having disjoined spatiotemporal regions would then appear to be a way no 'world' could be.

23 Stalnaker (1976) is neutral on the nature of properties while Bigelow and Pargetter (1990) and Forrest (1986a) take the properties to be universals.

24 A more formal treatment of the generation of world-natures is given by Forrest (1986a) who invokes (defined) property-forming operations such as product-forming, contraction, projection, conjunction and completion. In NR the informal characterization of the mode of combination of atomic properties into world-natures follows that of

Bigelow and Pargetter (1990: 207–10) who envisage the specification of the relevant atomic properties as a task for physical theory. Stalnaker (1976, 1984) offers no account of the composition of worldly ways out of elements.

25 I signal 'true' as a salient theoretical term of BR since here, but not in other cases, it figures immediately in the explanation of a key notion, viz. actualization.

26 See (11.2) below.

27 Bigelow and Pargetter (1990: 180) present Plantinga as 'promoting' the theory that possible worlds are maximal consistent sets of unstructured propositions. This variant is less reminiscent of Plantingan realism than of some hybrid position that seeks to combine a conception of the fundamental worldmaking elements as essentially unstructured (as PR does) with an account of possible worlds representing in a linguistic manner (as PR does not).

28 The difference between implicit and explicit entailment in this context may be exemplified as follows. The set of (interpreted) sentences S = {John is tall, John is male} represents explicitly that John is tall, that John is male and nothing else. S further represents implicitly, by entailment, that some male exists, that something tall exists, that something is tall and male, that it is not the case that each thing is either male or not tall, etc. The matter of implicit representation for AR in general looms large in Chapter 11.

29 Note that the relativized notion of actualization for worlds – v is actualized at w – is also explicated in terms of mutual entailment rather than identity of membership, for one can easily contrive maximal consistent sets of L-sentences that are extensionally distinct but which (intuitively) represent the same maximal possibility – consider one such set whose members are all atomic sentences and another whose members include some (complex) logical truths.

30 Another way in which AR might be developed, as noted by Rescher (1975) and McGinn (1981), is in the form of a mentalistic realism (MR) wherein possible worlds are identified as – not just associated or correlated with – appropriate constructs out of actual mental events, episodes or states. Since such worlds might be expected to be – *inter alia* – appropriately maximal despite the range of thoughts that (any) humans actually happen to think, MR might align itself with BR and identify the possible worlds as collections of Mentalese (language of thought) sentences. If MR eschews such a linguistic conception of thought, alignment with PR may prove more attractive. A *sui generis* conception of MR – in which *sui generis* mental entities combine in some *sui generis* mentalistic fashion to constitute possible worlds – is unattractive. Moreover, any version of MR will appear hopeless if it relies on the construction of all of the possible worlds out of actually tokened mental states (thoughts). So, notwithstanding its striking underdevelopment, I am disinclined to think that any remotely viable form of MR – if there is any such thing – would merit treatment as a species of AR distinct from those already recognized.

Notes

11 ACTUALIST REALISM: CONCEPTUAL APPLICATIONS

1   I emphasize that the proponents of AR typically do not claim that the favoured version of AR affords thoroughly non-modal analyses of the modal concepts. But given the various misconceptions about non-modal analysis that emerged in the case of GR (see Chapter 7), discussion of the issue in relation to AR is merited.
2   The secondary issue is whether, given the concept of possibility – either analysed non-modally or otherwise – the species of AR afford satisfactory analyses of the other concepts of counterfactual dependence, supervenience, essence, etc. I believe that the presumption that AR (generically) can match GR in these secondary analyses is often made rather easily, but I will not challenge it here.
3   See (5.4).
4   It is, of course, perfectly harmless for one who pursues this strategy to concede that we have an example of an impossibility in some interesting but restricted sense.
5   For a discussion that bears on this difficult question see Field (1989, 1993) – who invokes the extreme position in defence of the view that arithmetical truth is absolutely contingent – and, in reply, Hale and Wright (1994).
6   That these 'sources of modality' are innocuous was argued in Chapter 7 with respect to GR.
7   I will consider the related problems for sparser languages in discussing CR below.
8   There is another worry. Even if it has not been shown that the axiomatization is, in principle, incompletable, there are clearly substantial commitments involved in the claim that it is, in principle, completable. The conviction that the 'utopian' axiomatization is completable in principle appears to require that we are not irremediably ignorant about any modal truth (expressible in the worldmaking language). Lewis (1986a: 155) makes the point that, so long as modal ignorance persists on certain matters, it will be risky to write in a dubious axiom – say, that nothing is both positively charged and negatively charged – or to abstain from doing so. The risk of writing in is that we have a genuine possibility that no world represents, the risk of abstention is that we have a genuine impossibility that is represented by some world. It is also interesting to note that by pinning the hopes of a non-modal analysis on the knowability in principle of all (relevant) modal truths, BR would appear to be committed to a semantic antirealism – in the sense of Dummett (1978) – about modal discourse.
9   Another worry, although one that I will not develop, is that (B) ought properly to concern interpreted sentences and that some modal concept underlies that notion.
10 The Swiftian notion of a Lagadonian language is revived for philosophical purposes by Bigelow (1975) and gifted to BR for the purposes of constructing worldmaking languages by Lewis (1986a: Chapter 3). A nice account of the move away from actual natural languages to

Notes

Lagadonian languages for worldmaking purposes is presented in Bigelow and Pargetter (1990: 76–80).

11   That thing-like states of affairs would solve the problem of implicit representation is a point that Lewis (1992: 220) makes concerning the antirealist ('fictionalist') account of PW offered by Armstrong (1989). To take that course would be to achieve consistency, with respect to our triad, by asserting the conjunction of (ii) and (iii) while rejecting (i) – i.e. by rejecting realism.

12   The position that would emerge, then, would be very close to PR, save that robust CR may remain faithful to a conception of states of affairs as structured entities.

13   The requirement of compossibility may be articulated as the requirement that no simple state of affairs in the range set should be such that its existence (or obtaining) entails the nonexistence (non-obtaining) of any other. This is one of the necessary conditions for states of affairs to be mutually independent. The other, which in conjunction with the latter is sufficient, is that no state of affairs should be such that its existence (obtaining) entails the nonexistence (non-obtaining) of any other (cf. Armstrong 1997: 139). Clearly to state directly that the possible worlds are appropriate collections of independent states of affairs would be to appeal to an implicitly modal concept, given the characterization of independence in terms of the notion of entailment.

14   I assume that the concept of simple individual is non-modal, but I will say more below.

15   To adapt a point from Lewis (1986a: 152), as we shrink the range of simple properties to exclude impossible worlds so we expand the scope of the problem of implicit representation since the worlds represent explicitly only with respect to these simple worldmaking elements.

16   For discussion see Armstrong (1989: Chapter 6, 1997: Chapter 10), Hiipakka, Keinanen and Korhonen (1999) and MacBride (1999).

17   Given a range of properties, the simplicity of each would be sufficient for a range of properties to be wholly distinct from one another. More generally, and especially if NR or CR is not prepared to bank on the existence of simple properties, the challenge is to explicate in terms of their mutual distinctness the modal independence of the range of worldmaking properties. But here I focus on the simple case of mutual distinctness as achieved by simplicity.

18   If we have sets of operations that can produce *ex hypothesi* simple properties then there is trouble for the attempt to define simplicity in terms of the operations. In what follows, in order to give breathing space to the proposal, I will simply assume that an appropriate set of operations is available. But I note that the contraction operation introduced by Forrest (1986a) does have the undesirable feature in question.

19   This proposal implements in the first-order case the account of the conjunction of two properties as the contraction of their product in Forrest (1986a: 18).

20   Perhaps it is worth noting that there is no simple mereological solution in the offing to the problem of defining property complexity. The sort

Notes

of complexity that is required in world-natures, or structural universals more generally – see exposition of NR in Chapter 10 – is not generable by summing ('fusion') of properties (see Armstrong 1997: 34–8). But even if the property-forming relations cannot adequately be defined as mereological operations, a conceptual matter, it is another question whether whatever conjunctive properties exist might be identified with the sum of their conjuncts, an ontological matter.

21 I will return in Chapter 12 to the idea that such modal facts might ground an ontological rather than a conceptual complaint against certain versions of AR.

22 I acknowledge that in the matter of the modal content of the concept of a universal, the dialectic is more complicated than my brief account reflects. There are other, non-spatial, characterizations of the concept of a universal that ought to be considered and there is complex interplay between the consequences of these criteria and the truth-conditions of various modal claims about universals. At certain points in the dialectic one might, for example, seek to relieve the tension by allowing that some universals are particulars or at least that some universals might have been particulars. For a thorough discussion of the issues that takes these and other factors into consideration see MacBride (1999: esp. 484–93, 2001).

23 Perhaps we ought to exempt NR from the need to do work on the additional front of implicit representation. If explicit representation is achieved linguistically, and implicit representation is achieved by entailment, then Lewis's argument applies. But exemplary NR – like PR, but unlike BR and exemplary CR – does not conceive of the elements of world-natures as having powers of linguistic representation. Nor does exemplary NR conceive of the worldmaking elements (universals) as the kind of things that represent the existence of certain kinds of individuals by constituting the existence of such individuals. So it is pointless to saddle NR with the linguistic or constitutive accounts of representation and the difficulties that they bring. Instead, I will assume that NR like PR offers no account of how representation is achieved, that position on representation being addressed in Chapter 17.

12 ACTUALIST REALISM: ONTOLOGICAL APPLICATIONS

1 This is not to say that AR has no recourse to *surrogates* of GR non-actual individuals – ersatz individuals – for certain purposes, a point that is discussed extensively in Chapter 13 below. But, on pain of inconsistency with ontological actualism, the AR surrogates of non-actual individuals are not non-actual individuals. So when the surrogates of non-actual individuals are, for example, properties, the identification of properties with sets of the 'possible individuals' would amount only to the identification of properties with sets of properties.

2 It is worth pointing out that when the standard AR case is presented in this way it emerges clearly, as it does in the case of GR, that it is

Notes

ultimately the worldmaking elements, rather than the possible worlds themselves, that bear the load of the ontological identifications that are articulated in PW.

3 For one approach to the abstraction of individuals and properties as equivalence classes ('bundles') of tropes (including simple 'states of affairs') – albeit set against a Meinongian background – see Bacon (1995: Chapter 1).

4 So *qua* metaphysical theory, a species of AR need not be qualitatively less parsimonious – in the sense of Lewis (1973) and (9.1) – than GR.

5 Here I should emphasize that I am trying to establish the limitations of the capacity of AR to provide an account of truthmaking for modal claims regardless of whether the proponents of the various versions of AR have ever actually intended that their interpretation of PW should afford that kind of application.

6 Again, as in the case of GR I will not press the problem of how the account might be extended to (logically) complex cases from the basic case.

7 For further detail see (13.4) below.

8 I do not believe that this failure of symmetry and the consequent weakening of modal logic is something that CR is compelled to accept on philosophical grounds and I will show later (in (13.2)) how it can be avoided. But for the moment, the relevant consideration is that CR is entitled to this defence of the contingency of truth about possibility.

9 I sketch a justification as follows. First from truth of possibility claim to existence of state of affairs. Assume that there is a w at which *possibly Fa* is true. By the truth of *possibly Fa* at w there is a world v such that v is accessible from w and at v, Fa is true. By the truth of Fa at v, <F,a> obtains at v. By <F,a> obtaining at v, <F,a> exists at v. Since v is accessible from w, v exists at w, and if v exists at w then v is a subset of the range set R(w). But if v is a subset of R(w) and <F,a> is a member of v then F is a member of the base set B(w) and a is a member of B(w). But then <F,a> is a member of the range set R(w) and so, finally, <F,a> exists at w. Second, from existence of state of affairs to truth of possibility claim. Assume that there is a world w at which <F,a> exists. If so, <F,a> is a member of the range set R(w), and then the base set of w, B(w), must have as members F and a. Then there is a world v such that v = {<F,a>} and v is accessible from w. But if so there is a world v such that v is accessible from w and Fa is true at v. Thus, as required, at w it is true that *possibly Fa*.

10 Consider the world v = {<F,a>}. For every simple state of affairs s that is not identical to <F,a>, at v, s does not exist and *possibly Fa* is true.

11 Consider the world u which is the set whose members are all the simple states of affairs other than <F,a> and nothing else. At u, each basic possibility claim other than *possibly Fa* is true (since, at u, every simple state of affairs other than <F,a> obtains) and <F,a> does not exist.

12 Armstrong (1989) approaches the problem from the other, more natural, direction in attempting to extend his preferred account of truthmaking for non-modal claims to a PW (combinatorial antirealist)

Notes

account of truthmaking for modal claims. The difficulties encountered in seeking so to square the modal case with the non-modal case lead Armstrong (1997: 172–4) to renounce the PW approach to the specification of the truthmakers of modal claims.

13 ACTUALIST REALISM: SEMANTIC APPLICATIONS

1 Thus see e.g. the accounts of Plantinga (1974), Loux (1979), Roper (1982), Bigelow and Pargetter (1990) and Linsky and Zalta (1994). I would like to acknowledge, in particular, the influence of Linsky and Zalta (1994) on the structure of the present chapter.
2 The reader might find that the interpretation to be spelled out is not intuitive at all, hence my scare quotation. I take it that the thought is that given that modal talk, and especially about non-actual possibility, is talk about a domain of objects, then intuitively these objects are the possible worlds and other possibilia.
3 In the matter of ontological commitment I distinguish: (a) asserting the theory; from (b) assenting to the sentences that are usually taken to express the theory in the understanding that those sentences mean something other than what they appear to mean at face value. Various antirealists about possible worlds, in particular modalists (see Chapter 3) attempt to lay claim to the benefits of PW-semantics by way of (b) rather than (a).
4 As throughout I take commitment to sets to be unproblematic for all.
5 If R is restricted so that it holds over only some ordered pairs of worlds then some explanation is due of what this accessibility or relative possibility consists in. I will not press this point. See Lewis (1986a: 246) for scepticism about ad hoc appeal to unexplicated accessibility relations.
6 The problem is raised, but more tractably so, by other kinds of sentence – e.g.:

(2+) There could have been a purple cow.

In these cases, the thought is that the job of the 'possible individual' can be done by an actual individual – e.g. a non-purple cow – being assigned at another possible world to the extensions of both the predicates 'cow' and 'purple' (Plantinga 1974: 130). But that form of solution stretches only as far as de dicto possibilities are correlated with de re possibilities for actual individuals.
7 For modalist interpretations of PW see (2.6).
8 More cautiously, I should say here and throughout that this or that application of the PW-semantics *suggests* the validation of various modal theses since I am not prepared to present any applied semantics for any version of QML in such detail as would be required to demonstrate any such validation. Needless to say the validation of any given thesis does not inevitably follow from any of the features of models that concern us, since it is always possible to weaken the logic of the semantic theory or to block the validation by introducing any number of ad

Notes

hoc technical measures. What I am trying to present is a fair picture of the natural implications for validity of constraining models in the ways prescribed by the various solutions. The reader who wishes to pursue in detail questions of exactly which kinds of semantic theory validate precisely which theses of QML should consult Linsky and Zalta (1994) in the first instance and follow through the references there, particularly Garson (1984).

9 I maintain the default presumption on which the accessibility relation R is unrestricted so that, on every model, every possible world is accessible from every other.

10 Salient modal theses such as (BF) are conventionally expressed in necessity operator versions, but given the classical interdefinability of the modal operators (and first-order quantifiers) there will always be possibility operator equivalents. In the case of (BF) we have:

(BF*) $\Diamond \exists x[Fx] \to \exists x[\Diamond Fx]$.

The possibility operator equivalents are invoked since it is often easier to see whether there are counterexamples to these formulations. The example adduced in the text is a direct counterexample to (BF*).

11 I am simplifying the account by ignoring (putative) individuals that are necessarily abstract and (putative) actually concrete individuals that are necessary existents.

12 That CR with contracted world-domains so suggests that such theses are invalid is an observation attributed to Philip Quinn by Lycan (1979: 306–7). Armstrong (1989: 63) notes and accepts Quinn's point.

13 For the ambiguity of 'actual' and its cognates see references in and around Chapter 4 n.5 above.

14 The Lewis (1986a: 149–50) account of BR has it that the expressions that represent non-actual individuals should be incomplete expressions – open sentences that mirror the whole world at which the individual exists. There is no serious discrepancy here. Rather than think in terms of 'The F' we could just as well think in terms of '_ is the unique F'. Indeed the latter fits better if the worldmaking language has a standard first-order logical syntax. For then, as is well known, the orthodox Russellian treatment discerns in the logical syntax no singular terms that correspond to the definite descriptions in English sentences. Lewis does not present his open sentences as expressing uniqueness conditions. But this, I suspect, is related to his scepticism about the capacity of worldmaking languages to supply descriptions that are invariably unique (see Chapter 17 below). I will persist with the simple and natural idea that the representations of non-actual individuals are singular terms in the understanding that this marks no significant departure from Lewis's proposal.

15 For alternative CR the natural move is to join with PR and NR in addressing the D-problem by appealing to 'individual natures', perhaps *qua* abstractions from collections of states of affairs (cf. Hiipakka, Keinanen and Korhonen 1999). But the problem there, as always, is that

Notes

a *realism* about the associated possible worlds and their constituents would bring ontological commitment to the non-actual thick particulars that the existence of the constituents (states of affairs) is supposed to constitute.

16 This problem is the alethic modal analogue of the Geach (1967) problem of identity within propositional attitude contexts as generated by cases such as:

> (G) Hob believes that there is a witch and Nob believes that she (the same witch) blighted his sow.

17 In certain cases, such as the present, it may be feasible to contrive rigid representations for non-actual individuals, e.g. 'The person who develops if gametes b and c combine and develop into a person' (cf. Peacocke 1978: 479). Accordingly, we may be able to represent the existence at a world w of a particular individual, that it is the son of Richard and is famous, and also represent the existence at v of that very thing and its being not famous. However, there are two points that limit the significance of this observation. First, the representation in question is not quite apt to function in a truth-condition for (3). For the initial possibility operator generates a de dicto context and so the initial possibility does not concern 'a particular possible individual'. The point is clearer if we consider the true reading of the following variant on (5):

> (5+) It is necessary that any famous son of Richard be contingently famous.

Second, it is not obvious that one could formulate such a rigid representation corresponding to every individual possibility.

18 The case that we have considered is one in which we have a de re claim 'about a possible individual' that has been introduced explicitly by description. But the problem may affect other modal claims that feature names for which reference is taken to be fixed implicitly by description. Among the candidates for belonging to that class are names from fictive discourses.

19 Having chosen a set of individual-representations as surrogates for non-actual individuals the question often arises for AR whether actual individuals should be represented by such representations (here essences) or by themselves (individuals). The homogeneous conception of D, emerging from the former choice, makes the semantics simpler since it permits a common form of truth-condition for all possibility claims concerning individuals. The heterogeneous conception of D, emerging from the latter choice, complicates the semantics but allows the semantics to register different treatments of cases – possibilities concerning actual individuals versus possibilities concerning non-actual individuals – that many believe ought to be treated differently. Jager (1982) adopts the homogeneous approach in providing a detailed

Notes

PR application of the Kripke semantics; Lycan and Shapiro (1986) adopt a heterogeneous approach.

20 Forrest (1986a: 20–1) makes such an appeal to essences, albeit within the context of a semantic theory that is not written in the style of Kripke (1963).
21 Recall the equivalence of (BF) and (BF*) as indicated at n.10.
22 See (8.1) above.
23 I take this opportunity to note that Linsky and Zalta (1994: 455 n.33) appear to be guilty of *ignoratio elenchi* in objecting (further) against the PR semantics of Jager (1982) that it 'threatens circularity' by proposing to define co-exemplification in primitively modal terms when co-exemplification is supposed to be a notion that figures in the semantic theory of an object language that contains a modal operator. For it is no part of the PR agenda that modality should be explicable conceptually, or semantically, without appeal to any primitive modal concept.
24 Recall in this regard (from (8.3)), the methodological principle that for a semantic theory of modality to call for revision of opinion about modal logical principles is one thing but for it to call for revision of non-modal logical principles is another, far more detrimental, thing. Of course for those who hold that our non-modal predicate logic ought to be free anyway, the modal push towards a free logic will not be a problem.
25 For an account of the implications of weak and strong interpretations of the necessity operator see Davies (1978).
26 (SA) has attracted a fair amount of attention in the literature since it has been argued, in various ways, by Plantinga that the thesis of ontological actualism entails it. For further discussion of (SA) and its semantic implications see Plantinga (1976, 1985a and 1985b), Hinchcliff (1989), Fine (1985), Pollock (1985), Linsky and Zalta (1994), Bergmann (1996) and Hudson (1997).

14 ACTUALIST REALISM: SAFE AND SANE ONTOLOGY?

1 I believe that this avoidable confusion is courted by the presentation of AR as 'one-world actualism' a doctrine which has it that the actual world is presented as one kind of thing (blooming, buzzing, etc.) and the non-actual worlds as another (cf. Lycan 1991a and Stalnaker 1976).
2 Concerning PR in particular see McNamara (1993) and White (1977).
3 For discussion of this matter see – e.g. – Hale (1987: Chapter 3), Lewis (1986a: 81–6) and Hoffman and Rosenkrantz (1994: 182–7).
4 The discussion of (14.4) below on criteria of identity has some bearing on the question whether the distinctive entities of AR are abstractions from anything.
5 On reference to non-actual individuals see (5.6) and on knowledge of non-actual individuals see Chapter 9.
6 Historically, the demand for criteria of identity is most famously pressed, in different ways, by Frege (1884) and Quine (1948).
7 For the ensuing defence see Hale and Wright (2001).

Notes

8   In light of this point and the earlier discussion, I am quite out of sympathy with attempts to dismiss the significance of questions of criteria of identity in the case of abstract entities by hinting that it proves equally difficult to supply such criteria in the case of certain non-categorical concrete kinds. Thus, for example, Plantinga (1974: 1 n.1) so attempts to undermine the demand for a criterion of identity in the case of propositions.

9   It is not unknown for proponents of AR to raise questions about the intelligibility of the concept of set membership – or at least make the case that the concept in question does not obviously meet conditions of intelligibility that are wielded against concepts to which AR appeals. Thus the '*tu quoque*' response of van Inwagen (1986) to Lewis (1986a: Chapter 3) on 'magical ersatzism'. See (17.4) below.

10 For something in the way of justification of the negative claim see sections (14.5) and (14.6).

11 I acknowledge, as throughout, that AR – *qua* AR – might do without *sui generis* properties or states of affairs, but here I consider the salient and most popular developments of the species of AR in which such categories of entity are embraced. In particular, the distinctive ontological commitment of BR is to whatever the predicates of the worldmaking language are taken to be. In the version which appears most likely to achieve expressive adequacy, the worldmaking language of BR is Lagadonian and the predicates are properties. Once we envisage such a Lagadonian version of BR, we may say that all species of AR accept properties as an ontologically primitive category.

12 Here we pick up (from Chapter 13) the second horn of the McMichael (1983a) dilemma for the attempt to solve the D-problem in PW-semantics by identifying the universal domain as the individual essences. I know of no detailed discussion of the qualitative/non-qualitative distinction for properties. Among the cluster of features associated with non-qualitative properties is that proper names, indexicals or natural kind terms should figure essentially in our specification of them; that each constituent element at least, if not the whole complex, should be capable of multiple instantiation. Rather than rely on any detailed characterization of non-qualitative essences, I assume that they include the identity properties – being identical to Socrates, etc.

13 For such objections to Plantinga's conception of uninstantiated individual essences see Adams (1981), McMichael (1983a), Fine (1985), Menzel (1990) and Linsky and Zalta (1994: esp. 442 n.32).

14 The fundamental reason is lack of appropriate modal correlation of the existence of a putative truthmaker and the holding of the 'corresponding' modal truth.

15 The point is *ad hominem* to Plantinga. I do not mean to suggest that the arguments are good.

16 For the point about intensional entities in general, see (5.4). Again the present point about state of affairs is better construed as an *ad hominem* point to Plantinga (1987) rather than as a point that has any independent force.

Notes

17 One complaint that I do not make against the safety and sanity of AR ontology is commitment to primitive modal *entities*. I believe that the allegation of primitive modality is clearest when construed as a matter of conceptual content.
18 We shall see in Chapter 17 that AR has a '*tu quoque*' reply to Lewis's complaint against the intelligibility of the selection relation that underlies unrealized existence. The *tu quoque* concerns the safety of the set-membership relation. But if that reply succeeds it succeeds, at most, in securing a draw by showing either that both parties have a problem, if Lewis's objection to safety is a good one, or that neither party has a problem, if it is not.

15 ACTUALIST REALISM: PARADOX

1 The earliest explicit mention of PW-paradoxes I have found is in Adams (1974) wherein Perry is credited with such an objection to Adams' version of BR. Discussions of PW-paradox, other than those subsequently cited, may be found in Loux (1979: 53) and Jubien (1988: 307).
2 To exemplify, where the members of P(S*) are s_1, s_2 ... we have the corresponding and distinct propositions: that s_1 is a set, that s_2 is a set. ... We also have the corresponding and distinct propositions (for arbitrary r): that r is a member of s_1, that r is a member of s_2 ... etc.
3 It is of interest to note that Grim (1984: 190) argues from his central thesis to the non-existence of the following sets: the set of all things known by an omniscient being; the set of all propositions; the set of all falsehoods; the set of all necessary truths; the set of all contingent truths; the set of all contingent falsehoods; and the set of all atomic propositions.
4 A fourth strategy, which I will not consider here, is that of opting for a version of set theory in which Cantor's Theorem cannot be proved. Unsurprisingly, there are such non-classical versions of set theory. But there are also classical theories in which the subset axiom is so restricted that Cantor's Theorem cannot be proved. I am indebted here to Alan Weir.
5 Davies presents his example with acknowledgment to David Kaplan and Christopher Peacocke.
6 Thus the response of Lewis (1986a: 105). For a rejoinder to Lewis see Grim (1997: 149–51).
7 Kaplan (1995: 45ff.) appeals to the restriction strategy, recommending a Russellian approach in which intensions are stratified into types.
8 Clearly if there is no set of all of the possible states of affairs that obtain then, a fortiori, there is no set of all possible states of affairs.
9 McNamara (1993) argues that the argument of Plantinga (1974: Chapter IV) fails to establish the existence of a unique actualized world. But with considerations of paradox to the fore perhaps avoidance of commitment to a unique actualized world – for PR, the possible state of affairs that includes all obtaining states of affairs – is no bad thing.

Notes

10 For an informative preliminary discussion of property theory and paradox see Chihara (1998: 139–41).
11 See n.3 above.
12 Appeal to the restriction strategy in order to deal with PW-paradoxes is mooted by Adams (1974) and Grim (1984).
13 By CT, the power set of the real numbers is larger than the set of the real numbers. Recall that the standard justification for holding that the number of distinguishable possibilities is so large is that there might be a real continuum of spacetime points and that each of these might have one of two values independently of the values of any other points. See Chapter 4 n.21.
14 Grim (1984: 208) indicates that Lindenbaum's Lemma may offer a guarantee of consistency of certain maximal sets of sentences that are finite in length and claims that possible worlds, so construed, may prove to be 'important tools for the logician'. Perhaps so, but (as Grim is aware) it is another question whether appeal to such worlds affords any philosophical utility in the conceptual, metaphysical or semantic understanding of modalities and related notions.
15 Some of the general issues raised by the appeal to proper classes are broached in Menzel (1986), Grim (1986), Bringsjord (1989) and Chihara (1998: 133ff.).
16 Aside from the objections that will follow, the appeal to proper classes raises the following question for AR: how are the modal truths about proper classes to be represented?
17 This worry raises again the prospect that AR will need to appeal to some sort of multi-dimensional stratification in which the rank of an entity will depend on various rankings of the kinds of entity from which it is constructed – e.g. a collection might count as being of arbitrarily high rank because it has as a member a proposition that is of arbitrarily high propositional rank.
18 See Chapter 12.
19 Recall that the models of QML are sequences and so would normally be taken as sets. The members of the sequences, and so of the sets that constitute the sequences, include W, D and w*. PW-paradoxes may gain inroads here even in the case of the actualized world w*, since that is apt to be characterized as, or correlated with, the set of all truths *simpliciter*. If that collection of truths is taken as a proper class we have another obstacle to the provision of an applied PW-semantics for QML.
20 See (10.2) and (10.4) above.
21 Lycan (1991a) counts the availability of this account of representation as a major advantage of (generic) AR. The upshot of the present evaluation is that it will only be available to AR if she limits herself to pursuit of either the restriction strategy or the proper class strategy for avoiding PW-paradox.
22 Note here that there is no immediate bar on a possible world, so conceived, being a set member even if the collection of propositions that it represents is barred, on grounds of size, from being a set or being a member of a set. So the need to postulate a set of possible worlds in

order to provide an applied PW semantics for QML stands as no bar to such an application being available to those who take the presently discussed view of the collection of propositions.

23 There have been proposals of various semantic theories for QML that invoke non-maximal surrogates for possible worlds, such as situations (Barwise and Perry 1983), incomplete possibilities or even non-maximal 'worlds' (Forbes 1985: 18–22, 43–7 and Humberstone 1981). I will not attempt here to relate these proposals in detail to the general philosophical issues that have been identified for non-maximal solutions to the PW-paradoxes.

24 I would also venture that the apparent capacity of GR to deal with extraordinary modal claims by means of the redundancy interpretation of possibility (see Chapter 4) may prove an important advantage in this respect. If adequate, that interpretation indicates that GR is able to deal consistently with modal claims about the various intensional entities without extending or restricting (further) the ontological or conceptual resources that she deploys for the purposes of dealing with ordinary modal claims about spatiotemporally unified individuals.

16 ACTUALIST REALISM: TRANSWORLD IDENTITY AND TRANSWORLD IDENTIFICATION

1 That the problems are supposed to be so related is noted by, *inter alia*, Plantinga (1974: 93) and Loux (1979: 39).

2 The theses formulated in this section may appear unduly weak in two respects that require explanation. First, (TW1) and subsequent theses assert transworld identity for only some individuals rather than all while the stronger version is, indeed, typically intended. I opt for the weaker existential version since it is more easily attributed to all without qualification and allows all of the salient philosophical points to emerge. Second, writing the transworld identity theses so that quantification over individuals occurs in the position of widest scope produces under AR interpretation the restricted claim that there are *actual* individuals that are represented as existing by distinct possible worlds. Yet, typically, AR will make the stronger claim that transworld identity of represented individuals applies to represented individuals that do not actually exist as much as to represented individuals that do. Having acknowledged this point, I see no way of making this claim more precise without distorting its intended content. This difficulty flows from the intended non-factivity and opacity of representational 'at' contexts – an aspect of AR interpretation that was signaled in Chapter 10 and to which I will return in Chapter 17. Again, however, the immediate issues remain for the weaker version of the thesis.

3 Here we have cause to note again, by way of an exception, the non-salient combinatorial conception of worlds as sums of spacetime points (see (10.2) above).

4 As read by GR, (TW3) is the doctrine of genuine modal realism with overlap. This is the doctrine that Lewis (1986a: 198–202) takes to be

Notes

most deserving of the title 'transworld identity' but which he thinks comes to grief over the problem of accidental intrinsics. Recall also that GR is committed to the existence of 'transworld individuals', in the sense of individuals that have parts that are parts of different worlds, but not to any individual that is a proper constituent (part) of more than one world. On both points see (4.2) above.

5 Here I follow Lewis (1986a: 243) in so interpreting Chisholm but I will also consider an alternative interpretation below.
6 Given the availability of the foregoing response the suggestion that the problem might be addressed by restricting the scope of the principle of identity of indiscernibles to world-indexed properties (Loux 1979: 43–4) seems drastic and inadequately motivated.
7 Here is the first of many places in which a question of identity across worlds is supposed to be illuminated by analogy with a question of identity across time (Chisholm (1967), Loux (1979: 42)). The thought is that in face of the observation that Tom is not bald at t but bald at u, one would naturally defend the possibility of Tom existing at t and Tom existing at u, by appealing to Tom having (or lacking) baldness-at-u or by requiring that identicals have at any given time the same properties. Partly because of restrictions of space, and partly because I find the temporal comparisons unilluminating and even problematic, I will not appeal to these comparisons in any detail. For various further and detailed comparisons of questions of transworld identity with questions of diachronic identity see Kripke (1972: 51 n.18), Plantinga (1974: 95), Quine (1976), the response of van Inwagen (1985: 105ff.) to Tooley (1977), Forbes (1985: Chapters 5–6) and Lewis (1986a: 202–9).
8 It is not obvious that Chisholm himself intends one specific argument against TW1 as much as he intends the example to raise a series of difficulties that pertain to the thesis. The literature reflects a number of views about what 'the Adam–Noah argument' is. See e.g. n.11 below.
9 These ubiquitous essential properties have often been distinguished from, and treated more tolerantly than, those associated with a more full-blooded 'Aristotelian' essentialism of the kind that Quine abjured (see Parsons 1969).
10 In this chapter I use 'haecceitism' to refer to precisely this thesis about representation.
11 Loux (1979: 39) construes Chisholm as arguing from the Adam–Noah example that transworld identity (of represented individuals) is incompatible with the transitivity of identity. I am unconvinced that Chisholm intends such an argument and unclear about what the (unstated) argument is supposed to be. Perhaps the relevant argument is this. By hypothesis Adam (in W_1) and Noah (in W_1) are distinct. But if Adam (in W_1) is identical to a (in W_n) and a (in W_n) is identical to Noah (in W_1) then, by the transitivity of identity, Adam (in W_1) is identical to Noah (in W_1), contrary to the hypothesis. If so, then the argument can be blocked by denial of the minor premise, Adam (in W_1) is identical to a (in W_n), backed by an appeal to non-trivial essentialism. This is

the move that Loux commends to meet the argument that he has in mind and so, one way or another, we end up with the need to defend non-trivial essentialism.
12 See Lewis (1986d: ix–xvii).
13 For more detail on these matters see Lewis (1979).
14 For further discussion and explanation see Chapter 8.
15 Of course such unclarity can be explained epistemically, as a kind of ignorance about what the specific and determinate truth-conditions of the relevant essentialist claims are. But that is not the obvious explanation and even if it were adopted, the primary source of the malleability of our de re modal opinions would still be semantic rather than modal – it would be ignorance of the semantic facts rather than ignorance of the modal facts.
16 That such discipline is necessary (and sufficient) for truth-aptitude in a class of syntactically appropriate (declarative) sentences is the mainstay of a minimalist conception of truth-aptitude. See Wright (1992).
17 Consider, for example, contexts in which one might truly say that skin, wine or snow is white or that the football, the ball-bearing or the earth is spherical. For further discussion, see Lewis (1972, 1979).
18 There is an interesting distinction to be observed here within the AR camp between those who regard the purely qualitative account of representation de re as outright inadequate and those who hold only that such an account is not always adequate or, even just not always best. Those who have no objection in principle to representation in virtue of qualitative similarity may appeal judiciously to counterpart-theoretic representation where it is helpful to do so. This is the course that McMichael (1983a) commends to AR as an approach to de re representation of non-actuals in order to solve the iterated modality problem of Chapter 13. So the rejection of a purely qualitative account of representation de re is not to be conflated with insistence upon an entirely non-qualitative account.
19 For example, the possibility of compossible qualitatively indiscernible spheres (Adams 1981) or that a vertical rod may fall at different radial points on a plane and thereby realize different possibilities, etc. (Belot 1995, Melia 2001).
20 Lewis's stance here raises interesting questions. Lewis says that if we can have representation de re by naming then we don't need it to work by qualitative character. There are two thoughts here. The more palatable from a GR standpoint and more generally is that representation de re can be achieved by naming when the reference of a name is not determined by any purely qualitative description. The less palatable thought from a GR standpoint is that it can be a fact which resists qualitative explanation that a given name refers to a given individual. It looks as though GR can buy into the former rather than the latter by, for example, buying into a theory of reference that is broadly 'causal' rather than 'descriptive' and then giving a qualitative explanation of the relevant causal relations. If reference can obtain

by stipulation, then we should expect a qualitative explanation of how that is so.
21 Kripke, although one of the philosophers I have in mind in presenting this picture of AR, is by no means committed to the claim that our lack of firm opinions concerning essentialist claims is invariably due to ignorance of a determinate fact about essential properties rather than semantic or even metaphysical underdetermination. Thus, see his comments on whether the essences of certain kinds of particular thing (tables, nations, etc.) are fixed to any extent by the identity of their constituent particulars (Kripke 1972: 50–1).
22 There is a subsidiary thought here that is worth emphasizing. It is sometimes held that understanding a sentence that involves a proper name, 'Dylan', involves grasping the sense of that name and that such grasp of sense involves, in turn, having a certain kind of knowledge that is not obviously propositional knowledge (cf. Dummett (1973: Chapter 5)). The knowledge in question is knowing which individual is Dylan, and perhaps there are even special ways of knowing-which that are required. The point is that AR is free to buy into most if not all of this picture while maintaining that we understand de re modal claims about Dylan (and expressed by the use of the name 'Dylan') and avoiding commitment to the availability at every world of identifying conditions of the form, at w, for all y, y is identical to Dylan iff Qy. The most important consideration that blocks the commitment is this. It is one thing to require that in order to understand a name as it appears within a modal context one must have the ability to recognize which among the actual individuals is Dylan. It is another and altogether stronger claim that one would have to be able to recognize which of the individuals in another world-domain (and when presented in a certain way) is Dylan. A related point is made by Plantinga (1974: 96).
23 Here is exactly what Kripke says about the epistemic status of stipulation in this respect: '"Possible worlds" are *stipulated* not *discovered* by powerful telescopes. There is no reason why we cannot *stipulate* that, in talking about what would have happened to Nixon in a certain counterfactual situation, we are talking about what would have happened to *him*' (Kripke 1972: 44). 'Generally, things aren't "found out" about a counterfactual situation, they are stipulated' (Kripke 1972: 49). I believe that these comments have, *de facto*, given rise to a widely held view that Kripke advocates both (6) and (7).
24 I do not deny that radically idealistic versions of AR might be envisaged on which possible worlds literally do come into being as a result of our stipulations or other creative mental or linguistic acts. Nor do I deny that one might give AR expression to the radical conventionalist thought that the modal status of claims is a matter that is apt to be (communally) stipulated. My claim is that such idealism about modal ontology and modality is out of place with the main species of AR that have been discerned. So I am giving an account of what our species of AR ought to say if idealistic misconstrual of the role of talk of

stipulation in this context is to be avoided. McGinn (1981: 161–2) construes Kripke's remarks on stipulation as having exactly such idealist (antirealistic, constructivist) consequences for modal truth and epistemology. See also Rescher (1975: 96–7).

25 Such opinions need not be the products of a priori reflection alone, and hence the phenomenon of a posteriori necessities – *locus classicus* Kripke (1972) – that are 'known' by inference from both a priori and a posteriori premises.

26 Opinion about which properties of specific kinds of thing are essential might be presented as criteria of transworld identity – typically, necessary rather than sufficient conditions – for represented individuals of those kinds. Kripke (1972: 42) remarks that (some) questions of essential properties are equivalent to (some) questions about identity across possible worlds, and other philosophers, e.g. Forbes (1985), take themselves to be responding to 'the problem of transworld identity' when they propose accounts of the essential properties of certain kinds of individual. However, insofar as the problem of transworld identity is supposed to be a problem that threatens, in general, the coherence of the AR account of the truth-conditions of de re modal claims, it is difficult to see how kind-specific theories of essential properties of effort could address it adequately. If the coherence of the account of truth-conditions depends on the provision of criteria of identity then what would seem to be required are criteria that subsume all (represented) individuals. But that being so, and as Chihara (1998: 58) observes, there is still an enormous gap between what has been established concerning various kinds of individual and what is demanded. This is not to say that the demand is legitimate, but only to point out that the provision of piecemeal kind-centred criteria of transworld identity does not meet it.

17 ACTUALIST REALISM: REPRESENTATION

1 The other kind of explanation that I have not co-opted on behalf of any exemplary version of AR is that representation is 'pictorial' (Lewis 1986a: 65–74). Suffice to say, for present purposes, that pictorial representation is supposed to share with linguistic representation the vice of conflating distinct possibilities (1986a: 170–1).

2 Lewis (1986a: 144) retracts the (Lewis 1973: 90) allegations of expressive deficiency arising out of various finitistic constraints, later regarded as gratuitous, on the worldmaking language. It may also be worth remarking here that Lewis (1986a: 13–17) has quite different complaints of expressive deficiency that apply to modalist interpretations of PW (see Chapter 3) on which, unlike the case of AR, claims about possible worlds must ultimately be expressed in terms of the sentential modal operators of QML. In modalist interpretations, the modal content of PW has to be made explicit in the form of non-factive possibility operators in order to avoid commitment to worlds. But since AR accepts commitments to worlds the unanalysed modal content can be

Notes

left inside the world predicate. Quantification over such worlds is expressively liberating when it does not have to be constrained inside such non-factive contexts.

3 The quasi-technical notion of a term *for* a thing, which I import from Geach (1980: 70), is useful in this context. That 'a' is a term for a, is intended to express the idea that 'a' is apt to refer to a or that if 'a' were to refer to anything it would refer to a. But it is important that '_ is a term for a' is intended as an opaque context so that the truth of such a claim does not commit us to the existence of a. So the linguistic ersatzer can offer terms for non-actual entities without violation of ontological actualism.

4 Here I preserve and make explicit the distinctness of the entities that are the intended referents of the different items of vocabulary in the maximal description.

5 Haecceitism about properties is a more popular doctrine than haecceitism about individuals. (See, e.g., Armstrong 1989: 59.) Note however that if one rejects haecceitism for possible individuals, as Lewis does, the obvious alternative means of representing various intuitively distinct possibilities that appear to differ only haecceitistically is by appealing to distinct but indiscernible possible individuals. So, according to Lewis's critique, the linguistic ersatzer has a problem about capturing these possibilities on either approach, individual-centred or world-centred, to their representation.

6 It is of no effect here to invoke the idea that we can introduce such names because there is a world at which we do so, although the reasons differ from those that applied in the case of GR (see Chapter 5). That there is a world at which we name the (rigidified) actually alien colours is a representational claim that presupposes the capacity of L to express of some such colour that it is instantiated and named by us. That presupposition begs the present question.

7 If we envisage such expressions being underwritten by a PW-semantics for QML then we will require ersatz non-actual individuals – and in the second-order case, ersatz alien properties – to populate the universal domain D and to be available as the values of appropriate bound variables in local world-domains. See the end of (17.2) below. I say only that L permits such expression. A hard-line actualist may opt for modal denial, maintaining that that there could not have been any individuals other than those there actually are or that there could not have been any properties that were not constructs out of the actually instantiated properties. Such a hard-line actualist has no need to find entities to be the ersatz possible individuals or the ersatz alien instantiable properties.

8 One spells out in full what is intended (in this context) by there being an alien property that is instantiated by a as in (5) above.

9 What this shows in retrospect is that the pair (6) and (7), by deploying singular reference to properties, jointly expressed more than was necessary in order to articulate the haecceitistic difference between w and v.

10 See (16.1) above.

11 The irremediable absence of means of referring to alien properties

Notes

ensures that the worldmaking language of BR, and so the worlds of BR, are, in this sense, incomplete. However this is not incompleteness of the sort that is of any help in resolving the PW-paradoxes. The incompleteness generated by referential deficiency is incompleteness at the ground-floor level and does not restrict the vertical generation of higher-order intensions, propositions about propositions, etc. (See Chapter 15.)

12 It is at this point that we attempt to leave behind the thought that the unimprovable referential capacity of Lagadonian L settles that the expressive capacity of L is equally unimprovable.

13 Further suspicion about adequacy of interpretation might be most fruitfully directed on the principle (P2) and its unpacking, but I will not attempt to develop that thought here.

14 In this regard it is crucial that the truth-conditions for pixel sentences are fixed in a way that the representation by a world of an alien or non-actual possibility may be supposed not to entail the existence of any (ersatz) non-actual individual or alien property. On the right-side of (P1), for example, the statement of the existence of alien properties occurs inside the scope of the non-factive context, 'at w'.

15 The misrepresentation of possibilities is not for GR, as it is for linguistic AR, a matter of the expressive limitation of any language, since GR does not represent possibilities linguistically. In GR, cases of alleged misrepresentation are such that we can formulate, in line with the explanatory component of GR, a truth-condition for the relevant possibility claims, but a condition which goes unfulfilled since the ontological component of the theory fails to supply suitable worlds. The argument of (7.6) was that GR was victim to a kind of expressive limitation, but not in the sense that any possibility claim that one might formulate in English is inadequately represented by GR.

16 Divers (1997: 158–9) was so tempted.

17 For admission see Lewis (1986a: 73–4). On AR we can have a possible world at which there are no such things – the null state of affairs, or a maximal consistent set of propositions that entails that there is nothing (the empty set?). Unlike a genuine world, de dicto representation is not achieved in these cases reflexively by a concrete individual so that the existence of any representation represents the existence of some concrete thing. On the basis of this representational success for (magical) AR, van Inwagen (1996) purports – much more controversially – to explain why there is (a concrete) something rather than nothing in terms of the relative infrequency of such 'empty' worlds among the possible worlds.

18 Recall, from (5.4), that this is one aspect of the alleged advantage that AR has over GR through admitting impossible worlds.

19 The features of classical entailment should be borne in mind by anyone who would try to make anything of the capacity of AR to represent distinct necessities as distinct, since all worlds will (classically) entail all necessities.

20 It is tricky to classify NR in relation to Lewis's characterization, and

358

Notes

critique, of magicalism. On one hand Lewis's intent seems clear since: (a) he associates with magicalism those who have been identified here as proponents of NR (Forrest and Stalnaker); and (b) among the magicians' unhelpful specifications of the general AR representation schema, Lewis includes the specification of the elements as complex structural properties and the specification of the selected elements as ways things are (Lewis 1986a: 183). However, the classification of NR as a version of magical ersatzism stands in some tension with the initial supposition that the magicians' worlds have no relevant structure and the subsequent supposition that the worlds are simples that have no structure at all. For clearly, if elements are complex structural properties then maximal such elements are not simples, and the fact that the elements are supposed to be simples does play a role in the internalist horn of Lewis's dilemma (see main text below). Perhaps the thought is that the structure of NR worlds is not relevant structure, i.e. it is not structure that can supply an adequate compositional account of representation. But I will not consider the matter further. Suffice to say that, among our species, PR is the obvious target of Lewis's argument for commitment to magic, and NR may also be vulnerable to the argument.

21 There are two puzzling aspects of this phase of the argument. First, we appear to be offered an inference from the premise that the properties in question must be of the kind that (abstract) simples could instantiate to the conclusion that the only (concrete) things that could instantiate these properties are simple. In the absence of further explanation, the inference looks invalid. If some abstract simple has the property of representing that a donkey walks then – as the truth of the premise requires – it is true that the property of representing that a donkey walks is a property of a kind that a simple can instantiate. Yet representing that a donkey walks is a property that can be instantiated, and is instantiated, by many things that are not simple – so the conclusion is false. Perhaps the suppressed premise is that the only concrete entities that can share properties with abstract simples are themselves simple. Second, there also appears to be an unjustified transition from a claim about representational properties to a claim about properties represented. The kind of property which, by hypothesis, the concrete simples share with the abstract simples are representational properties – for example, representing that something has unit negative charge. Moreover, concrete individuals may have that representational property by instantiating the property of having unit negative charge. But it does not follow from these considerations that anything else, abstract or concrete, that shares the representational property also shares the property of instantiating unit negative charge. So more must be said before Lewis can rightly be said to have closed off the option of claiming knowledge of representational properties by acquaintance with their concrete instances.

22 This aspect of the PR account appears indispensable for it is crucial, in various respects, that the state of affairs of *Socrates' being a philosopher*

should not have Socrates as a constituent lest the contingent existence of the latter visit unwelcome contingency on the existence of the former. So there is no question of PR simply opting to go internal in order to avoid present embarrassment.

23 This specification of B-type properties is not very precise, but it needn't be. What really matters for what follows is that these are properties that sets could share even though they have no common members.

24 For a demonstration see van Inwagen (1986: 209).

25 The shift on the internal horn of the *tu quoque* from the internality of the relation to its range-internality appears to make no substantial difference. Swiftly, what made the internal horn of the dilemma work in the case of the selection relation was that if x stands in the selection relation to y, then there has to be an intrinsic property of x which determines that x stands in the selection relation to any duplicate of w. So it looks as though it was only the range-internality, and not the full-blown internality, of the selection relation that was exploited in the original dilemma.

26 Perhaps in this regard a crucial distinction to bear in mind is that between a theorist accepting that she lacks an explanation of how one of her primitive relational concepts could be grasped and her accepting that it has been shown that the concept in question could not be grasped.

Extended bibliography

Adams, R.M. (1974) 'Theories of Actuality', *Nous*, 8: 211–31. Page references to reprint in M.J. Loux (ed.) *The Possible and the Actual*, Ithaca: Cornell University Press (1979: 190–209).
—— (1981) 'Actualism and Thisness', *Synthese*, 49: 3–41.
Aho, T. (1994) *On the Philosophy of Attitude Logic*, Acta Philosophica Fennica, Vol. 57, Helsinki: Hakapaino Oy.
Armstrong, D.M. (1989) *A Combinatorial Theory of Possibility*, Cambridge: Cambridge University Press.
—— (1997) *A World of States of Affairs*, Cambridge: Cambridge University Press.
Ayer, A.J. (1936) *Language, Truth and Logic*, London: Gollancz.
Bacon, J. (1995) *Universals and Property Instances: The Alphabet of Being*, Oxford: Blackwell.
Barwise, J. and Perry, J. (1983) *Situations and Attitudes*, Cambridge, MA: Massachusetts Institute of Technology Press.
Beadle, A. (1997) 'Modal Fatalism', *Philosophical Quarterly*, 46: 488–95.
Belot, G. (1995) 'New Work for Counterpart Theorists: Determinism', *British Journal for the Philosophy of Science*, 46: 185–95.
Benacerraf, P. (1965) 'What Numbers Could Not Be', *Philosophical Review*, 74: 47–73.
—— (1973) 'Mathematical Truth', *Journal of Philosophy*, 70: 661–79.
Bennett, J.F. (1966) *Kant's Analytic*, Cambridge: Cambridge University Press.
Bergmann, M. (1996) 'A New Argument from Actualism to Serious Actualism', *Nous*, 30: 356–9.
Bigelow, J. (1975) 'Contexts and Quotation: Parts I and II', *Linguistische Berichte*, 38: 1–21 and 39: 1–21.
—— (1988a) *The Reality of Numbers*, Oxford: Clarendon.
—— (1988b) 'Real Possibilities', *Philosophical Studies*, 53: 37–64.
—— (1990) 'The World Essence', *Dialogue*, 29: 205–17.
Bigelow, J. and Pargetter, R. (1990) *Science and Necessity*, Cambridge: Cambridge University Press.
Black, M. (1960) 'Possibility', *Journal of Philosophy*, 57: 117–26.
Blackburn, S. (1984) *Spreading the Word*, Oxford: Clarendon Press.

—— (1986) 'Morals and Modals', in G. MacDonald and C. Wright (eds) *Fact, Science and Morality: Essays on A.J. Ayer's Language, Truth and Logic*, Oxford: Blackwell (119–42).

Bricker, P. (1996) 'Isolation and Unification', *Philosophical Studies*, 84: 225–38.

Bringsjord, S. (1985) 'Are There Set Theoretic Possible Worlds?', *Analysis*, 45: 64.

—— (1989) 'Grim on Logic and Omniscience', *Analysis*, 49: 186–9.

Carnap, R. (1947) *Meaning and Necessity*, Chicago: University of Chicago Press.

—— (1950) 'Empiricism, Semantics and Ontology', *Revue Internationale de Philosophie*, 4. Revised version reprinted in P. Benacerraf and H. Putnam (eds) *Philosophy of Mathematics: Selected Readings*, Cambridge: Cambridge University Press (1983: 241–57).

Chandler, H. (1976) 'Plantinga and the Contingently Possible', *Analysis*, 36: 106–9.

Chihara, C. (1998) *The Worlds of Possibility*, Oxford: Oxford University Press.

Chisholm, R. (1967) 'Identity Through Possible Worlds: Some Questions', *Nous*, 1: 1–8. Page references to reprint in M.J. Loux (ed.) *The Possible and the Actual*, Ithaca: Cornell University Press (1979: 80–7).

—— (1970) 'Events and Propositions', *Nous*, 4: 15–24.

—— (1971) 'States of Affairs Again', *Nous*, 5: 179.

Churchland, P. (1981) 'Eliminative Materialism and the Propositional Attitudes', *Journal of Philosophy*, 78: 67–90.

Cook, M. (1985) 'Names and Possible Objects', *Philosophical Quarterly*, 35: 303–10.

Copeland, J. (1996) 'Prior's Life and Legacy', in J. Copeland (ed.) *Logic and Reality: Essays in Honour of Arthur Prior*, Oxford: Clarendon (1–27).

Cresswell, M. (1972) 'The World is Everything That is the Case', *Australasian Journal of Philosophy*, 50: 1–13. Reprinted in M.J. Loux (ed.) *The Possible and the Actual*, Ithaca: Cornell University Press (1979: 129–45).

Davidson, B. and Pargetter, R. (1980) 'Possible Worlds and a Theory of Meaning for Modal Language', *Australasian Journal of Philosophy*, 58: 388–94.

Davidson, D. (1982) *Inquiries into Truth and Interpretation*, Oxford: Clarendon.

Davies, M. (1978) 'Weak Necessity and Truth Theories', *Journal of Philosophical Logic*, 7: 415–39.

—— (1981) *Meaning, Quantification and Necessity*, London: Routledge and Kegan Paul.

—— (1983) 'Actuality and Context Dependence II', *Analysis*, 43: 128–33.

Davies, M. and Humberstone, L. (1980) 'Two Notions of Necessity', *Philosophical Studies*, 38: 1–30.

DeWitt, B. and Graham, N. (eds) (1973) *The Many Worlds Interpretation of Quantum Mechanics*, Princeton: Princeton University Press.

Divers, J. (1994) 'On the Prohibitive Cost of Indiscernible Concrete Possible Worlds', *Australasian Journal of Philosophy*, 72: 384–9.

—— (1996) 'Supervenience for Operators', *Synthese*, 106: 103–12.
—— (1997) 'The Analysis of Possibility and the Possibility of Analysis', *Proceedings of the Aristotelian Society*, 97: 141–60.
—— (1998) 'Supervenience', *Philosophical Books*, 39: 81–91.
—— (1999a) 'A Genuine Realist Theory of Advanced Modalizing', *Mind*, 108: 217–39.
—— (1999b) 'Kant's Criteria of the A Priori', *Pacific Philosophical Quarterly*, 80: 17–45.
—— (1999c) 'A Modal Fictionalist Result', *Nous*, 33: 317–46.
Divers, J. and Hagen, J. (forthcoming) 'The Modal Fictionalist Predicament'.
Divers, J. and Melia, J. (2002) 'The Analytic Limit of Genuine Modal Realism', *Mind*, 111: 15–36.
Dummett, M. (1973) *Frege: Philosophy of Language*, London: Duckworth.
—— (1978) *Truth and Other Enigmas*, London: Duckworth.
—— (1981) *The Interpretation of Frege's Philosophy*, London: Duckworth.
Feldman, F. (1971) 'Counterparts', *Journal of Philosophy*, 68: 406–9.
Field, H. (1980) *Science Without Numbers*, Oxford: Blackwell.
—— (1989) *Realism, Mathematics and Modality*, Oxford: Blackwell.
—— (1993) 'The Conceptual Contingency of Mathematical Objects', *Mind*, 103: 285–99.
Fine, K. (1977) 'Postscript: Prior on the Construction of Possible Worlds and Instants', in A. Prior and K. Fine, *Worlds, Times and Selves*, London: Duckworth (116–61).
—— (1978) 'Modal Theory for Modal Logic Part I – The De Re/De Dicto Distinction', *Journal of Philosophical Logic*, 7: 125–56.
—— (1982) 'First-Order Modal Theories (III) – Facts', *Synthese*, 53: 43–122.
—— (1985) 'Plantinga on the Reduction of Possibilist Discourse', in J. Tomberlin and P. van Inwagen (eds) *Alvin Plantinga: A Profile*, Dordrecht: Reidel (145–86).
Fine, K. and Schurz, G. (1996) 'Transfer Theorems for Multimodal Logics', in J. Copeland (ed.) *Logic and Reality: Essays in Honour of Arthur Prior*, Oxford: Clarendon (169–214).
Forbes, G. (1983) 'Actuality and Context Dependence I', *Analysis*, 43: 123–8.
—— (1985) *The Metaphysics of Modality*, Oxford: Clarendon.
—— (1989) *The Languages of Possibility*, Oxford: Blackwell.
Forrest, P. (1982) 'Occam's Razor and Possible Worlds', *The Monist*, 65: 456–64.
—— (1986a) 'Ways Worlds Could Be', *Australasian Journal of Philosophy*, 64: 13–24.
—— (1986b) 'Neither Magic nor Mereology', *Australasian Journal of Philosophy*, 64: 89–91.
Forrest, P. and Armstrong, D. (1984) 'An Argument Against David Lewis' Theory of Possible Worlds', *Australasian Journal of Philosophy*, 62: 164–8.
Fox, J.F. (1987) 'Truthmaker', *Australasian Journal of Philosophy*, 65: 188–207.

Frege, G. (1884) *The Foundations of Arithmetic*. Page references to J.L. Austin translation, Oxford: Blackwell (1989 reprint).
Garson, J. (1984) 'Quantification in Modal Logic', in D. Gabbay and F. Guenthner (eds) *Handbook of Philosophical Logic: Volume II*, Dordrecht: Reidel (249–308).
Geach, P. (1967) 'Intentional Identity', *Journal of Philosophy*, 74: 627–32.
—— (1980) *Reference and Generality* (third edition) Ithaca: Cornell University Press.
Gibbard, A. (1975) 'Contingent Identity', *Journal of Philosophical Logic*, 4: 187–222.
Godel, K. (1947) 'What is Cantor's Continuum Problem?', *American Mathematical Monthly*, 54: 515–25. Reprinted in P. Benacerraf and H. Putnam (eds) *Philosophy of Mathematics: Selected Readings*, Cambridge: Cambridge University Press (1983: 470–85).
Grim, P. (1984) 'There is no Set of All Truths', *Analysis*, 44: 206–8.
—— (1986) 'On Sets and Worlds: A Reply to Menzel', *Analysis*, 46: 186–91.
—— (1997) 'Worlds by Supervenience: Some Further Problems', *Analysis*, 57: 146–51.
Haack, S. (1977) 'Lewis' Ontological Slum', *Review of Metaphysics*, 33: 415–29.
Hale, B. (1987) *Abstract Objects*, Oxford: Blackwell.
Hale, B. and Wright, C. (1994) 'A Reductio Ad Surdum? Field on the Contingency of Mathematical Objects', *Mind*, 103: 169–83.
—— (2001) *The Reason's Proper Study*, Oxford: Clarendon.
Hazen, A. (1976) 'Expressive Completeness in Modal Languages', *Journal of Philosophical Logic*, 5: 25–46.
—— (1979a) 'Counterpart Theoretic Semantics for Modal Logic', *Journal of Philosophy*, 76: 319–38.
—— (1979b) 'One of the Truths about Actuality', *Analysis*, 39: 1–3.
—— (1996a) 'Worlds as Complete Novels', *Analysis*, 56: 33–8.
—— (1996b) 'Actualism Again', *Philosophical Studies*, 84: 155–81.
Hellman, G. (1989) *Mathematics without Numbers*, Oxford: Oxford University Press.
Hiipakka, J., Keinanen, M. and Korhonen, A. (1999) 'A Combinatorial Theory of Modality', *Australasian Journal of Philosophy*, 77: 483–97.
Hinchcliff, M. (1989) 'Plantinga's Defence of Serious Actualism', *Analysis*, 49: 182–5.
Hintikka, J. (1957) 'Quantifiers in Deontic Logic', *Societas Scientarum Fennica*, Commentationes Humanarum Litterarum, 23.
—— (1961) 'Modality and Quantification', *Theoria*, 27: 119–28.
—— (1962) *Knowledge and Belief*, Ithaca: Cornell University Press.
—— (1963) 'The Modes of Modality', *Acta Philosophica Fennica*, 16: 65–82. Reprinted in M.J. Loux (ed.) *The Possible and the Actual*, Ithaca: Cornell University Press (1979: 65–79).
—— (1969) *Models for Modalities*, Dordrecht: Reidel.
—— (1975) *The Intentions of Intentionality and Other New Models for Modalities*, Dordrecht: Reidel.

Hochberg, H. (1994) 'Facts and Classes as Complexes and as Truthmakers', *The Monist*, 77: 170–91.

Hodes, H. (1984) 'On Modal Logics which Enrich First-Order S5', *Journal of Philosophical Logic*, 13: 423–54.

Hoffman, J. and Rosenkrantz, G. (1994) *Substance among Other Categories*, Cambridge: Cambridge University Press.

Hudson, H. (1997) 'On a New Argument from Actualism to Serious Actualism', *Nous*, 31: 520–4.

—— (1999) 'A True Necessary Falsehood', *Australasian Journal of Philosophy*, 77: 89–91.

Hughes, G.E. and Cresswell, M. (1996) *A New Introduction to Modal Logic*, London: Routledge.

Humberstone, L. (1981) 'From Worlds to Possibilities', *Journal of Philosophical Logic*, 10: 313–39.

Hume, D. (1739) *A Treatise of Human Nature*, ed. L.A. Selby-Bigge, Oxford: Clarendon (1888 edition).

Jackson, F. (1977) 'A Causal Theory of Counterfactuals', *Australasian Journal of Philosophy*, 55: 3–21.

Jager, T. (1982) 'An Actualist Semantics for Quantified Modal Logic', *Notre Dame Journal of Formal Logic*, 23: 335–49.

Jeffrey, R. (1965) *The Logic of Decision*, Chicago: McGraw-Hill.

Jubien, M. (1988) 'Problems with Possible Worlds', in D.F. Austin (ed.) *Philosophical Analysis*, Dordrecht: Kluwer (299–322).

Kanger, S. (1957) *Provability in Logic*, Stockholm: Acquist and Wiskell.

Kant, I. (1781) *Critique of Pure Reason*. Translation by N. Kemp-Smith, London: MacMillan (1929 edition).

Kaplan, D. (1967) 'Transworld Heirlines', paper presented at a joint symposium of the American Philosophical Association and the Association for Symbolic Logic, Chicago 1967. Page references to first published version (with postscripts) in M.J. Loux (ed.) *The Possible and the Actual*, Ithaca: Cornell University Press (1979: 88–109).

—— (1975) 'How to Russell a Frege-Church', *Journal of Philosophy*, 72: 716–29. Reprinted in M.J. Loux (ed.) *The Possible and the Actual*, Ithaca: Cornell University Press (1979: 210–24).

—— (1995) 'A Problem in Possible-World Semantics', in W. Sinnott-Armstrong, D. Raffman and N. Asher (eds) *Modality, Morality and Belief*, Cambridge: Cambridge University Press (41–52).

Kim, J. (1993) *Supervenience and the Mind: Selected Philosophical Essays*, Cambridge: Cambridge University Press.

King, P.J. (1995) 'Other Times', *Australasian Journal of Philosophy*, 73: 532–47.

Kraut, R. (1976) 'On the Philosophical Relevance of Possible-Worlds Semantics', *Philosophica*, 18: 91–111.

Kripke, S. (1959) 'Semantical Considerations on Modal Logic', *Journal of Symbolic Logic*, 24: 1–15; 323–4.

—— (1963) 'Semantical Considerations on Modal Logic', *Acta Philosophica Fennica*, 16: 83–94. Reprinted in L. Linsky (ed.) *Reference and Modality*, Oxford: Oxford University Press (1971: 63–87).

—— (1972) 'Naming and Necessity', in D. Davidson and G. Harman (eds) *Semantics for Natural Languages*, Dordrecht: Reidel (253–355; 763–9). Page references to revised and enlarged edition, *Naming and Necessity*, Oxford: Blackwell (1980).
—— (1980) 'Preface', in *Naming and Necessity*, Oxford: Blackwell (2–21).
—— (1982) *Wittgenstein on Rules and Private Language*, Oxford: Blackwell.
LePoidevin, R. and MacBeath, M. (eds) (1993) *The Philosophy of Time*, Oxford: Oxford University Press.
Lewis, D. (1968) 'Counterpart Theory and Quantified Modal Logic', *Journal of Philosophy*, 65: 113–26. Page references to reprinted version in his *Philosophical Papers: Volume I*, Oxford: Oxford University Press (1983: 26–39).
—— (1970) 'Anselm and Actuality', *Nous*, 4: 175–88. Reprinted in his *Philosophical Papers: Volume I*, Oxford: Oxford University Press (1983: 10–20).
—— (1971) 'Counterparts of Persons and their Bodies', *Journal of Philosophy*, 68: 203–11. Page references to reprinted version in his *Philosophical Papers: Volume I*, Oxford: Oxford University Press (1983: 47–54).
—— (1972) 'General Semantics', *Synthese*, 22: 18–67. Reprinted in his *Philosophical Papers: Volume I*, Oxford: Oxford University Press (1983: 189–229).
—— (1973) *Counterfactuals*, Oxford: Blackwell.
—— (1976) 'The Paradoxes of Time Travel', *American Philosophical Quarterly*, 13: 145–52.
—— (1978) 'Truth in Fiction', *American Philosophical Quarterly*, 15: 37–46. Reprinted in his *Philosophical Papers: Volume I*, Oxford: Oxford University Press (1983: 261–75).
—— (1979) 'Scorekeeping in a Language Game', *Journal of Philosophical Logic*, 8: 339–59. Reprinted in his *Philosophical Papers: Volume I*, Oxford: Oxford University Press (1983: 233–49).
—— (1983a) 'Postscripts to "Anselm and Actuality"', in his *Philosophical Papers: Volume I*, Oxford: Oxford University Press (1983: 21–5).
—— (1983b) 'Postscripts to "Counterpart Theory and Quantified Modal Logic"', in his *Philosophical Papers: Volume I*, Oxford: Oxford University Press (1983: 39–46).
—— (1986a) *On the Plurality of Worlds*, Oxford: Blackwell.
—— (1986b) 'Events', in his *Philosophical Papers: Volume II*, Oxford: Oxford University Press (1986: 241–69).
—— (1986c) 'Against Structural Universals', *Australasian Journal of Philosophy*, 64: 25–46.
—— (1986d) 'Introduction', in his *Philosophical Papers: Volume II*, Oxford: Oxford University Press (ix–xvii).
—— (1990) 'Noneism or Allism?', *Mind*, 99: 23–31.
—— (1991) *Parts of Classes*, Oxford: Blackwell.
—— (1992) Review of D.A. Armstrong, 'A Combinatorial Theory of Possibility', *Australasian Journal of Philosophy*, 70: 211–24.
—— (1996) 'Maudlin and Modal Mastery', *Australasian Journal of Philosophy*, 74: 683–4.

Extended bibliography

Linsky, B. and Zalta, E. (1994) 'In Defense of the Simplest Quantified Modal Logic', *Philosophical Perspectives*, 8: 431–58.
—— (1996) 'In Defense of the Contingently Nonconcrete', *Philosophical Studies*, 84: 283–94.
Linsky, L. (1971) 'Introduction' in L. Linsky (ed.) *Reference and Modality*, Oxford: Oxford University Press (1971: 1–16).
Loux, M.J. (1979) 'Introduction: Modality and Metaphysics', in M.J. Loux (ed.) *The Possible and the Actual*, Ithaca: Cornell University Press (15–64).
Lycan, W. (1979) 'The Trouble with Possible Worlds', in M.J. Loux (ed.) *The Possible and the Actual*, Ithaca: Cornell University Press (1979: 274–316).
—— (1988) Review of D. Lewis, 'On the Plurality of Worlds', *Journal of Philosophy*, 85: 42–7.
—— (1991a) 'Two – No, Three – Conceptions of Possible Worlds', *Proceedings of the Aristotelian Society*, 91: 215–27.
—— (1991b) 'Pot Bites Kettle: A Reply to Miller', *Australasian Journal of Philosophy*, 69: 212–13.
Lycan, W. and Shapiro, S. (1986) 'Actuality and Essence', *Midwest Studies in Philosophy*, 11: 343–77.
MacBride, F. (1999) 'Could Armstrong Have Been a Universal?', *Mind*, 108: 471–501.
—— (2001) 'Can the Property Boom Last?', *Proceedings of the Aristotelian Society*, 101: 225–46.
McGinn, C. (1976) 'A Priori and A Posteriori Knowledge', *Proceedings of the Aristotelian Society*, 77: 195–208.
—— (1981) 'Modal Reality', in R. Healey (ed.) *Reduction, Time and Reality*, Cambridge: Cambridge University Press (143–88).
—— (1983) *The Subjective View*, Oxford: Oxford University Press.
Mackie, J.L. (1976) *Problems from Locke*, Oxford: Clarendon.
—— (1977) *Ethics: Inventing Right and Wrong*, London: Penguin.
McMichael, A. (1983a) 'A Problem for Actualism about Possible Worlds', *Philosophical Review*, 92: 49–66.
—— (1983b) 'A New Actualist Modal Semantics', *Journal of Philosophical Logic*, 12: 73–99.
McNamara, P. (1993) 'Does the Actual World Actually Exist?', *Philosophical Studies*, 69: 59–81.
Marcus, R. (1985) 'Possibilia and Possible Worlds', *Grazer Philosophische Studien*, 25/6: 107–33. Page reference to reprinted version in R. Marcus, *Modalities: Philosophical Essays*, Oxford: Oxford University Press (1993: 189–213).
Maudlin, T. (1996) 'On the Impossibility of David Lewis' Modal Realism', *Australasian Journal of Philosophy*, 74: 669–82.
Meinong, A. (1910) 'The Theory of Objects', in R.M. Chisholm (ed.) *Realism and the Background of Phenomenology*, New York: The Free Press (1960: 76–117).
Melia, J. (1992) 'A Note on Lewis's Ontology', *Analysis*, 52: 191–2.
—— (1999) 'Holes, Haecceitism and two Conceptions of Determinism', *British Journal for the Philosophy of Science*, 50: 639–64.

—— (2001) 'On Reducing Possibilities to Language', *Analysis*, 61: 19–29.
Mellor, D. (1981) *Real Time*, Cambridge: Cambridge University Press.
Menzel, C. (1986) 'On Set Theoretic Possible Worlds', *Analysis*, 46: 68–72.
—— (1990) 'Actualism, Ontological Commitment and Possible World Semantics', *Synthese*, 85: 355–89.
✱ Menzies, P. and Pettit, P. (1994) 'In Defence of Fictionalism about Possible Worlds', *Analysis*, 54: 27–36.
Meredith, C. and Prior, A. (1956) 'Interpretations of Different Modal Logics in the "Property Calculus"'. First published in J. Copeland (ed.) *Logic and Reality: Essays in Honour of Arthur Prior*, Oxford: Clarendon (1996: 133–4).
Miller, R.B. (1989) 'Dog Bites Man: A Defence of Modal Realism', *Australasian Journal of Philosophy*, 67: 476–8.
—— (1990) 'There's Nothing Magical about Possible Worlds', *Mind*, 99: 453–7.
—— (1991) 'Reply of a Mad Dog', *Analysis*, 51: 50–4.
—— (1992) 'Concern for Counterparts', *Philosophical Papers*, 21: 133–40.
—— (1993) 'Genuine Modal Realism: Still the Only Non-Circular Game in Town', *Australasian Journal of Philosophy*, 71: 159–60.
Monadori, F. (1983) 'Counterpartese, Counterpartese*, Counterpartese$_D$', *Histoire Epistémologie, Langage*, 5: 69–94.
Montague, R. (1960) 'Logical Necessity, Physical Necessity, Ethics and Quantifiers', *Enquiry*, 3: 259–69.
Mulligan, K., Simons, P. and Smith, B. (1984) 'Truthmakers', *Philosophy and Phenomenological Research*, 44: 287–321.
Nagel, E. (1950) 'Science and Semantic Realism', Philosophy of Science, 17: 174–81.
Naylor, M. (1986) 'A Note on David Lewis's Realism about Possible Worlds', *Analysis*, 46: 28–9.
Nolan, D. (1996) 'Recombination Unbound', *Philosophical Studies*, 84: 239–62.
Nolt, J. (1986) 'What are Possible Worlds?', *Mind*, 95: 432–45.
✱ Noonan, H. (1994) 'In Defence of the Letter of Fictionalism', *Analysis*, 54: 133–9.
O'Leary-Hawthorne, J. (1996) 'The Epistemology of Possible Worlds: A Guided Tour', *Philosophical Studies*, 84: 283–302.
Parsons, T. (1969) 'Essentialism and Quantified Modal Logic', *Philosophical Review*, 78: 35–52. Reprinted in L. Linsky (ed.) *Reference and Modality*, Oxford: Oxford University Press (73–88).
—— (1980) *Nonexistent Objects*, New Haven: Yale University Press.
Peacocke, C. (1978) 'Necessity and Truth Theories', *Journal of Philosophical Logic*, 7: 473–500.
Plantinga, A. (1969) 'De Re et De Dicto', *Nous*, 3: 235–58.
—— (1970) 'World and Essence', *Philosophical Review*, 79: 461–92.
—— (1973) 'Transworld Identity or Worldbound Individuals', in Milton K. Munitz (ed.) *Logic and Ontology*, New York: New York University Press. Page references to reprint in M.J. Loux (ed.) *The Possible and the Actual*, Ithaca: Cornell University Press (1979: 146–65).

—— (1974) *The Nature of Necessity*, Oxford: Clarendon.
—— (1976) 'Actualism and Possible Worlds', *Theoria*, 42: 139–60. Page references to reprint in M.J. Loux (ed.) *The Possible and the Actual*, Ithaca: Cornell University Press (1979: 253–73).
—— (1985a) 'Self-Profile', in J. Tomberlin and P. van Inwagen (eds) *Alvin Plantinga: A Profile*, Dordrecht: Reidel (88–93).
—— (1985b) 'Replies to My Colleagues', in J. Tomberlin and P. van Inwagen (eds) *Alvin Plantinga: A Profile*, Dordrecht: Reidel (313–49).
—— (1987) 'Two Concepts of Modality: Modal Realism and Modal Reductionism', *Philosophical Perspectives*, 1: 189–231.
Pollock, J.L. (1985) 'Plantinga on Possible Worlds', in J. Tomberlin and P. van Inwagen (eds) *Alvin Plantinga: A Profile*, Dordrecht: Reidel (121–44).
Priest, G. (1987) *In Contradiction*, Dordrecht: Nijhoff.
Prior, A.N. (1957) *Time and Modality*, Oxford: Oxford University Press.
—— (1959) 'Thank Goodness That's Over', *Philosophy*, 34: 12–17.
—— (1970) 'The Notion of the Present', *Stadium Generale*, 23: 245–8.
Prior, A.N. and Fine, K. (1977) *Worlds, Times and Selves*, London: Duckworth.
Putnam, H. (1967) 'Mathematics without Foundations', *Journal of Philosophy*, 64: 5–22. Reprinted in P. Benacerraf and H. Putnam (eds) *Philosophy of Mathematics: Selected Readings*, Cambridge: Cambridge University Press (1983: 295–311).
—— (1971) *Philosophy of Logic*, London: Allen and Unwin.
—— (1975) 'The Meaning of "Meaning"', in his *Mind, Language and Reality: Philosophical Papers Volume II*, Cambridge: Cambridge University Press.
—— (1978) *Meaning and the Moral Sciences*, London: Routledge and Kegan Paul.
Quine, W.V.O. (1947) 'The Problem of Interpreting Modal Logic', *Journal of Symbolic Logic*, 12: 43–8.
—— (1948) 'On What There Is', *Review of Metaphysics*, 5: 21–38. Reprinted in his *From a Logical Point of View* (second edition), New York: Harper and Row (1961: 1–19).
—— (1951) 'Two Dogmas of Empiricism', *Philosophical Review*, 60: 20–43. Reprinted in his *From a Logical Point of View* (second edition), New York: Harper and Row (1961: 20–46).
—— (1953a) 'Reference and Modality', in his *From a Logical Point of View* (first edition), Cambridge, MA: Harvard University Press. Reprinted in his *From a Logical Point of View* (second edition), New York: Harper and Row (1961: 139–59).
—— (1953b) 'Three Grades of Modal Involvement', Proceedings of the XIth International Congress of Philosophy: Volume 14, Amsterdam: North-Holland. Reprinted in his *The Ways of Paradox and Other Essays* (revised edition), New York: Random House (1976: 158–76).
—— (1957) 'The Scope and Language of Science', *British Journal for the Philosophy of Science*, 8: 1–17. Reprinted in his *The Ways of Paradox and Other Essays* (revised edition), New York: Random House (1976: 228–45).

Extended bibliography

—— (1960) *Word and Object*, Cambridge, MA: Massachusetts Institute of Technology Press.
—— (1961) 'Reply to Professor Marcus', *Synthese*, 20. Reprinted in his *The Ways of Paradox and Other Essays* (revised edition), New York: Random House (1976: 177–84).
—— (1969) 'Propositional Objects', in his *Ontological Relativity and Other Essays*, New York: Columbia University Press (139–60).
—— (1976) 'Worlds Away', *Journal of Philosophy*, 73: 859–63. Reprinted in his *Theories and Things*, Cambridge, MA: Harvard University Press (1981: 124–8).
Rescher, N. (1975) *A Theory of Possibility*, Oxford: Blackwell.
Richards, T. (1975) 'The Worlds of David Lewis', *Australasian Journal of Philosophy*, 53: 105–18.
Roper, A. (1982) 'Towards an Eliminative Reduction of Possible Worlds', *Philosophical Quarterly*, 32: 45–59.
* Rosen, G. (1990) 'Modal Fictionalism', *Mind*, 99: 327–54.
* —— (1995) 'Modal Fictionalism Fixed', *Analysis*, 55: 67–73.
Rosenberg, A. (1989) 'Is Lewis's Genuine Modal Realism Magical Too?', *Mind*, 98: 411–21.
Routley, R. (1980) *Exploring Meinong's Jungle and Beyond*, Canberra: Australian National University Central Printery.
Roy, T. (1993) 'Worlds and Modality', *Philosophical Review*, 102: 335–61.
—— (1995) 'In Defence of Linguistic Ersatzism', *Philosophical Studies*, 80: 217–42.
Russell, B. and Whitehead, A. (1910) *Principia Mathematica: Volume I*, Cambridge: Cambridge University Press edition (1925–7).
Salmon, N.U. (1981) *Reference and Essence*, Princeton: Princeton University Press.
—— (1984) 'Impossible Worlds', *Analysis*, 44: 114–17.
—— (1996) 'Transworld Identity and Stipulation', *Philosophical Studies*, 84: 203–23.
Sanford, D. H. (1989) *If P then Q: Conditionals and the Foundations of Reasoning*, London: Routledge.
Schlesinger, G.N. (1984) 'Possible Worlds and the Mystery of Existence', *Ratio*, 26: 1–17.
Shalkowski, S. (1994) 'The Ontological Ground of the Alethic Modality', *Philosophical Review*, 103: 669–88.
Skorupski, J. (1980) 'Possibility', *Proceedings of the Aristotelian Society, Supplementary Volume*, 54: 89–104.
Sharlow, M.F. (1988) 'Lewis's Modal Realism: A Reply to Naylor', *Analysis*, 48: 13–15.
Simons, P. (1989) *Parts: A Study in Ontology*, Oxford: Oxford University Press.
—— (1993) 'Logical Atomism and Its Ontological Refinement: A Defense', in K. Mulligan (ed.) *Language, Truth and Ontology*, Dordrecht: Kluwer.
Skyrms, B. (1976) 'Possible Worlds, Physics and Metaphysics', *Philosophical Studies*, 30: 323–32.

—— (1981) 'Tractarian Nominalism', *Philosophical Studies*, 40: 199–206.
Smart, J.J.C. (1984) *Ethics, Persuasion and Truth*, London: Routledge and Kegan Paul.
Smith, B. (1999) 'Truthmaker Realism', *Australasian Journal of Philosophy*, 77: 274–91.
Stalnaker, R. (1968) 'A Theory of Conditionals', in N. Rescher (ed.) *Studies in Logical Theory*, Oxford: Blackwell.
—— (1976) 'Possible Worlds', *Nous*, 10: 65–75. Page references to reprint in M.J. Loux (ed.) *The Possible and the Actual*, Ithaca: Cornell University Press (1979: 225–34).
—— (1984) *Inquiry*, Cambridge, MA: Massachusetts Institute of Technology Press.
Taylor, C. (1998) 'Lewis's Modal Realism and the Possibility of Disjoint Spaces and Times', unpublished M.A. dissertation, University of Leeds.
Thomas, H.G. (1996) 'Combinatorialism and Primitive Modality', *Philosophical Studies*, 83: 231–52.
Tomberlin, J. (1996) 'Actualism or Possibilism', *Philosophical Studies*, 84: 263–81.
Tooley, M. (1977) 'Critical Notice of A. Plantinga, "The Nature of Necessity"', *Australasian Journal of Philosophy*, 55: 91–102.
Unger, P. (1984) 'Minimizing Arbitrariness: Towards a Metaphysics of Infinitely Many Isolated Concrete Worlds', *Midwest Studies in Philosophy*, 9: 29–51.
van Fraassen, B. (1980) *The Scientific Image*, Oxford: Clarendon.
—— (1995) '"World" Is Not a Count Noun', *Nous*, 29: 139–57.
van Inwagen, P. (1980) 'Indexicality and Actuality', *Philosophical Review*, 89: 403–26.
—— (1985) 'Plantinga on Trans-World Identity' in J. Tomberlin and P. van Inwagen (eds) *Alvin Plantinga: A Profile*, Dordrecht: Reidel (101–20).
—— (1986) 'Two Concepts of Possible Worlds', *Midwest Studies in Philosophy*, 11: 185–213.
—— (1996) 'Why Is There Anything At All?', *Proceedings of the Aristotelian Society, Supplementary Volume*, 70: 95–110.
—— (1998) 'Modal Epistemology', *Philosophical Studies*, 92: 67–84.
Vendler, Z. (1975) 'On the Possibility of Possible Worlds', *Canadian Journal of Philosophy*, 5: 57–73.
White, M.J. (1977) 'Plantinga and the Actual World', *Analysis*, 37: 97–104.
Wittgenstein, L. (1921) *Tractatus Logico-Philosophicus*. Translation by D.F. Pears and B.F. McGuinness, London: Routledge and Kegan Paul (1961 edition).
—— (1953) *Philosophical Investigations*, Oxford: Blackwell.
Wright, C. (1983) *Frege's Conception of Numbers as Objects*, Aberdeen: Aberdeen University Press.
—— (1987) 'Introduction', in his *Realism, Meaning and Truth*, Oxford: Oxford University Press.
—— (1992) *Truth and Objectivity*, London: Harvard University Press.

Yablo, S. (1993) 'Is Conceivability a Guide to Possibility?', *Philosophy and Phenomenological Research*, 53: 1–42.
Yagisawa, T. (1988) 'Beyond Possible Worlds', *Philosophical Studies*, 53: 175–204.
—— (1992) 'Possible Worlds as Shifting Domains', *Erkenntnis*, 36: 83–101.

Index

a priori knowledge: and analyticity 161–3; and causation 158–9; and concreteness 159–60; and contingency 160–1
abstention from use of possible-world talk/abstentionism 19–20, 24, 25, 40, 129, 304n.17, 306n.3
abstractness of worlds 229–31; *see also* a priori knowledge, causation, and concreteness; Lewis, on abstractness
actualism: analytic 62–5; ontological 169, 211; serious 224–6, 348n.26
actualist realism (AR) 21 *et passim*; species of 172
actuality, indexical theory of 44, 306n.5, 346n.13
Adam–Noah example 261, 263–74
Adams, R.M. 179, 268, 329n.19, 349n.13, 350n.1, 351n.12, 354n.19
advanced modalizing *see* modality, extraordinary/advanced
agnostic antirealism *see* antirealism
Aho, T. 298n.4
alien possibilities 81–2, 85, 87, 99, 100, 105–6, 114–21, 175, 277–81, 287, 315n.33, 317n.41, 320n.28, 325–6n.21, 326n.23, 357n.8, 358n.14
analysis *see* conceptual analysis/ elucidation; conceptual applications of PW
antirealism: about possible worlds 22–5; agnostic 23, 301n.12; error-theoretic 23, 301n.10; factualist (FA) 23; fictionalist 24, 301nn.16, 17, 342n.11; modalist 24, 301n.17, 323n.7, 332n.5, 345n.7; non-factualist (NFA) 22, 300–1n.10; semantic 341n.8; structure-based (SA) 23
applications (of PW): conceptual 26–32 *et passim*; cosmological 39; ontological 32–4 *et passim*; semantic 34–9 *et passim*
AR (actualist realism) *see* actualist realism
arithmetical Platonism *see* Platonism
Armstrong, D.M. 101, 175, 192, 216, 303n.12, 311n.4, 316n.35, 321–2n.38, 325n.15, 336n.25, 337n.6, 338n.10, 339n.17, 342nn.11, 13, 16, 342–3n.20, 344–5n.12, 346n.12, 357n.5; *see also* Forrest, P. and Armstrong, D.M.
Ayer, A.J. 300n.10

Bacon, J. 175, 310n.1, 344n.3
Barcan formula/principle (BF) and converse (CBF) 142, 212–21, 305n.2, 346n.10, 348n21
Barwise, J. and Perry, J. 175, 352n.23
Beadle, A. 329n.19
Becker principle 142–4, 331n.33; *see also* S4 principle
Belot, G. 354n.19
Benacerraf, P. 150, 165, 233
Bennett, J.F. 90

Index

Bergmann, M. 348n.26
BF (Barcan formula) *see* Barcan formula
Bigelow, J. 66, 175, 309n.28, 312n.10, 341n.10
Bigelow, J. and Pargetter, R. 92, 93, 111–12, 154, 177, 299n.12, 303n.11, 311n.5, 326n.3, 337n.4, 338–9n.16, 339n.23, 339–40n.24, 340n.27, 341–2n.10, 345n.1
Black, M. 315n.30
Blackburn, S. 23, 29, 134, 300n.9, 300–1n.10, 328n.14, 328–9n.17, 336n.24
book realism (BR) 21 *et passim*; exposition of 178–80
BR (book realism) *see* book realism
Bringsjord, S. 245, 246, 351n.15
Brouwer's principle/Brouwerian principle (B) 142–4, 216, 304n.21, 331n.33

Cantorian paradoxes *see* paradox(es), Cantorian
Cantor's theorem 243–5, 350n.4
Carnap, R. 156, 179
CBF (converse Barcan formula) *see* Barcan formula
Chihara, C. 112, 245, 247, 251, 271–2, 304n.18, 332n.7, 333–4n.12, 350n.10, 351n.15, 356n.26
Chisholm, R. 199, 257, 261–74, 353nn.5, 7, 8, 11
Churchland, P. 301n.11
combinatorial realism (CR) 21 *et passim*; exposition of 174–7
conceptual analysis/elucidation: explicit versus implicit 26–8; extensional versus intensional 29–32; modal versus non-modal 26, 28–9, 108–10; relation to ontological identification 32, 303n.9
conceptual applications of PW 26–32; and AR 181–95; and GR 47–51, 106–21
conditionals: counterfactual 11, 14, 50, 96–8, 299n.9; non-material 10–11; strict 11

Copeland, J. 301n.17, 304n.16
counterfactuals *see* conditionals, counterfactual
counterparts and counterpart relations 44, 50, 122–48 *et passim*
CR (combinatorial realism) *see* combinatorial realism
Cresswell, M. 175, 338–9n.16; *see also* Hughes, G. and Cresswell, M.
criteria of identity 10, 18, 30, 200, 228, 232–42, 257, 302n.3, 316–17n.37, 348n.4, 356n.26
CT (counterpart theory) *see* counterparts and counterpart relations

D-problem for AR 211–22
Davidson, B. and Pargetter, R. 318n.7
Davidson, D. 303–4n.15
Davies, M. 245, 306n.5, 313n.17, 329n.18, 348n.25, 350n.5
Davies, M. and Humberstone, L. 306n.5
DeWitt, B. and Graham, N. 39
Divers, J. 43, 154, 299n.11, 301n.17, 304n.17, 307n.14, 314n.21, 315n.32, 316n.35, 319n.22, 324n.12, 331n.34, 335n.17, 358n.16
Divers, J. and Hagen, J. 301n.16
Divers, J. and Melia, J. 307n.7, 322n.2
Dummett, M. 314n.26, 315n.28, 334n.13, 341n.8, 355n.22

epistemology *see* modal epistemology
error-theoretic antirealism *see* antirealism, error-theoretic
essences 14, 123, 327n.4, individual 220–2, 238–9
essential properties 14, 258–74
existentialism 221, 224
extensionality: and AR ontology 197; and counterpart theory 144–5; versus intensionality 9, 29–32, 302nn.6, 7
extraordinary modal claims *see*

374

Index

modality, extraordinary/ advanced

FA (factualist antirealism) *see* antirealism, factualist
Feldman, F. 330n.27
Field, H. 301n.11, 317n.4, 335n.21, 341n.5
Fine, K. 301n.17, 305–6n.2, 312n.12, 348n.26, 349n.13; *see also* Prior, A.N. and Fine, K.
Fine, K. and Schurz, G. 298–9n.4
Forbes, G. 143, 301n.17, 304n.17, 306n.5, 326n.2, 327–8n.9, 330n.28, 352n.23, 353n.7, 356n.26
Forrest, P. 177, 329n.19, 331n.1, 339nn.18, 23, 342–3n.24, 348n.20, 359n.20
Forrest–Armstrong paradox *see* paradox(es), Forrest–Armstrong
Forrest, P. and Armstrong, D.M. 101
Fox, J.F. 303n.12
Frege, G. 162, 233, 302n.3, 311n.7, 314n.26, 318n.10, 348n.6
Fregean: objection to quantification over possibilia 59, 77–85, 317n.41; Platonism *see* Platonism; rejection of supervenience of epistemological status on facts about referents 159–60

Garson, J. 345–6n.8
Geach, P.T. 326n.2, 347n.16, 357n.3
general relativity 93–4
genuine realism (GR) 21 *et passim*; exposition of 43–6; minimal (MGR) versus replicating (RGR) 83–4; misrepresentation of possibilities by 284–5, 322n.6; ontological component of *see* GRO; possibilist (PGR) versus impossibilist (IGR) 69–77; worldly (WGR) versus unworldly (UGR) 93–4, 103–4, 322n.6
Gibbard, A. 330n.29
Godel, K. 162
Godelian intuitionism 162–3

Grim, P. 245, 246, 247, 248, 253, 350nn.3, 6, 351nn.12, 14, 15
GR *see* genuine realism
GRO (ontological component of genuine realism) 45–6: completeness of 107, 117–21; consistency of 107; knowledge of 151–65

Haack, S. 60
haecceitism *see* representation
Hagen, J. *see* Divers, J. and Hagen, J.
Hale, B. 314n.26, 348n.3
Hale, B. and Wright, C. 162, 302n.3, 335n.19, 341n.5, 348n.7
Hazen, A. 125, 127, 141–3, 222, 253–4, 304n.17, 306n.5, 309n.28, 328n.10, 331n.31
Hellman, G. 301n.18
Hiipakka, J., Keinanen, M. and Korhonen, A. 175, 342n.16, 346–7n.15
Hinchcliff, M. 348n.26
Hintikka, J. 178, 298–9n.4, 304n.16, 330n.28
Hochberg, H. 303n.12
Hodes, H. 304n.17, 306n.5
Hoffman, J. and Rosenkrantz, G. 348n.3
HP (Hume's Principle) *see* Hume's Principle
Hudson, H. 312–13n.13, 348n.26
Hughes, G. and Cresswell, M. 304n.18, 309n.28
Humberstone, L. 352n.23; *see also* Davies, M. and Humberstone, L.
Hume, D. 300–1n.10
Humean supervenience *see* supervenience
Hume's Principle (HP) 161–2, 233, 302n.3, 316–17n.37
Husserl, E. 339n.18
hyperintensionality 200, 313n.17, 329n.18

identity *see* criteria of identity; necessity of identity
IGR (impossibilist genuine realism) *see* genuine realism, possibilist (PGR) versus impossibilist (IGR)

375

Index

impossible worlds and impossibilia 52, 59, 67–77, 109–10, 174, 181–3, 187–95, 202, 267, 285, 298–9n.4, 312–13n.13, 313nn.16, 18, 314n.25, 324n.11, 324–5n.14, 342n.15, 358n.18
incredulous stares 153–4
indiscernible worlds 51, 83–4, 308–9n.21, 312n.12, 316nn.35, 36, 323n.4, 326n.22
intensionality *see* extensionality; hyperintensionality
interpretations: of possible-world discourse (PW) 16–18; realist versus antirealist 19–21
intuitionism *see* Godelian intuitionism; Kantian, intuitionism
island universes 62–3, 87, 93–9, 104, 311n.5
iterated modality 9, 40; problem of for AR 218–19, 280–1, 354n.18

Jager, T. 347–8n.19
Jeffrey, R. 179
Jubien, M. 350n.1

Kanger, S. 304n.16
Kant, I. 90
Kantian: intuitionism in mathematical epistemology 162–3; objection to GR 87–91
Kaplan, D. 245–6, 257, 268, 270–2, 350n.7
Kaplan paradoxes *see* paradox(es), Kaplan
Keinanen, M. *see* Hiipakka, J., Keinanen, M. and Korhonen, A.
Kim, J. 299n.11
King, P.J. 91–2, 318n.11, 318–19n.18
Korhonen, A. *see* Hiipakka, J., Keinanen, M. and Korhonen, A.
Kripke, S. 143, 299n.12, 300–1n.10, 319n.19, 326n.2, 330n.28, 335n.17, 348n.20, 356n.25; as actualist realist 337n.5; his intuitive application of his semantics for QML 210–26; on irrelevance of counterpart theory 125–34, 327n.5; semantics *see* Kripkean semantics; on transworld identity/identification 270–2, 353n.7, 355n.21, 355–6n.24
Kripkean semantics 19, 30, 35–6, 304nn.16, 18 *et passim*; and AR 210–26; and GR 57, 60, 309n.28; sketch of for QML 36–9

Lagadonian languages 84, 180, 189, 215, 217, 219, 275, 281–2, 286, 341–2n.10, 349n.11, 358n.12
Leibniz, G. 326n.2, 339n.18
Leibniz's law 199, 236, 240
LePoidevin, R. and MacBeath, M. 328n.16
Lewis, D.: on abstractness 230, 300n.8, 315n.28, 318n.7, 348n.3; on accessibility relations 331n.35, 345n.5; on accidental intrinsics 306n.4, 352–3n.4; on the actual world 228; on alien possibilities 115, 119, 315n.33, 320n.28; on analytic actualism 63–4; as author of GR 43; on claim to realism 300n.5; on conceivability and possibility 318n.12; on counterpart theory 122–48, 326n.2; on discrimination of intensional entities 72; on doxastically modal analysis 110–11; on epistemology of GR 149–65; on ersatz individuals 346n.14; on expressive limitations of QML 309n.26, 356–7n.2; on expressive power of modal English and PW 304n.17; on haecceitism 268, 354–5n.20; on impossibilia 67–8, 76; on indexicality of 'actual' 44–5, 306n.5; on indiscernible worlds 83–4; on intensional roles 307n.12; on justification of GR 57–8, 310n.30; on linguistic ersatzism/BR 84, 275–81, 317n.39, 356–7n.2; on magical ersatzism/PR 197, 286–92, 359n.20, 359–60n.21; on Meinongian quantification 310n.1; on methodology in

376

linguistics 331n.39, 354n.17; on misrepresentation by GR 284–5; on number of possibilities 251, 308–9n.21; on ontological identifications 51, 308n.19; on primitive modal content in BR analyses 182–8; on propositional content 308n.18; on recombination 101–3, 115, 175; on revisionary implications of GR 329n.19; on sets and individuals 307n.8, 318n.6; on transworld identity 258, 270, 352–3n.4, 353nn.5, 7; on truthmakers 56; on unity of worlds 86–99; on universals 193, 309n.24

Lindenbaum's Lemma 351n.14

Linsky, B. and Zalta, E. 214–15, 221–3, 345n.1, 345–6n.8, 348nn.23, 26, 349n.13

Linsky, L. 302–3n.8, 305–6n.2

Locke, J. 301n.11

Loux, M.J. 262, 310n.1, 345n.1, 350n.1, 352n.1, 353nn.6, 7, 353–4n.11

Lycan, W. 29, 59, 60, 109–10, 150, 260–1, 298–9n.4, 310n.1, 311n.3, 313n.18, 324nn.11, 12, 13, 324–5n.14, 336–7n.1, 337n.5, 346n.12, 348n.1, 351n.21

Lycan, W. and Shapiro, S. 188, 219, 268, 347–8n.19

MacBeath, M. *see* LePoidevin, R. and MacBeath, M.

MacBride, F. 195, 342n.16, 343n.22

McGinn, C. 65–6, 77, 163, 228, 311n.9, 312n.12, 316n.34, 316–17n.37, 323–4n.8, 334n.14, 335n.20, 336nn.24, 25, 340n.30, 355–6n.24

Mackie, J.L. 301n.11

McMichael, A. 223, 326n.2, 349n.13, 354n.18

McNamara, P. 348n.2, 350n.9

Marcus, R. 315n.30

Maudlin, T. 316n.36

Meinong, A. 59, 310n.1

Meinongian conception of quantification/existence 59–65, 310n.1, 311n.3, 344n.3

Meinongian realism about possible worlds 59, 175, 310n.1

Melia, J. 155, 278–84, 354n.19; *see also* Divers, J. and Melia, J.

Mellor, D.H. 328n.16

mentalistic realism (MR) 340n.30

Menzel, C. 246, 252, 253, 349n.13, 351n.15

Menzies, P. and Pettit, P. 307n.14

Meredith, C. and Prior, A.N. 304n.16

mereology 46, 103, 307n.9

MGR (minimal genuine realism) *see* genuine realism, minimal (MGR) versus replicating (RGR)

Miller, R.B. 90, 109, 134–8, 146, 313n.16, 314n.25, 319n.19, 320n.30, 324–5n.14, 328–9n.17

modal epistemology: GR and 149–65; PW and illumination of 39; received view of 164; and stipulation of possible worlds 272–4; underdevelopment of 164

modality: absolute versus relative 8–9; alethic versus non-alethic 6–7; cases versus kinds 3–4; de dicto versus de re 43, 130, 171, 305–6n.2; extraordinary/advanced (versus ordinary) 47–50, 54, 56, 67, 71, 74–5, 82, 84, 88–90, 94–8, 126, 161, 284, 307n.14, 315n.33, 316n.36, 318n.6, 319n.22, 321n.35, 322n.1, 331n.34, 335n.18, 352n.24; iterated *see* iterated modality

Mondadori, F. 327n.8

Montague, R. 304n.16

MR (mentalistic realism) *see* mentalistic realism

Mulligan, K., Simons, P. and Smith, B. 303n.12

Nagel, E. 300–1n.10

nature realism (NR) 21 *et passim*; exposition of 177–8

Naylor, M.B. 68, 313n.15

NE (necessity of existence) *see* necessity of existence

Index

necessity of existence, principle of (NE) 213–21, 225
necessity of identity 141–3, 187, 330n.30
NFA (non-factualist antirealism) *see* antirealism, non-factualist
Nolan, D. 101–3, 321–2n.38
Noonan, H. 307n.14
NR (nature realism) *see* nature realism

ontological: actualism *see* actualism, ontological; commitment (to possible worlds) 19–25; component of GR *see* GRO; economy, quantitative and qualitative 154–5, 344n.4; identifications 32–3, 51, 196–201, 252, 303nn.9, 13; priority and reduction 112–14; *see also* applications (of PW), ontological

paradox(es) 321–2n.38; Cantorian 243–56; Forrest–Armstrong 101–3, 321–2n.38; Kaplan 245–6; of recombination 100–3, 321–2n.38
Pargetter, R. *see* Davidson, B. and Pargetter, R.; Bigelow, J. and Pargetter, R.
parsimony *see* ontological, economy
Parsons, T. 310n.1, 353n.9
Peacocke, C. 347n.17, 350n.5
Peano axioms 161
Perry, J. 350n.1; *see also* Barwise, J and Perry, J.
Pettit, P. *see* Menzies, P. and Pettit, P.
PGR (possibilist genuine realism) *see* genuine realism, possibilist (PGR) versus impossibilist (IGR)
Plantinga, A.: on claim to realism 300n.5; on criteria of identity 349n.8; distinction between pure and applied semantics 36–9; on the existence of a unique actualized world 350n.9; on individual essences 220–2; on Meinongian character of GR 60–2; objections to counterpart theory 125–9, 330nn.27, 30; on ontological identifications 199, 349n.15; on PW-semantics 345n.1; on serious actualism 348n.26; on transworld identity and transworld identification 270–1, 352n.1, 353n.7, 355n.22; on world books 178, 246–7; on world-indexed properties 262; *see also* Plantingan realism
Plantingan realism (PR) 21 *et passim*; exposition of 173–4
Platonism, arithmetical/mathematical/Fregean/neo-Fregean 150, 152, 161–3, 233–4, 314n.26, 315n.30
Pollock, J.L. 348n.26
possible-world discourse (PW) 15; abstentionism about 19; applications of 18–19, 26–40; contested sentence of 17–18; interpretations of 16–18, 19–21; psychological/pictorial aspects of 40
PR (Plantingan realism) *see* Plantingan realism
Priest, G. 76
Prior, A.N. 25, 56, 301n.11, 326n.2, 328n.16; *see also* Meredith, C. and Prior, A.N.
Prior, A.N. and Fine, K. 301n.17
propositional attitudes 7, 298–9n.4, 301n.11, 305n.2, 308n.18, 329n.19, 347n.16
Putnam, H. 162, 301n.18, 320–1n.31, 334n.13; see also Quine–Putnam
PW (possible-world discourse) *see* possible-world discourse
PW-paradox *see* paradox(es)
PW-semantics *see* Kripkean semantics, sketch of for QML; semantic applications of PW

QML (quantified modal logic) *see* quantified modal logic(s)
Q-problem for AR 211, 259
quantified modal logic(s) (QML) 35 *et passim*; sketch of Kripkean semantics for 36–9; *see also*

378

Index

semantic applications of PW
quantum mechanics, many worlds interpretation of 39–40
Quine, W.V.O. 30–1, 78, 162, 175, 302n.7, 302–3n.8, 303n.14, 324n.10, 338–9n.16, 348n.6, 353n.7
Quine–Putnam: conception of mathematical epistemology 162–3, 335n.21
Quinn, P. 346n.12

realism about possible worlds 19–21; *see also* actualist realism; book realism; combinatorial realism; genuine realism; Meinongian realism about possible worlds; mentalistic realism; nature realism; Plantingan realism
referential opacity/transparency 141, 145, 302n.7, 330n.29
relations, external versus internal 286–92, 360nn.22, 25
relativity *see* general relativity
representation 172; haecceitistic 264–74, 276–84, 357n.5; implicit (versus explicit) 180, 189–91, 217, 253–5, 273, 285, 340n.28, 342n.11, 343n.23; linguistic 275–84; magical 284–92
Rescher, N. 340n.30, 355–6n.24
RGR (replicating genuine realism) *see* genuine realism, minimal (MGR) versus replicating (RGR)
Richards, T. 60, 150, 335n.20
Roper, A. 155, 178, 186, 345n.1
Rosen, G. 24, 134–5, 307n.14, 328–9n.17, 329n.19
Rosenberg, A. 90, 92, 317n.1, 318n.12
Rosenkrantz, G. *see* Hoffman, J. and Rosenkrantz, G.
Routley, R. 310n.1
Roy, T. 281
Russell, B. 78
Russell, B. and Whitehead, A.N. 301n.15
Russellian: response to paradoxes 350n.7; treatment of definite descriptions 346n.14

S4 principle 127, 142, 304n.21
S5 principle 142, 205, 207, 216, 304n.21
SA (structure-based antirealism) *see* antirealism, structure-based
Salmon, N.U. 125–6, 127, 142, 327nn.6, 7
Sanford, D. 299n.9
Schlesinger, G.N. 39, 329n.19, 331n.1
Schurz, G. *see* Fine, K. and Schurz, G.
semantic applications of PW 34–9; and AR 210–26; and GR 57
semantics, pure versus applied 36–9
Shalkowski, S. 112–14, 192, 325n.16
Shapiro, S. *see* Lycan, W. and Shapiro, S.
Sharlow, M. 313n.16
Simons, P. 303n.12, 307n.9; *see also* Mulligan, K., Simons, P. and Smith, B.
Skyrms, B. 39, 58, 159–60, 175, 338n.10
Smith, B. 303n.12; *see also* Mulligan, K., Simons, P. and Smith, B.
Stalnaker, R. 177, 299n.9, 336–7n.1, 339nn.22, 23, 339–40n.24, 348n.1, 359n.20
states of affairs: in alternative CR 176; in CR 174–7, 338nn.12, 14, 15; in PR 173–4, 239–42; in PR as safe and sane ontology 227–8; thing-like 190–1, 337n.6, 338n.15, 339n.17, 342n.11; various conceptions of distinguished 337n.6; versus representations of 338n.15
stipulation: semantic, and modal epistemology 272–4
supervenience: of epistemological status on character of referents 160–1; Humean 146, 266, 331n.37; representation by 253–4; strong, weak and global 12–13, 319n.22; of truth on being 56–7,

379

206, 309n.25; of truth on degree of utility 156

Tarskian semantics for modal languages 35–6
Taylor, C. 318n.13
tenseless truth-conditions for tensed sentences 131–2
Tooley, M. 353n.7
transworld identity and transworld identification 257–74
truthmakers for modal truths 33–4; and AR 201–9; and GR 51–7

UGR (unworldly genuine realism) see genuine realism, worldly (WGR) versus unworldly (UGR)
Unger, P. 329n.19
universals 53, 103, 178, 193–5, 231, 309n.24, 321n.37, 339n.23, 342–3n.20, 343n.22

V-problem for AR 211, 223–6
van Fraassen, B. 301n.12, 322n.42, 333n.11

van Inwagen, P. 39, 173, 197, 228, 270, 289–92, 306n.5, 311n.3, 336n.24, 336–7n.1, 349n.9, 353n.7, 358n.17, 360n.24

Weir, A. 350n.4
WGR (worldly genuine realism) see genuine realism, worldly (WGR) versus unworldly (UGR)
White, M.J. 348n.2
Whitehead, A.N. see Russell, B. and Whitehead, A.N.
Wittgenstein, L. 300–1n.10, 338n.9
Wright, C. 300n.1, 314n.26, 331n.38, 334n.13, 354n.16; see also Hale, B. and Wright, C.

Yablo, S. 336n.24
Yagisawa, T. 29, 68, 71–6, 100, 103–5, 163, 298–9n.4, 309n.28, 313nn.16, 18, 314n.20, 22, 318n.7, 328–9n.17, 333n.11

Zalta, E. see Linsky, B. and Zalta, E.